UNDE

JESUS

A GUIDE TO HIS LIFE AND TIMES

STEPHEN M. MILLER

BARBOUR
PUBLISHING

Previously released under the title *The Jesus of the Bible*.

© 2009 by Stephen M. Miller

The author is represented by The Steve Laube Agency LLC, Phoenix, Arizona.

ISBN 978-1-61626-914-2

eBook Editions:
Adobe Digital Edition (.epub) 978-1-62029-686-8
Kindle and MobiPocket Edition (.prc) 978-1-62029-685-1

Cover design: Christopher Tobias, Tobias' Outerwear for Books

Published by Barbour Publishing, Inc., P.O. Box 719, Uhrichsville, Ohio 44683, www.barbourbooks.com

Our mission is to publish and distribute inspirational products offering exceptional value and biblical encouragement to the masses.

Printed in the United States of America.

INTRODUCTION

I'm a tad blue as I write today. If you read this book from front to back, this is the first of my scribbling you'll see. But it's the last I've written—at the end of a year I spent with Jesus.

Now don't worry. I'm not getting metaphysical on you. Jesus didn't suddenly appear in my home office, as he did inside the locked house where his disciples were hiding after the Crucifixion. I didn't get to look Jesus in the eye, shake his hand, or talk with him over a cup of coffee. He probably wouldn't like coffee anyhow. But I did get to study his life, his teachings, and the world in which he lived. For an entire year. And the publisher paid me to do it.

The gent who said you can't have your cake and eat it, too, was crazy. I just did. That gentleman, by the way, was playwright John Heywood. Writing a collection of proverbs in 1546—in the Old English style of the original King James Version of the Bible—he put it this way: "Wolde you bothe eate your cake, and haue your cake?"

I think that translates: "Would you both eat your cake, and have your cake?"

Yes, I wolde.

But now the year is hanging in my rearview mirror. And I'm sad about that. If I were J. K. Rowling saying good-bye to Harry Potter, I'd be crying. But I expect to see Jesus again.

Over the past 12 months, I read his story in the Bible's four Gospels—Matthew, Mark, Luke, and John. I read stories about him in other ancient writings by early church leaders, Jewish writers, and Roman historians of his century. I read, too, what some of the brightest Bible scholars today make of all this history.

I've read more words this past year than a redbud has red buds—maybe more than an orchard of redbuds has red buds. I know that sounds like an exaggeration, but I'm not a preacher.

I did it all with just one question in mind: How can I paint a picture of Jesus for people who don't know much about him?

That's who I write for.

Bible-savvy Christians are certainly allowed to read this book. I won't thump them if I catch them; that would be unkind. If they do read it, I wish them well and hope they find insights and inspiration in the story of Jesus. But I didn't write for them.

I wrote for some folks in my extended family who think Jesus is a myth. And for some of my friends who admire the teachings of Jesus but who never took the time to get to know the man behind the teachings. And for neighbors in my community who want to learn more about Jesus but don't want to fall asleep while they're doing it.

The last thing I want to do is kill a tree to make another boring book. Especially about Jesus. That would be so not green, magnified to celestial proportions.

A WORD OF THANKS

My name's on the cover, but I'm just one guy in the choir singing this song. A few of the others singing shoulder to shoulder beside me:

My family. Linda, my wife, along with our children, Becca and Brad. They've let me work at home as a full-time freelance writer. They never once kicked me out.

Steve Laube, my agent, who won't take notes during our meetings because he thinks it's important to look people in the eye when they're talking. It's his only bad habit, far as I can tell. How he manages to get his notes right is beyond me.

Paul K. Muckley, my editor, one of the most gracious people I know. A rarity among editors; trust me, I know this. As for you other writers of lavishly illustrated Bible reference books, I saw him first.

Shalyn Sattler, my publisher's marketing maven. She's probably the best in the choir at living the Golden Rule—doing for others what she wishes they would do for her. She sends people free stuff, copies of my books among them. (But you have to be on the list. They'll tell you that at the Pearly Gates, too, I've heard.)

David Lindstedt, Kelly McIntosh, Annie Tipton, and Ashley Schrock also played key roles in the production process.

God bless each one of these people.

And God bless you as you read this book—and more importantly, as you read his Book.

Stephen M. Miller
www.StephenMillerBooks.com

CONTENTS

—— **BEHIND THE STORY** ————————————————

1. JESUS IN HISTORY (TIME LINE) 7
2. JESUS' HOMELAND 9
3. RESTLESS HOPE OF THE JEWS: FREEDOM 13
4. JESUS' FAMILY TREE 22
5. MARY AND JOSEPH ENGAGED 30

—— **THE STORY** ————————————————————

6. JESUS IS BORN 35
7. WISE MEN COME 44
8. ESCAPE TO EGYPT 52
9. A BOY IN NAZARETH 57
10. YOUNG JESUS AT THE TEMPLE 65
11. JESUS BAPTIZED 72
12. JESUS TEMPTED 79
13. JESUS STARTS TEACHING 85
14. JESUS CHOOSES 12 DISCIPLES 91
15. MIRACLE 1: WATER INTO WINE 99
16. JESUS HEALS THE SICK 104
17. REJECTED IN HIS HOMETOWN 113
18. JESUS' MOST FAMOUS SERMON 118
19. THE LORD'S PRAYER 130
20. JESUS ON FASTING 136
21. JESUS AND DISCIPLES BREAK SABBATH RULES 142
22. JESUS' FAVORITE TEACHING METHOD: PARABLES 149
23. PARABLE OF A FARMER PLANTING SEEDS 157
24. PARABLE OF THE GOOD SAMARITAN 162
25. PARABLE OF THE LOST SON 168

26. PARABLE OF THE SHEEP AND GOATS 173
27. A ROMAN SOLDIER ASKS JESUS FOR HELP 178
28. JESUS STOPS A STORM 183
29. JESUS FEEDS 5,000 187
30. JESUS SHINES AT THE TRANSFIGURATION 192
31. JESUS AND THE TAX MAN ZACCHAEUS 196
32. THE SECRET OF ETERNAL LIFE 200
33. JESUS RESURRECTS LAZARUS 206
34. JEWISH LEADERS PLOT TO KILL JESUS 212
35. A SHADY LADY POURS PERFUME ON JESUS 220
36. THE FIRST PALM SUNDAY 226
37. SIGNS OF THE END TIMES 231
38. THE LAST SUPPER 240
39. JESUS PRAYS ONE LAST PRAYER 247
40. JESUS ARRESTED 252
41. JESUS ON TRIAL BEFORE PILATE 259
42. JESUS EXECUTED AND BURIED 265
43. JESUS BACK FROM THE DEAD 273
44. JESUS' ASSIGNMENT FOR HIS FOLLOWERS 281

BEYOND THE STORY
45. JESUS AND THE SECOND COMING 285
INDEX 292

BEHIND THE STORY
JESUS IN HISTORY

BIBLE EVENTS

37 BC–AD 4 Herod the Great rules as history's last king of the Jews; appointed by Rome

20 BC Herod begins a 46-year-long renovation of the Jerusalem Temple

6 BC Jesus is born

4 BC–AD 39 Herod Antipas, son of Herod the Great, rules Galilee as governor

AD 5 Apostle Paul is born (dies AD 64)

AD 29 Jesus begins his ministry (some place his ministry from AD 26 to 30)

AD 33 Jesus is crucified and resurrected

AD 35 Paul becomes a Christian

AD 43 Paul begins 10,000 miles of missionary trips

AD 50 Paul writes what is probably the first book in the New Testament: 1 Thessalonians

AD 64 Romans execute Peter and Paul

WORLD EVENTS

30 BC Mark Antony and Cleopatra commit suicide after losing a Roman civil war to Octavian

27 BC Octavian takes the name of Caesar Augustus

7 BC The planet Jupiter (representing kings) aligns with Saturn (representing Jews) in the Pisces constellation (representing what is now Israel)

5 BC A star explodes into a nova

AD 14–37 Emperor Tiberius rules Roman Empire

AD 26–37 Pilate serves as governor of Judea in what is now southern Israel

AD 36 High priest Caiaphas is fired by Vitellus, the same Roman official who fired Governor Pilate at about the same time

AD 37–41 Caligula, famous for his cruelty and sexcapades, reigns as emperor

AD 43 Romans invade England

AD 50 The French (Gauls) introduce the Romans to soap

AD 66–73 Jews rebel against the Roman occupying force, temporarily driving out the invaders

AD 70 Rome mounts a counter-strike against the Jews, destroying Jerusalem and the Jewish Temple—which is never rebuilt

AD 85 John is exiled to prison island, Patmos

AD 95 In exile, John writes the last book in the Bible: Revelation

AD 64 Most of Rome burns; Nero blames Christians

AD 68 Nero commits suicide

AD 79 Mount Vesuvius erupts, destroying Pompeii near Naples, Italy

AD 80 Colosseum is dedicated in Rome; Christians are killed as entertainment

AD 90 Heresy surfaces in the church, teaching that Jesus was a spirit being who only looked human

Dates are approximate and debated among experts.

BC = Before Christ. The creator of this calendar got the date of Jesus' birth wrong by perhaps six years or more. King Herod, who tried to kill the baby Jesus by slaughtering all Bethlehem boys age two and under, died in 4 BC.

AD = *Anno Domini*. That's Latin for "in the year of the Lord."

JESUS' HOMELAND

Jesus' homeland—barely the size of New Jersey—lies on a narrow strip of land between the desert and the deep blue sea. That's the Syrian Desert and the Mediterranean Sea.

Tiny though the Jewish homeland was by international standards, its location was strategic—for soldiers on the march, caravan merchants on the move, or travelers on their way to visit long-distance relatives. Israel, as we call the land today, provided the most hospitable land bridge connecting southland regions, such as Egypt and the rest of Africa, with nations and empires to the north, such as Greece and Rome.

Travelers headed north or south typically decided to pass through Israel rather than risk the hazards of traveling by sea or desert.

During Jesus' few years of ministry, he never traveled more than about 70 miles (113 km) from his hometown of Nazareth. Yet in those relatively meager miles, he covered a continent's worth of varying landscapes. The country is that geographically diverse: from barren deserts to lush tropics, sandy beaches to snowcapped mountains, and fertile fields to desolate wastelands.

Israel's landscape also lays claim to fame in several geological categories:

- **World's biggest scar.** The Jordan River, Sea of Galilee, and Dead Sea all lie on the north end of a massive rift valley extending deep into Africa—a break in the earth's crust that's more visible from space than the Grand Canyon.
- **World's lowest dry ground**. At about 1,300 feet below sea level (396 meters), the shoreline of the Dead Sea is the lowest dry spot on earth.
- **World's lowest freshwater lake**. That's the Sea of Galilee, at 700 feet below sea level (213 meters). Some 13 miles long and 7 miles at its widest (21 x 11 km), it's a little smaller than Lake Tahoe, on the border of California and Nevada.
- **World's lowest riverbed**. The Jordan River starts above the Sea of Galilee and plunges downhill for 70 miles (113 km) below the lake, emptying into the Dead Sea.

HILL COUNTRY

Rolling hills make up most of Israel. The biggest highland area is the ridge on which Jerusalem sits. It's about 80 miles long and 20 miles wide (130 x 30 km). And it's the reason Jerusalem-bound travelers in Jesus' time always said they were going up to Jerusalem. Whether travelers were coming from the north, south, east, or west, they always had to climb the Judean hills to reach Jerusalem.

The famous Mount of Olives, where Jesus prayed the night of his arrest, is actually a tiny ridge of hills that is part of this highland area called the Judean hills.

When Joshua and the Israelites invaded Israel more than 1,000 years before Jesus, they chose this area to fight most of their battles. That's because the hills gave a tactical advantage to their lightly armed militia over the heavily armed and slow-moving Canaanites, with their chariots.

Jesus was a man of the hills. He grew up in Galilee, among the gently rolling hills of northern Israel. His hometown of Nazareth sits atop a ridge near the sprawling Jezreel Valley—also known as the Valley of Armageddon, where some say the final battle between good and evil will take place.

THE PLANET'S BIGGEST SCAR

Called the Great Rift Valley, this tear in the earth's crust stretches 4,000 miles (6,400 km)—from Syria, through Israel, all the way to the country of Mozambique near the southern tip of Africa. That's the distance from Anchorage to Miami, as the snowbird flies. Or from Moscow to Madrid and back again.

The entire rift valley, a trench that averages about 30–40 miles (48–64 km) across, is prone to earthquakes, such as the one that occurred the moment Jesus died: "The curtain in the sanctuary of the Temple was torn in two, from top to bottom. The earth shook, rocks split apart, and tombs opened" (Matthew 27:51–52).

Another tremor followed on Sunday morning, at the Resurrection: "Suddenly there was a great earthquake! For an angel of the Lord came down from heaven, rolled aside the stone, and sat on it" (Matthew 28:2).

The Bible reports many other earthquakes. One terrified a Philistine army that was preparing to fight the Jews (1 Samuel 14:15). Another was big enough to serve as a calendar landmark for the ministry of the prophet Amos: "He received this message in visions two years before the earthquake, when Uzziah was king of Judah" (Amos 1:1). And God may have used an earthquake to bring down the walls of Jericho, which lies inside the rift valley, near the Jordan River.

SWAMPS, LAKES, FERTILE PLAINS

There's a saying in Israel today: "You go to Jerusalem to pray and Tel Aviv to play."

In Jesus' time, that was half right. The beach city of Tel Aviv didn't exist. It was a swamp. So was part of the basin north of the Sea of Galilee, where snowmelt from Mount Hermon and runoff from streams gathered into a marshland lake called Hulah before meandering into the Sea of Galilee.

There were so many swamps in the region that Israelis started importing eucalyptus trees from Australia after the modern nation of Israel was created in 1948. These trees consume water like a herd of thirsty, limp-humped camels.

Former swamps have been reclaimed and turned into cities or farmland. Swampy Lake Hulah is gone, too, replaced by productive farms.

The most fertile farmland region in Jesus' day was in his part of the country—Galilee—which is dominated by the massive freshwater lake known as the Sea of Galilee. Some locals call it *Yom Kinneret*—literally "sea harp" in Hebrew. That's because it's shaped like a harp. At 13 miles long and 7 miles across (21 x 11 km), it's the nation's major source of freshwater, and the main water supply feeding the Jordan River. Underground springs pump water into the lake, adding to the rainwater runoff and the mountain snowmelt.

Many of the hills slope gently enough for farmers to plow the ground and plant crops. The vast Jezreel Valley was—and still is—ideal farmland rich in black loam. That's a soil perfect for farming, because it retains nutrients while allowing water to flow freely and irrigate the crops.

SOUTHERN BADLANDS

South of Jerusalem, the land turns harsh. Hot. Dry. Occasional shrubs cling to life in the Negev, a nearly lifeless region sometimes described as a desert and sometimes as a wilderness. But it looks like neither.

There aren't many Sahara Desert–type vistas of sand with dunes piled up like waves on freeze-frame. And there are certainly no forests like we might expect in a "wilderness."

The farther south a person travels, the more the land looks like Mars—or the South Dakota badlands. Aside from an occasional oasis or a spring, there are few signs of life.

That's changing today—fortunately for the people living there, because the Negev makes up nearly two-thirds of Israel's land.

This stretch of once-barren land between the Dead Sea and the Red Sea's Gulf of Aqaba seems to be witnessing a prophecy fulfilled:

"Even the wilderness and desert will be glad in those days. The wasteland will rejoice and blossom with spring crocuses. Yes, there will be an abundance of flowers and singing and joy! The deserts will become as green as the mountains of Lebanon, as lovely as Mount Carmel or the plain of Sharon" (Isaiah 35:1–2).

Irrigation worked the miracle. Even hard-packed, rocky soil comes to life when water is added. Perhaps that'll be good news for Martian colonies one day.

WHEN ISRAEL WAS PALESTINE

We call the country *Israel*. But for most of the past 2,000 years, people called it by another name: *Palestine*.

Throughout its 4,000-year history as the Jewish homeland—which began in Abraham's time—this patch of land has gone by the name of Israel for only a few centuries.

The Jews picked this name after Joshua and other refugees from the exodus out of Egypt settled in the land. They divided the real estate among the 12 tribes named after the sons of Jacob, Abraham's grandson. Then this coalition of tribes adopted the name God had given Jacob: "Your name will no longer be Jacob. . . . From now on you will be called Israel" (Genesis 32:28).

The nation became known as Israel in either the 1400s BC or the 1200s BC. Bible experts debate which century. Unfortunately, the united nation of Israel collapsed just a few centuries later, shortly after King Solomon died in about 970 BC. The tribes split into two nations: Israel in the north and Judah in the south.

A couple hundred years after that, in 722 BC, Assyrian invaders from what is now Iraq wiped the northern kingdom of Israel off the political map. Babylonian invaders did the same to Judah in 586 BC.

That's the year the Jews became a race without a country.

Some Jews began returning about 50 years later and rebuilt Jerusalem. But they never regained the sovereignty and glory of their Golden Age under King David and King Solomon. Instead, the region again became home to a mix of races.

Greek Palestine. The Greeks were the first on record to call the area Palestine—after the warrior race that gave us Goliath: the Philistines. In Hebrew, the Philistines were called *pelistim*. Their homeland was called *peleset*. The Greek translation of this Hebrew word was *palastium* (pal lus TEE um). This finger of land included the modern-day Gaza Strip, a coastal territory now controlled by the Palestinian Authority. The Greek historian Herodotus, traveling in the area during the 400s BC, met some descendants of the Philistines and dubbed the entire territory Palastium.

Latin Palestine. The Romans picked up on the Greek name after invading the area, adapting the word to fit their Latin language: *Palaestine*.

Emperor Hadrian, in the early AD 100s, renamed the Roman province of Judea, in what is now southern Israel, Palestine Province. By the AD 300s, the entire area became known as Palestine.

The name Israel was reborn only in 1948, after the United Nations created a sovereign safe haven for the Jewish race decimated by the Holocaust of World War II. This restored Jewish homeland came at the expense of many Arab Palestinians living there.

Since 1948, Arab Palestinians scattered throughout Israel and the Middle East have been trying to regain their homeland. Attempting to trade land for peace, the Israelis have given the Palestinians control of small, selected plugs of the country. Most Palestinians want more. But many Jews say the Palestinians don't deserve any of the land because God promised it to the descendants of Abraham, Isaac, and Jacob.

RESTLESS HOPE OF THE JEWS: FREEDOM

If Jesus wanted an easy life on earth, he showed up at the wrong time. The Promised Land had become the Occupied Land.

By the time Jesus opened his mouth to deliver his first sermon, in about AD 29, the nation of Israel had been occupied by invaders for nearly a century. Israel wasn't even a nation anymore. It was just an assortment of county-sized provinces ruled by governors answering to a dictator 1,500 miles (2,400 km) away in Rome.

Some Jews were fine with this.

- Society's elite had cozied up to the invaders, earning positions of power and prestige.
- Top Jewish leaders were handpicked by the Romans. That included the high priest—a position God said should be limited to descendants of Aaron.
- Jewish entrepreneurs, such as tax collectors, got rich by collaborating with the invaders.

Most Jews, however, hated the Romans—and hated any fellow Jews who cooperated with Rome.

More than anything, most Jews hungered for freedom. They wanted their country back. They wanted the glory of Israel revived. And they wanted God to deliver on his promise: "When the people cry to the Lord for help against those who oppress them, he will send them a savior who will rescue them" (Isaiah 19:20).

Even the most perceptive Jewish scholars of the time seem to have had no idea that the savior God would send was someone who would rescue them from sin, not from the Romans. Nor did they have a clue that the Romans would remain in their homeland for three more centuries, or that the resurrection of the Jewish nation would have to wait nearly 2,000 more years—until 1948, when the United Nations established Israel as a safe haven for Holocaust-surviving Jews.

EXPECTING THE MESSIAH AT ANY MOMENT

Time was ripe for God to once again step into Jewish history. Many observant Jews, if not most, believed it.

They believed it because of what they read in their Bible, which Christians call the Old Testament. Prophets several centuries before Jesus had described a future for the Jews that looked very much like the harsh life under Roman occupation. And these prophecies said that God would send an "anointed one" to save them.

Anointed one is a title. It refers to anyone in Bible times selected by God for the

continued on p.14

continued from p.13

special purpose of saving his people. Kings, such as David, were called "anointed ones." The Hebrew word for this title is *Masiah*, or Messiah. And the word translating this into the Greek language popular in Jesus' day is *Christos*. In English, it's *Christ*. So "Jesus Christ" wasn't the Savior's formal name. It was his name and title. Instead of Jesus, PhD, it was Jesus, Messiah.

Jews were praying for Christ to come and expecting him any day. Here are a few prophecies that led them to this belief:

- **David's kingdom is forever.** "The Lord declares that he will make a house for you [David]—a dynasty of kings! For when you die and are buried with your ancestors, I will raise up one of your descendants. . . . Your house and your kingdom will continue before me for all time, and your throne will be secure forever" (2 Samuel 7:11–12, 16).
- **David's dynasty will be resurrected.** "For the time is coming," says the Lord, "when I will raise up a righteous descendant from King David's line" (Jeremiah 23:5).
- **A child is born.** "The people who walk in darkness will see a great light. . . . You will break the oppressor's rod, just as you did when you destroyed the army of Midian. . . . For a child is born to us, a son is given to us. The government will rest on his shoulders. And he will be called: Wonderful Counselor, Mighty God, Everlasting Father, Prince of Peace. His government and its peace will never end. He will rule with fairness and justice from the throne of his ancestor David for all eternity" (Isaiah 9:2, 4–7).

When Jesus arrived, David's dynasty had been dead for 600 years. But the Jews were expecting a political resurrection. They were in for a surprise. They got a king who said, "My Kingdom is not of this world" (John 18:36), and who promised everlasting life in heaven rather than a prosperous life on earth.

Expecting a warrior, they got a pacifist. Expecting a new and improved Israel, they got the Kingdom of God. Expecting freedom from slavery to the Romans, they got freedom from slavery to sin and the judgment that follows.

Most Jews wouldn't buy it. They couldn't believe Jesus was the Messiah.

This is why the New Testament Gospel writers worked so hard to make the case for Jesus as Messiah—reporting his godlike miracles along with the many prophecies he fulfilled. The most famous prophecy is about God's suffering servant, who would die for the sins of others: "The Lord laid on him the sins of us all" (Isaiah 53:6).

When asked bluntly if he was the Messiah, Jesus answered, "I Am" (Mark 14:62).

HOW THE JEWS LOST THEIR COUNTRY

Iraqi invaders wiped Israel off the political map.

Actually, there were two Jewish nations and two Iraqi invasions. There was the kingdom of Israel in the northern half of modern-day Israel, and the kingdom of Judah in the southern half. Assyrians from what is now northern Iraq overran the northern Jewish country in 722 BC. And Babylonians, headquartered near what is now Baghdad, decimated Judah in 586 BC—leveling Jerusalem and exiling the survivors.

All of this must have come as quite a shock to Jews who believed what God had told Abraham: "I will give the entire land of Canaan [now called Israel]. . .to you and your descendants. It will be their possession forever" (Genesis 17:8).

The trouble is that the Jews didn't hold up their end of the bargain. The contract God made with Jews in the time of Moses required them to obey God's laws. But the Jews didn't. Century after century, they disobeyed, while God patiently continued warning them. After the Jews ignored generations of warnings delivered by various prophets, they finally got what the contract said they'd get: "The Lord will bring a distant nation against you. . . . You will be torn from the land you are about to enter and occupy. For the Lord will scatter you among all the nations from one end of the earth to the other" (Deuteronomy 28:49, 63–64).

The Jews never fully recovered.

Eventually, the Iranians came to their rescue. Actually, they were Persians living in what is now Iran. The Persians crushed the Babylonian Empire about 50 years after Jerusalem fell, and then freed Babylon's political prisoners. Some Jews returned to their homeland and started rebuilding the cities. But the Jews still weren't free. The Persians ruled them.

Next came Alexander the Great and his Greek army, marching through the Jewish homeland in 332 BC on his way to conquer Egypt. The Jews didn't even try to resist. By that time, Alexander had already scattered the Persian army and was well on his way to establishing the largest empire the world had ever seen— stretching some 3,000 miles (4,800 km) from Greece to the border of India. It was there in India that Alexander apparently picked up a bug that stoked a fever, killing him at age 33. His generals then divvied up the empire.

One of those generals left a successor: Antiochus IV Epiphanes, who so provoked the Jews that they revolted and won their independence for about a century. Antiochus provoked them by remodeling the Jewish Temple into a temple for Zeus. And he ordered the Jews not to practice their religion. Under threat of execution, Jews weren't allowed to

- circumcise their boys, a ritual that ushered them into the Jewish faith;
- read their Bible;
- treat the Sabbath as a holy day of worship and rest; or
- refuse to eat pork, a nonkosher food that Jewish law said they should never eat.

Many Jews chose death rather than abandon their faith and adopt Greek religion and culture. Antiochus often made the dying hard. Once, he built a huge copper pot, which he used to cook seven Jewish brothers who refused to bow to an idol. The youngest boy was age seven.

In retaliation for such crimes, one Jewish family—the Maccabees— organized an army of guerrilla fighters. Within about three years, the Jews had fought off their oppressors, who were headquartered in what is now Syria.

JEWISH MONKS PREPARE THE WAY FOR THE LORD

"Prepare in the desert the way for the Lord" (Isaiah 40:3 NCV).

One group of Jews decided to do just that. They moved to the desert, where they waited for the Messiah.

They took ritual baths every day to keep themselves pure. That way, when the Messiah showed up, they'd be ready instantly to join his army and help drive out the Romans—as holy minutemen.

"All the children of righteousness are ruled by the Prince of Light and walk in the ways of light," they wrote on one of their scrolls, titled *War of the Sons of Light against the Sons of Darkness*. "But all the children of falsehood are ruled by the Angel of Darkness and walk in the ways of darkness."

These fanatical Jews considered themselves "Sons of Light" who would one day ride into battle with the Messiah's army and defeat the "Sons of Darkness," a tag they put on all godless people in the world, especially Romans.

Ironically, the Sons of Darkness defeated the Sons of Light. The Romans destroyed the desert settlement in AD 68 while crushing a nationwide Jewish revolt.

These isolationist Jews were called Essenes, a name most often translated as "pious ones." When the Jewish nation temporarily won its independence in 167 BC, the war leaders took over—appointing themselves as kings and priests. In disgust, a group of suddenly unemployed priests moved 14 miles (22 km) east of Jerusalem, where they built a community called Qumran, near the Dead Sea. There, they preserved copies of sacred Jewish writings—including copies of the Bible discovered in 1947 that were 1,000 years older than the scrolls that scholars had used to produce the King James Version of the Bible. Scholars now use these Dead Sea Scrolls to help create new Bible translations.

The Essenes weren't just isolationist scrollworms. They were end-time fanatics. But "end time" for them didn't mean the end of humanity. It meant the end of evil. They expected a heaven-sent warrior to defeat evil and set up something close to heaven on earth. And they had plenty of Bible passages to back them up, including:

- **Earth-shaking leader.** "Out of the stump of David's family will grow a shoot—yes, a new Branch bearing fruit from the old root. And the Spirit of the Lord will rest on him. . . . The earth will shake at the force of his word, and one breath from his mouth will destroy the wicked" (Isaiah 11:1–2, 4).
- **Foreigners be gone.** "For in that day," says the Lord of Heaven's Armies, "I will break the yoke from their necks and snap their chains. Foreigners will no longer be their masters. For my people will serve the Lord their God and their king descended from David—the king I will raise up for them" (Jeremiah 30:8–9).
- **Living in perfect peace.** "In that day the wolf and the lamb will live together. . . . The baby will play safely near the hole of a cobra. . . . Nothing will hurt or destroy in all my holy mountain, for as the waters fill the sea, so the earth will be filled with people who know the Lord" (Isaiah 11:6, 8–9).

Unfortunately for the Essenes, they didn't live to see this wonderful era of peace. The utopia that many prophets describe still seems to wait somewhere in the future. Tragically for these Essenes—who had devoted their lives to waiting for the Messiah— they missed him by less than a day's walk.

But the newly liberated Jewish nation never did resurrect the glory of ancient Israel—perhaps in part because they didn't follow the ancient form of government, with a king from David's family and priests from Aaron's family. Instead, leaders of the revolt created their own dynasty of combo rulers: priest-general-king. Three in one. A religious leader, a military leader, and a political leader—a multipurpose ruler one halo shy of deity. They called their dynasty the Hasmoneans, after the oldest leader's tribal name. But in the years that followed, they fought among themselves for the right to rule—brother killing brother.

This new system of government and religion upset many Jews. Some, who considered themselves the legitimate priests, left Jerusalem. They set up their own monklike community 14 miles (22 km) east of Jerusalem, in the Judean badlands at Qumran near the Dead Sea. Believing that God would soon send a messiah to restore Israel, they spent their time waiting—passing time by copying sacred Jewish writings that became known as the Dead Sea Scrolls.

Jewish Bible scholars known as Pharisees hated the new system, too. They staged a riot when the priest-general-king Alexander Janneus tried to act in his self-appointed capacity as priest by leading a worship service during the annual Feast of Tabernacles. Pharisees and their supporters pummeled him with lemons. A sourpuss, Alexander responded in his self-appointed capacity as general. He called in the troops, who killed some 6,000 protestors. This prompted a revolt that took Alexander nine years to quell.

In the process, he captured 800 Pharisee leaders—and crucified them. A Jew crucifying fellow Jews. This wasn't just a torturous death; it was a religious statement. Jews considered people crucified as cursed of God: "Anyone who is hung on a tree is under God's curse" (Deuteronomy 21:23 NIV).

JEWS INVITE ROME TO INVADE

After Alexander Janneus died, his wife ruled the country and appointed one of their two sons, Hyrcanus II, as high priest and heir to the throne. He took over as king when his mother died. But his brother, Aristobulus II, wasn't happy about it. He seized control and demoted his brother, ordering him to serve only as high priest.

Civil war erupted. Rome had been a friend to the family, so the brothers called on a Roman general to arbitrate the dispute.

Bad decision.

For two centuries before the rise of Hyrcanus and Aristobulus, the once-modest village of Rome had been in the process of building an empire—one enemy or opportunity at a time. The Romans had already swallowed up all of Italy and its offshore islands—Sicily, Sardinia, Corsica—along with parts of Africa, Spain, France, Greece, Turkey, and Syria. All of these regions were forced to play host to occupying forces and to pay tribute to Rome: money, crops, and other supplies.

In a lapse of judgment, the feuding Jewish brothers apparently expected the

WHO'S WHO OF TROUBLED TIMES

Alexander the Great (356–323 BC), young Greek king who conquered much of the Middle East and spread Greek language and culture throughout the nations.

Alexander Janneus (ruled 103–76 BC), Jewish Hasmonean leader who declared himself the Jewish king, general, and high priest—three in one; crucified fellow Jews who opposed him.

Antigonus (ruled 40–37 BC), Hasmonean son of Aristobulus II; temporarily snatched the Jewish homeland back from Herod the Great; Herod later defeated Antigonus, with Roman help, and executed him.

Antiochus IV Epiphanes (ruled 175–163 BC), Syrian ruler who forced Jews in Israel to stop practicing their Jewish religion, sparking a successful Jewish war for independence.

Antipater (ruled Judea 47–43 BC), father of Herod the Great; he was an Arab leader in what is now southern Israel until Caesar made him ruler of Judea, a region including Jerusalem.

Aristobulus II (ruled 67–63 BC, died 49 BC), Jewish Hasmonean who stole political power from his brother, Hyrcanus II, until the Roman general Pompey arrived and exiled Aristobulus to Rome.

Hasmoneans (ruled 167–63 BC), a dynasty of Jewish leaders from the Maccabean family; they led Jews in a successful guerilla war of independence against Antiochus IV Ephiphanes and then ruled the Jewish homeland for a century.

Herod Antipas (ruled 4 BC–AD 39), son of Herod the Great and governor of Jesus' homeland of Galilee throughout Jesus' lifetime; he executed John the Baptist.

Herod the Great (ruled 37–4 BC), appointed by the Romans as king of the Jewish homeland. Insanely protective of his power, he executed many in his own family and ordered the slaughter of Bethlehem baby boys in an attempt to kill Jesus.

Herod Philip (ruled 4 BC–AD 34), son of Herod the Great and governor of what are now parts of Syria and Jordan.

Hyrcanus II (high priest 79–40 BC, died 30 BC), high priest during the Hasmonean Dynasty and early Roman rule; executed by Herod the Great.

Maccabees. See "Hasmoneans."

Mark Antony (about 82–30 BC), Roman general who recommended Herod to become king of the Jews; lost civil war against Octavian, who became Caesar Augustus; committed suicide with his lover, Queen Cleopatra of Egypt.

Phasael (ruled 46–40 BC), brother of Herod the Great; appointed by his father, Antipater, as ruler of Jerusalem.

Pilate (ruled about AD 26–37), governed the Roman province of Judea, the territory surrounding Jerusalem; ordered the crucifixion of Jesus.

Pompey (106–48 BC), Roman general who first invaded the Jewish homeland and put a local Arab ally, Antipater, in charge of the region.

Romans to kindly help them out of this jam and then go back home.

They were half right.

A Roman general named Pompey was only too happy to bring some military muscle into the Jewish homeland. He arrived in 63 BC, siding with Hyrcanus. He captured Jerusalem and exiled Aristobulus to Rome, along with his family and many supporters. Pompey restored Hyrcanus to his role as high priest and then declared him a prince—not a king—who was now subject to Rome.

Romans had come to stay.

HEROD THE NOT-SO-GREAT

Jewish people did have one more king to come—their last king of the homeland. Unfortunately, he was an Arab by race. Not a Jew.

Herod was the son of a ruler from Idumea, a small region in what is now southern Israel. The people living there were Arabs descended from Jacob's brother, Esau.

Though Herod wasn't a Jew by race, he was a Jew by conversion—forced though it was. Decades before Herod's time, self-liberated Jews of the Hasmonean Dynasty ordered the Idumeans to convert to the Jewish religion or die.

Herod's father, Antipater, was the ruler of Idumea—and a gifted survivor by nature. Naturally, he decided that his family would convert. He made a similar survival choice decades later, after Julius Caesar defeated Pompey in a civil war. Antipater switched loyalties from loser Pompey to winner Caesar. In return, Caesar made him governor of the Jewish homeland. Hyrcanus retained his job as high priest and as a prince with about as much political mojo as today's crown prince of England—whose mojo would fit in a tea bag.

Antipater the Arab gave important jobs to his two oldest sons: Herod became governor of Galilee; Phasael ruled Jerusalem. At the time, Herod was 25—just one year older than Alexander the Great had been when he marched through the Jewish homeland. Herod seems to have had the same fire in his soul and would eventually share Alexander's superlative title, becoming known as Herod the Great.

A ruthless leader, Herod quickly placated Galilee, though it was a famous hole-in-the-wall populated by lawbreakers. His leadership skills didn't escape notice in Rome, where the senate was on the lookout for foreign rulers capable of pacifying and running distant provinces. When his father was assassinated, Herod become the dominant leader of the region—though not yet a king.

Then Rome made the mistake of releasing Antigonus, the exiled son of Aristobulus, one of the feuding brothers of the defunct Hasmonean Dynasty. This young man had inherited his father's violent craving for power, and he rallied support for his cause from among the Parthian Empire in what is now Iran and Afghanistan. In 40 BC, Antigonus drove Herod out of Jerusalem and captured Herod's brother Phasael, who committed suicide rather than endure torture and mutilation. Antigonus also cut off the ears of Hyrcanus, the high priest, a mutilation that disqualified him from serving any longer as high priest.

Herod sailed to Rome, where he appealed for help in taking back the Jewish territory for Rome—and, more important, for himself. Mark Antony remembered how Herod had pacified rough and tough Galilee. So at Antony's recommendation, the senate declared Herod king of Judea. Herod raised an army of mercenary troops, and with Roman reinforcements, he took back Jerusalem then captured and executed Antigonus, the rebel leader.

In appreciation, Rome expanded Herod's kingdom, giving him most of what are now the livable parts of modern-day Israel, along with Roman provinces in present-day Syria and Jordan.

Herod quickly secured his hold on power by eliminating potential rivals. These included 45 nobles who had supported the rebel leader, along with most of the Sanhedrin, the Jewish high council that managed Jewish affairs a bit like a combined Supreme Court/Congress.

To retain his hold on power, Herod later ordered the execution of many people he considered threats, including family members he thought were plotting a coup. These included

- Hyrcanus, the now-earless former high priest and last remaining leadership link to the ruling family of Jews from the Hasmonean Dynasty;
- Mariamne, his wife, who was also the granddaughter of Hyrcanus;
- Mariamne's mother and brother;
- his two sons by Mariamne; and
- a third son by another wife.

All this family slaughter led Caesar Augustus to crack an alliterative pun: "I would rather be Herod's pig (*bys*, in Rome's preferred language of Latin) than his son (*buios*)."

It was a solid one-liner, sure to draw a laugh from anyone who knew the Jews. Herod, who was at least a marginally practicing Jew, wouldn't have ordered a pig slaughtered, because pork wasn't kosher. Yet he slaughtered his own sons.

Vicious though he was, Herod tried to endear himself to the masses. He built wonderful facilities throughout his kingdom, including entire cities, such as the harbor town of Caesarea, and aqueducts to bring water into cities such as Jerusalem. But his most memorable project was the Jerusalem Temple, which he expanded and remodeled beyond even what King Solomon, in all his glory, had been able to accomplish.

Still, most Jews never did warm up to Herod. They considered him an outsider teamed up with the Romans against them. And they thought the same of Herod's sons, who inherited much of the kingdom.

PILATE AND HEROD'S BOYS

Herod died in 4 BC, perhaps just a couple of years after Jesus was born. Herod left a will that split his kingdom among three of the sons he hadn't killed.

Rome accepted Herod's wishes but demoted all three men. One got to keep the title of king, but he ended up with just a part of the Jewish homeland. The other two sons got diminished titles, reducing their status to that of governors.

- **Herod Archelaus** (ruled 4 BC–AD 6) became king of Judea, the Roman province surrounding Jerusalem. He managed to upset the Jews so much that Rome fired him a decade later and replaced him with a series of Roman governors, including Pilate, who became infamous for ordering the crucifixion of Jesus.
- **Herod Antipas** (ruled 4 BC–AD 39) served Rome by governing Galilee and Perea as *tetrarch*, a title less prestigious than *king*.
- **Herod Philip** (4 BC–AD 34) served as tetrarch over several small provinces—Gaulanitis, Trachonitis, Batanea, and Auranitis—in what is now Syria.

By the time Jesus stepped into this scene by launching his ministry in about AD 29, the Jews were fed up from nearly a century of Roman occupation—more than 60 years of that under the rule of Herod and his family.

They ached for freedom to live as Jews led by fellow Jews in a sovereign Jewish nation.

They thought all they needed was a divine spark—a bold savior with the anointing, spirit, and power of God. Someone like King David, who would rally the nation and lead them to victory.

Instead, they were sent Jesus, who would lead them to God.

JESUS' FAMILY TREE

Reporting the story of Jesus, Matthew missed his lead. That's what students of journalism might say after reading his first few sentences.

A good lead instantly hooks a reader—perhaps with a shocking quote, a jaw-dropping revelation, or maybe an intriguing question. If Matthew were writing today, he might launch into the story by reporting that Jesus healed the sick, walked on water, and rose from the dead.

Instead, Matthew the Gospel writer starts with the most mundane information

WHO DID WHAT IN THE JEWISH FAMILY?

It was a man's world in Jesus' day. Men ruled the roost. But they couldn't keep the family well fed and secure by themselves. Everyone had to help out in some way.

Father. As head of the family, a Jewish father controlled the family's life. He also had a wide-ranging to-do list:

- Provide income to sustain the family with food, clothing, shelter—often working in this agricultural society as shepherd, farmer, fisherman, or merchant.
- Teach sons the family trade, along with the Jewish laws.
- Maintain the house, repairing the clay walls and roof after rainstorms.
- Arrange the marriages of daughters.
- If wanting to divorce his wife, write a short letter saying so; this letter served as a legally binding document dissolving the marriage.

Mother. A mother's main job was to manage the home front by taking care of the children and keeping food on the table. Chores:

- Provide children for her husband.
- Carry water each day from the village well, usually in the cool of the day— morning or evening.
- Grind wheat or barley kernels into flour for making the daily loaves of bread.
- Prepare the meals.
- Spin wool and flax (a fibrous plant) into thread.
- Make and repair the family clothes.
- Teach daughters how to cook, sew, and do the other household chores.

Son. Boys grew up helping their father in the field or the shop and learning to read by studying the sacred Jewish writings at home or in the synagogue. Only sons—not daughters—could inherit the family estate.

Daughter. Girls stayed at home with their mother, learning the chores their mothers did. Most girls weren't taught to read or write and weren't permitted in the synagogue schools, which were devoted especially to religious training.

Servant. Like slaves in recent centuries and illegal immigrants today, servants often did the jobs no one else wanted to do:

- washing the feet of guests;
- serving meals to the family;
- hauling water from the well;
- guarding the flock; and
- helping with the harvest by hand-cutting stalks of grain and picking olives, grapes, and other produce.

possible: a list of Jesus' relatives. "This is a record of the ancestors of Jesus the Messiah" (Matthew 1:1).

That's it. Matthew's lead. His attempt to hook readers.

But the thing is, it worked. For readers of Matthew's time, this genealogy was everything a good lead should be. It reached right up off the scroll, grabbed the reader by the ears, and yelled out loud and clear, "Jesus is the promised Messiah we've all been waiting for. And you won't believe who's in Messiah's family."

WHY GENEALOGIES WERE SO IMPORTANT

Matthew's genealogy was a legal document. By comparing it to other genealogies, Jews could confirm that Jesus met the two most important ancestral requirements for the Messiah that God had promised to send:

- Jesus was a Jew descended from Abraham; and
- he was related to King David, which made him a legit contender for Israel's throne.

There were other genealogies to confirm the family links that Matthew alleged. Many were safely secured inside the Temple compound, especially genealogies about the families of priests and kings. These were important because Jewish law said only descendants of King David could serve as king, and only descendants of Moses' brother, Aaron, could serve as priests.

So if a Jew wanted to work in the Jerusalem Temple as a priest, he needed to prove that he was swimming in Aaron's gene pool.

The Bible tells about some who couldn't prove their claim. When Jews in the mid-500s BC returned to their homeland from a 50-year exile in what is now Iraq—then called Babylon—some insisted they were descended from priests. But they didn't have the paperwork.

"Three families of priests—Hobaiah, Hakkoz, and Barzillai—also returned. . . . They searched for their names in the genealogical records, but they were not found, so they were disqualified from serving as priests" (Ezra 2:61–62).

Some people returning to Israel were even disqualified as Jews: "Another group returned [652 people]. . . . However, they could not prove that they or their families were descendants of Israel" (Ezra 2:59).

Genealogies were a big deal, not only among the Jews.

Romans, too, expected people to be able to trace their heritage back several generations. This determined their social status—and their tax level. Roman citizens were taxed at lower rates than citizens of conquered lands. A Roman noble could refuse to let his daughter marry if the would-be husband couldn't trace his aristocratic bloodline back five generations.

Most people in Matthew's day couldn't read or write. So it was common to commit a genealogy to memory—or at least the highlights of it.

Many Bible experts say Matthew's genealogy was tailored for memorization.

For one thing, it's condensed. At first glance, it looks like it traces every generation from Abraham to Jesus. But it doesn't. It skips many generations. Matthew names only 14 men spanning the 1,000 years from Abraham to David. But in a single century, there can easily be three generations of men leading their families: grandfather, father, and son. And that would add up to 30 generations over 10 centuries. So Matthew may have skipped half or more of the generations.

Many Bible scholars see Matthew's list as divided into three groups of 14. Perhaps that's partly to help people memorize it.

But it could also be to promote Jesus as the Messiah, descended from King David. Hebrew letters had number equivalents. And as shorthand to conserve space on scrolls, Jews wrote only consonants, not vowels. They would have written David's name in letters comparable to our English letters *dvd*. In Hebrew, *d* equals 4 and *v* equals 6.

Do the math. David's name is 4 + 6 + 4. That equals 14.

So the list of names in Matthew's genealogy, as well as the arrangement of those names, identifies Jesus as the Messiah.

WHY DOESN'T MATTHEW'S GENEALOGY MATCH LUKE'S?

The Gospel of Luke also reports a genealogy of Jesus. But it's disturbingly different from Matthew's. It actually appears that Luke is barking up the wrong family tree. Or maybe Matthew got it wrong.

In the 500 years between Joseph and Zerubbabel—one of the Jewish leaders returning from exile in Babylon—Matthew lists only nine names. Luke doubles that, perhaps evidence that Matthew condensed his version of the genealogy.

But there are differences more perplexing than this. Matthew said Joseph's father was Jacob, but Luke says it was Heli. Again, this is possible evidence that Matthew skipped a generation and jumped directly to Joseph's grandfather or beyond. There are also many other names that show up in Luke's list that never got a mention by Matthew.

Bible experts offer theories about why the two lists don't mesh. Here are a couple of the more popular ones:

- **Theory 1.** Matthew traced Jesus' genealogy through his legal ancestry by Joseph's adoption. Luke traced Jesus' blood connection to David through Mary.

- **Theory 2.** Matthew and Luke both worked from Joseph's family tree, but for different reasons, drawing from different sources, and highlighting different ancestors. Matthew wanted to show Jesus' legal claim to David's throne. But Luke, a Gentile, traced Jesus' lineage beyond Abraham—all the way back to Adam. That's because Luke wanted to spotlight Jesus' connection to all humans through Adam—not just his connection to the Jews through Abraham.

Whatever the reason behind the different genealogies, there's little doubt that Matthew and Luke both got their main point right: Jesus belongs in the family tree of Abraham and David.

There's support for this outside the Bible: from early Christian writers, Roman historians, and even the Jewish community.

- **Church writers.** Augustine, a church leader in the AD 300s, expressed the church's prevailing view that Jesus was "the son of God in his divine nature and the son of David in the flesh."
- **Historians.** Romans interrogated the grandsons of one of Jesus' brothers because they were descended from David, according to *Church History*, a book written in the early AD 300s by Eusebius. Also, Julius Africanus, a historian from the late AD 100s, reported that Jesus' relatives said they were David's descendants.
- **Jews.** Though most Jews insisted Jesus wasn't the Messiah, they didn't deny his connection to David. Jesus' genealogy was a matter of public record.

ADOPTION THICK AS BLOOD

Even if Jesus had been related to David only through his adoption by Joseph, Mary's husband, that in no legal way diminished Jesus' connection to David. Even if Jesus had been grafted onto David's family tree, he was still part of the tree.

In that society, an adopted son was a full son, with all the rights and respect due a son by birth. Jews treated their adopted children that way. So did the Romans.

Before Abraham had a son, he expected to adopt one of his servants. Abraham and his wife were both old and apparently infertile. So Abraham told God, "Eliezer of Damascus, a servant in my household, will inherit all my wealth" (Genesis 15:2). God assured Abraham that this wouldn't be necessary. But if it had been, Eliezer would have been considered Abraham's son no less than Isaac was later.

Among the Romans, family ties of adoption were strong enough to secure even the throne. Julius Caesar, a man without a son, adopted Octavian, who later became Emperor Augustus. And Augustus adopted Tiberius, who assumed control of the empire when Augustus died.

SHADY WOMEN

Testosterone ruled. Women weren't considered worth a mention in most genealogies. Yet Matthew named four from distant history. That's strange enough. But the four he plucked from the family tree seem like rotten apples not fit to hang out with the Messiah.

If Matthew felt that he had to mention a few token women, why didn't he go for the revered mothers of Judaism—matriarchs such as Sarah, Rebekah, Rachel, and Leah? These respected women—wives of Abraham, Isaac, and Jacob—produced the grandsons and sons who gave their names to the tribes of Israel.

SEX SCANDALS

All five women in Matthew's genealogy of Jesus risked public hostility over what looked like sexual misconduct. Tamar, Rahab, and Bathsheba had sex outside of marriage. The Virgin Mary was accused of it. And Ruth crawled under the covers of a wealthy man she had just met.

FIVE LADY BIRDS OF A FEATHER

	TAMAR	RAHAB	RUTH	BATHSHEBA	MARY
Sex scandal	Had sex with father-in-law, delivered twin sons	Prostitute in Jericho	Put on perfume and sneaked under covers of a man	Had affair with King David; got pregnant	Got pregnant, but not by fiancé, Joseph
At risk	Sentenced to death by burning	Risked charges of treason for helping Jewish spies	Risked being accused of prostitution	Risked death, the penalty for adultery	Risked broken engagement and possibly execution
Outcast	For being unmarried and pregnant	For being a hooker	For being a widow without a son to take care of her	For adultery	For being unmarried and pregnant
Mistreated	Abandoned by the man who was supposed to provide her with a husband	Apparently forced to choose between prostitution or begging	As a widow, all her assets were confiscated; she was left homeless	"Invited" to have sex with the king	Joseph decided to break the engagement
Cleared	Father-in-law admitted mistreating her	For her courageous help, she was allowed to join the Israelites	Boaz married her; their son was the grandfather of King David	David took the blame and married her; they had a son: King Solomon	Angel told Joseph that Mary was pregnant by Holy Spirit; Joseph married Mary
Race	Probably Canaanite	Canaanite from Jericho	Arab from Moab (modern-day Jordan)	Possibly Hittite (from modern-day Turkey) like her first husband	Jew who gave birth to Savior of all races—Jew and non-Jew

Instead, Matthew picked these women from the family tree:

- **Tamar**, a widow who tricked her father-in-law into thinking she was a hooker; she had sex with him, got pregnant, and had twin sons;
- **Rahab**, a hooker who ran her business out of Jericho;
- **Ruth**, an Arab who took a bath, put on perfume, dressed in her best clothes—and then slipped under the covers of a sleeping man; and
- **Bathsheba**, a married woman who had an affair with King David and got pregnant.

Why on earth would Matthew choose the likes of these women—especially if he wanted to puff up Jesus' lineage? These are skeletons that Jesus' enemies should have dragged out of the closet to deflate Matthew's claim that Jesus was the Messiah.

Actually, there's an outside chance that Ruth is the only famous Bible character that Matthew intended to mention. Adding her name to the list makes at least some sense because she was David's great-grandmother. Tamar and Rahab weren't specifically identified as the one-time and the full-time hookers. And Bathsheba isn't mentioned by name in the original Greek version but is only implied by the phrase "widow of Uriah." Still, most Bible experts agree that these infamous women from early Jewish history are exactly who Matthew had in mind.

Bible scholars are left guessing why Matthew chose them. Here are three of the most popular theories:

1. As sinners, they foreshadowed the salvation that Mary's son would bring. Matthew chose these women not because of their merits, but because of their sin. In a way, they were opening acts for the main attraction, who would "save his people from their sins" (Matthew 1:21).

In addition, these sinful women helped elevate the status of Mary, who had done nothing wrong.

Tamar's sin was to disguise herself as a prostitute so her father-in-law would get her pregnant and produce a son who would take care of her in her old age. Tamar's first two husbands—brothers of each other—had died. Fearing that his younger son, Shelah, might also die if he married Tamar, Judah refused to honor Jewish law and give Tamar to Shelah when he came of age. Instead, Judah abandoned her to poverty as a widow.

Rahab's sin was prostitution. Yet Joshua rewarded her with citizenship in Israel for protecting his spies as they scouted out Jericho. Ancient Jewish writings say she married Joshua. But Matthew, apparently drawing from a lost source, says she married Salmon and gave birth to Boaz, who married Ruth. That would have made Rahab Ruth's mother-in-law.

Ruth's sin apparently began when she crawled under the covers of a sleeping

Boaz. Yet this was a type of marriage proposal. Boaz was a close relative of Ruth's dead husband, and the ancient social security system called for the closest male relative to marry the widow, take care of her, and provide her with children if possible. If Ruth committed any sin, it was probably the intent or the action of having sex with Boaz that very night. Naomi had advised Ruth to "go and uncover his feet and lie down there. He will tell you what to do" (Ruth 3:4). "Feet" was often a euphemism for "private parts." But there's no indication that Ruth and Boaz had sex that night. In fact, Jewish writings preserve Ruth's reputation, while declaring the other three women sinful.

Bathsheba's sin—the most famous sin of the four—was to commit adultery with King David. This Bible story, however, portrays her as passive—as someone obliging Israel's Alpha Male back when men were men and everyone else was pitifully less. There's no indication that she resisted or consented. Yet Jewish law prohibited adultery. And the law presumed that a woman would scream if raped: "The woman is guilty because she did not scream for help" (Deuteronomy 22:24).

2. As foreigners, they foreshadowed salvation for Gentiles. Historians don't know for sure that all four women were Gentiles. But two were. Rahab was a Canaanite from Jericho, and Ruth was an Arab from Moab, an ancient nation in what is now Jordan.

Tamar is presumed to be Canaanite for two reasons. She lived in Canaan. And she showed up early in Jewish history, before the 12 tribes of Israel had been established as a nation. As for Bathsheba, she may have been a Jew, but it's more likely she was a Hittite, from what is now Turkey, like her husband Uriah the Hittite.

3. As sexually scandalous, they foreshadowed Mary's scandal. This is the most popular view at the moment. Like Mary, all four women got involved in unusual sexual encounters, targeting them for public scandal.

As a result—again like Mary—each woman

- *found herself outside the boundaries of respectability set by the men who ran their society.* Rahab, Tamar, and Bathsheba engaged in sex outside of marriage. Mary was thought to have done so. As for Ruth, she became a destitute widow when her husband died without leaving her a son. Women were treated like minors are today, with no legal rights to property.

- *risked condemnation for what she did.* Pregnant and unmarried, Tamar was publicly accused of sexual sin and condemned to burn to death—an uncommonly harsh sentence. She escaped only by revealing that her accuser was the father of her children. Rahab probably drew whispers for the rest of her life. Boaz kept Ruth's secret. David took the criticism for getting Bathsheba involved in the affair. And Joseph kept Mary's "indiscretion"

quiet, planning to divorce her privately.
- *was vindicated*. Rahab was welcomed into the Israelite community. Tamar's father-in-law stopped the execution by declaring, "She is more righteous than I am" (Genesis 38:26). Ruth married Boaz and gave birth to David's grandfather. Bathsheba was not held responsible for complying with the king's request, and she later married David and produced the son who took over when David died: Solomon.

Parallels like these have led many Bible experts to speculate that Matthew included Rahab, Tamar, Ruth, and Bathsheba in Jesus' genealogy for one main reason: to prepare readers for the story of yet another socially misfit woman caught up in a sex scandal but destined to be wonderfully vindicated.

RUTH: ARAB MOTHER OF THE JEWS

Not all founding mothers of the Jewish nation were Jews.

Ruth—the woman who gave birth to what became Israel's longest and most revered dynasty of kings—was an Arab from what is now Jordan.

She came from a nation called Moab and a race distantly related to the Jews—but a race descended from incest between a father and his daughters. The Jews descended from Abraham, but the Moabites descended from Abraham's nephew, Lot. After God destroyed Lot's hometown of Sodom, Lot and his daughters found shelter in a cave. The daughters thought everyone on earth had been destroyed. So to continue the human race, they got their father drunk and had sex with him.

Both daughters became pregnant. The oldest daughter gave birth to a son she named Moab, ancestor of Ruth's Moabite nation. The youngest daughter gave birth to a son she named Ammon, ancestor of the Ammonite people, who also lived in what is now Jordan. Jordan's modern-day capital of Amman is a name that comes from the Ammonite nation.

Arabs in these two neighboring nations refused to give food and water to the Jews during the exodus out of Egypt; in fact, they even hired a wizard to put a hex on Israel. As a result, God declared that "no Ammonites or Moabites, or any of their descendants for ten generations, can become part of Israel, the Lord's people" (Deuteronomy 23:3 CEV).

God made an exception for Ruth. Well before 10 generations had passed, Ruth—one exceptional Moabite—shows up in the Messiah's family tree.

She had married a Jew of Bethlehem who immigrated to her homeland during a drought in Israel. When her husband, and his brother and father, died in Moab, the widowed Ruth and her mother-in-law, Naomi, moved back to Bethlehem. There, Ruth met and married Boaz, a relative of her former husband. The couple had a son, Obed, who had a son, Jesse, who had a son, David.

David, Ruth's great-grandson, grew up to become Israel's most respected king and the founder of a 400-year family dynasty of kings that included beloved leaders such as Solomon and Hezekiah.

MARY AND JOSEPH ENGAGED

When Joseph discovered that his fiancée, Mary, was at least three months pregnant, he suddenly found himself trapped in a lose-lose scenario.

He had only two options, both painful:

- break the engagement, as Jewish law demanded; or
- ignore the law and marry her as if the child were his. But by doing this, he would forfeit his reputation as a godly man—because, in effect, by marrying a pregnant bride he would have been admitting that he had disobeyed Jewish law by having sex with Mary before the wedding.

Joseph's dilemma probably began less than a year earlier, when he first got engaged.

The Bible doesn't say how Joseph proposed or how old he and Mary were. But if they followed the typical Jewish custom reported in the Talmud, a collection of ancient Jewish commentary and laws, they were both teenagers—and Joseph's father made the proposal offer to Mary's father. (For a discussion of the theory that Joseph was an elderly widower, see "Joseph's First Family," page 31.)

The Talmud advised young women to marry when they were able to bear children—after their menstrual cycle began, at about age 12 or 13. It recommended that young men wait a bit longer—until sometime between the ages of 14 and 18. But it wasn't unheard of for a woman not to marry until her twenties, and it was quite common for men to wait that long.

Laws in neighboring countries and empires were similar. In Egypt, young women typically married between the ages of 12 and 14, and young men between 14 and 20. In the Roman Empire at the time of Augustus, when Mary and Joseph were engaged, the legal minimum age was 12 for young women and 14 for young men. But it was common for women to wait until their early teens and for men to wait until their early or middle twenties.

In Jewish communities—and throughout the Middle East—parents usually arranged the marriages of their children. The father of a young man would approach the father of a young woman and propose the marriage.

A girl over the age of 12½ could refuse her father's choice, according to the Talmud (which was written after the time of Joseph and Mary but is said to draw from teachings during that time and before). The Bible offers examples of both—parents giving freedom to the young couple in selecting their mates, and parents imposing their own will. For example, Samson picked a non-Jewish wife against the wishes of his parents. "He told his father and mother, 'A young Philistine woman in Timnah caught my eye. I want to marry her. Get her for me'" (Judges 14:2). And the widowed Ruth actually proposed to her second husband, Boaz. "Spread the corner of your covering over me," she told him, "for you are my family redeemer" (Ruth 3:9). She was invoking Jewish law that required a relative of her first husband to save her from poverty by marrying her.

JOSEPH'S FIRST FAMILY

Was Mary Joseph's second wife?

That's what some Christians speculate—especially Roman Catholics and Eastern Orthodox Christians. Both groups teach that Mary not only was a virgin when she married Joseph, but remained a virgin the rest of her life.

There are at least a couple of problems with that theory:

- **Jesus had four brothers and some sisters.** Hometown critics of Jesus said, "He's just the carpenter's son, and we know Mary, his mother, and his brothers—James, Joseph, Simon, and Judas. All his sisters live right here among us" (Matthew 13:55–56).
- **Joseph "did not have sexual relations with her until her son was born" (Matthew 1:25).** This implies they had sexual relations afterward.

This second problem is easily resolved, say some Catholic and Orthodox scholars. The Greek word translated as "until" doesn't imply sexual relations afterward any more than it excludes it.

As for the first problem, many Christian speculate that Jesus' "brothers and sisters" were actually other relatives, such as cousins. But there were also ancient stories that said these were Joseph's children by an earlier marriage.

Some early Christian writings not included in the New Testament—and considered fiction by most Bible experts—say that Joseph married his first wife when he was 40 years old. Depending on the story, her name was Melcha or Escha or Salome. They lived together for 49 years and had four sons and two daughters. A few years after his wife died, Joseph, in his early nineties, got engaged to Mary.

This would certainly explain why there's no mention of Joseph when Jesus began his ministry 30 years later. But it raises a question, too. Matthew's readers knew that couples were generally young when they got married. If Joseph was so much older than Mary, why didn't Matthew say so, rather than allow his readers to assume the mistaken notion that Joseph was a young man?

DICKERING OVER MONEY

Once two fathers agreed that their son and daughter would marry, they began to dicker. The negotiation covered two areas: what the groom's family should pay to the bride's family, and what the bride's dowry would bring into the marriage.

Bride price. The groom's family would pay the bride's family for the loss of their daughter's help around the house. Once married, the bride would move in with her husband, or with her in-laws if her husband didn't have a home.

There was no set price, which is why the fathers dickered.

But there were some general guidelines. For example, if a man stole a young woman's virginity, Jewish law said he had to marry her and pay her father 50 shekels of silver (Deuteronomy 22:29). That's about 1.25 pounds or 570 grams in weight. At today's prices, with silver selling for about $10 a troy ounce, the value would be about $150. During Bible times, 50 shekels was the going price for a male slave in his prime (Leviticus 27:3).

Some fathers were better negotiators than others. Laban, for example, talked the penniless Jacob into paying a much higher than usual price for each of Jacob's two wives: seven years of working for their father (Genesis 29:18, 27).

Outside the Bible, the Jews had other guidelines for setting the bride price. Some of these guidelines show up in writings from after the time of Joseph and Mary, but they are thought to reflect practices that were common in Joseph's day as well. Rabbis suggested 200 silver denarii for a virgin and 100 denarii for a widow. A single denarius was the daily wage for a common laborer. So the price of engagement for a laborer was about seven months of salary for a virgin; and about half that for a widow.

If we were to convert the ancient wages to a modern-day minimum wage of $7.25 ($58 per day), we're talking $11,600 for a virgin and $5,800 for a widow.

Dowry. Bride families also had a price to pay: the dowry. They gave their daughter a collection of assets, such as jewelry and money. Her husband could use these assets, but he would have to return them if he later divorced the woman.

In Joseph and Mary's time, it was common for the two families to put their agreement in writing, or at least to agree orally in front of several witnesses. This was, in essence, a prenuptial agreement, a marriage contract. One such contract, dating to AD 128, said that the woman brought a dowry of 500 denarii—200 of it in jewelry and clothing, and the remaining 300 in currency.

Bride gift. A groom would sometimes give his bride a gift to symbolize their commitment to each other. Romans sometimes used engagement rings, but Jews didn't adopt this practice until sometime after Joseph and Mary.

—— MORE THAN A MODERN-STYLE ENGAGEMENT ——

Jewish engagements usually stretched out for about a year. But they were more final than engagements today.

- The couples weren't called fiancé and fiancée. They were called husband and wife.
- If one person died before the wedding, the other was considered a widow or widower.
- A child born to the couple during the engagement was considered their legitimate child and legal heir.
- The only way to break an engagement was through divorce.

Only two of the four Gospels, Matthew and Luke, tell us about Mary's pregnancy during the engagement.

But by comparing the two stories, it's a fair guess that Mary was more than three months along before Joseph realized it—perhaps even four months or more. In Luke's timeline, the angel Gabriel told the Virgin Mary that she was about to become pregnant by the Holy Spirit. "A few days later Mary hurried to the hill country of Judea" (Luke 1:39), which is in the southern region of

Israel, near Jerusalem. She went there to visit a relative named Elizabeth, who was herself already six months pregnant. "Mary stayed with Elizabeth about three months and then went back to her own home" (Luke 1:56). Mary probably stayed for Elizabeth's delivery—a son, who would later be known as John the Baptist.

HOW TO GET DISENGAGED

The Bible doesn't say when or how Joseph discovered the pregnancy. But once he did, he decided to divorce Mary, as Jewish law required. Greek and Roman laws agreed. To do otherwise would have condoned Mary's apparent adultery. And that would have branded Joseph as a moral bottom dweller.

Joseph's pain could have been eased a bit by divorcing Mary publicly— if money eases heartache. The law allowed him to confiscate her dowry. One marriage contract from the ancient Middle East puts it this way: "If Demetria [bride] is discovered doing any evil to the shame of her husband, Heraklides, let her be deprived of everything she brought [to the marriage]. But let Heraklides prove whatever he sues Demetria about before three men on whom they both agree."

For Joseph, this approach was not an option.

"Joseph, her fiancé, was a good man and did not want to disgrace her publicly, so he decided to break the engagement quietly" (Matthew 1:19). All he needed to do was write a short note of divorce and let two or three witnesses read it.

Here's a divorce letter written in AD 72 at Masada, a community in what is now southern Israel. The names of Joseph and Mary have been inserted in place of the original names:

> "I, Joseph, divorce and release of my own free will today you, Mary, who had been my wife before this time. You are free on your part to go and become the wife of any Jewish man you wish. This is for you a writ of release and a bill of divorce. . . . At any time that you ask me, I will replace this document for you."

Mary and her family would have appreciated this gentle approach more than most Jews in Israel. That's because they lived in Galilee, a region in northern Israel where parents tried to keep the engaged couples from spending time alone with each other. Jews in the southland were more relaxed about this.

But not in Galilee. Not according to ancient Jewish reports.

Galilean Jews based their practice on an old adage still common in some Middle Eastern communities: If a man and woman are left alone for 20 minutes, they'll have sex.

Before Joseph could divorce Mary, "an angel of the Lord appeared to him in a dream. 'Joseph, son of David,' the angel said, 'do not be afraid to take Mary as your wife. For the child within her was conceived by the Holy Spirit. And she will have a son, and you are to name him Jesus, for he will save his people from their sins.' . . . When Joseph woke up, he did as the angel of the Lord commanded and took Mary as his wife. But he did not have sexual relations with her until her son was born. And Joseph named him Jesus" (Matthew 1:20–21, 24–25).

IT'S ONLY A DREAM

Why would something as flighty as a dream convince Joseph that something as bizarre as a virgin birth was about to happen? And to his fiancée, of all people?

Wouldn't the odds favor a goat cheese sandwich gone bad as the suppertime source of his weird dream?

Fact is, people in ancient times believed that dreams connected humanity to the heavens. Middle Eastern people at a crossroads in their lives would sometimes seek guidance from the gods by sleeping in holy places, such as temples. Assyrians (from what is now Iraq) wrote books about how to interpret dreams. So did the Egyptians.

One such book, written by an Egyptian scribe named Kenhirkhopeshef, is full of dream scenes and how to interpret them. For example, if you see yourself in a dream as

- **dead,** you'll live a long life;
- **making love to your wife in the daytime,** the gods will discover what you've done wrong in your life;
- **eating crocodile meat,** you'll become a politician—a village official.

The Bible confirms that God often used dreams to communicate to people of all sorts—prophets and pagans alike.

Prophets. "If there were prophets among you, I, the Lord, would reveal myself in visions. I would speak to them in dreams" (Numbers 12:6).

Pagans. "That night God came to Abimelech in a dream and told him, 'You are a dead man, for that woman you have taken is already married!' " (Genesis 20:3).

God also gave some people the gift of interpreting dreams. "God gave Daniel the special ability to interpret the meanings of visions and dreams" (Daniel 1:17).

So when Joseph fell asleep and dreamed what may have been an especially vivid dream about Mary giving birth to the Messiah, it caught his attention. He may have confirmed the message by asking Mary what the angel had told her. Both got the same basic information, with Joseph's message reported in Matthew and Mary's message reported in Luke:

- Mary would give birth to a son conceived by the Holy Spirit (Matthew 1:20; Luke 1:35).
- The child would save his people (Matthew 1:21; Luke 1:33).
- He would be named Jesus (Matthew 1:21; Luke 1:31).

JESUS IS BORN

She gave birth to her first child, a son.
She wrapped him snugly in strips of cloth
and laid him in a manger.

LUKE 2:7

B orn in a barn, the King of kings and Savior of the world didn't get off to a particularly regal start.

Judging from his humble birth, Jesus looked like he was doomed to spend his life as a social bottom dweller who would make no mark in the world larger than a grave.

- His mother got pregnant without any help from her husband.
- His adoptive father was a common worker, a carpenter.
- His family lived in Nazareth, a hole-in-the-wall village in northern Israel.

As the newborn Jesus lay in a feeding trough built for livestock, life didn't seem to be looking up—not as far as a casual observer could see.

But the casual observer wasn't there earlier to witness angels assuring Joseph and Mary otherwise. And for some shepherds tending their sheep near Bethlehem, what they observed in the nighttime sky on Jesus' birthday was anything but casual. Heaven's army hovered overhead, praising God and directing them to "the Savior—yes, the Messiah, the Lord" (Luke 2:11).

IS DECEMBER 25 REALLY CHRISTMAS?

No, Virginia, Santa Claus got the date wrong.

That's if you go with the odds—which are 365 to one that Jesus was born on some other day. The odds get longer when we add a clue from Luke:

"That night there were shepherds staying in the fields nearby, guarding their flocks of sheep" (Luke 2:8).

They were sleeping outside—at night—in the dead of winter?

Most Bible experts say they doubt it. Bethlehem lies on nearly the same latitude as Waco, Texas, and Savannah, Georgia. But the average low temperature in December hovers around freezing—even lower in January. Outdoor grazing generally stretched from early spring to late fall: March to November.

The real birth date of Jesus has been lost to history.

Some early church leaders didn't even want to celebrate Jesus' birthday. They argued that he's not like some pharaoh, Herod, or pagan god. Origen made that case in the AD 200s.

Others disagreed and pitched their favorite dates:
- *January 2*, Hippolytus (about AD 170–236);
- *March 21*, a Latin essay (about AD 243) insisting March 21 was the day God created the sun; and
- *May 20*, Clement of Alexandria (about AD 150–215).

continued on p.36

continued from p.35

As far as we can tell, Christmas was first celebrated on December 25 in AD 336, after Emperor Constantine legalized Christianity.

Many scholars say that church leaders picked this date to bump aside a trio of winter solstice holidays that were popular among Romans. Winter solstice is when the sun starts to make its comeback, when the long nights of winter begin to shorten and move toward the long days of summer.

Christmas commandeered these pagan holidays:

Saturnalia. Celebrated December 17–24, this was one of Rome's best-known festivals. It honored the god Saturn, father of Jupiter (Greek: Zeus). Businesses, schools, and public offices closed to allow people to party hearty and exchange gifts.

Here's how Seneca, a Roman philosopher writing in AD 50, describes the flurry of activty: "It is now the month of December, when most of the city is in a bustle. . . . Loose reins are given to the public for their wild parties; everywhere you may hear the sound of great preparations."

Birthday of the Unconquered Sun. In the Latin language of the Romans, this celebration was called *Natalis Solis Invicti.* This festival marked the beginning of the end of a dark and dreary winter and the coming of springtime and summer.

Birthday of the Sun of Righteousness. This honored the birthday of Mithras, the sun god worshipped by people in what is now Iran—and by many Roman soldiers. Mithraism was a bloody cult, which may have been one of the attractions for soldiers. As the story goes, Mithras was born with a knife. He later rode and killed the cosmic bull, whose blood fertilized all vegetation and gave life to the planet. Cult members worshipped Mithras by killing bulls and standing in a pit below the corpses to let the blood wash over them.

They were literally washed in the blood of the bull. Christians, on the other hand, thought of themselves as "washed. . .in the blood of the Lamb" (Revelation 7:14).

In time, Christians argued that their celebration on December 25 had nothing to do with trying to Christianize pagan sun worship. As one anonymous Christian explained in the AD 300s, "We hold this day holy, not like the pagans because of the birth of the sun, but because of him who made it."

GETTING THE YEAR RIGHT

Oddly, Jesus was born in a BC year. Before Christ.

Go figure.

As a result, our entire calendar spins around the wrong birth year of Jesus.

Calendars today tag years of ancient history as BC or AD. The AD stands for *Anno Domini*, Latin for "in the year of our Lord."

But the monk who invented the AD calendar by starting it with the year of Jesus' birth got the birthday wrong—by six years, maybe more.

The monk's name was Dionysius Exiguus. In English, we'd call him Dennis the Little. And given what he did to our calendar, some might suggest Dennis the Menace. He lived in Rome 500 years after the time of Jesus, and he created the calendar at the pope's request. Where Dennis came up with the date for Jesus' birth, he didn't say.

Matthew and Luke put the birth of Jesus in the final years of Herod the Great, the Rome-approved king of the Jews. He's the king who ordered the slaughter of all the boys in Bethlehem ages two and younger, in an attempt to kill Jesus. Herod died in 4 BC. If one of his last acts was to order the Bethlehem slaughter, and if Jesus maxed out the age limit of two, then he would have been born sometime around 6 BC. Some scholars guess 7 BC.

But there's a problem with these dates as well.

If we merge Luke's story with surviving Roman history written in the same century, we'd have to mark Jesus' birthday a decade after King Herod died. Luke said Jesus was born during "the first census taken when Quirinius was governor of Syria" (Luke 2:2). But Josephus, a first-century historian, says that Quirinius wasn't appointed governor until the Roman year equal to AD 6.

Bible experts offer several theories for solving the dilemma:

- A partial inscription leaves the door open to the possibility that Quirinius served an earlier term as well—from 10 to 7 BC. Unfortunately, his name isn't on the inscription.
- Quirinius may have been governing the region before his official appointment.
- The reference to the "first" census of Quirinius could also be translated "before." So the revised sentence would read: "This census was before the one that Quirinius conducted."
- The census Luke reported could have been the "first" of two censuses that Quirinius conducted. The second would have been the one Josephus reported.

POP QUIZ

Who does the following stone inscription from the first century describe?

"The birth date of our God has signaled
the beginning of good news for the world."

Jesus?

Try Caesar Augustus—the Roman emperor who ruled when Jesus was born and who was worshipped as a god.

Luke begins the story about Jesus' birth by mentioning Augustus: "At that time the Roman emperor, Augustus, decreed that a census should be taken" (Luke 2:1).

A few sentences later, Luke describes the birth of Jesus with words that sound like a spin-off of the inscription describing Augustus: "I bring you good news that will bring great joy to all people. The Savior—yes, the Messiah, the Lord—has been born today" (Luke 2:10–11).

Some wonder whether Luke was taking a jab at Augustus, essentially saying, "You're not the real savior of the world. Jesus is."

But it's just a guess, because Luke doesn't tend to buck the empire elsewhere in his writings, which include the book of Acts.

BETHLEHEM BOUND

Taxes were on the mind of Caesar Augustus when he ordered the census. God used these Roman taxes imposed on the Jews in a good way—to help fulfill a seven-hundred-year-old prophecy about the Messiah:

> "But you, O Bethlehem Ephrathah, are only a small village among all the people of Judah. Yet a ruler of Israel will come from you, one whose origins are from the distant past. . . . He will be highly honored around the world. And he will be the source of peace."
>
> MICAH 5:2, 4–5

It's a mystery why Joseph and Mary had to go to Bethlehem for the census. "All returned to their own ancestral towns to register for this census. And because Joseph was a descendant of King David, he had to go to Bethlehem in Judea, David's ancient home" (Luke 2:3–4).

That sounds like a fine explanation. But there's no evidence that the Romans ever conducted a census this way. Perhaps they delegated this census to the local provinces. If so, the Jews could have planned it. Tied as the Jews were to their family heritage, it would have made sense for them to go back to their ancestral, tribal hometowns for a census.

Augustus ordered a census periodically to enroll people for taxes. This registration gave him an idea of the revenue he could expect. People in provinces throughout the empire were taxed per person, as well as by a percentage of their assets.

It's unclear why Mary—nine months pregnant—accompanied Joseph on the long trip from Nazareth to Bethlehem. Depending on the route they traveled, it could have taken them three to five days to cover the 70 to 90 miles (110 to 145 km). And if she were still just his "fiancée" (Luke 2:5), their fellow countrymen wouldn't have taken kindly to their traveling alone. Galileans generally frowned on engaged couples spending time alone.

But Bible experts say that *fiancée* could be Luke's shorthand way of showing that Joseph and Mary hadn't consummated their marriage. And Mary's late-term pregnancy may have been the very reason she went along—she wanted Joseph with her when Jesus was born.

VIRGIN BIRTH

In the story of Jesus' birth, there's one tidbit that's absolutely unique: He was born to a woman who hadn't had sexual intercourse.

There are plenty of myths about women getting pregnant by one of the gods. Legend says Rome started that way. Twin brothers Romulus and Remus, the founders of Rome, were said to have been born to Rhea Silvia, a virgin devoted to the goddess Vesta to remain a virgin her entire life. But as the legend goes, Mars, the god of war, got her pregnant.

Bible experts say Rhea Silvia's experience doesn't come close to the Bible's description of Mary's conception: "While she was still a virgin, she became pregnant through the power of the Holy Spirit" (Matthew 1:18).

Irenaeus, a theologian from the AD 100s, explained that just as the Spirit of God created life at the beginning of time, the Holy Spirit created new life in Mary—a fresh start for humanity.

There's no indication that the Holy Spirit took physical form and implanted sanctified semen in Mary. Throughout the New Testament, the Holy Spirit is portrayed as a spiritual entity, not a physical one. Even the description of the Spirit descending on Jesus "like a dove" (Matthew 3:16) is intended to describe the arrival of heavenly power. It's not a clue that the third member of the Trinity is a bird.

Only Matthew and Luke report the virgin birth. Some scholars conclude that this meager mention shows that the teaching was inserted into the Bible by a creative editor. Others insist there was no need for other New Testament writers to defend the teaching, because Christians already knew about it and believed it.

Matthew linked the virgin birth to a prophecy by Isaiah 700 years earlier:

All of this occurred to fulfill the Lord's message through his prophet: "Look! The virgin will conceive a child! She will give birth to a son, and they will call him Immanuel, which means 'God is with us.'"

MATTHEW 1:22–23

Actually, most scholars say Isaiah was talking about a young woman in his time. And the Hebrew word he used for *virgin* could refer to any young woman —virgin or not. But Matthew apparently saw this prophecy pulling a double shift, applying to Mary as well. So Matthew used the Greek word for *virgin* that means just that—not "young woman."

In the AD 100s, Celsus, a Greek philosopher and critic of Christianity, said the Greek word for *virgin* (*parthenos*) was probably a subtle wordplay to reveal the true name of Jesus' father: a Roman soldier called Panthera, which was a common name. Years later, rabbis picked up this theory and tweaked it a tad. They, too, said the story might have been a poetic play on words to disguise the fact that Mary got pregnant by a Roman soldier. The Greek word for *soldier* is *pandera*.

But by the time of Celsus, Christians widely embraced the virgin birth of Jesus, and the teaching showed up in their statements of faith. Sometime between centuries one and five, church leaders declared the virgin birth as one of the key tenets of the Christian faith: "He [Jesus] was conceived by the power of the Holy Spirit and born of the Virgin Mary" (Apostles' Creed).

CHURCH OF JESUS' BIRTH

Since the first century AD, legend says, Christians have venerated a cave beneath what is now Bethlehem's Church of the Nativity. The legend says Jesus was born in this very cave.

The cave got tagged a sacred site at least as early as AD 135. Emperor Hadrian did the tagging when, after he crushed a Jewish revolt in the region, he decided to destroy all sacred Jewish and Christian shrines. In their place, he built Roman shrines—which had the opposite effect he intended. His shrines preserved the locations of the holy sites.

Ironically, the shrine that Hadrian built over the cave stable in Bethlehem was devoted to Adonis—a Greek god famous for his resurrection. Adonis supposedly spent each winter in Hades and came back to earth each spring.

Two hundred years after Hadrian built this shrine, Emperor Constantine legalized Christianity. For the first time in history, Christians were allowed to build churches. When Constantine's mother, Helena, visited the Holy Land in the early AD 300s, she learned that the shrine to Adonis marked the birthplace of Jesus. So she ordered the Church of the Nativity built over the cave.

The church was completed in about AD 330. Though it has suffered over the long centuries, much of the original church has survived. Persian invaders (from what is now Iran) destroyed most of the Holy Land churches and synagogues in the AD 600s but left this one standing. Legend says it's because they saw art inside of people from their culture: wise men from the East.

BORN IN A BARN

When Joseph and Mary arrived at the tiny hilltop village of Bethlehem, about six miles south of Jerusalem, they couldn't find lodging. Some Bible translations call it an "inn" (*katalyma* in Greek). But it probably wasn't a typical hotel.

Luke talked about a public hotel in the parable of the Good Samaritan. That's where the Good Samaritan took an injured man he found alongside the road. But for that inn, Luke used a different Greek word: *pandocheion*.

Bible experts guess that the lodging Joseph and Mary couldn't find was a guest room in a private home, or perhaps a caravansary—where travelers such as caravan merchants would water their livestock and rest for the night. There was a caravansary on the outskirts of Bethlehem, along the main route to Egypt.

Joseph and Mary ended up spending the night in a shelter for livestock. Christian writers in the AD 100s said the shelter was a cave. The hills around Bethlehem are laced with caves where animals take shelter in bad weather. Some poor people today still make their homes in these caves.

DELIVERING BABY JESUS

Luke, a physician, tells us more about the birth of Jesus than any other Gospel writer. Yet even the doc manages only two sentences about the delivery: "She gave birth to her first child, a son. She wrapped him snugly in strips of cloth and laid him in a manger" (Luke 2:7).

Jesus the first son. "First son" doesn't necessarily mean that Mary had other children after Jesus. Catholic and Orthodox Christians teach that she didn't and that the brothers and sisters reported in Matthew 13:55–56 were other relatives, such as cousins, or perhaps Joseph's children from a previous marriage.

But *first son* does identify two important facts about Jesus, say many Bible experts:

- Jewish law required that the firstborn son be devoted to God in a special ceremony, and Jesus was that son.
- "First son" meant that Jesus had the rights of the family's first son, which included a leadership role in the family and twice as much inheritance as any other son in the family.

Childbirth techniques. A Roman physician from the AD 100s, Soranus, wrote about childbirth in his book *On Midwifery and the Diseases of Women*.

Birthing stool. Soranus' how-to book on delivering a baby had the pregnant woman sitting on a birthing stool, with someone holding on to her from behind.

Midwife. A midwife usually handled the delivery, even if a male doctor was available to direct. There was a sense that women were better suited to treat women. And this helped with worries about modesty.

Lubricating oil. The midwife saturated the mother's vagina with olive oil to help ease the delivery.

Stretching the birth canal. The midwife inserted a finger from her left hand into the mother's vagina. Making circular motions, she would gently widen the birth canal with her left hand while lubricating it with oil in her right hand between contractions.

Pushing. When the child was ready to greet the world, the midwife would tell the mother to take a deep breath and push. The midwife would grab the child and pull it out when the uterine muscles were relaxed, not contracted.

Cutting the cord. The umbilical cord was cut four finger-widths from the baby's belly and then tied with wool yarn.

Evaluation of the child. The midwife checked the child for deformity, strength in crying, and pain responses. This was to see if the child was "worth raising." (See "Kid Killers," page 56.)

Cleaning. If the child was a keeper, the midwife sprinkled it with powdered salt to protect against infection. Then she rinsed the baby in warm water and rubbed it with olive oil. She added drops of oil to the eyes to wash away the thick residue from the uterus.

Wrapping. Finally, the midwife wrapped the baby tightly in strips of cloth—swaddling clothes—about two inches wide. The ancients said this would help the child grow straight. It also protected the child from potential eye injury caused by its own fingernails. The child was kept swaddled for about six months, though changed as necessary, washed, rubbed in oil, and dusted with dried, powdered myrtle leaves.

Placed in a feeding trough. Wrapped, the baby was placed on a pillow filled with soft hay.

SPECIAL INVITATION FOR SHEPHERDS

Luke shifts the scene from Bethlehem to a nighttime field on the outskirts of town. If this pasture is what's known today as the Shepherds' Field, as tour guides often suggest, it's about two miles (3 km) from the village.

Suddenly an angel appeared, lighting the night and terrifying the shepherds.

"Don't be afraid!" the angel said. "I bring you good news that will bring great joy to all people. The Savior—yes, the Messiah, the Lord—has been born today in Bethlehem, the city of David!" (Luke 2:10–11).

Then an army of angels appeared and began praising God.

The scene faded again to the dark of night as the angels disappeared.

Why such a special invitation for lowly shepherds, at the bottom of the cultural barrel? Most Bible experts see a theme in this story: empathy and compassion for the poor. Jesus came in humility to bring the good news of salvation to the poorest people.

Some 30 years later, Jesus said as much during a worship service in his hometown of Nazareth: "The Spirit of the Lord is upon me, for he has anointed me to bring Good News to the poor" (Luke 4:18).

The shepherds—sometimes called the world's first evangelists—rushed to Bethlehem and told Joseph and Mary, and anyone else who would listen, what the angel had just told them.

RITUALS FOR BABY JESUS

Mary remained ritually unclean for the first week after the birth. But on the eighth day, she and Joseph had Jesus circumcised, as Jewish law required:

"From generation to generation, every male child must be circumcised on the eighth day after his birth" (Genesis 17:12). It was part of the covenant agreement between God and the Jews; in a sense, a contract signature written in blood.

After the first week, Mary still had another 33 days of seclusion—during which she was not allowed to take part in religious ceremonies. The ban would have been 66 days had Mary delivered a girl. But after the six weeks had passed, Mary and her family went to Jerusalem to perform two rituals: purification and dedication.

Mary's purification. Mary brought a purification offering to the Temple. The law called for two animals: a year-old lamb and a pigeon or dove. But if a family couldn't afford this—and Mary's family couldn't—the woman could bring "two turtledoves or two young pigeons" (Leviticus 12:8).

Jesus' dedication to God. God told the Jews, in the time of Moses, "Dedicate to me every firstborn among the Israelites. The first offspring to be born, of both humans and animals, belongs to me" (Exodus 13:2). Kosher animals, such as cattle, sheep, and goats, were sacrificed. But children had two options. They could work in the Temple if they belonged to a family of priests. Or they could go about their lives away from the Temple if their parents gave the priest an offering of five silver shekels. That's about two ounces or 60 grams. In Roman times, that much silver equaled about three weeks of work for an average laborer.

The priest on duty when Joseph and Mary brought Jesus to the Temple was Simeon.

Somehow, Simeon recognized Jesus as the Messiah—which startled Joseph and Mary.

Then Simeon gave Mary a chilling prophecy:

"This child is destined to cause many in Israel to fall, but he will be a joy to many others. He has been sent as a sign from God, but many will oppose him. . . . And a sword will pierce your very soul."

LUKE 2:34–35

Some wonder if that final sentence is a clue about how Mary would feel when one day she would look up and see her son dying on a cross.

WISE MEN COME

Jesus was born in Bethlehem in Judea,
during the reign of King Herod. About that time
some wise men from eastern lands
arrived in Jerusalem.
MATTHEW 2:1

As late as two years after Jesus was born, Bible experts say, a team of VIP stargazing fortune-tellers from a country east of Israel showed up in Jerusalem. They came with a dangerous question and an incredible story.

"Where is the newborn king of the Jews? We saw his star as it rose, and we have come to worship him" (Matthew 2:2).

This question was dangerous because of who they were addressing: the current king of the Jews, Herod the Great. He didn't have any newborn son. In fact, he had already executed two of his sons, one wife, and miscellaneous other relatives he suspected of plotting coups. He would later kill a third son with his dying request.

All of this pretty much confirms that the wise men were from way out of town. They had no idea what Herod was like.

Matthew's story drops us into a whirl of questions—most of which he doesn't bother to answer. These include the most basic questions reporters are supposed to cover—journalism's five *w*'s:

- Who were these wise men?
- Where did they come from?
- What kind of star led them to the Jewish homeland?
- When did they arrive?
- Why was Jesus still in Bethlehem?

Fortunately, historians from Matthew's own century help us fill in the blanks with some reasonable answers—and a few educated guesses.

WHO WERE THE WISE MEN?

The word *magi*—plural of *magus*—means "magician." As in "Simon Magus," the sorcerer who wanted to buy the disciples' power to fill people with the Holy Spirit. "Let me have this power, too" (Acts 8:19). He got a lecture instead.

But the magi who showed up at Jesus' doorstep weren't what we think of today as magicians or sorcerers. The earliest known reference to magi showed up about 600 years before Jesus. They were priests in Persia, modern-day Iran. In time, their neighbors in what is now Iraq (then Babylon) adapted the word to describe experts in astrology, fortune-telling, magical incantations, and wisdom. Magi often served kings as respected counselors.

Matthew—the only writer in the Bible who reports the story of the wise men—gives only one clue about their homeland. He said they came "from eastern lands" (Matthew 2:1).

Guesses include regions today called Iraq, Iran, and the Arabian Peninsula—home to countries such as Saudi Arabia, Yemen, and Oman. Yemen, in southern Arabia, was an excellent source of two gifts the magi brought: frankincense and myrrh. But most scholars say that Iraq and Iran are more likely where the magi came from, because that's where astrology flourished.

If the magi came from Babylon, near modern-day Baghdad, and followed one of the shorter caravan routes, their journey would have covered about 900 miles (1,450 km). Add another 300 miles (480 km) if they came from Susa, the former Persian capital.

The trip from Babylon would have taken about two months, if the magi traveled at the typical rate of about 20 miles (30 km) a day six days a week. Before they left home, they would have needed time to organize and equip their caravan and armed escort. And if these ancient scholars were anything like scholars today, it could have taken them a year or more to study the star, research relevant legends, and agree on a course of action.

Perhaps that would explain why it took them two years to reach the Jewish homeland. At least that's the timeline Matthew implies when he reports that Herod "sent soldiers to kill all the boys in and around Bethlehem who were two years old and under, based on the wise men's report of the star's first appearance" (Matthew 2:16).

WE THREE KINGS

With all due respect to the Christmas carol "We Three Kings," Matthew never said there were three—or that they were kings. At least the song gets "we" right; there were certainly more than one.

Christian writers started calling them kings as early as the AD 200s, because the magi supposedly fulfilled a prophecy hidden in the lyrics of a Jewish song: "All kings will bow before him" (Psalm 72:11).

The idea that there were three magi probably came from the three gifts they brought: gold, frankincense, and myrrh. Some legends say there were as many as 12 wise men.

Names for the three magi first showed up several hundred years later, including on a Latin list of important people written in the 700s: "On January 1, the magi brought him gifts and worshipped him. The names of the Magi were Balthasar, Melchior, and Gaspar."

As legends continued to develop, Balthasar became known as a king of Arabia, Melchior as a king of Persia, and Gaspar as a king of India.

Adventurer Marco Polo, from what is now Italy, traveled throughout Persia in the 1200s, where he said he visited the tombs of the magi, reporting that the corpses still had beards and hair. At that time, however, the church already venerated the supposed remains of the magi in a great cathedral in Cologne (in present-day Germany).

— WHAT STAR DID THEY SEE? —

It's one of the most intriguing mysteries in the story of Jesus' birth. What exactly did the wise men see?

There are lots of theories, but unfortunately no bell ringers that track perfectly with the details in Matthew's account. Here are some of the possibilities, each with a glitch:

- **A comet or a supernova that the Chinese observed during March and April in 5 BC.**

The timeline is right since most Bible experts say Jesus was probably born between 7 and 4 BC.

Glitch: Whatever the star was, it led the magi to the Jewish homeland and then seemed to disappear. Then "the star they had seen in the east guided them to Bethlehem. It went ahead of them and stopped over the place where the child was" (Matthew 2:9). Comets and supernovas don't act like that.

- **Halley's Comet, visible in 12 BC.**

After Bible times, the first church leader on record to speak of the star said it was a comet. Origen, writing from Egypt in the early AD 200s, said: "We think that the star which appeared in the east was a new star and not like any of the ordinary ones. . . . It is to be classed with the comets which occasionally occur."

Glitch: Most scholars say Jesus wasn't born that early. Seven BC is considered the earliest likely date of his birth.

- **A glowing spirit being or an astral phenomenon, perhaps like the pillar of light that led Moses and the Israelites through the exodus badlands on their way to the Promised Land.**

Some Bible experts warm up to this idea. There is at least one parallel between Israel's pillar of light and the magi's star. The pillar would come and go, leading the Israelites when they needed to move on. The Star of Bethlehem seemed to do the same thing. It got the magi to Jerusalem but seemed to fade out before reappearing and leading them on to Bethlehem.

Glitch: Why, then, describe it as a star? Matthew's first readers knew what magi did for a living—that they looked to the stars for clues about the future. So Matthew's readers would have envisioned a star in the sky, not a pillar of light.

- **An angel delivering a message.**

Some biblical scholars like this idea, too, for three reasons:

1. Bible writers sometimes used the word *star* as a metaphor to describe angels: "This is the meaning of the mystery of the seven stars you saw in my right hand. . . . The seven stars are the angels of the seven churches" (Revelation 1:20). Similar metaphors show up in the books of Job and Daniel.

2. Ancient Jewish and Christian writers often described angels as guides pointing people somewhere.

3. There's also support for the idea from a book written in the AD 500s—an Arabic version of *The Gospel of the Infancy*. Describing the magi's trip home,

the book says: "There appeared to them [the magi] an angel in the form of that star that had before guided them on their journey. And they went away, following the guidance of its light, until they arrived in their own country."

Glitch: Why would Matthew describe the phenomenon as a star and make no mention of an angel?

- **An unusual conjunction (alignment) of Jupiter and Saturn in the Pisces constellation in 7 BC.**

This popular theory from the 1970s is based on ancient history and confirmed by modern astronomical calculations. It seems to make sense to some Bible students because, on the ancient horoscope,

❏ Jupiter—the largest planet in our solar system—represented kings.

❏ Saturn represented Jews. This is confirmed by the first-century Roman historian Tacitus. He said the god Saturn protected the Jews because they worshipped on Saturday, the day that honored him. Babylonian records also confirm the connection between Saturn and the Jews.

❏ The constellation Pisces (meaning "fish") represented the land of Israel. Though scholars can't trace the connection between Pisces and Israel back beyond a rabbi in the 1400s, there is evidence that Pisces represented at least the Mediterranean fishing region of nearby North Africa.

On the basis of this background, some scholars speculate that the magi saw Jupiter and Saturn lining up in Pisces and would have concluded that a new king of the Jews had been born in Israel. This conjunction happened three times in 7 BC: around May 29, September 20, and December 5, give or take a few days. Modern calculations confirm this triple conjunction—a rare event that happens about once a millennium.

That means the wise men didn't follow an actual star; they simply went where the astrological signs pointed: to the Jewish homeland.

There are a bunch of variations on this theory. One points to 6 BC, when Jupiter and Saturn rose in the eastern sky inside the constellation of Aries the Ram. Unlike the case for Pisces, there are ancient documents that say Aries represented the Jewish homeland.

Another theory bundles three years of events into a single scenario. The triple conjunction of 7 BC along with Saturn and Jupiter drawing close together in Aries in 6 BC got the attention of the magi. They started their journey when they saw the comet or supernova in 5 BC.

Glitch: One problem with the triple conjunction theory is that Matthew's story seems to involve an astral phenomenon that moved. Also, a Babylonian almanac from this era doesn't consider the conjunction important enough to mention.

- **Halley's Comet in AD 66.**

Writing in the *Journal of the British Astronomical Association* in 2004, astronomer R. M. Jenkins speculated that Matthew's story was fictional, probably based on a similar event in AD 66.

Jenkins said Matthew was following a Jewish style of writing called midrash, which is Bible commentary that includes "what must have happened," filling in the gaps as necessary. One apparent gap was that Jesus' story needed to fulfill predictions about a coming star: "A star will rise from Jacob" (Numbers 24:17).

So Jenkins speculated that Matthew, inspired by the events of AD 66, filled in the gap by creating the story of the magi.

Roman records from the first century confirm that a group of magi made a long trek to Rome in AD 66 under the light of Halley's Comet, which shined brightly over Jerusalem. This was the year the Jews launched their doomed revolt against Rome, which ended in the destruction of Jerusalem and the Temple. The Roman historian Josephus, himself a Jew, wrote that a comet appeared as a warning of disaster. "Among the warnings was a comet of the type called Sword, because their tails appear to represent the blade of a sword. It appeared above the city [Jerusalem]."

Chinese records add measurements, showing that when the comet first appeared, it rose in the eastern sky—as Matthew's story seems to imply: "We saw his star as it rose" (Matthew 2:2). Also, it moved toward the west—each night edging a little farther west in relation to other stars.

The magi of AD 66 were led by a fellow wise man, King Tiridates of Armenia. The group was on its way to Rome to meet Emperor Nero. Three Roman historians—Suetonius, Pliny, and Dio Cassius—all considered the arrival of these magi important enough to report.

"I have come to you, my god, to worship you as I do Mithras [Persian god of light]," Tiridates said as he bowed before the emperor.

Delighted, Nero raised him by the hand, kissed him, replaced the turban on Tiridates' head with a crown, and declared him king of Armenia. Tiridates was king to begin with, but now he had Rome's seal of approval.

Afterward, Dio Cassius reported, "The king did not return by the route he had followed in coming." That echoes what Matthew said about the magi: "When it was time to leave, they returned to their own country by another route" (Matthew 2:12).

If Matthew did feed off this Roman story, he would have used it to make his point not only that Jesus is the Messiah, but also that Jesus—not Nero—is God. Context clues in the Gospel suggest that Matthew wrote his Gospel after the Romans destroyed the Jerusalem Temple in AD 70.

Glitch: It's hard for some to believe that Matthew would have included a fictional story alongside factual stories that can be verified from other sources. For many, it would make more sense that he crafted an authentic story in a way to help his first readers see parallels to similar events from their time—in this case as a means of comparing the divinity of Jesus to the supposed divinity of Nero.

WHY THE WISE MEN FOLLOWED

Whatever the "star" was, there were historical reasons the magi followed it and political reasons they ended up in the Jewish homeland.

As for history, comets, exploding stars, and planetary conjunctions were sometimes interpreted as signs of an important leader's birth or death. A "radiant constellation" is said to have clued earlier magi in on the birth of Alexander the Great.

As for politics, the magi knew that many Jews thought the Messiah would come at any time. Jews lived among them—descendants of Jews forced to move to Babylon from Israel when the Babylonians leveled Jerusalem 600 years earlier.

Suetonius confirms that people far and wide knew about the Jewish hopes for a new leader: "Throughout the entire East there had spread an old and persistent belief. . .[that] men coming from Judea would seize power."

Jewish writings connect this savior king to a star:

- "What I saw in my vision hasn't happened yet. But someday, a king of Israel will appear like a star" (Numbers 24:17 CEV).
- "Shining star, son of the morning! You have been thrown down to the earth, you who destroyed the nations of the world. For you said to yourself, 'I will ascend to heaven and set my throne above God's stars. I will preside on the mountain of the gods' " (Isaiah 14:12–13).
- "I, Jesus, have sent my angel to give you this message for the churches. I am both the source of David and the heir to his throne. I am the bright morning star" (Revelation 22:16).

WORRYWART HEROD

When the wise men showed up in Jerusalem looking for the newborn king of the Jews, King Herod probably had good reason to worry that the end was near—at least for his dynasty.

Magi, as royal advisors, probably came with an armed escort and a caravan large enough to sustain them for the long journey.

Even more worrisome, if they came from Iraq or Iran, as most scholars suggest, they came from the Parthian Empire. About 35 years earlier, the Parthians ran King Herod out of his own country and captured Herod's brother Phasael, who killed himself rather than face mutilation.

These Parthians had allied themselves with some Jews in a family that ruled before Herod: the exiled Hasmonean Dynasty. Antigonus, son of a former Hasmonean ruler, led the coup, hoping to restore his family to power.

He died trying.

Herod came back a few years later with a Roman army. He recaptured Jerusalem, executed Antigonus, and drove the Parthians out of the region.

Afterward, whenever Herod caught wind of a coup—real or imagined—heads rolled. Before he finally died, he had executed half a dozen close family members, including one wife, one father-in-law, one mother-in-law, and three sons. One of those sons, the crown prince, was killed just five days before Herod died.

As far as Herod was concerned, the magi brought wind of yet another coup in the making.

Because the Messiah's imminent arrival was on nearly every Jew's mind—as confirmed by both the New Testament and the famous Dead Sea Scrolls, which were written during that time—Herod presumed the wise men were talking about the Messiah.

Consulting his religious advisors—experts in the Jewish Bible—Herod learned that they expected the Messiah to be born in Bethlehem. They got the idea from a prophecy: "But you, O Bethlehem. . .a ruler of Israel will come from you, one whose origins are from the distant past" (Micah 5:2).

Considering himself sly enough to outfox both the wise men and God, Herod sent the magi on a scouting mission:

"Go to Bethlehem and search carefully for the child. And when you find him, come back and tell me so that I can go and worship him" (Matthew 2:8).

Mentally delete *worship* and insert *kill*. Herod did.

The magi made the six-mile (10 km) trip from Jerusalem to Bethlehem. "On coming to the house, they saw the child with his mother Mary" (Matthew 2:11 NIV).

The word for *child* is one that refers to either a baby or a toddler. Jesus may have been as old as two, since Herod, a few days later, would order all Bethlehem boys two and under executed. The word *house* shows that Joseph's family was no longer staying in a stable. Perhaps Joseph found carpentry work in Bethlehem and decided to stay awhile. Matthew later hints as much. He says that when Joseph led his family out of Egypt and back to Israel after Herod died, he intended to return to Judea—in southern Israel, where Bethlehem was. But in a dream he learned that Herod's wicked son now ruled that region. "So the family went and lived in a town called Nazareth" (Matthew 2:23). That was in northern Israel, in the region of Galilee ruled by the most tolerant, least psychotic son of Herod.

When the wise men saw young Jesus, "they bowed down and worshiped him" (Matthew 2:11). The irony in Matthew's story is that the people worshipping Jesus aren't the folks anyone would have expected. It wasn't the high and mighty Jewish scholars. It was pagan foreigners—sinners who looked for guidance from stars instead of from God.

Many Bible experts say this was Matthew's point—that he included this story to show that Jesus came for everyone, not just for the Chosen People.

GIFTS FIT FOR A KING

The magi knew how to pick regal gifts.

Their combo criteria for this perfect gift:

- expensive;
- hard to get;
- easy to carry; and
- simple to exchange for cash or goods.

They brought gold and two kinds of imported scents: frankincense and myrrh.

Gold. This could have come in any form: coins, jewelry, or perhaps intricately designed bowls and cups.

Christian symbol: Church leaders said this choice of gift was no coincidence. Gold represents Jesus as king.

Frankincense. Imported from hot, dry climates, this hardened, light-colored sap is drained from Boswellia trees in the Arabian Peninsula and in North African nations such as Somalia and Ethiopia.

Use: Priests of many faiths—Judaism included—burned it as a sweet-smelling incense.

Christian symbol: Church leaders said it symbolized Jesus' divinity. That's beause Jewish priests used it as part of the recipe for the only incense allowed inside the Temple.

Myrrh. Found high in semidesert regions of Somalia in North Africa, Yemen in the Arabian Peninsula, and parts of India, myrrh is a reddish sap harvested from Commiphora bushes.

Use: Sold in either liquid or solid form, it was used as a perfume in the days before deodorant, and as an anointing oil for corpses to hide the smell of decay. It also had medicinal uses—it was mixed with wine to reduce pain.

Christian symbol: Church leaders said myrrh symbolized the death and burial of Jesus. During the Crucifixion, Jesus was offered "wine drugged with myrrh, but he refused it" (Mark 15:23). At the burial that followed, Jesus' body was wrapped with "seventy-five pounds of perfumed ointment made from myrrh and aloes" (John 19:39).

ESCAPE TO EGYPT

*An angel of the Lord appeared to Joseph in a dream.
"Get up! Flee to Egypt with the child and his mother,"
the angel said. "Stay there until I tell you to return,
because Herod is going to search for the child to kill him."*
MATTHEW 2:13

No other writer in the Bible bothered with some of Matthew's most important stories, spotlighted at the front of his Gospel. The story of Joseph, Mary, and young Jesus fleeing to Egypt is one of them.

Like other Gospel writers, Matthew chose his stories for a reason. More than any other Gospel writer, Matthew had an eye to Jewish history. He saw what others apparently missed, such as

- dozens of Old Testament prophecies fulfilled by Jesus; and
- parallels between the life of Jesus and the long history of Israel.

In Matthew's mind, the story of Jesus' escape to Egypt did both: It fulfilled prophecy. And it connected Jesus to the Jewish people in ways that only the promised Messiah could be connected.

Jesus was the Messiah. That's the throbbing heart of Matthew's message. He passionately drives that message home by quoting twice as many Jewish prophecies as any other Gospel writer. Churning out one prophecy after another—57 in all—Matthew piles up the evidence for Jesus as the Messiah. Mark, the runner-up in prophecy quotes, comes in with only 30.

WISE MEN, HOLY FAMILY ON THE RUN

After the star-following magi worshipped Jesus and showered his family with treasures, God warned them in a dream not to report back to King Herod, who had said he wanted to worship the baby.

The dream—which many people in the ancient Middle East trusted as insight from heaven—essentially warned that Herod had some creative worship rituals in mind. Such as grabbing the baby by the ankles and bashing its head against a stone wall—a common method of quickly killing a child.

The magi took a different route back to their homeland. If they came from what is now Iraq or Iran, they may have traveled south around the tip of the Dead Sea, catching the caravan route north through what is now Jordan and Syria. Or they could have traveled west and caught the northbound caravan route up the Mediterranean coast.

Joseph had a dream, too—his second reported. The first dream, perhaps a couple of years earlier, had convinced Joseph to marry his very pregnant fiancée. Now a second dream warned him to take his family and flee to Egypt.

THE WANDERING JEW

Jews traveled more than most people in New Testament times—scattering themselves all over the Roman Empire and beyond, from Italy to Iran. Yet their law required healthy Jewish men to go to Jerusalem for important annual festivals, such as Passover.

Fortunately for the Jews, Rome invented paved roads.

Earlier empires built a system of roads throughout the Middle East. But the Romans insisted on all-weather roads paved with stone slabs and sloped high in the middle for good drainage. They wanted to make sure their armies could get to where they were needed in any troubled province.

"All roads lead to Rome" was only a slight exaggeration. Roman leaders were more concerned about connecting Rome to its far-flung provinces than with connecting provinces to each other. So most of the main routes did lead to Rome or to Mediterranean seaports that Rome controlled.

By land. Walking on foot, a person could generally cover 15–20 miles (26–32 km) a day. Along some main roads, inns were spaced about 20 miles (32 km) apart. One 2,000-year-old rest stop discovered in 2004 included a chariot service station, a gourmet restaurant, and a hotel with central heating. But most inns probably weren't even close to what travelers considered comfortable, safe, or reputable. Preferring the hospitality of locals, some people took letters of recommendation so they could avoid the inns. Famous Romans of the day, such as Horace and Pliny, wrote in their books about fleabag inns and mattresses stuffed with bedbugs. Less notable travelers scribbled their reviews on the hotel walls, sometimes praising the local working ladies and sometimes complaining about the food or the service. Graffiti at Mule Driver's Inn: "We have wet the bed, innkeeper. I confess we have done wrong. If you want to know why, there was no chamber pot."

By sea. Sailing could be the fastest, cheapest, and most comfortable way to travel long distances. One heavily traveled route was the 1,000-mile-plus (1,600 km) voyage from Egypt—Rome's main supplier of grain—to Italy. Booking passage would cost an entire family a fare equal to just two or three days of salary. With favorable winds they would arrive in about 10 days. Summer was the safest time to sail. Spring and fall were risky. Winter was for emergencies only.

By air. Okay, a few feet in the air. Donkeys, at about three feet tall, were the travel beast of choice for most Jews. Affordable and sure-footed, they could handle Israel's rugged terrain better than horses. But they weren't much faster than walking on foot—about 20 miles (32 km) a day. With a horse, most travelers could manage 25–30 miles (40–48 km)—and 50 (80 km) or more on urgent business. The book of Acts reports that Peter left Joppa in the morning and traveled 30 miles (48 km) along the main coastal route, arriving in Caesarea later that day (Acts 10:23–24). Camels, able to cruise 20 miles in a single hour, were the preferred choice for travelers needing a combo of speed, stamina, and thirst resistance. Fat in a camel's hump can store enough water to sustain the animal for up to seven days in extreme heat. The camel can rehydrate itself by gulping down about 25 gallons (95 liters) of water in 5–10 minutes.

BABY BODIES IN BETHLEHEM

Once King Herod realized he had been outsmarted by the magi, he pulled the trigger on Plan B—for Butchery.

"He sent soldiers to kill all the boys in and around Bethlehem who were two years old and under, based on the wise men's report of the star's first appearance" (Matthew 2:16).

Bethlehem was a tiny village. Only 123 Jews returned there after the nationwide exile to Babylon some 500 years earlier. The village remained small. Historians estimate that in Jesus' time, about a thousand people lived in the area. And given the high infant mortality, estimated at about 30 percent in those days before sterile medical practices, scholars say there were probably only one or two dozen boys to slaughter.

Certainly this would have horrified the locals. But it didn't make international headlines. In fact, there's no surviving mention of it outside Matthew's report.

Most Bible history experts say this should come as no surprise—nor should it cause anyone to doubt Matthew's story. The tragic event fits Herod's violent pattern, especially during the final, paranoid years of his life when he killed anyone he suspected of trying to overthrow him—including three of his own sons.

Herod died in 4 BC—and most Bible experts place Matthew's story of the holy family's escape to Egypt during the final year of Herod's life. If the scholars are right, the slaughter in Bethlehem would have competed with stories such as these, which made it into Roman history books written during the first century:

SEEING JESUS IN THE EXODUS

Matthew seemed to expect his Jewish readers to pick up on parallels between Jesus in Egypt and the Jews in Egypt during the time of Moses.

By simply telling Jesus' story, without commentary, Matthew seems to be sending a subtle message that he wants the readers to discover for themselves: Just as God brought Israel out of Egypt and made a covenant to protect them, God brought the Messiah out of Egypt to make a new covenant to save all people.

JEWS IN EGYPT	JESUS IN EGYPT
Pharaoh, king of Egypt, ordered all the male Jewish infants killed.	Herod, king of the Jews, ordered all the male infants in Bethlehem killed.
Moses fled from his home in Egypt when his life was in danger.	Jesus' family fled from their home in Bethlehem when Jesus' life was in danger.
God ordered Moses to return to his home in Egypt after the king died.	God ordered Jesus' family to return to their home after King Herod died.
God's order: "Return to Egypt, for all those who wanted to kill you have died" (Exodus 4:19).	God's order: "Take the child and his mother back to the land of Israel, because those who were trying to kill the child are dead" (Matthew 2:20).
Moses delivered Israel from slavery.	Jesus delivered people from their slavery to sin.

- *4 BC—five days before Herod died.* He ordered the execution of his oldest son, Antipater, who was next in line for the throne.

- *4 BC.* On the brink of death, Herod arrested what first-century Roman historian Josephus called "the most illustrious men of the whole Jewish nation, from every village." Corralled in a hippodrome, they were to be executed as soon as Herod died—to make sure the Jews mourned instead of celebrated. But after Herod died, his sister ordered the men released unharmed.

- *4 BC.* Herod ordered two Jewish scholars and their rabbis burned alive for destroying a golden eagle emblem he had erected at the Jerusalem Temple. The eagle showed that Rome protected the Temple. The Jews said God should get the credit.

- *6 or 7 BC.* Herod ordered his two sons by his favorite wife, Mariamne, executed: Alexander and Aristobulus.

Bible experts say it's no wonder Josephus and other Roman historians of the day skipped mentioning the slaughter of a few children in an obscure shepherding village.

HEROD'S GRISLY DEATH

Within months—perhaps weeks—of ordering the young boys of Bethlehem slaughtered, King Herod died an agonizing death. Poetic justice, some say. Religious leaders at the time said God punished Herod for ordering some rabbis burned to death.

The story of Herod's death is recorded in *Wars of the Jews*, a seven-volume history written by Josephus about 80 years after Herod died.

Modern medical detectives who have studied Herod's symptoms speculate about the cause of death. Some attribute it to complications from gonorrhea. Others suggest chronic kidney disease complicated by a genital infection.

Here are paraphrased excerpts from Josephus' description of Herod's death:

Disease consumed him. Painful symptoms wracked his entire body in pain. He had only a slight fever. But his skin itched terribly all over. His intestines hurt all the time. His feet and abdomen were swollen. And his genitals were rotting with gangrene which had become infested with maggots.

Beside all this, he had trouble breathing and couldn't breathe at all when he sat up. He also suffered from convulsions. . . .

Hoping for a cure, he went across the Jordan River to the hot springs at Callirrhoe [beside the Dead Sea in what is now Jordan]. There, the doctors decided to also bathe him in warm oil. They gently lowered him into a bathtub filled with oil. His eyes closed and when he was lifted out, he seemed to be dying. But the screams of his servants revived him. . . .

Overcome with pain, unable to eat, and convulsing with coughs, he tried to kill himself. He took an apple and asked for a knife to peel it. Then he looked around and saw that no one was near him. Suddenly he raised the knife with his right hand, as if preparing to stab himself. His cousin Achiabus ran over to him, grabbed his hand, and prevented the suicide. . . .

Herod [age 69] died 37 years after Rome made him king. [He died in March 4 BC at his winter palace in Jericho.]

FUGITIVES GO HOME

After Herod's death, Joseph had two more dreams. One revealed that it was okay to go back to Israel. But the second warned him away from Judea—in southern Israel, where Bethlehem is located. This suggests that Joseph had intended to return to Bethlehem.

The danger in Judea was that Rome had appointed Herod's 19-year-old son, Archelaus, as king of Judea, Samaria, and Idumea—roughly the southern half of modern-day Israel. He was such a vicious ruler that Rome dethroned him 10 years later and banished him to what is now France (then Gaul). The emperor banished him because Archelaus ordered troops to slaughter 3,000 rioting Jewish pilgrims who came to Jerusalem for the Passover festival.

Joseph probably bypassed Bethlehem and Jerusalem by following the coastal road north alongside the Mediterranean Sea. He moved his family back to Nazareth, in a northern Israel region called Galilee. Herod's more tolerant 17-year-old son, Herod Antipas, ruled this area as a governor.

The move back to Nazareth "fulfilled what the prophets had said: 'He will be called a Nazarene' " (Matthew 2:23).

Trouble is, there are no prophets in the Bible who said that.

Bible experts guess that Matthew was referring to a prophecy with a word that sounded similar to *Nazarene—neser*. It means "branch." Predicting the coming of the Messiah, the prophet Isaiah had said: "Out of the stump of David's family will grow a shoot—yes, a new Branch [*Neser*] bearing fruit from the old root. . . . In that day the heir to David's throne will be a banner of salvation to all the world" (Isaiah 11:1, 10).

KID KILLERS

It was common in Jesus' time for parents to kill unwanted newborn children.

People of many cultures—the Romans included—allowed parents to kill their newborns. The most common method was to abandon them outdoors. People did this if the child looked deformed or unable to survive, or if it was a girl when the father wanted a son.

A letter from Jesus' time says as much. In 1 BC, a man named Hilarion wrote this note from Alexandria, Egypt, to his pregnant wife, Alis:

"If you have the good luck to deliver another child, if it's a boy keep it. But if it's a girl, set it outside and let it die" (Papyrus Oxyrhynchus 744).

This ancient practice of abandoning children also shows up in the writings of a prophet:

"On the day you were born, no one cared about you. Your umbilical cord was not cut, and you were never washed, rubbed with salt, and wrapped in cloth. No one had the slightest interest in you; no one pitied you or cared for you. On the day you were born, you were unwanted, dumped in a field and left to die" (Ezekiel 16:4–5).

Some Romans preferred infanticide to abortion—considering abortion too risky for the woman, because it usually involved taking toxic drugs to induce the miscarriage.

The Jews, however, would have none of this. Two Roman historians from the first century confirm the Jewish practice of keeping their children:

- "Sacred Jewish law orders all the offspring to be brought up, and forbids women either to cause an abortion or to discard the fetus" (Josephus, a Roman Jew).
- "Jews think it criminal to kill any unwanted child" (Tacitus).

A BOY IN NAZARETH

*Jesus grew in wisdom and in stature and
in favor with God and all the people.*

LUKE 2:52

Born in what amounts to a barn and raised in a dip of a village as a carpenter's son, Jesus spent his growing-up years as a humble peasant. But if a humble upbringing is what he wanted most, he should have been born a girl.

The trouble is that, as a girl, Jesus would have missed out on the synagogue education that most Bible scholars say he obviously got. At a mere 12 years of age—still a child by ancient Jewish standards—he impressed the Jerusalem scholars with insights from scripture. Synagogue-run classes for boys apparently got their start shortly before Jesus was born. But they were closed to girls.

Rabbi Eliezer, a leading first-century scholar, later explained the no-girl code: "Anyone who teaches his daughter the Law [Jewish scripture] is teaching her *tiflut*," a word often translated "immorality." In other words, it's a sin to hang pearls on a pig. The pig is too dumb to appreciate it.

Jesus grew up in a world where men were men, and everyone else was pitifully less.

HOMETOWN NAZARETH

Jesus really did live in a dip of a village—literally. Nazareth was nestled in a large dip eroded into a ridge off the main caravan route.

Some scholars estimate that no more than 500 villagers shared the single spring of water on a plug of ground no larger than 60 acres. That's about 900 yards by 200 yards (823 x 183 meters)—the max size of villages identified in etchings on local tombs during the days of King Herod the Great.

Much of the village was probably open farmland—a patchwork of tiny farms cultivated by locals trying to grow enough crops to see them through the year. Archaeologists have uncovered grain silos along with olive and wine presses.

Crops probably included grains such as wheat and barley and vegetables such as beans and lentils, along with vineyards, olive orchards, and fig trees. Though first-century historian Josephus never bothered to mention Nazareth, he did say the Galilean region where the village was located was fertile and heavily farmed:

> *Every inch of the soil has been cultivated by the locals. The land everywhere has such rich soil producing wonderful grazing fields, and such a wide variety of trees that even the laziest people are tempted to take up a career in farming.*

Located almost halfway between the Sea of Galilee, which lies 15 miles (24 km) east, and the Mediterranean coast, 20 miles (32 km) west, Nazareth got adequate rain for the fields and forests. Resting in a highland plateau some 1,300 feet above sea level (400 meters), Nazareth also collected runoff water

BIZARRE TALES OF JESUS AS A BOY

At five years old, Jesus was already developing a mean streak—doing what any normal kid might do if he had superhuman powers: killing playmates who irritated him.

This shocking story and others like it appear in a laughably fictional book about Jesus' childhood. The book, *Infancy Gospel of Thomas*, may have been written in the AD 100s, more than a century after Jesus' time.

A writer identifying himself only as Thomas the Israelite said Jesus was playing by a stream on the Sabbath, using mud to dam up tiny pools of water—a no-no on the sacred day of rest. A passing villager saw this and reported it to Jesus' father, Joseph, who scolded young Jesus in front of his playmates.

One little boy apparently decided to express his support for the Sabbath. He took a branch and broke the clay dams, which drained the tiny pools. "You idiot!" Jesus said. "What did the ponds do to you? Now you're going to dry up, too." Instantly the boy shriveled to death—like a grape fast-forwarding into a raisin.

Other strange tales of Jesus in this book:

- **Killing another playmate.** A boy running through the village bumped into Jesus, who cried out, "Your little journey is over." The boy dropped dead.
- **Blinding the playmate's parents.** The boy's parents complained to Joseph. Jesus promised to stop killing his playmates. But first he struck the boy's parents blind.
- **Raising a dead playmate.** A third playmate accidentally fell off the roof of a house. Other children blamed Jesus, who defended himself by raising the boy from the dead. Jesus then asked the resurrected boy if he had pushed him down. "No, Lord," the boy answered. "You didn't push me down, but you did raise me up."
- **Healing a cut foot.** When a man chopping wood accidentally cut his foot and was on the verge of bleeding to death, Jesus touched the foot and healed it.
- **Waterproofing a cloak.** Carrying water back from the well, six-year-old Jesus accidentally broke the jug. So he gathered water into his cloak and carried it home.
- **Stretching wood.** When Joseph was building a bed frame for a rich man, he cut one of the crossbeams too short. Jesus stretched it to match the other beam.
- **Healing a snake bite.** A poisonous snake bit Jesus' brother James, who was gathering firewood. As James lay dying, Jesus blew on the wound. His breath healed James and exploded the snake—in a miracle of the snakebite and the snake bits.

If Jesus had done any of these bizarre miracles, it seems odd that his neighbors, years later, would have been surprised to learn that the adult Jesus had become a miracle worker. (See "Rejected in His Hometown," page 113.)

But they were. And they said so: " 'Where does he get this wisdom and the power to do miracles?' Then they scoffed, 'He's just the carpenter's son' " (Matthew 13:54–55).

from the surrounding hills. Archaeologists digging in the area have uncovered cisterns—plaster-lined, waterproof pits for storing water.

SURVIVING CHILDHOOD

Growing up anywhere in the Roman Empire—Nazareth included—a child had about a fifty-fifty chance of surviving to adulthood. Those are roughly the same odds for children today in undeveloped areas that don't have the benefit of medical treatment.

Jewish parents in Jesus' day loved their children. Even the girls. And they sang about their kids:

> *Children are a gift from the Lord; they are a reward from him. Children born to a young man are like arrows in a warrior's hands. How joyful is the man whose quiver is full of them!*
>
> PSALM 127:3–5

Unfortunately, disease and accidents kept thinning out the quiver. Ancient Roman epitaphs on tombs tell what sent youngsters to the grave:
- Fell into a well.
- Fell from a window.
- Burned in a fire.
- Crushed by a pile of stakes that collapsed (a three-year-old was helping his parents stack the wood).
- Choked on fruit (perhaps a grape, which is still a threat to small children).
- Kicked by a horse.
- Run over by a wagon.
- Struck by a misthrown javelin.
- Stung by a scorpion.

Skeletons in Pompeii, Italy, that became encrusted with volcanic ash from Mount Vesuvius' eruption in AD 79 have revealed surprising facts about childhood diseases and development at the time.

Many children seemed to skip the growth spurt that's common today in children ages 9–14. Disease blocked the growth, according to Ray Lawrence, a researcher at the Institute of Archaeology and Antiquity at the University of Birmingham.

Writing in *History Today*, Lawrence said, "At one house, thought to have been the residence of a certain Julius Philippus, eight of the nine skeletons discovered reveal evidence of major diseases during childhood that prevent the body from producing calcium for the formation of bones or teeth. The typical disease that prevents bone and tooth formation is tuberculosis."

One of these skeletons was of an 11-year-old child who had survived four bouts of disease—at ages 4 and 5 and twice at age 7.

If adult skeletons at Pompeii are any measure of average height throughout the empire, boys surviving to adulthood reached an average height of five feet five inches. Girls grew into women about five feet tall.

FUN AND GAMES

As a little boy, Jesus probably played some of the same games that children play today. Pictures chiseled into stone funeral monuments show children throwing nuts and balls to each other or whacking them with a stick along the ground, much like hockey without the ice or polo without a horse. Some of the balls were made from leather, stuffed with wool or cloth and sewed with string or leather strips.

Kids played with marbles, too, though not made from glass like most marbles today. In Jesus' time, marbles were made from clay or rock—including marble. Rules of the game haven't been discovered yet, but like kids today, perhaps they used their thumbs as a spring to shoot a marble at a target on the ground. And maybe they targeted marbles inside a circle in an attempt to knock them out of the circle and claim them as a prize.

Board games were a favorite, too. Some board patterns have survived—chiseled in stone or painted on walls. By the looks of them, some were similar to checkers, backgammon, and tic-tac-toe. Many of these games were chiseled right into the pavement where people sat with little to do:

- doorways to houses where servants guarded the entrance;
- city gates where people congregated or waited to meet others; and
- military quarters where soldiers passed their time while off duty.

Children played running games, too: tag, racing, jumping, and even a form of hopscotch—which seems to have started as an agility exercise for Roman soldiers.

A few toys have survived: dolls, jacks, rattles, whistles, spinning tops, and animals on wheels.

GAME CENTRAL

Children in Jesus' day played catch with balls, as illustrated in a Roman sculpture from a stone coffin.

Some played with hoops, as Middle Eastern boys and girls still do. Pictures from Roman times show children using sticks to push hoops along a path or to toss hoops into the air, trying to see how long they can keep the hoops aloft.

Board games were popular all over the Middle East. "Three in a row" is one that dates to the century in which Jesus lived. This game pitted two players against each other. If the ancient rules were like modern ones, the object was for players to align their colored pieces in horizontal or vertical rows of three. Each time a player created a line, that player got to take one of the opponent's pieces.

The three-square pattern, along with other board game designs, has shown up chiseled in stone on the floor at the Jerusalem post where Roman soldiers stayed: the Fortress of Antonia. Overlooking the Temple, this fortress may have been where soldiers would later mock Jesus by dressing him in a royal robe and crowning him with thorns.

SCHOOL: NO GIRLS ALLOWED

Lucky for Jesus, public education got up and running just in time for his childhood.

Ancient Jewish writings say that a rabbi named Simeon ben Shetah started some schools in the first century BC, and that a priest named Joshua ben Gamla expanded this to establish schools for all Jewish boys in the century in which Jesus lived.

But these were boys-only schools. Girls had to learn at home from their parents.

Elementary ed. For the first few years of life, Jewish boys and girls were cared for mainly by their mother—and were often nursed for two or three years. As soon as they could talk, the children began learning about what it meant to be Jewish.

God's law required parents to teach their children God's commandments:

"You must commit yourselves wholeheartedly to these commands that I am giving you today," [Moses reminded the Jews in his farewell speech before he died.] "Repeat them again and again to your children. Talk about them when you are at home and when you are on the road, when you are going to bed and when you are getting up."

DEUTERONOMY 6:6–7

Girls learned them, too. At the very least, they had to know about laws that affected life in the home—such as what kinds of food were kosher for Jews to eat.

Jewish boys started elementary school in the local synagogue at about age five. Unlike Roman children, Jewish boys didn't generally study art, secular literature, and math. They studied the Bible—rich in history, sacred literature, and philosophy. They studied half a day for six days a week, resting on the Saturday Sabbath.

They started by learning the Hebrew alphabet, reading, and then memorizing the Jewish laws and history. Laws of ritual purity in Leviticus were probably among the first they studied. They also studied the Psalms, a collection of songs that revealed a lot about God.

Advanced ed. At age 10, the boys moved up a level. They had already studied the Jewish Bible, with a concentration in the written laws of Moses preserved in the first five books of the Bible—Genesis through Deuteronomy. Next they moved on to the interpretation and application of those laws.

The boys already knew they weren't supposed to work on the Sabbath. But now they needed to learn how some of the revered rabbis from history defined *work*. Some rabbis said people were guilty of working on the Sabbath if they walked more than half a mile—about a thousand paces.

The boys memorized these oral laws, which the Jews eventually preserved in a collection of sacred traditions called the Mishnah.

As a grown-up, Jesus would reveal that he disagreed with many of these interpretations. Many Jewish scholars considered it work to treat sick people on the Sabbath, except in cases of life or death. But Jesus justified his Sabbath-day healings by explaining that suffering humans deserved at least as much compassion as suffering animals. If one of the livestock falls into a hole on the Sabbath, Jesus reminded his scholar-critics, "don't you rush to get him out?" (Luke 14:5).

This Q&A approach is a technique that Jesus learned from school, where the rabbis would grill their young students with questions about both the written and oral law.

Q: What should you do if you find mold in your house?

A: Contact the priest. He will "put the house in quarantine for seven days. On the seventh day the priest must return for another inspection" (Leviticus 14:38–39). If the mold is still there, the affected part of the house is removed and replaced. If the mold continues to spread, the house will be torn down.

Adult ed. At age 13, Jewish boys were treated as men responsible for their actions and for obeying the laws they had been learning. Jewish boys today mark that event with a happy celebration called a bar mitzvah. As part of the celebration, a boy would get to read scripture during worship on the first Sabbath after his thirteenth birthday. Jesus missed his bar mitzvah. He was born about 500 years too soon. The Jews hadn't yet invented the celebration.

By age 15, Jewish young men began to study the wisdom of Jewish sages that was later written down in the Gemara, a collection of analysis and commentary on Jewish teachings. At 18, the young men were considered ready for marriage, and by age 20 they were ready for a career—often in the family business.

LEARNING A TRADE

About the time Jesus started studying the Jewish sages, in his midteens, he may also have been starting his formal apprenticeship—learning his father's trade.

Joseph was a *tekton*, a Greek word often translated "carpenter." But it could also simply mean "builder." Joseph may have worked out of his home, with his shop opening onto the street. If he specialized in carpentry, he probably made wooden plows, yokes, pitchforks, doors, carts, wagons, ladders, and furniture.

To become a carpenter, Jesus would have needed to master a wide variety of tools that are often much harder to master than today's power tools. Among them:

- axes, saws, and wedges for chopping trees and cutting out the beams and boards;
- bow drills for drilling holes;

- hammers and mallets for driving iron nails and wooden pegs; and
- wood chisels, planes, and awls for precisely shaping the wood.

Joseph and his sons may have found work in neighboring Sepphoris, a city about three miles (5 km) north of Nazareth. Craftsmen from all over the region were rebuilding Sepphoris throughout Jesus' childhood.

Romans had burned down the city when they crushed a Jewish revolt there after Herod the Great died in 4 BC. But Herod's son Herod Antipas, who ruled Galilee, decided to rebuild the city and make it his capital. Jewish historian Josephus said Herod brought in builders from neighboring villages throughout Galilee, who helped turn the city into the "ornament of all Galilee." Herod built a palace, city walls and towers, and a theater seating at least 3,000. There were an upper and a lower city, each with its own market. And there were many shops, inns, synagogues, and schools.

The rebuilding continued for decades, ending about the time Jesus started his ministry. Some scholars speculate that the rebuilding is what kept Jesus busy until then.

It's possible, though, that Jesus never embraced carpentry. For two reasons:

- **Not all young men decided to work in the family business.** Lucian, a writer from the AD 100s, said he skipped out on the family business of stonemasonry. He said he left after his uncle beat the marble out of him. Lucian had accidentally broken a slab of stone with a poorly placed chisel blow.
- **Not all parents wanted their children to stay in the family business.** Some parents worked out arrangements with gifted artisans or merchants to expand the horizons of their children. There were many trades to choose from, including blacksmith, potter, shepherd, farmer, basket weaver, cloth weaver, tent maker, and tanner.

In AD 42, a boy named Papontos entered into a five-year contract to become the apprentice of a weaver. He agreed to work for free, in exchange for on-the-job training. The contract doesn't say how old Papontos was. But the one clue suggests he was at least 14—when Romans would have considered him a man of taxable age. In the contract, the weaver agreed to pay the young man's tax.

The Bible says nothing specific about Jesus' education and apprenticeship. Jesus could have been a synagogue-school dropout and a slow-motion carpenter. But the Bible's implication is that he excelled at both school and work.

Hint 1: Scholars who talked with him when he was a 12-year-old "were amazed at his understanding" (Luke 2:47).

Hint 2: Luke wrapped up the childhood stories with this telling summary:

"Jesus became wise, and he grew strong. God was pleased with him and so were the people" (Luke 2:52 CEV).

HUMBLE HOMES

Houses of most villagers were simple, boxlike buildings—one story, sometimes two.

Builders often set the house on a foundation of stones at least one layer deep. Then they raised walls from mud bricks and coated them inside and out with water-resistant plaster.

Most homes had a flat roof built on beams that supported a blanket of woven branches and a thick layer of mud and plaster. Homeowners had to compact the roof after each heavy rainfall. Some used limestone rollers that looked like landscaping rollers. Most used their feet.

People used the roof like homeowners today use their deck, patio, or porch. They usually climbed up by a ladder or an outdoor stairway. There, they could work in the cool breeze of the outdoors, relax in the early evening, or sleep in the open air on hot nights.

Jews built a railing around the roof to protect people from falling off—especially children.

Inside most houses were three or four rooms, including a multipurpose living room for cooking, eating, sleeping, and entertaining. Joseph's home may have included a shop room where he worked as a carpenter.

Wooden doors probably hung on leather hinges and were locked at night with a wooden beam or a metal bar slid into brackets anchored to the wall.

Small windows let in only a little light. Set high, they allowed cooking smoke and heat to escape while trapping the cooler air inside the house—a smart idea in the hot Middle East.

YOUNG JESUS AT THE TEMPLE

They found Jesus sitting in the temple,
listening to the teachers and asking them questions.
Everyone who heard him was surprised at how
much he knew and at the answers he gave.

LUKE 2:46–47 CEV

O f all the Bible stories about Jesus, only one gives us a glimpse into his personality as a child—just one reports him doing something and saying something.

And what he did looks like misbehavior.

What he said sounds a tad like he was talking back to his mother.

He was 12 years old at the time—one birthday away from the time when the Jews would have considered him a man responsible for his own actions. The setting: crowded Jerusalem during the annual springtime religious festival of Passover, when Jews scattered from all over the Middle East came back to the Holy City. They came to honor God for freeing their ancestors from slavery in Egypt more than 1,000 years earlier, during the time of Moses.

The apparent misbehavior: Jesus slipped away from his parents and their caravan returning home to Nazareth. He stayed in Jerusalem without his parents' permission. This forced Mary and Joseph to rush back to Jerusalem to look for their son.

The apparent back talk: When his parents finally found him three days later at the Temple and his mother scolded him, young Jesus said they should have been smart enough to figure out where he was.

We're left to wonder whether Jesus got a spanking.

Some scholars, however, argue that this was not a case of "Spare the rod, spoil the child," because there was really no misbehavior or back talk.

PASSOVER IN JERUSALEM

Especially in Jesus' time, the Jewish capital of Jerusalem was at its busiest and most jam-packed during the springtime holiday of Passover.

There's a combo reason:

- Passover was a freedom celebration commemorating the birth of Israel as a nation.
- The Jews weren't free. Their homeland was occupied by the Romans, and had been for about 80 years.

The Jews brought to town an air of expectancy. They hoped and prayed

KNOW YOUR JEWISH HOLIDAYS

Jesus and his parents went to Jerusalem for the weeklong celebration of two festivals in one: Passover followed immediately by the Festival of Unleavened Bread. This visit was one of three pilgrimage festivals when God expected Jewish men to worship him in Jerusalem. The list of festivals appears in Leviticus 23.

FESTIVAL	DATE	PURPOSE
New Year's Day, also called Festival of Trumpets (Rosh Hashanah in Hebrew)	September (Tishri 1 on the Jewish lunar calendar)	Commemorates Creation and the Jewish nation's responsibilities on earth. Begins 10 days of self-examination before the annual day of repentance.
Day of Atonement (Yom Kippur)	September or October (Tishri 10)	Most solemn day of the year, when Jews repent of their sins.
Festival of Booths, or Tabernacles (Sukkot)*	September or October (Tishri 15)	Weeklong remembrance of when the Jews of the Exodus lived in huts (sukkot); also celebration of the end of harvest in a fruitful land.
Passover (Pesah)	March or April (Nisan 15)	Celebrates God's freeing of the Jews from slavery in Egypt.
Festival of Unleavened Bread (made without yeast)*	March or April (linked with Passover, from Nisan 15–21, or 22 for some Jewish groups)	Recalls the Jews' quick departure from Egypt; there was no time for bread to rise.
Festival of First Fruits	March and April (when farmers harvest their first grains: flax and barley)	Celebrates the beginning of harvest.
Pentecost, also called Festival of Weeks (Shavuot)*	May or June (Sivan 6 in Israel, Sivan 7 outside Israel)	Celebrates the beginning of wheat harvest. Festival names come from the timing: 50 days (pentecost means "fifty") or seven weeks after Passover.

*= A pilgrimage festival requiring able-bodied men to celebrate in Jerusalem if possible (Exodus 23:14–17).

that God, who had once freed their ancestors from slavery in Egypt, would perform an encore—that he would send the long-awaited Messiah to free them from Rome. They wanted their Jewish nation born again, sovereign and free.

Passover comes from a passage that describes the tenth plague. That's the plague that finally convinced the pharaoh of Egypt to free the Jews. God said he would kill all the oldest males in Egypt. As for the Jews: "I will pass over you. This plague of death will not touch you when I strike the land of Egypt" (Exodus 12:13).

The Jews followed a lunar calendar, marking their months by the turn of the full moon. Passover took place on Nisan 15, which usually falls somewhere in April—around Easter. Jesus was crucified during Passover.

To give the Jews strength to flee Egypt, God told them to eat a meal. He prepared the menu, rich in symbolism. At twilight on the fourteenth day of Nisan, the Jews sacrificed a lamb and roasted it. "Do not break any of its bones," God said (Exodus 12:46). One Gospel writer later said this foreshadowed the death of Jesus, whose bones weren't broken. "These things happened in fulfillment of the Scriptures that say, 'Not one of his bones will be broken' " (John 19:36).

Nisan 15 began at sundown. That marks the beginning of Passover, when the enslaved Jews in Moses' day ate their freedom meal of roasted lamb, "bitter salad greens and bread made without yeast" (Exodus 12:8). Unleavened bread symbolized a fast-food meal eaten on the run, since the Jews didn't have time to wait for yeast to puff up the bread dough. They'd be on the move before daybreak.

God told the Jews to celebrate this freedom day forever:

This is a day to remember. Each year, from generation to generation, you must celebrate it as a special festival to the Lord. This is a law for all time.

EXODUS 12:14

Joseph took his family to Jerusalem every Passover, because this was a pilgrim holiday. Any Jewish men able to make the trip were instructed to do so: "All men must appear before the Lord your God at the place he chooses" (Deuteronomy 16:16). God chose Jerusalem as the place for his Temple—the only worship center where Jews were allowed to offer sacrifices to him.

SACRIFICES 101

By law, Jews in Jesus' time were permitted to offer sacrifices to God only at the Jerusalem Temple.

There were many sacrifices they could offer, but the most common are described in Leviticus 1–7:

Burnt offering. This purified the worshipper from sin. The worshipper killed and burned an animal on the altar. Rich people killed a bull. Most others killed a male goat or sheep. Poor people killed a dove or pigeon.

Grain offering. Jews brought grain from the harvest as a way to thank God for providing food for them. Worshippers could bring the grain as flour, baked goods, or roasted kernels. The priests burned some of it and kept the rest as part of their salary.

Peace offering. A worshipper burned part of an animal as an expression of thanks to God. The worshipper ate the rest of the animal, either alone or with family and friends.

Sin and guilt offerings. These animal sacrifices purified a person who had committed specific types of sins, such as stealing or lying, or unintentional sins such as making a rash promise that was impossible to keep.

LONG WALK TO JERUSALEM

Joseph and his family traveled in a caravan. That explains why, on the trip home, they didn't miss Jesus until the end of their first day on the road.

"They assumed he was among the other travelers. But when he didn't show up that evening, they started looking for him among their relatives and friends. When they couldn't find him, they went back to Jerusalem to search for him there" (Luke 2:44–45).

Traveling by caravan was safer than traveling alone. Any route to Jerusalem led through desolate territory, with no other human in screaming range. But the sheer number of travelers in a caravan could discourage bands of robbers from attempting a holdup.

Jews often avoided the most direct route to Jerusalem. It ran through the central highlands and was no easy trek. More important, it took them through a region and city both named Samaria. Jews and Samaritans were a bit like the feuding Hatfields and McCoys.

The Samaritans descended from Jews who had intermarried centuries earlier with Assyrian invaders from what is now Iraq. Blue-blooded Jews treated the Samaritans as half-breeds. Worse, the Samaritans revered only the first five books of the Bible—which the Jews claimed the Samaritans had distorted with editing. So the Jews said the Samaritans practiced a warped version of Judaism. (For more background on the hatred between these two groups, see page 162 in "Parable of the Good Samaritan.")

The caravan could have taken the international trade route along the Mediterranean coast. But even that was hilly. They would have had to travel west and pass through the Carmel Mountains to get to the coastal road. Then south at Joppa, near modern-day Tel Aviv, they could have turned southeast, climbing over the Judean hills leading to Jerusalem.

More likely, they cut through the Jezreel Valley and then followed the Jordan River to Jericho. The only tough hills they faced were on the day-long walk up the desolate badlands into Jerusalem. Walking is how most people traveled. The path took them more than half a mile up, from 1,000 feet (300 meters) below sea level in Jericho to 2,500 feet (760 meters) above sea level in Jerusalem, 20 miles (32 km) southwest. The entire trip from Nazareth—about 90 miles (145 km)—probably took around four days.

A KID WOWS THE SCHOLARS

At 12 years old, Jesus was well into his biblical studies. Some historians say this was probably the most academically intense year for Jewish boys, because at age 13 they were considered men, responsible for knowing and obeying Jewish law.

This was probably Jesus' last visit to the Temple as a child.

King Herod had started dismantling and rebuilding the Temple in about 20 BC—in a massive project that continued at least 46 years (John 2:20). Herod actually moved a mountain of dirt to expand the Temple hilltop—creating the largest temple platform in the ancient world. At 172,000 square yards (157,000 square meters), it was large enough to hold 27 football fields, end zones included.

Groups of Jews gathered in any of several massive courtyards that were framed with roof-topped colonnades for protection from the sun and rain. Here is where many Jewish scholars held religion classes and led Q&A sessions, inviting queries from visiting Jewish pilgrims.

Jesus may have spent much of his Passover week here. He may not have gotten word that his Nazareth contingent was heading home.

A gifted student, Jesus impressed the Jerusalem scholars with his questions, as well as his answers to questions they asked. The Bible doesn't say what they discussed—Jewish laws would be a good guess. But some books written more than a century later claim to fill in the gap of missing information, though most scholars today say it would take quite a stretch to believe what these books say.

The *Infancy Gospel of Thomas*, possibly written in the AD 100s, says Jesus asked well-informed questions about Jewish law and that he interpreted key points of the law along with some parables the prophets told. It adds that when Mary showed up, a group of scholars—scribes and Pharisees—praised her for raising such a brilliant child. "Blessed are you among women," they said. "God has blessed the fruit of your womb. For we have never seen nor heard such glory, virtue, and wisdom."

The *Arabic Gospel of the Infancy*, compiled in the AD 500s from earlier sources, goes much further. It says Jesus taught the scholars a thing or two or three: religion, astronomy, and medicine.

Religion. "He explained the books, the law, the principles, the rules, and the mysteries contained in the books of the prophets—topics no human being could ever hope to understand."

Astronomy. Asked by an astronomer if he had studied astronomy, Jesus "explained the number of the spheres, and of the heavenly bodies, their natures and operations. . .their course, direct and retrograde. . .and other things beyond the reach of reason."

Medicine. Asked by a scientist if he had studied medicine, he "explained to him physics and metaphysics. . . .the powers and fluids of the body and their effects, also the number of organs and bones, veins, arteries, and nerves. . .the effect of heat and dryness, of cold and moisture, and what causes these effects. . . and other things beyond the reach of any created intellect."

With that, the scientist rose to his feet and declared to the 12-year-old: "Lord, from this time on I will be your disciple and slave."

Whatever Jesus taught the scholars, his mother was ticked.

Mary and Joseph had just spent three days looking for him. Perhaps

- one day traveling home, only to discover he wasn't with the caravan;
- one day back to Jerusalem; and
- another day scouring the crowds of Jerusalem.

By the time they found him, they could have been almost home.

"Son," his mother said to him, "why have you done this to us? Your father and I have been frantic, searching for you everywhere" (Luke 2:48).

Any parent who has ever misplaced one of their kids can understand the emotions washing over Mary. She might have wondered if she should hug him or spank him—or both.

Without hearing the tone of Jesus' voice, it's easy to imagine him sounding like a sassy little know-it-all. "But why did you need to search?" he asked. "Didn't you know that I must be in my Father's house?" (Luke 2:49).

Sassiness isn't the only way to read this, especially if Jesus was sincere.

Luke says that Mary and Joseph didn't understand what Jesus meant. Scholars aren't sure either. But they enjoy guessing.

Perhaps the most widely accepted theory is that Jesus was saying he had to be involved in teaching people about the things of God. The Temple was the perfect place for that because crowds came there to encounter God in worship and teaching.

Did 12-year-old Jesus know everything about his past, present, and future?

No. Even at the end of his adult ministry he didn't know when he would return to earth. "No one knows the day or hour when these things will happen, not even the angels in heaven or the Son himself. Only the Father knows" (Matthew 24:36).

But the answer he gave Mary as a boy on the verge of becoming a man certainly implies that though he didn't know everything about his future, he knew something.

ANCIENT LEGENDS OF BRILLIANT BOYS

We shouldn't take Luke seriously when he puffs the 12-year-old Jesus, reporting that his wisdom astonished the top Jewish scholars. So say some historians, arguing that overstating the attributes of heroes was a common literary technique in ancient writing: acceptable exaggeration—history written by a fan.

Others insist that Luke's one-sentence brag about Jesus is mild compared to other ancient brags—and worthy of belief.

Kid Alexander the Great, future conqueror of the Middle East. As a young boy, he visited with representatives sent by the king of Persia (modern-day Iran). "He won their approval by his friendliness, and by asking no childish or trivial questions, but by asking about the distance they traveled, what the journey was like, what the king was like, and the fighting skills of both the king and his soldiers." (*The Life of Alexander*, part 1, written in the AD 100s.)

Baby Octavian, future emperor of Rome when Jesus was born. "When Augustus was still an infant, his nurse put him for the night in his cradle on the ground floor. The next morning he was gone. After a long search he was found in the high tower with his face toward the rising sun." (*The Life of Augustus*, section 94, written in the AD 100s.)

Teen Josephus, first-century Jewish historian. "When I was about 14 years of age, people praised me for my love of learning. The high priests and leading men of the city frequently came to me to ask my opinion about the accurate understanding of points of the law." (*The Life of Flavius Josephus*, section 2, written about AD 100.)

JESUS BAPTIZED

*Jesus went from Galilee to the Jordan River
to be baptized by John.*
MATTHEW 3:13

Jesus' baptism is one of the few stories about him that's important enough to show up in all four Bible books about his life: Matthew, Mark, Luke, and John.

Raising Lazarus from the dead didn't get that kind of coverage. It appears only in the Gospel of John.

The parable of the Good Samaritan didn't. Only Luke covered that story.

Jesus' miracle of turning water into wine didn't. John again was the sole reporter.

What was so important about Jesus getting dipped in the Jordan River?

The tougher question is why Jesus bothered getting baptized at all. In a ritual symbolizing spiritual purity, John the Baptist was dipping people who had asked God to forgive them of their sins.

Did Jesus need forgiveness, too?

WHO WAS JOHN THE BAPTIST?

John isn't just a famous character in the Bible.

He shows up in a Roman history book, in a story that tracks with the Bible. This story credits John with helping an Arab army crush a Jewish army.

The astonishing story appears in a 20-volume collection called *Antiquities of the Jews*. It was written in Jesus' century by Josephus, a Jewish historian who was also a Roman citizen.

Josephus spun the story around a clash between John the Baptist and Herod Antipas, ruler of Jesus' home region of Galilee. Son of Herod the Great, Herod Antipas stole his own brother's wife and married her. John publicly condemned him: "It is against God's law for you to marry your brother's wife" (Mark 6:18).

Herod's new wife wasn't happy about John's implication that she was committing incest and adultery. So she arranged to have John's head handed to her on a platter, according to Mark 6.

Josephus added some interesting background.

Before Herod could marry his sister-in-law, Herodias, the marriage agreement required him to divorce his current wife, Phaesalis, daughter of an Arab king. Her father, King Aretas, ruled parts of what are now Syria, Jordan, and Saudi Arabia. Relations between Herod and Aretas were already strained over border disputes. And now—shamed by the return of his rejected daughter—

Aretas went to war. He crushed Herod's defenses and took part of Herod's territory along the west bank of the Jordan River.

Josephus writes:

> *Some of the Jews thought the destruction of Herod's army came from God, as a fitting punishment for what he did to John, who was called the Baptist. Herod had killed John, a good man who commanded the Jews to exercise virtue, both in righteousness to one another and in faithfulness to God.*
>
> *John said it was in this spirit that they should be baptized. He said God would accept this baptism, not to wash away sins but to purify the body. John presumed that before baptism the person's soul was already purified by righteousness.*

ANTIQUITIES OF THE JEWS

Luke placed John's short ministry on history's timeline. It began in "the fifteenth year of the reign of Tiberius, the Roman emperor" (Luke 3:1). Tiberius inherited the empire from Augustus in AD 14. Based on this, scholars estimate that John began his ministry sometime between the end of AD 27 and the middle of AD 29—perhaps only a few months before Jesus launched his ministry. Both men were dead by about AD 33.

Relative of Jesus. John was a distant relative of Jesus, because their mothers were related. The angel Gabriel made that connection when he announced the birth of both boys, John first and Jesus six months later. Gabriel told Mary, "Your relative Elizabeth [John's mother] has become pregnant in her old age! People used to say she was barren, but she's now in her sixth month" (Luke 1:36).

Mary rushed down to see Elizabeth, who already knew that both unborn boys were destined for greatness.

- **John.** Elizabeth's husband had certainly told her what Gabriel said about John: "He will prepare the people for the coming of the Lord" (Luke 1:17).
- **Jesus.** Someone also clued Elizabeth in about Mary's boy: "God has blessed you above all women, and your child is blessed," Elizabeth told Mary. "Why am I so honored, that the mother of my Lord should visit me?" (Luke 1:42–43).

Mary and Elizabeth probably told their sons these stories. And perhaps the families visited each other, especially when Mary and Joseph brought their family to Jerusalem for the festivals. Elizabeth's husband, Zechariah, was one of the many Temple priests.

John probably could have been a priest, too. But he became a prophet, living in the Judean badlands. Some Bible experts speculate that he lived for at least a time with the Essenes of Qumran, a community of isolationist Jews

14 miles (23 km) east of Jerusalem. These Jews taught that the Messiah could come at any moment. So they purified themselves daily in a ritual similar to baptism. They're most famous for writing the Dead Sea Scrolls.

Why did John choose to live in the desert? He said he saw himself fulfilling a 700-year-old prophecy about the Messiah's advance man. When Jewish scholars asked John who he was, he quoted Isaiah 40:3: "I am a voice shouting in the wilderness, 'Clear the way for the Lord's coming!' " (John 1:23).

Given the relationship between John and Jesus, it shouldn't come as a surprise that when Jesus showed up, John cried out to the crowd, "Look! The Lamb of God who takes away the sin of the world! He is the one I was talking about when I said, 'A man is coming after me who is far greater than I am, for he existed long before me' " (John 1:29–30).

THE NOT-QUITE-MIGHTY JORDAN

If the world's most famous rivers threw a potluck party, with each river bringing food proportionate to its size, the Nile would bring all the meat, the Mississippi would bring all the drinks, and the Jordan would bring a can of olives for the chef's salad.

Even calling the Jordan a river would make the eyes of the Ohio roll on. From the Jordan's source of snowmelt and rain drain at the peak of Mount Hermon, the river doesn't stretch even 120 miles (193 km) before emptying into the Dead Sea. That's only about half the length of Israel, a tiny country the size of New Jersey.

The Mississippi cuts a 2,300-mile (3,700 km) swath through 10 states—from Minnesota to Louisiana. The Ohio stretches nearly half that distance. The Nile—the longest river in the world, and the Jordan's next-door neighbor—flows north 4,100 miles (6,600 km) through nine African countries before emptying into the Mediterranean Sea at Egypt.

Yet the Jordan is no less famous than greater rivers. For one reason. This is where John baptized Jesus.

By his presence alone, Jesus had a way of transforming something tiny and unimportant into something huge and significant. Even when tensions rise in the Middle East, pilgrims still flock to Bethlehem, where they kneel and pray at the birthplace of Jesus. And they renew their baptism in the Jordan River, often collecting vials of water for their ministers to use in rituals such as infant baptisms.

Jordan River Specs:
65 miles (105 km) long as the dove flies (Sea of Galilee to Dead Sea)
135 miles (220 km) long as a fish swims the winding curves
2–10 feet (1–3 meters) deep
30 yards (27 meters) across, on average
1,300 feet (400 meters) below sea level at its lowest

WHO INVENTED BAPTISM?

By the time John came along, there was nothing new about water baptism as a religious cleansing ritual.

Egyptians baptized the newly born and the newly dead. Water purified the babies and symbolized new life for the dead.

Sumerians in the world's first-known civilization, in what is now Iraq, used water to ritually purify worshippers of Enki, their god of water and creation.

Hindus took purification baths in the Ganges River.

The Jews took ritual cleansing baths, too—for many reasons:

- **Conversion.** Non-Jews who converted to the Jewish religion apparently took a ritual bath. It cleansed them and initiated them into the faith.
- **Contamination.** Jews took a ritual bath before worshipping God at the Temple. It cleansed them from any ritual impurities—such as touching a non-Jew or a dead corpse, or after recovering from a skin disease. Jewish purification rituals are recorded in Leviticus 12–16.
- **Sex-related purification.** Jewish women had to take a ritual bath after each menstrual cycle and after delivering a baby. Jewish men had to take a bath after a "bodily discharge" (Leviticus 15:2), which would include wet dreams and possibly sexual intercourse. Bible experts debate what "discharges" this law covers.

The monklike Jews of Qumran took ritual baths every day—sometimes several times a day. They apparently expected the Messiah to arrive at any moment and launch a freedom fight to restore Israel: the Sons of Light against the Sons of Darkness.

They described this war in a Dead Sea Scroll called the War Scroll, probably written around the time of Jesus—between 50 BC and AD 50, according to some archaeologists. The Qumran Jews wanted to stay ritually clean so they could join the army of the Sons of Light whenever it arrived.

Bible experts debate where John got the idea for his unique take on baptism: "I baptize with water those who repent of their sins and turn to God" (Matthew 3:11).

Qumran was his source, some say. Like John, these Jews recognized that water didn't cleanse a person's spirit. That cleansing started with repentance. One big difference between John's one-time baptisms and the ritual baths at Qumran is that the Qumran Jews baptized themselves over and over.

Other scholars say that John probably drew from the Jewish baptism ritual designed for Gentile converts. Yet other experts argue that this ritual probably didn't exist at the time of John, because there's no clear reference to it in Jewish writings of that century. Other experts, however, say there are implications that it existed. And they point to this excerpt from a collection of prophecies written before the time of Jesus: "Sinful people, repent…wash your body from head to toe in streams of running water, and lift your hands to heaven, asking forgiveness.… God will forgive you and not destroy you" (*Sibylline Oracles*, book 4).

If John got the ritual from any of these sources, he changed it quite a bit. He was baptizing fellow Jews, not Gentiles. And he did it in a single event, not over and over. Perhaps John got the idea from heaven, delivered in a dream or by an angel.

WHY DID JESUS GET BAPTIZED?

Christian scholars agree on this much: Jesus didn't get baptized to repent of his sins and turn to God.

As Jesus' top disciple put it: "Christ did not sin or ever tell a lie" (1 Peter 2:22 cev).

But baptism for repentance is what John offered. So why did Jesus insist on taking the plunge?

Even John didn't understand. "John tried to talk him out of it. 'I am the one who needs to be baptized by you,' he said, 'so why are you coming to me?' " (Matthew 3:14).

"It should be done," Jesus answered, "for we must carry out all that God requires" (Matthew 3:15).

If ever an answer begged for a follow-up question, this is the one. And the question would be this: "What do you mean, 'all that God requires'?" Generally, when the Bible reports a cryptic statement of Jesus, Bible experts offer a puzzling array of possible explanations. But not in this case. Most top Bible scholars agree that Jesus was essentially saying that this act of baptism was the next logical step in God's plan of salvation.

It's not that Jesus needed to repent. What he needed was to link the beginning of his ministry with the work of the advance man predicted by the prophets:

- "Look! I am sending my messenger, and he will prepare the way before me. Then the Lord you are seeking will suddenly come to his Temple. The messenger of the covenant, whom you look for so eagerly" (Malachi 3:1).
- "Listen! It's the voice of someone shouting, 'Clear the way through the wilderness for the Lord!' " (Isaiah 40:3).

All four Gospel writers report the baptism of Jesus, not because they thought he needed forgiveness, but because they had connected the dots. They knew John was the Messiah's predecessor. And they marked this first public meeting of the two as the beginning of Jesus' ministry.

Bible experts say Jesus' baptism also has a second layer of meaning.

When Jesus stepped into the water, he stood with the people he came to save. He was right there with them, identifying with their humanity and their need. More than just an example to follow, he became the reason to follow—the source of God's salvation sent from heaven to walk among people who needed God by their side.

PROPHECIES FULFILLED IN JESUS' BAPTISM

Many Jewish scholars in Jesus' day said that certain prophecies in their Bible described the Messiah—especially some of the prophecies in the book of Isaiah. Matthew's report of Jesus' baptism links some of these messianic markers directly to the baptism of Jesus.

PROPHECY	FULFILLMENT
Righteousness. "When he sees all that is accomplished by his anguish, he will be satisfied. And because of his experience, my righteous servant will make it possible for many to be counted righteous, for he will bear all their sins" (Isaiah 53:11).	"It is proper for us in this way to fulfill all righteousness" (Matthew 3:15 NRSV). Jesus' explanation about why he needed to be baptized.
Heavens open, Spirit descends. "Oh, that you would burst from the heavens and come down!" (Isaiah 64:1). "Look at my servant. . .my chosen one. . . . I have put my Spirit upon him" (Isaiah 42:1).	"The heavens were opened and he saw the Spirit of God descending" (Matthew 3:16).
Pleasing to God. "He is my chosen one, who pleases me" (Isaiah 42:1).	"This is my Son, whom I love, and I am very pleased with him" (Matthew 3:17 NCV).
Precious son of sacrifice. "Take your son, your only son—yes, Isaac, whom you love so much—and go to the land of Moriah. Go and sacrifice him" (Genesis 22:2).	"This is my own dear Son" (Matthew 3:17 CEV). Jesus begins the long journey to his execution as a sacrifice for the sins of the world.
God's Son. "The Lord said to me, 'You are my son. . . . I will give you the nations as your inheritance, the whole earth as your possession' " (Psalm 2:7–8).	"A voice from heaven said, 'This is my Son' " (Matthew 3:17 NCV).

ON THE WINGS OF A DOVE

While Jesus was being baptized, "he saw the Spirit of God descending like a dove and settling on him" (Matthew 3:16).

This scene sparks a lot of questions. Is the Holy Spirit a bird? Was the dove literal—flesh and feathers? Who saw the Spirit descend?

Some Bible experts say it's likely that no one but Jesus saw anything; others say the crowd must have witnessed something unusual. Perhaps they heard a voice. Matthew's phrasing implies as much: "This is my dearly loved Son" (Matthew 3:17), instead of "You are my dearly loved Son," as God would say if he were speaking directly to Jesus.

Whatever the crowd witnessed, most scholars say they probably didn't see a dove at the baptism. The dove was likely just a metaphor, a way of describing the gentle arrival of God's Spirit.

Why all four Gospel writers use the dove symbol remains a mystery. But there are two popular theories.

A new world. The writers may have expected their Jewish readers to connect the Spirit hovering over Jesus in the Jordan River with the Creation story: "The Spirit of God was hovering over the surface of the waters" (Genesis 1:2).

This connection implies that the baptism of Jesus signaled the beginning of a new day and a new world. One particular prophecy about the Messiah helps link these two ideas: "Look at the new thing I am going to do. . . . I will make a road in the desert" (Isaiah 43:19 NCV).

Peace replaces judgment. Jewish readers may have connected the baptism dove with the dove that Noah released after the flood: "The dove returned to him in the evening with a fresh olive leaf in its beak" (Genesis 8:11).

Jesus' baptism may have signaled that God's old contract with humanity was over—a contract that emphasized rules and punishment for breaking those rules. In its place emerged a new contract based on peace, symbolized by the olive branch. This is a peace that's available for followers of Jesus: "I am leaving you with a gift—peace of mind and heart. And the peace I give is a gift the world cannot give. So don't be troubled or afraid" (John 14:27).

IS BAPTISM A MUST?

Some Christian groups teach that baptism is a requirement for salvation. No baptism, no getting past Saint Peter at heaven's gate.

Many Roman Catholics teach this. So do Eastern Orthodox churches, such as the Greek Orthodox Church. For biblical support, they turn to quotes from Jesus:

- "Go and make disciples of all the nations, baptizing them in the name of the Father and the Son and the Holy Spirit" (Matthew 28:19).
- "I assure you, no one can enter the Kingdom of God without being born of water and the Spirit" (John 3:5).

But most Protestant denominations argue that baptism is not a requirement for salvation. "Born of water," Protestants argue, is a vague phrase that could mean many things, including physical birth or spiritual birth through Jesus. The "spiritual birth" theory draws its support from prophets who used metaphors of water and spirit to predict what salvation life would be like when the Messiah came:

"I will sprinkle clean water on you, and you will be clean. Your filth will be washed away. . . . And I will put my Spirit in you" (Ezekiel 36:25, 27).

Most Protestant churches teach that baptism is a wonderful rite of inauguration into the faith, but that salvation is secured by nothing more than genuine faith in Christ. For biblical support, they most often turn to a letter that Paul wrote to Christians in Rome: "If you confess with your mouth that Jesus is Lord and believe in your heart that God raised him from the dead, you will be saved" (Romans 10:9).

JESUS TEMPTED

Jesus was led by the Spirit into the wilderness
to be tempted there by the devil.
MATTHEW 4:1

Déjà vu is what some Bible students feel when they read the story of Satan tempting Jesus. They can't put their finger on it, but they sense something familiar.

Three Gospels tell this story: Matthew, Mark, and Luke. Mark condenses it to just a couple of sentences—not enough to connect it to any past event. But the déjà vu emerges in the more detailed versions of Matthew and Luke—whose stories are so much alike that many Bible experts say they probably got their facts from the same source.

Several scenes in Jesus' story trigger the déjà vu.

Trigger: After Jesus' river baptism, he went to the desolate Judean badlands.
Source: After crossing through the sea, Jews on the Exodus went into the badlands of the Sinai Peninsula.

Trigger: Jesus fasted 40 days in the mountainous badlands.
Source: Moses fasted 40 days on Mount Sinai.

Trigger: Tempted to turn rocks into bread, Jesus told Satan, "People do not live by bread alone, but by every word that comes from the mouth of God" (Matthew 4:4).
Source: Moses said the same thing to the Jews after God tested their faithfulness during 40 years in the badlands: "He humbled you by letting you go hungry. . . . He did it to teach you that people do not live by bread alone; rather, we live by every word that comes from the mouth of the Lord" (Deuteronomy 8:3).

The déjà vu doesn't stop here. Satan tempted Jesus three times. Each time, Jesus replied with a quote from that very moment in history when the Jews of the Exodus were living in the badlands.

It's as if the Gospel writers weren't just reporting an interesting story about Jesus. It's as if these writers—along with Jesus—wanted the Jews to see themselves not only in history but in his story.

After reading both stories side by side, some Bible experts conclude that through Jesus' temptation, God was performing an encore—testing the faithfulness of Jesus just as he had once tested the Jews. The difference: Jesus passed the test.

— HEADING TO THE DESOLATE MOUNTAINS —

Jesus left the Jordan River Valley, where John the Baptist had baptized him and where the Holy Spirit had descended on him and empowered him to face the rough weeks ahead. The Bible doesn't say exactly where John baptized Jesus or to where Jesus retreated. But there are clues that both events took place near Jericho, close to where the Jordan River empties into the Dead Sea:

- John introduced Jesus to the crowds "in Bethany, an area east of the Jordan River, where John was baptizing" (John 1:28). Most Bible experts say this was probably just across the river from Jericho. But Bethany's location is uncertain.
- Ancient tradition says that Jesus was tempted in the badlands on Jericho's side of the river, on a 1,200-foot-high (366 meters) mountain called Jebel Quarantal (Arabic for "Mountain of 40 Days"). This rock chalk ridge a few miles northwest of Jericho overlooks the river valley. Five hundred years after Jesus, Roman Emperor Justinian ordered a church built on this mountain to commemorate the temptation.

Why Jesus went to a mountainous wasteland, the Bible doesn't say. But this may have been the same area where John the Baptist lived in isolation before he began his ministry. Also, many religions in ancient times taught that people are closer to the gods when they stand on a mountain—and that demons live in barren lands such as deserts. On a badlands mountain, Jesus may have been seen as putting himself in an ideal spot for hearing from both God and Satan.

— 40 DAYS OF FASTING —

Luke says that Jesus fasted and prayed for 40 days before Satan arrived. Among the Jews, fasting was a religious ritual. Instead of eating a meal, they would spend the time in prayer—often seeking God's direction or help during a crisis. Huge concerns often led to extended fasts.

At the birth of Israel as a nation, when Moses began to receive God's laws that would govern the people, Moses fasted on Mount Sinai "forty days and forty nights" (Exodus 34:28). And now as Jesus prepared to launch a ministry that would show people how to be born again and that would replace laws written on stone with laws written on the heart, Jesus fasted 40 days. (For more on fasting, see "Jesus on Fasting," page 136.)

"Forty" may not have been literal days marked on a calendar. The number may have meant a long stretch of time—weeks. People writing the stories of Moses and Jesus may have chosen this round number because it had a connection to another long event: the 40 years that Jews of the Exodus spent in the badlands south of Israel.

This suggests yet another connection between Jesus and the Jews, some scholars say. The Jewish people spent 40 years in the badlands before beginning their God-appointed task of reclaiming the lost Promised Land. Jesus spent 40 days in the badlands before launching his God-appointed ministry of reclaiming lost souls.

THE HUNT FOR SATAN

A Bible latecomer, Satan makes his grand entrance into scripture only when he arrives to tempt Jesus. That's the first time Satan shows up as a spiritual being.

Before that, *Satan* wasn't used as a person's name. It was just a Hebrew word that meant "accuser." Old Testament writers used that word to describe all kinds of people—including revered characters such as David, Solomon, and even God when he angrily accused Israel of sin.

The talking snake in the Garden of Eden? It was just that, as described in the Creation story—a talking snake.

Job's tormenter? He was just "the accuser," someone who addressed the heavenly council with a proposal to test Job's loyalty.

It took many centuries for Jewish and Christian writers to begin identifying these two culprits as Satan—the incarnation of evil and the leader of a demonic coalition devoted to destroying humanity. An end-time visionary best known for looking forward in time, John the apostle also looked backward and revealed the identity of Eden's snake: "the ancient serpent called the devil, or Satan" (Revelation 12:9).

Satan's first known appearance as an individual came a little more than a century before Jesus. A Jewish Pharisee, writing sometime between 105 and 135 BC, looked forward to a utopian time when people would "live in peace and in joy, and there shall be no Satan or any evil destroyer" (*Jubilees* 23:29).

In the centuries that followed, new insights about Satan continued to emerge in Jewish and Christian writings.

The Talmud, a collection of ancient Jewish teachings, presents an array of ideas about Satan:
- Satan came into the world with Eve, as a created being;
- he flies; and
- he can assume various forms, such as a bird, a deer, or a beggar.

New Testament writers present Satan as "the ruler of this world" (John 12:31). But they also doom him as history's biggest loser. In a vision of the future, John reports that "the devil, who had deceived them, was thrown into the fiery lake of burning sulfur, joining the beast and the false prophet. There they will be tormented day and night forever and ever" (Revelation 20:10).

The evolution in humanity's understanding of Satan doesn't mean that people invented him. Jesus certainly spoke of Satan and other demons as real spiritual entities. But the gradual emergence of information does suggest that for several millennia, Satan operated under the cloak of humanity's ignorance. It took Jesus to bring him into the light of day, revealing him as the evil creature he is.

TEMPTATION 1:
TURN STONES TO BREAD AND EAT

When Jesus was at his weakest and hungriest, Satan arrived.

It's Satan's first appearance in the New Testament. And he comes not as an abstract symbol of evil, but as a living entity—a spirit being intent on derailing the ministry of Jesus.

Paul describes Satan and his demons this way: "We are not fighting against flesh-and-blood enemies, but against evil rulers and authorities of the unseen world, against mighty powers in this dark world, and against evil spirits in the heavenly places" (Ephesians 6:12).

Satan's first temptation of Jesus seems more compassionate than dangerous. "If you are the Son of God, tell these stones to become loaves of bread" (Matthew 4:3). Satan knew Jesus was God's Son. For this reason, some Bible scholars say Satan's initial urging might have had a softer touch: "Since you're God's Son, why suffer this hunger? Feed yourself."

After all, what's wrong with a hungry man eating? Or with Jesus miraculously producing bread?

Scholars don't agree on what was wrong with Satan's suggestion. But they have theories:

Independence from God. One of the most popular theories is that Satan was trying to convince Jesus to assert his independence from God. Satan wanted to convince Jesus to use his power to escape hardship instead of following the course God had set: a course that would begin with suffering and lead to death.

Competing with God. Given the many connections between the temptation of Jesus and the Jewish exodus out of Egypt, some Jews may have seen the miracle of turning stones into bread as an attempt to one-up God, who had provided the Jews with manna to eat during the Exodus.

A trick to prove Jesus is the Messiah. The Jews expected that the Messiah would do miracles. That's why a group of Jewish scholars once asked Jesus to "show us a miraculous sign to prove your authority." Jesus refused, saying, "Only an evil, adulterous generation would demand a miraculous sign" (Matthew 12:38–39).

TEMPTATION 2:
JUMP AND WATCH ANGELS CATCH YOU

Satan takes Jesus to the highest point at Jerusalem's sprawling Temple complex. Most Bible experts say this probably wasn't a physical relocation, but a realistic vision or a vivid dream—like those God often used to communicate to prophets.

Matthew and Luke didn't say exactly where on the Temple Jesus saw himself. But Josephus, a first-century Jewish historian, described the highest point of the Temple complex—which may have been the southeast corner of the towering wall.

He said if you stood on top, where Jewish leaders blew their ram's horns to call people to worship, the long look down would leave you feeling weak in the knees. That's because you were not only looking down from the heights of the wall but also looking beyond the base of the wall, deep into the Kidron Valley below. The estimated height—nearly a sheer drop from the top of the wall to the valley floor—was 450 feet (137 meters).

Like Jesus, Satan knew the Bible—and quoted it. He pulled from a psalm that might seem tailored for a jumper: "The Lord will keep you safe. . . . He will spread his wings over you and keep you secure. . . . God will command his angels to protect you wherever you go. They will carry you in their arms, and you won't hurt your feet on the stones" (Psalm 91:3–4, 11–12 CEV).

Again, readers are left wondering what sin Jesus thought he would be committing if he took this literal leap of faith. After all, Satan was right. Angels were available to protect Jesus. That became clear later, when Peter drew his sword to stop the temple officers from arresting Jesus.

"Put away your sword," Jesus told him. . . . "Don't you realize that I could ask my Father for thousands of angels to protect us, and he would send them instantly? But if I did, how would the Scriptures be fulfilled that describe what must happen now?" (Matthew 26:52–54).

Theories about what was wrong with Satan's suggestion:

Manipulating God. One especially popular idea is that it would have forced God to do what he had promised to do: protect his children—as he had done with the Jews during the Exodus, saving them from the Egyptian army. The Temple, especially, was considered a holy place where God would protect his people.

Just another trick to prove Jesus is the Messiah. One ancient Jewish manuscript that may date to before the time of Jesus said this: "When the king, the messiah, reveals himself, he will come and stand on top of the temple" (*Pesiqta Rabbati* 36).

TEMPTATION 3:
WORSHIP SATAN AND INHERIT THE EARTH

In the Gospel of Luke, this is the second temptation. But Matthew uses this one as his closer, perhaps because of the climactic offer Satan made to Jesus: the entire world.

In a temptation with a view, Satan took Jesus to a mountain and showed him all the nations on the planet. Then Satan offered to let Jesus rule all these nations "if you will kneel down and worship me" (Matthew 4:9).

But Jebel Quarantalis, the mountain where tradition says this happened, offers only a wonderful view of the river valley—not of the entire world. No mountain has a view like that—except a mountain in a vision or a dream.

This is the one temptation in which it's clear to everyone who knows Jewish law that Satan is urging Jesus to sin. All of the hundreds of Jewish laws in the Old Testament are based on 10 basic laws: the 10 Commandments. The first and most important of those 10 is this: "Deeply respect God, your God. Serve and worship him exclusively" (Deuteronomy 6:13 THE MESSAGE).

Jesus quoted this passage and then ordered Satan to leave. It's an order Satan apparently had no choice but to obey.

PASSING THE TEST

Was this a test or a temptation? Some say it was both. The Greek word for "tempt" can also mean "test."

Remember the story of Job? An "accuser," presumed to be Satan, asked God for permission to bombard Job with suffering. The accuser's goal: tempt Job to curse God.

God approved the plan. But how could he? The Bible says, "Do not say, 'God is tempting me.' God is never tempted to do wrong, and he never tempts anyone else" (James 1:13). God does, however, test us: "Abraham offered Isaac as a sacrifice when God was testing him" (Hebrews 11:17).

The difference between "testing" and "tempting" is the motive, many Bible scholars say. God may test a person's character or a person's loyalty. But God will not tempt a person to do something wrong.

Satan tempts people, hoping to lure them away from God. Adam—the first human—gave in. Jesus didn't. The apostle Paul wanted people to realize what kind of a difference Jesus made because of his victory over Satan—at the Temptation as well as at the Crucifixion.

"Everyone was going to be punished because Adam sinned. But because of the good thing that Christ has done, God accepts us and gives us the gift of life. Adam disobeyed God and caused many others to be sinners. But Jesus obeyed him and will make many people acceptable to God" (Romans 5:18–19 CEV).

JESUS STARTS TEACHING

*Instead of staying in Nazareth, Jesus moved
to Capernaum. This town was beside Lake Galilee. . . .
Then Jesus started preaching, "Turn back to God!
The kingdom of heaven will soon be here."*
MATTHEW 4:13, 17 CEV

All four Gospel writers report the story of Jesus starting his ministry, but not one of them would have passed Journalism 101. Reporters are taught to get answers to five key questions: who, what, when, where, and why. But all four Gospel writers skip the "when" question. Because of that, readers can't be sure when Jesus began his ministry—or how long it lasted.

Piecing together clues from the Gospels, such as references to Jesus visiting Jerusalem during the annual Passover holiday, most Bible experts say Jesus' ministry spanned about three years:

- one year of obscurity;
- one year of popularity; and
- one year of increasing hostility from Jewish leaders.

But which three years?

AD 26–30, say some scholars. Luke said, "Jesus was about thirty years old when he began his public ministry" (Luke 3:23). If Jesus had been born sometime between 4 and 6 BC, as Bible experts commonly suggest, he would have been between the ages of 30 and 32.

AD 29–33, say an increasing number of other experts. A strong clue for this later date is Luke's report that John the Baptist began his ministry in the fifteenth year of Tiberius' reign (Luke 3:1)—which Roman history reveals couldn't have been any earlier than AD 27. So if Jesus had started his work in AD 26, he would have gotten the jump on his advance man. If this later date is correct, Jesus may have been 36 when he started his preaching ministry and 39 when he died.

Whatever the date when Jesus started his work, "John [the Baptist] had been arrested" (Matthew 4:12). He was in jail by order of Herod Antipas, ruler of Galilee. John's execution would follow.

The time for the Messiah's advance man was over. And the time for the Messiah had begun.

GALILEE, IDEAL MINISTRY CENTER

"When Jesus heard that John had been arrested, he left Judea and returned to Galilee" (Matthew 4:12). Judea was in southern Israel, where John had lived and baptized. Galilee was in the north, beside a huge lake called the Sea of Galilee.

Exactly where Jesus started preaching is a puzzler, too. The Gospel reporters not only skipped the "when" question but also missed "where" as well. Or at least they jumped to different points on the geographical timeline when referring to those start-up weeks or months.

Matthew says, "He went first to Nazareth, then left there and moved to Capernaum, beside the Sea of Galilee" (Matthew 4:13). Mark says only that Jesus went "into Galilee" (Mark 1:14). Luke says that Jesus went to Galilee and "taught regularly in their synagogues" before going to Nazareth (Luke 4:15). And John says that Jesus actually started recruiting some of his disciples while he was still in Judea, where John baptized (John 1:42–43).

This variation has led some Bible experts to conclude that Jesus' ministry didn't start with a big-bang miracle. From the time that John the Baptist publicly introduced Jesus as both the "Messiah" (John 1:31) and the "Lamb of God who takes away the sin of the world" (John 1:29), Jesus began a gradual move out of obscurity.

All four Gospel writers agree, however, that Jesus returned to Galilee. It was natural for him to go there. It was home. Nazareth was his hometown, and he probably returned to the village several times during his ministry—not just that one famous time when the hometown folks rejected him and tried to "push him over the cliff" (Luke 4:29).

For several reasons, Galilee was a great location for Jesus to start his ministry:

Galilee was far from the followers of John the Baptist. John had developed a following in the southland. Jesus moved to the northland, a several-day walk away. This would have eased tensions between what could have been perceived as a rivalry between competing religious movements. Certainly John and Jesus wouldn't have clashed. But their followers might have engaged in some arguments: "My master is holier than yours."

Galilee was far from Jerusalem's Bible experts. Top Jewish scholars of the day didn't always interpret their Bible the way Jesus did. By distancing himself for a time from these leaders, called Pharisees and Sadducees, Jesus gave himself time to get his message out—before the Jewish leaders united to silence him.

Galileans were more tolerant and open-minded. Far from Jerusalem, Galileans were inclined to think for themselves instead of letting so-called experts in Jewish law do their thinking for them. Galileans also had to be tolerant to get along with their neighbors. They were surrounded by non-Jews on three sides, and Mediterranean fish on the fourth. The Samaritans lived south of them, in the heart of the Jewish homeland. Other Gentiles lived north in what is now Lebanon, and east in what are now Syria and Jordan. Living among mixed cultures and doing business with them tends to mellow out the hard lines, making it easier for the people to get along with each other.

Galilee was a small region of close-knit Jewish communities. Galilee wasn't much bigger than some modern-day counties—and smaller than some.

It stretched about 50 miles (80 km) north to south and 30 miles (50 km) east to west, from the Sea of Galilee to the Mediterranean Sea. Surrounded by Gentiles, Galilee was a tiny island of Jews who knew each other. Word of a miracle worker like Jesus would have spread quickly among them.

Galilean weather was mild, allowing year-round ministry. The area lies on the same latitude as the sun-soaked cities of San Diego, Dallas, and Charleston.

The Sea of Galilee acted as a natural amphitheater. This freshwater lake lay in the depths of the land like the last few sips of murky soup at the bottom of a bowl. Sloping hills surrounded the lake. Crowds could sit on the hillside— theater seating style—and hear Jesus as he addressed them from the shoreline or from a boat anchored near the shore.

Galileans, like most Jews, were anticipating the Messiah's arrival. Though surrounded by the territories of non-Jews, Galilee was a Jewish land filled with Jews eager for the promised Messiah to come and drive out the occupying Romans and then reestablish the Jewish nation to its past glory.

Galilee fulfilled the prophecy of where the Messiah would appear. Matthew is the only Gospel writer who reports the connection between Jesus' ministry in Galilee and Isaiah's 700-year-old prediction that most Jews associated with the Messiah: "The land of Zebulun and Naphtali will be humbled, but there will be a time in the future when Galilee of the Gentiles, which lies along the road that runs between the Jordan and the sea, will be filled with glory. The people who walk in darkness will see a great light" (Isaiah 9:1–2).

If ever there was a prophecy about the Messiah, this chapter is one. It's the chapter that goes on to say, "For a child is born to us, a son is given to us. The government will rest on his shoulders. And he will be called: Wonderful Counselor, Mighty God, Everlasting Father, Prince of Peace. His government and its peace will never end" (Isaiah 9:6–7).

Zebulun and Naphtali were two of Israel's 12 tribes, both located in Galilee. Jesus' hometown of Nazareth rested inside Zebulun's territory. Capernaum, Jesus' ministry headquarters, lay within Naphtali's borders.

"Galilee of the Gentiles" may refer to the fact that this region was surrounded by Gentiles and spiritually darkened by that influence. "The road that runs between the Jordan and the sea" was an international trade route from Damascus into Israel and south toward Egypt along the Mediterranean coast.

JESUS' MESSAGE IN A SENTENCE

Modern-day prophets of doom carrying posters saying REPENT! THE END IS NEAR may have gotten their inspiration from Jesus.

"Jesus began to preach, 'Repent of your sins and turn to God, for the Kingdom of Heaven is near' " (Matthew 4:17).

The difference between the two messages is that instead of delivering bad news, Jesus delivered good news. He offered hope—a way of escaping the punishment that Jewish law said people deserved for their sins.

Yet it was a vague message, open to interpretation. People could read into it any number of expectations. But most Jews were expecting the Messiah. And they were expecting a certain kind of messiah. Someone who would

- drive out the Roman occupiers;
- restore Israel as a sovereign nation; and
- rebuild the nation in all its past glory.

But Jesus wouldn't turn out to be a political messiah who would save the Jews from their enemies. He would be a spiritual messiah who would save the Jews—and anyone else who believed in him—from their sins. As he would one day tell the Roman governor Pilate, "My kingdom is not of this world" (John 18:36 NIV).

That's apparently not the message Jesus wanted to communicate at the beginning of his ministry. Instead of saying, essentially, "I'm the Messiah, but I have a surprise for you—I'm a pacifist," he opted for another approach.

With his insights, his fulfillment of prophecies about the Messiah, and his jaw-dropping miracles, he helped many people take the first step toward him. He convinced them he was the Messiah. Then he gave them time to adjust their preconceived notions about the Messiah to the reality standing in front of them.

What would have confused most Jews is that many prophecies about the Messiah talk about a wonderfully changed world, with Israel a nation of honor, and with all nations—and even nature—living in peace. Heaven on earth. With prophecies such as these, it's easy to overlook the other prophecies about a suffering servant of God. (See "Jesus—Messiah or Not?" below.)

Many Christian Bible experts say all of these prophecies will be fulfilled eventually, but that Jesus fulfilled only some of them during his First Coming. These scholars use a cryptic phrase to describe this mysterious, double aspect of the Kingdom of God: "already and not yet." Jesus brought God's Kingdom to earth—God's rule over those willing to be ruled by him. But the Kingdom hasn't come in its full form. When it does, all that exists will become the Kingdom of God.

But for now, at the beginning of his ministry, Jesus was content to let his neighbors know that the Messiah they had been waiting for was standing among them.

JESUS—MESSIAH OR NOT?

Christians say Jesus was the Messiah that Old Testament prophets said would come to save people. And Christians have a list of fulfilled prophecies to defend their position.

Jews, on the other hand, insist that Jesus wasn't the promised Messiah. And they have a list of unfulfilled prophecies to defend their position.

continued on p.89

continued from p.88

CHRISTIAN THESIS: JESUS IS THE MESSIAH

PROPHECY	FULFILLMENT
Related to David. "Out of the stump of David's family will grow a shoot" (Isaiah 11:1).	**Jesus' family tree.** "This is a record of the ancestors of Jesus the Messiah, a descendant of David" (Matthew 1:1).
Virgin birth. "The Lord himself will give you the sign. Look! The virgin will conceive a child! She will give birth to a son and will call him Immanuel (which means 'God is with us')" (Isaiah 7:14).	**Virgin Mary.** "You will conceive and give birth to a son. . . . "Mary asked the angel, "But how can this happen? I am a virgin." The angel replied, "The Holy Spirit will come upon you" (Luke 1:31, 34–35).
Birthplace Bethlehem. "But you, O Bethlehem Ephrathah, are only a small village among all the people of Judah. Yet a ruler of Israel will come from you, one whose origins are from the distant past" (Micah 5:2).	**Jesus is born.** "The Savior—yes, the Messiah, the Lord—has been born today in Bethlehem, the city of David!" (Luke 2:11).
Riding a donkey. "Rejoice, O people of Zion! Shout in triumph, O people of Jerusalem! Look, your king is coming to you. He is righteous and victorious, yet he is humble, riding on a donkey—riding on a donkey's colt" (Zechariah 9:9).	**Jesus rides into Jerusalem.** "They brought the colt [young donkey] to Jesus. . . . As he rode along, the crowds spread out their garments on the road ahead of him. When they reached the place where the road started down the Mount of Olives, all of his followers began to shout and sing as they walked along, praising God" (Luke 19:35–37).
Suffering servant. "He was led like a lamb to the slaughter. . . . My righteous servant will make it possible for many to be counted righteous, for he will bear all their sins" (Isaiah 53:7, 11).	**Crucifixion.** "The Son of Man came not to be served but to serve others and to give his life as a ransom for many" (Mark 10:45).
Feeling deserted. "My God, my God, why have you deserted me? Why are you so far away? Won't you listen to my groans and come to my rescue?" (Psalm 22:1 CEV).	**Jesus cries from the cross.** "My God, my God, why have you deserted me?" (Matthew 27:46 CEV).
Alive again on third day. "In two days he will put new life in us; on the third day he will raise us up so that we may live in his presence" (Hosea 6:2 NCV).	**Resurrection Sunday.** "The Jews in Jerusalem killed him by hanging him on a cross. Yet, on the third day, God raised Jesus to life" (Acts 10:39–40 NCV).

continued on p.90

continued from p.89
JEWISH THESIS: JESUS IS NOT THE MESSIAH
Jews point to the following unfulfilled prophecies—along with many others—which some Christian scholars say should be read as symbolism or as events still in the future:

- **Political peace.** "I will remove the battle chariots from Israel and the warhorses from Jerusalem. I will destroy all the weapons used in battle, and your king will bring peace to the nations. His realm will stretch from sea to sea and from the Euphrates River to the ends of the earth" (Zechariah 9:10).
- **Heaven on earth.** "In that day the wolf and the lamb will live together; the leopard will lie down with the baby goat. The calf and the yearling will be safe with the lion, and a little child will lead them all" (Isaiah 11:6).
- **Justice reigns.** "Look, a righteous king is coming! And honest princes will rule under him. . . . Even the hotheads will be full of sense and understanding. . . . In that day ungodly fools will not be heroes. Scoundrels will not be respected" (Isaiah 32:1, 4–5).
- **All nations worship in Jerusalem.** "In that day Jerusalem will be known as 'The Throne of the Lord.' All nations will come there to honor the Lord. They will no longer stubbornly follow their own evil desires" (Jeremiah 3:17).
- **Peace, wealth in Jerusalem.** "I will give Jerusalem a river of peace and prosperity. The wealth of the nations will flow to her" (Isaiah 66:12).

WAS JESUS HANDSOME?
Jesus was homely, according to the oldest surviving reports.

Perhaps fortunately for Jesus, those reports aren't old enough to be reliable. They're from church leaders who wrote about two centuries after Jesus. These churchmen took their cue from a literal reading of prophecy, not from descriptions or artwork passed down from earlier generations.

The Jews had no art to pass down. They taught it was wrong to portray humans in any kind of art, partly because so many people worshipped idols pictured as humans.

The prophecy that led church leaders to conclude Jesus was ugly came from Isaiah: "There was nothing beautiful or majestic about his appearance, nothing to attract us to him" (Isaiah 53:2).

But a century later, Christian writers and artists decided he must have been handsome. For support, they pointed to the lyrics of a sacred song about Israel's ideal king, the Messiah: "You are the most handsome of all" (Psalm 45:2).

There is one letter, traced back at least to the 1400s, that claims to come from Publius Lentulus, governor of Judea before Pilate's appointment to that job. Actually, there's no record that Publius existed. But in a letter to the Roman senate, he supposedly describes Jesus in detail:

> *He is a man of medium size. . . . His hair is of the color of a ripe hazel-nut, straight down to the ears, but below the ears wavy and curled. . . . It is parted in two on the top of the head, in the custom of the Nazarenes. . . . His face has no wrinkles or spots, but a slightly reddish complexion. His nose and mouth are perfectly formed. His beard is full but not long, and divided at the chin. . . . He is a handsome man.*

JESUS CHOOSES 12 DISCIPLES

Jesus went up on a mountain to pray,
and he prayed to God all night. At daybreak
he called together all of his disciples and
chose twelve of them to be apostles.

LUKE 6:12–13

It's no wonder Jesus captured people's attention. For a rabbi—a teacher well versed in sacred Jewish writings—his approach to just about everything he did in his ministry was incredibly unrabbi-like.

His miracles seemed more like something a prophet would do. His teachings seemed more like the wishful thinking of a heretic. And his choice of disciples was nearly as unexpected as a herd of flying pigs—not at all kosher.

The fact that he chose disciples was strange enough. It was supposed to work the other way around. Religion students typically picked the masters they wanted to study under, much like doctoral students today select a preferred mentor.

As strange as it was for Jesus to do the choosing, he escalated *bizarre* to a new level in the choices he made.

He didn't go for the brainiacs, the holy elite, or the rising stars in Jewish scholarship:

- Instead of brainiacs, he chose fishermen—at least four.
- Instead of holy elite, he chose a taxman—whom the high and holy considered ritually unclean "scum."
- Instead of rising stars in Jewish scholarship, he seems to have chosen at least one follower from a rising freedom fighter movement called the Zealots.

This was a mismatch of plaids and stripes that seemed destined to clash itself to death. On the one hand, a taxman was perceived as a traitorous Roman sympathizer. On the other hand, a Zealot freedom fighter wanted nothing more than to get rid of Romans and their sympathizers.

And who would expect anything but fish from a fisherman? Even after spending perhaps three years with Jesus, two of these fishermen—Peter and John—would draw a bland evaluation from Jewish scholars who sized them up as "ordinary men with no special training in the Scriptures" (Acts 4:13).

Yet Jesus matched these men on the same team. His team. This dirty dozen became his chosen people. Jesus expected great things from them—nothing less than the fulfillment of prophecy: "You will do more than restore the people of Israel to me. I will make you a light to the Gentiles, and you will bring my salvation to the ends of the earth" (Isaiah 49:6).

Wishful thinking at its best.

NET FISHING 101

Fishermen used three kinds of nets: cast, drop, and tow.

Cast. Usable by a single fisherman, the cast net was designed as a circle about 20–25 feet across (6–8 meters). Lead sinkers on the edge pulled it down like a falling parachute, trapping fish between the net and the lake bottom.

Drop. Long and narrow like a fence, the seine net could be dropped over the side of the boat to hang vertically in the water—with weights on the bottom edge and floats on the top. Fishermen could use the net to surround a school of fish. Then they pulled in the net using ropes at the right and left sides—turning the net into a U filled with fish.

Tow. The trammel net, reinforced with three layers of netting, stretched nearly 200 yards (183 meters) between two boats. As fishermen rowed their boats forward, fish got trapped in the net.

Many fishermen worked at night, when it was harder for fish to see the nets and when fishermen could use torches to lure curious fish toward the boat.

— INVITATION FROM A RABBI ——

When it came to matching rabbis with disciples, a famous rabbi of the first century expressed the customary method. His name was Gamaliel, a Pharisee who taught the apostle Paul. Gamaliel offered this advice for students who wanted to become Jewish scholars:

Find a teacher and lose your ignorance.

ABOT 1:16

It was up to each student to find a rabbi who would teach him how to interpret the Jewish laws. Serving much like an apprentice, the student would spend as much time as possible with the rabbi, learning from his words and actions.

The object was to retain as much knowledge as possible. Or as one rabbi in ancient times put it, to hold on to the knowledge like a "plaster-sealed cistern, not letting one drop of water escape."

Jewish law, especially the hundreds of laws preserved in the first five books of the Bible, is what most rabbis of Jesus' day taught. These scholars debated how to interpret the laws and how to apply them to life. For example, the Law said Jews shouldn't work on the Sabbath. But at what point did an activity become work? (For more on Sabbath rules, see "Jesus and Disciples Break Sabbath Rules," page 142.)

Rabbi Jesus, however, didn't seem to spend much time teaching his disciples about the Law. Instead, he taught them about the God behind the Law.

Jesus said that was the purpose of the Law in the first place: "Don't misunderstand why I have come. I did not come to abolish the law of Moses or the writings of the prophets. No, I came to accomplish their purpose" (Matthew 5:17).

The Bible never explains why Jesus chose the 12 he did—though history bears out the wisdom of his choices. Even Judas Iscariot had an important role to play. What's clear is that Jesus chose working-class men, mostly from his own region, Galilee, and from his own level in society.

DISCIPLE UNDER THE BED

One story in the Talmud—a collection of sacred Jewish commentary and history about Jewish law—tells of an eager disciple hiding under his master's bed. The student said he wanted to learn how the Law applied to sex:

> Kahana sneaked into Rabbi Abba's bedroom and hid under the bed. There, Kahana heard the rabbi and his wife engage in happy, intimate pillow talk—followed by exuberant sex.
> Afterward, Kahana spoke from under the bed. "You sound like a man who's never had sex before."
> Shocked, the rabbi replied, "Kahana, what are you doing here? Get out! You're being rude!"
> "No I'm not," Kahana answered. "This is a matter of Law. And I have to study it."

BABYLONIAN TALMUD, BERAKHOT 62A

THE FIRST FOUR DISCIPLES—AND THEN SOME

How Jesus went about inviting the disciples to join his ministry is a bit of a puzzle, because it's difficult to blend all four Gospel accounts. The writers drew from sources that saw the events from different perspectives.

The Gospels of Matthew and Mark both say Jesus invited brothers Peter and Andrew first, while they were "throwing a net into the water" (Matthew 4:18). Then, farther up the lakeshore, Jesus invited the brothers James and John, who were repairing their nets in a boat. All four fishermen worked for Zebedee, father of James and John. All four instantly left what they were doing and followed Jesus—though there's no indication they had ever met him before.

Luke tells a different story. The four men were washing their nets after a night of fishing. They had caught nothing. Jesus asked Peter to push his boat into the water so Jesus could use it as a floating stage to address the crowd. Afterward, Jesus told Peter to row out farther and drop his net in the water. The huge haul ripped some of the netting. Peter and his partners rowed their harvest back to shore, where Jesus told them, "From now on you'll be fishing for people!" (Luke 5:10). That's when they left everything and followed him. Later, Jesus invited a tax collector to join the disciples: Levi, probably a nickname for Matthew.

The Gospel of John adds a third version to the mix. It says Jesus' first disciples were a couple of transfers from the ministry of John the Baptist: Andrew and an unnamed colleague—perhaps his partner John, the writer of this

Gospel, who had a humble habit of not mentioning himself in the book. The two joined Jesus after John the Baptist identified him as the Messiah. Andrew introduced his brother Peter to Jesus. And perhaps John told his brother James. The next day, Jesus added two more disciples: Philip and Nathanael.

Perhaps all these versions are accurate, at least from the perspective of the various witnesses. There could have been multiple meetings between Jesus and his first disciples. And it's possible that the fishermen dropped what they were doing more than once to follow Jesus somewhere.

Yet the story gets a tad more complicated.

Jesus had scores of disciples following him. At one point he sent "72 other disciples" on a mission. He sent them into neighboring villages with these instructions: "Heal the sick, and tell them, 'The Kingdom of God is near you now' " (Luke 10:9).

SETTLING ON AN EVEN DOZEN

At some point, Jesus decided to create an elite group of 12 disciples.

Why 12? Some numbers had powerful symbolic meanings to the Jewish people. Twelve had a connection to the founding of the Jewish nation. God instructed Moses to organize the country into a dozen tribal clans.

It's as if Jesus was sending the message that God's people were being born again. They were getting a fresh start, a new covenant, and a bright future.

Jesus would extend this symbolic connection at the Last Supper, promising the disciples that they'd have authority over the original 12 tribes—that the era of the new covenant would take precedence over the old system of Jewish laws. "When the world is made new and the Son of Man sits upon his glorious throne, you who have been my followers will also sit on twelve thrones, judging the twelve tribes of Israel" (Matthew 19:28).

Before Jesus selected his elite dozen from the scores of disciples following him, the Gospels of Mark and Luke both report that he "went up on a mountain to pray, and he prayed to God all night. At daybreak he called together all of his disciples and chose twelve of them to be apostles" (Luke 6:12–13).

The word *apostle* indicates a promotion for the 12. *Disciple* comes from a Greek word that means student or apprentice. But *apostle* refers to a trusted emissary—a messenger.

In the years that followed, the title of apostle would become reserved for only the most honored leaders in the first generation of Christians. These were leaders whom Jesus personally sent out to spread his teachings.

WHO'S WHO OF THE 12 APOSTLES

In every Bible list of the 12 disciples, and there are four—in Matthew, Mark, Luke, and Acts—the same name always pops up first.

Peter. He was the leader of the 12. The spokesman who confronted Jesus when others had questions they were afraid to ask. The first to say out loud that Jesus was the Son of God. And the first to preach a sermon after the resurrected Jesus ascended to heaven.

Peter was also one of Jesus' three best friends—an inner circle that included brothers James and John. Only these three were allowed to accompany Jesus at critical moments in his ministry, such as when Jesus resurrected the daughter of Jairus, when he met with Elijah and Moses on a mountain and was transfigured into a glowing celestial presence, and when he prayed in the Garden of Gethsemane on the night of his arrest.

AKA. Simon, Cephas, Rocky. His name was originally Simon, son of John. Jesus renamed him Peter, the Greek word for "rock." (That's Cephas in Aramaic, the language most Jews spoke, having brought it home with them from exile in Babylon 500 years earlier.)

Hometown. Bethsaida, by the Sea of Galilee. But he apparently moved to nearby Capernaum, where he had a home.

Occupation. Fisherman on the Sea of Galilee. He and his brother Andrew worked as partners with James and John, the sons of Zebedee.

Claim to fame. After temple officers arrested Jesus and took him to trial, Peter waited outside. There, a servant girl asked if he was one of Jesus' followers. "Woman," he said, "I don't even know him!" (Luke 22:57).

Ministry highlight. After Jesus returned to heaven, Peter preached the disciples' first-known sermon, leading about 3,000 Jews to faith in Jesus and jump-starting the Christian movement. That seemed to fulfill a prediction Jesus had made: "Upon this rock I will build my church" (Matthew 16:18).

Manner of death. "Crucified at Rome with his head downward," wrote Origen, a church leader in the AD 200s. This seemed to fulfill what Jesus had told Peter would happen: " 'When you are old, you will stretch out your hands.' . . . Jesus said this to let him know by what kind of death he would glorify God" (John 21:18–19).

Andrew. Brother of Simon Peter. Andrew was the disciple who brought to Jesus the boy with five small loaves of bread and two fish—from which Jesus fed more than 5,000.

Hometown. Bethsaida. But he may have lived in Capernaum with Peter.

Occupation. Fisherman and partner with Peter, James, and John.

Claim to fame. He introduced Peter to Jesus, saying, "We have found the Messiah" (John 1:41).

Manner of death. Crucified on an X-shaped cross, according to the *Acts of Andrew*, a book written in the AD 200s.

James, son of Zebedee. Along with his brother John, as well as Peter, James was one of Jesus' three closest friends.

Hometown. Somewhere near the twin fishing villages of Capernaum and Bethsaida.

Occupation. Fisherman in partnership with his brother John and the brothers Peter and Andrew.

Claim to fame. First apostle to die a martyr's death, and the only one whose martyrdom is reported in the Bible.

Manner of death. "King Herod Agrippa [son of Herod the Great] began to persecute some believers in the church. He had the apostle James (John's brother) killed with a sword" (Acts 12:1–2).

John, son of Zebedee. Brother of James—the two of whom Jesus nicknamed "Sons of Thunder." Perhaps they were Zealots, wanting to overthrow Rome. But more likely they earned the nickname because of their fiery tempers. When a Samaritan village refused to welcome Jesus, the bold brothers said to Jesus, "Lord, should we call down fire from heaven to burn them up?" (Luke 9:54). Jesus declined the offer.

Hometown. Somewhere near Capernaum and Bethsaida.

Occupation. Employed by his father as a fisherman in partnership with John, Peter, and Andrew.

Claim to fame. He and James brought their mother to Jesus so she could ask a favor: "In your Kingdom, please let my two sons sit in places of honor next to you, one on your right and the other on your left" (Matthew 20:21). This infuriated the other disciples.

Ministry highlight. John was probably the unidentified "beloved disciple" to whom Jesus, hanging on the cross, entrusted the care of his mother, Mary. Many scholars also consider John the author of the Gospel of John, the three letters of John, and Revelation, too.

Manner of death. Early church leaders said he died of natural causes at an old age, around AD 100, in Ephesus.

Philip. At the Last Supper, he asked Jesus to show them God the Father. Jesus replied, "Anyone who has seen me has seen the Father!" (John 14:9).

Hometown. Bethsaida.

Occupation. Unknown.

Ministry highlight. He introduced Jesus to Nathanael, also known as Bartholomew.

Manner of death. Crucified in Turkey, according to church tradition.

Bartholomew. Appears in every New Testament list of apostles, including in Acts, but is not mentioned otherwise.

AKA. Nathanael. That's what many scholars speculate. His full name may have been Nathanael bar Tholami (son of Tholami).

Hometown. Cana, assuming he is Nathanael.

Occupation. Unknown.

Claim to fame. When Philip invited him to come and meet Jesus the Messiah, Nathanael replied, "Can anything good come from Nazareth?" (John 1:46).

Ministry highlight. Church tradition says he took the gospel to India.

Manner of death. One tradition says he was skinned alive and beheaded in India. Another says he was stuffed in a sack and tossed in the sea.

Matthew. Perhaps the most unlikely of all disciples.

AKA. Levi, according to the Gospels of Mark and Luke. This may have been a nickname or part of his full name: Matthew Levi.

Hometown. Most likely Capernaum, because that's where Jesus met him.

Occupation. Tax collector. He operated a toll booth, probably on the main trade route that ran near Capernaum.

Claim to fame. Jesus invited the likes of him—a tax collector—to join the band of disciples. Most Jews hated tax collectors because tax men got rich by overcharging people.

Ministry highlight. After accepting Jesus' invitation, he threw a party for Jesus—inviting his tax collector colleagues. When Jewish scholars saw this, they asked Jesus' other disciples, "Why does your teacher eat with such scum?" (Matthew 9:11).

Manner of death. Executed with an ax or a sword in Ethiopia, according to the most popular tradition.

Thomas. After learning that Jesus expected to die in Jerusalem, Thomas courageously urged the other disciples, "Let's go, too—and die with Jesus" (John 11:16).

AKA. Doubting Thomas, "nicknamed the Twin" (John 21:2).

Hometown. Probably somewhere in Galilee.

Occupation. Unknown.

Claim to fame. After the other disciples told him they had seen the resurrected Jesus, he replied, "I won't believe it unless I see the nail wounds in his hands, put my fingers into them, and place my hand into the wound in his side" (John 20:25).

Ministry highlight. Early church writers said he started the church in India. Today, the Syro-Malabar Catholic Church of India, with three million members, claims Thomas as founder.

Manner of death. Tradition says he was speared to death in India.

James, son of Alphaeus. Outside the list of apostles, he's not mentioned in the Bible.

AKA. Possibly the same person as "James the younger" (Mark 15:40), perhaps to distinguish him from the older apostle named James.

Manner of death. Crucified in Egypt, according to one tradition. In Iran, according to another.

Simon the Zealot. His name shows up in the Bible only in the list of apostles. The descriptor "Zealot" could refer to his personality—as a go-getter. But most Bible experts say it probably links him to the Jewish rebel movement by that name. About 40 years after the time of Jesus, Jewish Zealots led the nation into a doomed revolt against Rome.

AKA. Simon the Cananean. "Cananean" is "an Aramaic term for Jewish nationalists" [or *Zealots*] (Matthew 10:4 footnote).

Manner of death. Crucified, or hacked to death, in Iran, with Judas the son of James, according to tradition.

Judas, son of James. He shows up only once outside the list of apostles. He asked Jesus why he was revealing his identity only to the disciples and not to the world (John 14:22). It's a question Jesus sidestepped by telling Judas simply to do as he was told.

AKA. Called Thaddaeus in Matthew and Mark. This may have been his nickname or the name of the village from which he came.

Manner of death. Martyred with Simon the Zealot, according to tradition.

Judas Iscariot. He is always listed last—for good reason.

Hometown. Probably Kerioth, a village whose location is now unknown. Iscariot, scholars say, likely means "man of Kerioth." Judas' father was also known by that last name: "Simon Iscariot" (John 6:71). There was a city by that name in southern Israel. If that's where Judas came from, he may have been the only non-Galilean among the disciples. Some scholars say the name Iscariot may reveal that Judas was a rebel, since the name sounds a bit like Sicarii, a group of Jewish freedom fighters much like the Zealots.

Occupation. Unknown.

Claim to fame. For a reward, he helped Jewish authorities arrest Jesus.

Ministry highlight. "In charge of the disciples' money, he often stole some for himself" (John 12:6).

Manner of death. He hanged himself (Matthew 27:5). Then his body "fell headfirst into the field. His body burst open, and all his insides came out" (Acts 1:18 CEV). Perhaps the rope or tree branch from which he hanged himself broke.

MIRACLE 1: WATER INTO WINE

When they started running low on wine at the wedding banquet,
Jesus' mother told him, "They're just about out of wine."
JOHN 2:3 THE MESSAGE

Of all the miracles Jesus could have performed to launch his ministry—healing the sick or raising the dead—his first miracle on record was to liven up a party with enough wine to get more than 1,000 people drunk. At least by today's measure of drunkenness.

It figures. That's what his Pharisee critics might have said.

These Jewish scholars would later watch Jesus enjoying himself at a party and declare, "He's a glutton and a drunkard" (Matthew 11:19).

Not likely.

Drunks get bad press in the Bible. They're spoken of as sinners and fools: "What sorrow for those who get up early in the morning looking for a drink of alcohol and spend long evenings drinking wine to make themselves flaming drunk" (Isaiah 5:11).

Yet the apostles who knew Jesus and wrote his story in the New Testament portray him as neither sinner nor fool: "There is no sin in him, and sin is not part of his program" (1 John 3:5 THE MESSAGE).

This miracle at Cana is a puzzling story for many Christians—even troubling. They can't understand why Jesus would do something like this at all, let alone as his miracle of first impression. And they don't understand why John, one of his best friends, would taint Jesus' reputation by telling everyone and his brother about it. Why not do like the other three Gospel writers—skip it?

With good reason, John not only didn't skip it but also turned it into his lead miracle headline.

PARTYING IN CANA

The party was a wedding celebration in Cana, a village whose location is lost to history. Drawing from the meaning of *Cana*, "place of reeds," most scholars today guess that the ruins of this village lie under a yet-to-be excavated mound of dirt overlooking a marshy plain full of reeds.

First-century coins found at the mound suggest this was the site of a village in Jesus' day. Khirbet Cana is what the locals call the place. *Khirbet* is Arabic for "ruins." It's about a nine-mile (14 km), three-hour walk north of Jesus' hometown of Nazareth.

Mary, Jesus' mother, showed up on the guest list. So did Jesus and the five disciples that John 1:35–51 says he had recruited so far. These were brothers Peter and Andrew; Philip; Nathanael, who lived in Cana; and an unidentified disciple, probably John—the anonymous writer who most scholars say wrote this Gospel.

Perhaps Mary and her family were related to someone in the wedding or were close friends. One copy of this story written in the AD 200s says in the preface that the groom was John, the writer of this story and one of Jesus' closest disciples. Another tradition adds that Mary and John's mother were sisters, which would have made Jesus and John cousins.

Whatever Mary's relationship to the newlyweds, she acted like more than just a guest. She may have been helping run the celebration. Two clues:

- Mary knew the wine was running out even before two key people—the groom, who hosted the party and provided the food and drinks, and the master of ceremonies, who kept the banquet running smoothly; and
- the servants followed her directions.

WEDDING RECEPTION, AD 30

After a long engagement—typically a year—it was time for the wedding. Fall weddings were popular in this farming community, after the harvest was in and the people were enjoying the fruits of their hard work.

Parents of the bride and groom had already negotiated the financial arrangements:

Groom's cost. The groom had paid the "bride fee" to compensate his father-in-law for the loss of his daughter, who was considered an asset. The groom or his family typically hosted the wedding reception.

Bride's cost. The bride's father agreed on the dowry of assets she would bring to the marriage—perhaps money, jewelry, clothes, household furnishings, and servants.

On the wedding day, it was customary for the groom to walk to his bride's home. Accompanying him was a procession, including his best man, his family, and friends. The bride waited for him, dressed in her wedding clothes and attended by her bridesmaids, family, and friends. If the groom arrived at night, he would be greeted by a row of ladies lighting the darkness with lamps—a familiar scene Jesus used in a parable, the story of 10 bridesmaids (Matthew 25:1).

At the door, the groom asked for his bride. When she came to him, he lifted her veil and praised her with cheers of joy—a cue for his friends to do the same.

Then began the ancient version of the wedding march. But instead of father and bride, it was groom and bride. Together they led a procession of both families to the groom's home, where he would host a wedding feast—the climax of this happy ceremony.

Flowers decorated the house. Food and wine crowded the tabletops and the nooks in the walls. Music filled the air as guests began to arrive, singing and dancing, presenting their wedding gifts, and offering words of blessing to the newlyweds.

If the family was relatively well off, the celebration might last a week. But for farmers, fishermen, and carpenters, one good day might be all they could afford, and all their family and friends would expect.

NO WINE BEFORE IT'S TIME

Running out of wine wasn't like running out of ice at a barbecue. It was a big deal.

Many family and friends had invested a lot of time and money, some of them traveling days or weeks to join the celebration. They came to honor the couple with their presence and their presents—and these guests had every right to expect honor in return, through the hospitality of food and wine. Ancient records show that on rare occasions some disgruntled guests sued when they didn't receive hospitality on a par with their investment.

At the very least, running out of wine would have left the groom looking like a poor planner, or worse, a cheapskate. And sending out for wine at a moment's notice could have gotten expensive, because any merchants selling wine in this small village would have recognized a seller's market when they saw one.

Mary took the problem to her son.

"Dear woman, that's not our problem," Jesus replied. "My time has not yet come" (John 2:4).

In this Gospel, when Jesus talked about his "time," he was talking about his crucifixion.

Case in point: "Now the time has come for the Son of Man to enter into his glory. . . . Now my soul is deeply troubled. Should I pray, 'Father, save me from this hour'? But this is the very reason I came!" (John 12:23, 27).

Somehow, Jesus saw a connection between his destiny and what his mother was asking him to do. Perhaps he connected dots like these:

- Turning water into wine would mark him as a miracle worker, thrusting him into the public eye.

ANCIENT MARRIAGE CONTRACT

Date: Year 17 of Caesar Augustus' reign (13 BC)
Groom: Apollonius, son of Ptolemaeus
Bride: Thermion, daughter of Apion

Thermion and Apollonius agree they have come together to share a common life.

Apollonius confirms that he has received from Thermion a dowry of a pair of gold earrings weighing three quarters and. . .silver drachmai [part of the contract describing the dowry is lost].

From now on, Apollonius will provide his wife, Thermion, with clothing and all other necessities in proportion to his income. He will not mistreat her, run her off, or bring in another wife. If he does, he will give Thermion one and a half times the value of her dowry along with all of his property—as if this were ordered by a court of law.

Thermion will fulfill her obligations toward her husband. She will not leave the house for a day or a night without the consent of her husband. Nor will she dishonor him or their family, or engage in sexual relations with another man. If she does any of this, she will forfeit her dowry and pay whatever fines are levied by the court if the case goes to trial.

- Many Jews would see the miracle as a sign—the beginning of the Messiah's reign. Long ago, prophets had said that when the Messiah came, wine would flow like water: "Then the terraced vineyards on the hills of Israel will drip with sweet wine!" (Amos 9:13).
- This miracle would start the clock on the countdown to the Cross. Jewish leaders would soon take notice of Jesus and eventually arrange his execution.

Immediately after refusing to do anything about the problem, Jesus did something about the problem.

What changed his mind? Curious Bible scholars would like to know.

Some speculate that God confirmed the time was right. Others argue that the time wasn't right, and for that reason Jesus did the miracle in low profile—with only his mother and the servants knowing about it.

SAVING THE BEST FOR LAST

At Jesus' direction, the servants filled six stone jars with water. Jewish households typically kept containers like this filled with water to wash away ritual defilement, such as that from touching a dead animal. Clay jars wouldn't work. They had to be discarded if a ritually unclean person touched them. But stone containers were defilement-proof.

Each jar could hold "twenty to thirty gallons" (John 2:6). That's a total of at least 120 gallons (454 liters), and as much as 180 gallons (681 liters).

"Now dip some out, and take it to the master of ceremonies," Jesus told the servants.

Fine wine poured into the cup.

Three five-ounce glasses of table wine—a total of 15 ounces (.44 liters)—could raise the blood alcohol content of an average-sized person well beyond the .08 percent used today as a measure of impairment. There are 128 ounces in a gallon, and 15,360 ounces in 120 gallons. Do the math. Divide 15 ounces into 15,360 ounces. Jesus had miraculously produced enough wine to render at

---

WINEMAKING THE NATURAL WAY

Harvest was a happy time in Jesus' day—as it still is for farmers. It's payday for a year's hard work:

- pruning in the winter;
- propping up the vines during the spring and summer; and
- picking grapes late in the summer or early in the fall—depending on the type of grape and the vineyard's location.

Some grapes went straight to the mouth or to the dinner table. Others were dipped in olive oil and dried in the sun to become raisins.

But most were carted off to the winepress in August or September to become wine by October or November.

least 1,024 people unfit to drive a donkey cart.

This wasn't the watered-down budget wine sometimes served late into the party, when anything crossing the palate tasted like a blur.

"A host always serves the best wine first," the master of ceremonies said to the groom after drinking wine from heaven's vineyard. "Then, when everyone has had a lot to drink, he brings out the less expensive wine. But you have kept the best until now!" (John 2:10).

WEDDING PLANNER

The "master of ceremonies" who declared Jesus' wine the toast of the feast was a bit like a wedding planner. He was in charge of the event, the seating arrangements, entertainment, and food.

One Bible book offers advice for such a person: Wisdom of Jesus, Son of Sirach. This is a book written in about 200 BC and included in the Apocrypha, a collection of sacred Jewish writings preserved in many Catholic and Eastern Orthodox Bibles.

"If you get chosen to direct a banquet party, don't act as if you're better than your guests. Put your guests first. Only when you've taken care of their needs is it okay to relax and join the party as one of them. Do this and you'll earn high praise from the people who entrusted you with such an honor" (Sirach 32:1–2 author's paraphrase).

AND THE POINT IS

John summed up the short story in two short sentences: "This miraculous sign at Cana in Galilee was the first time Jesus revealed his glory. And his disciples believed in him" (John 2:11).

Matthew, Mark, and Luke each report an average of about 20 miracles by Jesus. John reports only seven—carefully selected and tagged as "signs" that Jesus is the Son of God.

1. Turns water into wine (John 2:1–12). Jesus, who was part of the God-head that created the world, still has the Creator's power.

2. Heals a little boy long-distance (John 4:46–54). Jesus isn't limited by geography.

3. Heals a lame man on the Sabbath (John 5:1–17). Jesus isn't limited by time. Some Jews said it was wrong to practice medicine on the day of rest. Jesus said it's okay to do good on any day.

4. Feeds 5,000 people (John 6:1–14). Jesus then declared himself the bread of life—the source of both physical and spiritual nourishment.

5. Walks on water (John 6:16–21). Jesus isn't just the Creator; he's also the Master of his creation.

6. Heals the blind (John 9:1–41). Jesus, "the light of the world," gives sight to the blind—physical and spiritual.

7. Raises Lazarus from the dead (John 11:17–44). Jesus, "the resurrection and the life," is more powerful than death.

JESUS HEALS THE SICK

A vast crowd brought to him people who were lame,
blind, crippled, those who couldn't speak, and many others.
They laid them before Jesus, and he healed them all.

MATTHEW 15:30

Jesus healed 35 people.

That's the total body count in the combined stories of Matthew, Mark, Luke, and John—the four Gospel accounts of Jesus' ministry. These are the 35 men, women, and children whose stories are told ever so briefly—sometimes in just a few sentences.

Yet Jesus probably healed thousands of others whose stories aren't recorded at all. Sometimes he healed all the sick people in an entire village: "As the sun went down that evening, people throughout the village [Capernaum] brought sick family members to Jesus. No matter what their diseases were, the touch of his hand healed every one" (Luke 4:40).

That's one of two reasons the crowds swarmed him—he never met a disease he couldn't cure. The other big attraction was his skill as an insightful speaker with a unique, commonsense slant on Jewish teachings.

This tag team of ministries—teaching and healing—drove his mission statement, which the prophet Isaiah wrote for him 700 years earlier. Jesus quoted it during a worship service in his hometown synagogue:

> *"The Lord's Spirit has come to me, because he has chosen me to tell the good news to the poor. The Lord has sent me to announce freedom for prisoners, to give sight to the blind, to free everyone who suffers."*
>
> LUKE 4:18 CEV

It's what Jesus would spend his entire ministry doing.

PHYSICAL PROBLEMS JESUS CURED

ILLNESS	PATIENT	MATTHEW	MARK	LUKE	JOHN
Demon possession	Man in Capernaum synagogue	–	1:23–26	4:33–35	–
	Men living in Gadarene cemetery	8:28–34	5:1–15	8:27–35	–
	Daughter of Canaanite woman	15:21–28	7:24–30	–	–
	Boy suffering from seizures	17:14–18	9:17–19	9:38–43	–
	Man possessed, blind, mute	12:22	–	11:14	–
	Man possessed, mute	9:32–33	–	–	–
	Mary Magdalene with seven demons	–	16:9	8:2	–
Blindness	Man at Bethsaida	–	8:22–26	–	–
	Men sitting by Jericho road	20:29–34	10:46–52	18:35–43	–
	Man possessed, blind, mute	12:22	–	11:14	–
	Two men asking Jesus for mercy	9:27–31	–	–	–
	Man born blind	–	–	–	9:1–7
Leprosy	Man with advanced leprosy	8:2–4	1:40–42	5:12–13	–
	10 men in a village	–	–	17:11–19	–
Fever	Peter's mother-in-law	8:14–15	1:30–31	4:38–39	–
	Son of Capernaum official	–	–	–	4:46–54
Paralysis	Man carried on mat by friends	9:2–7	2:3–12	5:18–25	–
	Servant of Roman soldier	8:5–13	–	7:1–10	–
Lameness	Woman with curved back	–	–	13:11–13	–
	Invalid man at Bethesda pool	–	–	–	5:1–9
Inability to speak	Man possessed, mute	9:32–33	–	–	–
	Man possessed, blind, mute	12:22	–	11:14	–
Deaf, poor speech	Man from Ten Towns region	–	7:31–37	–	–
Shriveled hand	Man at synagogue	12:9–13	3:1–5	6:6–10	–
Excessive bleeding	Woman, perhaps with menstrual disorder	9:20–22	5:25–29	8:43–48	–
Swollen arms, legs	Man at Pharisee's home	–	–	14:1–4	–
Dismembered ear	Slave of high priest, arresting Jesus	–	–	22:50–51	–

— A DOZEN DISORDERS ————————————————

If we could round up the 35 people Jesus healed and usher them into interrogation rooms based on their former ailments, we'd need a dozen rooms.

The three largest rooms would be for the

- 11 cured of leprosy;
- 8 exorcized of demons; and
- 7 cured of blindness.

A few patients would have to dart from one room to the next, including a man cured of three ailments: demon possession, blindness, and the inability to talk.

Leprosy. Not everyone in the Bible who was reported to have had leprosy had what doctors today call Hansen's Disease—an infection caused by the bacterium *Mycobacterium leprae*. This disease produces lesions on the skin, including light patches that numb the nerves so the patient doesn't feel pain. Wounds unnoticed and left untreated can develop infections that require amputation.

In Bible times, Jewish priests diagnosed the skin disorders of their fellow Jews. The Mishnah, a collection of laws and teachings passed down by word of mouth before being written down in about AD 200, said the priests looked for one of four shades of white patches on the skin:

- bright white, like snow
- soft white, like Jerusalem's limestone Temple
- eggshell white
- wool white

Most likely, the priests misdiagnosed many patients who merely had a skin problem such as eczema, psoriasis, or rash-producing lupus.

Some Jews, however, may well have had the genuine disease—such as the man Jesus met "with an advanced case of leprosy" (Luke 5:12). Jesus reached out and touched him, and the skin lesions disappeared.

Demon possession. Stories about Jesus exorcizing demons are hard for many people to relate to today. Missionaries in developing countries assure us that demons are alive and well and possessing people in cultures where superstition and pagan worship flourish. But most of us in developed nations have never seen such a thing.

So when we read the Bible's diagnosis of demon possession, we want a second opinion. Consider the symptoms of one of Jesus' patients, a boy: "Whenever this spirit seizes him, it throws him violently to the ground. Then he foams at the mouth and grinds his teeth and becomes rigid" (Mark 9:18). Couldn't that be epilepsy?

Epilepsy doesn't talk.

But Jesus and the evil spirit in this boy had words.

"'I command you to come out of this child and never enter him again!'

Then the spirit screamed and threw the boy into another violent convulsion and left him" (Mark 9:25–26).

In each of the stories of demon possession, Jesus talked to the evil spiritual entities. The most famous was actually a gang of spirits called Legion. Mark and Luke say there was just one patient; Matthew says there were two. The spirits addressed Jesus as "Son of the Most High God" and begged him not to send them back to the darkness. So he cast them into a herd of 2,000 pigs. The animals responded immediately by committing lemming-like suicide. They charged off a steep hill and plummeted into the Sea of Galilee. The Bible doesn't explain why Jesus did this or what effect it had on the demons.

Jesus wasn't the only person casting out demons at this time in history. Other exorcists used various techniques: burning incense, wearing amulets, making special sounds, using dog hair or palm branches, as well as reciting incantations. One ancient exorcism incantation actually began by invoking the name of Jesus: "I summon you by the God of the Hebrews, Jesus. . . ." This incantation shows up in the Greek Magical Papyri, a collection of spells and mystical insights compiled over five centuries, from the 100s BC to the AD 400s.

Jesus, however, didn't use any memorized string of words or religious accessories. He simply told the demons to get gone.

EXORCISM IN A ROMAN HISTORY BOOK

Josephus, a Jewish writer and Roman citizen who lived in Jesus' century, said he watched a Jewish exorcist named Eleazar free a man from a demon:

> Here's how he did it. He had a ring tied to a baaras root [perhaps mandrake, which is shaped a bit like a human]. It was the same kind of root Solomon used to exorcise demons. Eleazar put the ring to the possessed man's nose, and then pulled the demon out through the man's nostrils. Instantly, the man collapsed. Eleazar started reciting incantations he had composed, which mentioned Solomon and ordered the demon never to come back.
>
> To assure witnesses that the demon had come out, Eleazar ordered it to knock over a cup of water he set up in the room.
>
> ANTIQUITIES OF THE JEWS 8:2, 5 AUTHOR'S PARAPHRASE

Blindness. This disease was probably more common in Bible times than it is today—for the same reason it's more common in undeveloped parts of the world that don't have access to good sanitation or antibiotics and other medical treatment.

Bacteria attack the eyes, producing infections such as trachoma—which is highly contagious and spreads by direct contact: touching the secretions fro' the eyes or nose, or clothing with secretions on it. Trachoma is the world's le' ing cause of preventable blindness, affecting 40 percent of the children in ' of the poorest countries. Risk factors: poverty, poor hygiene, crowded living conditions, few latrines, high number of flies, children ages 3–5.

Trachoma is easily treated today with a single dose of the antibiotic azithromycin, sold under the brand name of Zithromax. But left untreated, this infection can produce sores on the cornea, followed by blindness.

One ancient treatment was to apply various concoctions to the ailing eyes. There's just such a story in the Apocrypha, a collection of Jewish writings that appears between the Old and the New Testaments in many Catholic and Eastern Orthodox Bibles. A man named Tobit became blind after bird droppings fell into his eyes. An angel named Raphael told the man's son, Tobias, to "smear the gall of the fish on his eyes" (Tobit 11:8 NRSV). That's the wetness from the fish's insides. It cured Tobit.

This treatment is remarkably similar to one of the cures recorded in a first-century collection of books called *Natural History*, by Pliny:

> *The fat of all kinds of fish—freshwater and saltwater—melted in the sun and mixed with honey is an excellent treatment for improving eyesight.*
> REMEDIES FROM AQUATIC ANIMALS, BOOK 32

Perhaps playing catch-up, the National Eye Institute, a branch of the U.S. National Institutes of Health, launched a study in 2006 to see if fish oil can slow the progression of age-related macular degeneration, the leading cause of vision loss among people above age 60. It's a disease that causes part of the retina to thin, destroying the sharp vision directly ahead that's needed for reading or driving.

Jesus, who cured at least seven blind people and more likely hundreds, generally did nothing more than speak the cure or touch the person. But on one occasion he did use a technique that would have been familiar to the patient, a man born blind. Perhaps to help increase the man's faith, "he spit on the ground, made mud with the saliva, and spread the mud over the blind man's eyes" (John 9:6). Then he told the man to wash off the mud.

That's similar to a combo of treatments recommended in Pliny's *Natural History*:

- "To cure inflammation of the eyes, wash the eyes each morning with spit from your overnight fast" (*Remedies from Living Creatures*, book 28, chapter 10).
- "To protect your eyes from developing eye diseases including inflammation of the eyes, do this and you will never again develop an eye disease. Each time you wash the dust off your feet, touch your eyes three times with the muddy water" (*Remedies from Living Creatures*, book 28, chapter 10).

FEVER BE GONE

Rabbi Alexandri, a Jewish scholar in ancient times, said healing a person with a fever—as Jesus did for Peter's mother-in-law—is a bigger miracle than the one that saved Shadrach, Meshach, and Abednego from the fiery furnace.

"Any fire started by a human can be put out by a human. But a sick person is engulfed by a fire sent from heaven. What human can possibly put that out?" (Talmud, *Nedarim* 41a).

Other ailments. Jesus healed several other kinds of physical problems—some as mundane as a fever, and some as astonishing as reattaching a severed ear. That's the ear Peter hacked off a man who helped arrest Jesus the night before the Crucifixion.

One of Jesus' most intriguing medical cases was this: "A woman in the crowd had suffered for twelve years with constant bleeding. She had suffered a great deal from many doctors, and over the years she had spent everything she had to pay them, but she had gotten no better. In fact, she had gotten worse" (Mark 5:25–26). She touched Jesus' robe, and the bleeding stopped.

This woman may have suffered from menorrhagia, a disease that produces excessive or prolonged menstrual bleeding. Normally, a menstrual period lasts four to five days, occurring every 21 to 35 days and producing about two or three tablespoons of blood. A woman with menorrhagia, however, can soak a pad or tampon for several consecutive hours, losing six tablespoons (about a third of a cup) or more of blood.

Medical books written in the first century show exactly how this woman could have gone broke trying to find a cure. There were scores of treatments. Here are just a few from various books in Pliny's *Natural History* collection.

- the red seed or the root of paemonia, a flowering plant;
- the clymenus plant, perhaps honeysuckle, described as especially effective in stopping a uterus from bleeding;
- lysimachia, a flowering plant in the primrose family, taken in a drink or applied topically;
- seeds from hemlock pine trees (not poison hemlock), pounded and mixed with water;
- polyp, a type of sea creature such as the Portuguese man-of-war jellyfish—smash the creature and apply it topically;
- ashes or the dried blood of a burned frog applied topically;
- stomach contents of a deer, mixed with vinegar and applied topically;
- stomach contents of a rabbit or ashes of a rabbit's fur applied topically;
- ashes of donkey excrement—especially of a male donkey—mixed with vinegar and applied with wool; and
- ashes of a horse's head or thigh mixed with vinegar and applied topically.

Pliny's list of cures goes on and on—with more than enough treatments to bleed a patient of her life's savings.

DID SIN CAUSE SICKNESS?

People got sick because they sinned—so God was punishing them. That was conventional Jewish wisdom of the day.

The Talmud, a collection of ancient Jewish writings, connects sin and sickness: "A sick man does not get well until all his sins are forgiven." For biblical support, the writer, identified as Rabbi Alexandri, pointed to a psalm: "He forgives all my sins and heals all my diseases" (Psalm 103:3).

Rabbi Jesus, however, said it wasn't that simple.

On the one hand, Jesus' healing ministry confirms that there are times when sin produces sickness. After he healed a man who had spent 38 years as an invalid, Jesus warned, "Now you are well; so stop sinning, or something even worse may happen to you" (John 5:14).

Sometimes, however, sin has nothing to do with the sickness. When Jesus' disciples saw a man born blind, they presumed it was because of sin.

"Rabbi," they asked him, "why was this man born blind? Was it because of his own sins or his parents' sins?"

"It was not because of his sins or his parents' sins," Jesus answered. "This happened so the power of God could be seen in him" (John 9:2–3). Then Jesus healed the man.

IS FAITH THE CURE?

It's easy to see why many Christians argue that if we can just work up enough faith, we can count on getting cured. Folks hang that theory on quotes from Jesus himself:

- "Daughter, your faith has made you well" (Mark 5:34).
  —To a woman with excessive bleeding
- "Because of your faith, it will happen" (Matthew 9:29).
  —To a pair of blind men
- "Because you believed, it has happened" (Matthew 8:13).
  —To a Roman officer with a sick servant
- "You can pray for anything, and if you have faith, you will receive it" (Matthew 21:22).
  —To his disciples
- "You don't have enough faith," Jesus told them. "I tell you the truth, if you had faith even as small as a mustard seed, you could say to this mountain, 'Move from here to there,' and it would move. Nothing would be impossible" (Matthew 17:20–21).
  —To his disciples, who couldn't exorcise a demon

Also, when Jesus returned to his hometown of Nazareth, the people's lack of faith limited Jesus' healing miracles: "Because of their unbelief, he couldn't do any miracles among them except to place his hands on a few sick people and heal them" (Mark 6:5).

Faith was certainly important. But the Bible shows that it wasn't the source of Jesus' power.

Remember the story of Jesus reattaching the ear of one of the men arresting him? Jesus didn't do this in response to the faith of that traumatized man standing there with his ear in his hand. Faith was probably the last thing on his mind.

Sometimes Jesus performed healing miracles to convince faithless people to grow some faith. When this didn't work, "he was amazed at their unbelief" (Mark 6:6). That's when he "began to denounce the towns where he had done so many of his miracles, because they hadn't repented of their sins and turned to God" (Matthew 11:20).

WHY JESUS DID MIRACLES

Compassion was not the big reason.

For one thing, every person Jesus healed eventually died.

And for another, when he healed the invalid at Jerusalem's pool of Bethesda, he walked right past "crowds of sick people—blind, lame, or paralyzed" (John 5:3).

Many Bible experts say that Jesus' main reason for healing people was to convince the Jews that their wait for the Messiah was over.

Jesus said as much in a message he sent to John the Baptist. John, in jail, had sent word to Jesus asking whether Jesus was really the Messiah. Jesus told the messenger: "Go back to John and tell him what you have heard and seen—the blind see, the lame walk, the lepers are cured, the deaf hear, the dead are raised to life, and the Good News is being preached to the poor" (Matthew 11:4–5).

Jesus knew that John, a prophet himself, would understand that this fulfilled what the Old Testament prophets had said would happen when the Messiah came.

"Your God is coming," Isaiah once wrote. "He is coming to save you. And when he comes, he will open the eyes of the blind and unplug the ears of the deaf. The lame will leap like a deer, and those who cannot speak will sing for joy!" (Isaiah 35:4–6).

Whoever this man was—and it would take his resurrection to convince even his closest disciples that he was divine—God had sent him.

In time, after Jesus ascended and the church began to grow, healing miracles diminished and no longer remained a primary focus of Christian ministry. But they were crucial for Jesus' ministry because they proved he was the very person his disciple Peter once declared he was: "You are the Messiah, the Son of the living God" (Matthew 16:16).

AFFLICTION	TREATMENT
Human bite, snake bite	Apply ear wax.
Toothache	Rub with wood that has been struck by lightning.
Intermittent fever (malaria)	Wrap in wool a piece of nail used in a crucifixion and apply to neck of patient.
Stiff, inflamed joints	Apply mud mixed with body oil sweat from a wrestler.
Water in ear	If right ear, tilt waterlogged ear onto right shoulder and hop around on left foot. If left ear, do the opposite.
Ringing ears	Mix one spoonful each of breast milk, Attic honey (gourmet honey from Athens area), and urine of child who hasn't reached puberty. No indication whether this goes in ears or mouth.
Crusty secretions from the eyes	Wash eyes with the gravy of a hyena's freshly roasted liver.
Ugly bruises	Rub with cheese and honey to reduce color.
Broken bone	Wrap bone with ashes of the jawbone of a wild boar or pig. Boiled bacon works, too. The bone will heal more quickly.
Itching	Apply mud mixed with donkey urine or donkey bone marrow.
Insomnia	Eat rabbit meat.
Depression	Boil calf excrement in wine; drink.
Pain in the neck	Rub neck with butter or bear grease.
Stomachache	Eat beef stew cooked in vinegar and wine.

REJECTED IN HIS HOMETOWN

When he came to the village of Nazareth,
his boyhood home, he went as usual to the synagogue
on the Sabbath and stood up to read the Scriptures. . . .
The people in the synagogue were furious.
Jumping up, they mobbed him.
LUKE 4:16, 28–29

It was what Jesus said that got him in trouble. Without actually using the *m* word, he managed to make it clear that he was the Messiah whom God had promised to send.

That would have been tough enough for the home folks to believe, because they knew Jesus was a carpenter, not a king. But he also invoked God's holy Word to make his "blasphemous" case. Then he refused to back up his claim. No Messiah-proving miracles. He would neither put up nor shut up.

When the home folks expressed their doubts about his incredible claim, he gave them a short course in Jewish history that sounded a tad like a parable. The moral: God would eat pork with a pagan before he'd share a meal with the likes of you Nazareth Jews.

Hometown boy or not, Jesus sounded as if he had grown up into a false prophet. Jews knew what to do with false prophets: "The false prophets or visionaries who try to lead you astray must be put to death. . . . In this way you will purge the evil from among you" (Deuteronomy 13:5).

Stoning criminals was the typical form of execution in this land lumped with more than its fair share of stones. But instead, they decided to throw him at the stones. They'd dump him over a cliff at the edge of town, like a sack of garbage.

SERMON IN A SYNAGOGUE

It's impossible to know exactly when this sermon took place. The Gospels of Matthew, Mark, and Luke each tell the story; yet only Luke, reporting the episode in the greatest detail, placed it at the beginning of Jesus' ministry—right after the Temptation.

Luke probably wasn't following a chronological timeline, many Bible experts say. After all, he reported that this story came after Jesus had taught and healed people "in Capernaum" (Luke 4:23). Perhaps Luke put the story up front as a literary technique—foreshadowing:

1. Jesus' rejection in Nazareth foreshadowed his later rejection by the Jewish nation.

2. Jesus' mistreatment as a prophet at home foreshadowed that he would suffer the fate of many Jewish prophets. He would die at the hands of his own people.

Whatever the timing, at some point in his ministry Jesus found himself addressing the hometown crowd during a Sabbath-day synagogue service.

This is the oldest known report of what took place during ancient synagogue services. But to fill in some of the detail, scholars turn to the ancient teachings of Jewish rabbis in writings such as the Mishnah.

The Mishnah wasn't written until about AD 200. But it preserves teachings and history passed on by word of mouth from centuries earlier. This includes reports about how the Jews worshipped in the synagogue. By the time of Jesus, the Jews had been worshipping in synagogues for perhaps five centuries. So the worship rituals were well established.

It took at least 10 men to get a synagogue up and running. During each service, the Jews would:

- Recite the closest thing they had to a creed: Deuteronomy 6:4–9. It's called the *Shema* ("hear"). And it begins, "Listen, O Israel! The LORD is our God, the LORD alone." It's the Jewish version of Christianity's Apostles' Creed—a statement of core beliefs.
- Recite a collection of prayers. (To read some prayers from this collection, see "How Jews Prayed in Jesus' Day," page 131.)
- Read a passage from the Law—one of the first five books of the Bible. This was read in the Hebrew original and translated into Aramaic, the most popular Jewish language at the time. The Jews had picked up Aramaic during their exile in Babylon (modern-day Iraq).
- Read a passage from the Prophets.
- Sing psalms and other songs of worship.
- Listen to a sermon about the Bible passage.
- Close with a benediction.

In later centuries, the Jews selected the Bible passages ahead of time—cycling through the entire set of readings every three years. But it's uncertain whether they used this cycle in Jesus' day. Many Bible experts say Jesus probably selected the passage himself, rather than providentially coming to Nazareth just in time for this particular reading.

Jesus read two passages from the prophet Isaiah. If ever Jesus had a mission statement, this is it: "The Spirit of the LORD is upon me, for he has anointed me to bring Good News to the poor. He has sent me to proclaim that captives will be released, that the blind will see, that the oppressed will be set free, and that the time of the LORD's favor has come" (Luke 4:18–19, paraphrasing Isaiah 61:1–2; 58:6).

When Jews in ancient times read these two passages from Isaiah, they believed the prophet was talking about the Messiah. Based on many passages in Isaiah and in other books of prophecy, the Jews understood that God would send his special servant to save the Jewish nation from their oppressors and restore the glory of Israel.

Jesus' first zinger in the worship service came after he read that passage. It was apparently his preamble to a sermon he never got to preach: "The Scripture you've just heard has been fulfilled this very day!" (Luke 4:21).

Translation: "The Messiah is here. And it's me."

JUST A CARPENTER

There had to have been a pause—a moment for the audacity and sheer chutz-pah of Jesus' statement to sink in.

Once it did, the deeply offended crowd scoffed, "He's just a carpenter, the son of Mary and the brother of James, Joseph, Judas, and Simon. And his sisters live right here among us" (Mark 6:3).

Carpenters got no respect—not when it came to matters of the brain. Carpenters and other laborers who depended more on their backs than their brains were considered essential to the community, but too lowbrow for high thought.

Consider a few examples from ancient history:

Peg the philosopher. A few decades after Jesus, a carpenter's son dared to step into the academia of Athens. He became a philosopher in a city famous for philosophy. His name was Secundus. But they called him Peg. As in "dumb as a wooden nail." He never made the big time, though one of his students did: Herodes Atticus. Herodes later disowned Peg as his mentor.

Too dumb to understand smart people. One book in the Apocrypha, a collection of Jewish books written between the time of the Old and New Testaments, joins the ancient crowd in demeaning workaday grunts. After admitting that "no city can get by without them," the writer goes on to say they're so busy with their business that they don't have time to study and seek wisdom. This lack of wisdom is why "they don't sit in the chair of a ruler or a judge. They don't even understand the decisions a judge makes. Nor can they talk intelligently about lofty ideals such as discipline or judgment" (Sirach 38:32–33 AUTHOR'S PARAPHRASE).

Nothing special about wood. Celsus was a philosopher in the AD 100s who attacked Christianity and demeaned what he saw as a wood theme in the religion: "Everywhere they [Christians] speak in their writings about the tree of life. . . . I imagine because their master was nailed to a cross and was a carpenter by trade. Maybe if he happened to be thrown off a cliff. . .there would have been a cliff of life" (*Against Celsus*, book 6, chapter 34).

A Christian scholar named Origen wrote a rebuttal in his book *Against Celsus*. But instead of defending Jesus' calloused hands, Origen seemed to consider it an unwinnable debate. He simply said that Celsus didn't know what he was talking about: "Celsus appears to me to confuse matters which he has imperfectly heard." End of discussion.

Nazareth continued its attack on Jesus by saying he'd grown up right in front of their eyes—as if that disqualified him as the Messiah.

The implication is funny, because they dissed themselves without realizing it. They actually sounded as if they agreed with the disciple Nathanael, wh after hearing that the Messiah had come from Nazareth, replied, "Nazareth! Can anything good come from Nazareth?" (John 1:46).

Apparently not.

PUT UP OR SHUT UP

Jesus replied with an old saying that doesn't seem to fit the context: "You will undoubtedly quote me this proverb: 'Physician, heal yourself'—meaning, 'Do miracles here in your hometown like those you did in Capernaum' " (Luke 4:23).

What made Jesus think the proverb "Physician, heal yourself" meant he should perform miracles?

This particular proverb wasn't one that people quoted word for word. It was a general idea that shows up in several ancient Greek and Jewish writings—each time expressed in a different way.

Here's one version of it from an article written in the AD 100s: "You seem like a pharmacist coughing—while trying to sell us a sure-fire cure for coughing" (*Apology for "On salaried posts in great houses"*).

If we apply the idea behind this criticism to Jesus' situation, it's as if he's anticipating that the Jews are about to say something like this: "You seem like a carpenter trying to tell us you're the Messiah. We've already seen your woodwork, so show us your miracles."

In other words, put up or shut up. How can a physician heal others if he can't heal himself? How can a pharmacist cure the cough of others if he can't cure his own cough? How can a carpenter be the Messiah if he can't do anything more miraculous than frame a doorway?

Perhaps Jesus knew that no amount of miracles would persuade these people. So he essentially told them they weren't worth the trouble. And he did it in a way that suggested their ancestors weren't worth the trouble, either. Ancestors of the Jews

- **mistreated prophets.** In what became the first time on record for Jesus to identify himself as a prophet, he reminded the worshippers that the Jews had a long history of rejecting their homegrown prophets. Ancient Jewish writings report that King Manasseh ordered Isaiah sawn in half. King Zedekiah ordered Jeremiah thrown into a muddy pit. Amos, Hosea, and a long line of other prophets wasted their words on deaf ears.

- **got bypassed by the miracle workers.** Drawing from one of the lowest spiritual moments in Jewish history—when evil Ahab and Jezebel reigned—Jesus reminded the hometown folks of miracles that two prophets had done for non-Jews. Elijah, during a three-and-a-half-year drought, miraculously provided flour and olive oil for a widow living in what is now Lebanon. And Elisha cured a Syrian soldier from leprosy.

Here's the clincher—the spark that lit the riot. Jesus said the prophets performed these miracles for the unchosen, unholy, Gentile "dogs"—as some Jews described non-Jews—even though "there were many widows in Israel" and "many lepers in Israel."

The force of these words might have translated into something like this: "God would prefer the companionship of a flea-bitten Gentile dog to the sorry company of you or your mother."

For the benediction, the Jews escorted Jesus to a nearby cliff.

Somehow, he escaped: "He passed right through the crowd and went on his way" (Luke 4:30). Perhaps he slipped away in the confusion. Or maybe it was a miracle—the only one he felt they deserved.

JEWISH CRIMES TO DIE FOR

There are two dozen capital offenses preserved in the laws of Moses—the four books of Exodus, Leviticus, Numbers, and Deuteronomy.

There's no indication that the Jews regularly imposed the ultimate penalty in each case. In fact, there are many instances in which they didn't punish the offender at all. One of the more famous examples was when some Jewish leaders brought to Jesus a woman caught in the act of adultery. With Jesus' help, she walked.

Nazareth Jews tried to execute Jesus for the crime of being a false prophet.

Criminal by nearly any standard
- Murder (Exodus 21:12, 14)
- Sacrificing a child to an idol (Leviticus 20:2)
- Kidnapping (Exodus 21:16)
- Lying to convict a person of a capital offense (Deuteronomy 19:16–19)
- Failure to control a violent animal that ends up killing someone (Exodus 21:29)
- Ignoring the verdict of a judge (Deuteronomy 17:12)

Bad kids
- Hitting either parent (Exodus 21:15)
- Persistent disobedience toward parents (Deuteronomy 21:18–21)
- Showing disrespect toward either parent (Exodus 21:17)

Spirit world
- Witchcraft (Exodus 22:18)
- Consulting with mediums or spirits of the dead (Leviticus 20:27)

Sex sins
- Sex with an animal (Leviticus 20:15)
- Raping an engaged woman (Deuteronomy 22:23–24; rape of other single women drew a fine and a shotgun wedding)
- Adultery (Leviticus 20:10)
- Incest with mother or stepmother (Leviticus 20:11)
- Incest with daughter-in-law (Leviticus 20:12)
- Marrying a mother and her daughter (Leviticus 20:14)
- Homosexuality (Leviticus 20:13)
- Priest's daughter becoming a prostitute (Leviticus 21:9)
- Nonvirgin passing herself off as a virgin to get married (Deuteronomy 22:20–21)

Breaking religious laws
- False prophecy (Deuteronomy 13:5)
- Worshipping idols (Deuteronomy 13:6–9)
- Using God's name disrespectfully (Leviticus 24:16)
- Working on the Sabbath day of rest (Exodus 31:15)

JESUS' MOST FAMOUS SERMON

One day as he saw the crowds gathering,
Jesus went up on the mountainside and sat down.
His disciples gathered around him,
and he began to teach them.
MATTHEW 5:1–2

Matthew calls it the Sermon on the Mount.

Luke lowers the elevation, calling it the Sermon on the Plain. He also lowers the word count, keeping only about one-fourth of what Matthew reports. There's Matthew's three chapters—5–7—compared to Luke's 33 verses—6:17–49.

Actually, Jesus may have preached sermons like this many times, to different crowds, as he traveled around—especially this message, a masterpiece that captures the essence of his life and teachings.

But because the message covers so many faith-stretching ideas, many Bible experts say they doubt Jesus preached it in a single sermon. His revolutionary ideas delivered at the rapid-fire pace reflected in this sermon would have overwhelmed any listener. Instead, scholars suggest that Matthew and Luke pulled highlights from many sermons and wove them into one.

Or perhaps Jesus presented the ideas in a series of sermons over several days—a bit like an evangelist on a weekend crusade.

SERMON ON THE MOUNT OR ON THE PLAIN?

A walk along the rolling hills of Galilee helps explain why Matthew and Luke may have written about the same sermon, yet with Matthew describing the place as a hillside and Luke calling it a plain.

The location of the Chapel of the Beatitudes, marking the traditional site of the sermon, offers a perfect example. The chapel sits on the crest of a gently sloping hilltop. But a stone's throw away lies a level field. Crowds jockeying for position within the sound of Jesus' voice may have taken seats on the soft grass of both the hillside and the plain.

THE BEATITUDES

Matthew's account starts with the sermon's most famous section: the Beatitudes.

Some preachers call these sayings the "Be Happy Attitudes"—a prescription for eternal happiness. *Beatitudes* is from the Latin word *beatitudo*, meaning "blessed." Jesus made a list of attitudes that God wants to see in people. These are attitudes for which God blesses people by welcoming them into his

Kingdom—a spiritual world ruled by him, now on earth and forever in heaven.

Luke's account starts the same way, but with a shorter list.

In a swift current of poetry that Jesus could have recited in under 30 seconds, he rattles off his list of Beatitudes—flipping conventional wisdom upside down in the process.

Many Jews of the day thought God blessed people by giving them health, wealth, and happiness. They said this was God's way of rewarding people for living a good life. The healthiest, wealthiest, and happiest people were considered the cream of God's crop—the best of the best.

Too bad for the sick, poor, sad folks. God was certainly punishing them. At least that was the conventional way of thinking. That's why when the disciples saw a blind man, they asked Jesus, "Why was this man born blind? Was it because of his own sins or his parents' sins?" (John 9:2).

As for the question, Jesus said the disease was for this moment in time—to showcase God's power. Then Jesus healed the man.

And as for the widespread misconception that God limits his blessing to society's elite, Jesus offered good news and bad news.

First the bad news. It's for the rich. They might feel blessed now, but Jesus said a lot of them were in for a rude awakening on the flip side of the grave: "What sorrow awaits you who are rich, for you have your only happiness now. . . . Your laughing will turn to mourning" (Luke 6:24–25).

Now the good news. It's for society's bottom dwellers. The healthy, wealthy, and jolly folks may have had a great life, but the sick, poor, and sad are going to have a great eternal life. For God is giving these seemingly unfortunate souls the keys to his kingdom.

- God blesses those who are poor: "The Kingdom of Heaven is theirs."
- God blesses the sad and the crying: "They will be comforted."
- God blesses those who suffer from injustice: "They will be satisfied."
- God blesses the peacemakers: "They will be called the children of God."

So said the Son of God, a pacifist whom the prophets said would be known as the "Prince of Peace" (Isaiah 9:6).

These Beatitudes came as quite a surprise to many Jews of the day. There's one particular Beatitude that helps people today see just how surprising these teachings were back then. In our competitive culture, we know that it's usually the aggressive go-getters and blatant self-promoters who tend to hack off the biggest hunks of real estate, cash, and other trademarks of success—hoarding them all.

But Jesus said, "God blesses those who are humble, for they will inherit the whole earth" (Matthew 5:5).

These are people who may not steal off with a huge slice of the fiscal pie.

But they have eternal dividends waiting for them in the Kingdom to come. As for the selfishly rich, the happy, and the well fed—Luke says they had better enjoy themselves while they can, because in God's spiritual Kingdom, which is as real as the physical world, they're bankrupt.

JESUS CONDENSED
Sermon on the Mount Headlines

Golden Rule
"Do to others whatever you would like them to do to you. This is the essence of all that is taught in the law" (Matthew 7:12).

Anger
"Settle your differences quickly" (Matthew 5:25).

Revenge
"Do not resist an evil person" (Matthew 5:39).

Judging
"The standard you use in judging is the standard by which you will be judged" (Matthew 7:2).

Enemies
"Love your enemies! Pray for those who persecute you!" (Matthew 5:44).

Charity
"Don't do your good deeds publicly, to be admired by others" (Matthew 6:1).

Money
"You cannot serve both God and money" (Matthew 6:24).

Assets
"Don't store up treasures here on earth. . . . Store your treasures in heaven" (Matthew 6:19–21).

Worry
"I tell you not to worry about everyday life—whether you have enough food and drink, or enough clothes to wear" (Matthew 6:25).

Prayer
"Don't babble on and on. . . . Your Father knows exactly what you need" (Matthew 6:7–8).

TROUBLING SOUND BITES

Jesus followed the Beatitudes with a shopping list of holy behavior he wanted to see in his followers. To some readers, the list seems outrageous, unattainable— and, for that very reason, cruel.

A sampler's platter of his hard-to-swallow sayings:

- "Be perfect."
- "Love your enemies."
- "Don't worry about tomorrow."

Jesus wasn't being as stern as it seems, many scholars insist. He was giving us a goal on which to fix our eyes, like a wandering hiker taking bearings from a distant mountain peak. This is a life route Jesus wants us to do the best we can to follow, scholars say, because he knows where the journey leads: to blessings, to the Kingdom of heaven, and to God.

SERMON HIGHLIGHTS

"You are the salt of the earth. . . . You are the light of the world" (Matthew 5:13–14). A Roman encyclopedia writer from Jesus' time may help explain what Jesus was talking about. His name was Pliny, and he was born in about AD 23—just four or five years before Jesus started his ministry. In *Natural History*, a collection of 37 volumes mainly about nature, Pliny writes, "There is nothing more useful than salt and sunshine."

Perhaps Jesus was telling his disciples that the world needs them—so they should make themselves useful.

"I did not come to abolish the law of Moses or the writings of the prophets. No, I came to accomplish their purpose" (Matthew 5:17). That seems a strange thing for Jesus to say, given some of the prophecies about him.

The "law of Moses" refers to a contract—or covenant—between God and the Jewish people. If the Jews lived by these rules, which are preserved in the book of Deuteronomy, God promised to bless them. But the prophets said the Jews broke the contract by persistently disobeying God. And the prophet Jeremiah said a day was coming when God would make a new contract with the people. "I will put my instructions deep within them, and I will write them on their hearts" (Jeremiah 31:33).

At the Last Supper, the night before his execution, Jesus raised a cup of wine representing the blood he would shed a few hours later: "This cup is the new covenant between God and his people—an agreement confirmed with my blood, which is poured out as a sacrifice for you" (Luke 22:20).

New Testament writers later declared that Jesus' death and resurrection rendered the old set of Jewish laws obsolete. "When God speaks of a 'new' covenant, it means he has made the first one obsolete. It is now out of date" (Hebrews 8:13).

So it seems to some readers that Jesus, contrary to what he said in this sermon, did come to abolish the law—or at least to retire it. That's the effect his ministry would have on his followers.

But most Bible experts insist that Jesus wasn't lying. Nor was he trying to ease his Jewish listeners into a false sense of security so he could gently nudge them away from their Jewish faith and toward a new religion. Jesus knew that the law had one purpose, which he summed up in a double-barreled commandment: "'You must love the LORD your God with all your heart, all your soul, and all your mind'. This is the first and greatest commandment. A second is equally important: 'Love your neighbor as yourself.' The entire law and all the demands of the prophets are based on these two commandments" (Matthew 22:37–40).

Jesus came to help people honor this spirit of the law.

Many Jewish leaders, on the other hand, got all tangled up in observing the letter of the law and in creating loopholes that allowed them to treat God with disrespect and their neighbors like dirt.

For example, instead of requiring grown children to take care of their needy parents, as required by one of the 10 Commandments—the core Jewish law—"Honor your father and mother," leaders created an amendment. Children could declare their assets unavailable by setting them aside as an offering for God (Mark 7:11). As if God needed the money. The Jews eventually dropped this amendment, but only after more than a century of debate—which Jesus may have helped to start.

Half a dozen don'ts: anger, lust, divorce, swearing an oath, retaliation, hating enemies (Matthew 5:21–48). Drawing on a phrase that he repeats every time he starts a new topic during this part of the sermon—"You have heard. . . but I say"—Jesus points people to principles behind several key Jewish laws.

Anger. Jews knew they were not supposed to murder; the law is number six in the 10 Commandments, just after "Honor your parents." But Jesus said God doesn't even want people to get angry. But when they do, Jesus offered this advice: "Settle your differences quickly" (Matthew 5:25).

Lust. For married folks, lust is adultery stage one. As a preventative, Jesus

DIVORCE AMONG THE JEWS

Jesus argued for marriage and against divorce. He sided with God, who said, "Remain loyal to the wife of your youth. 'For I hate divorce!' " (Malachi 2:15–16).

Consider the following quotes of Jesus:

- "A man who divorces his wife, unless she has been unfaithful, causes her to commit adultery. And anyone who marries a divorced woman also commits adultery" (Matthew 5:32).
- "Since they [the married couple] are no longer two but one, let no one split apart what God has joined together" (Matthew 19:6).

These words of Jesus seem harsh and intolerant, especially to women and men trapped in abusive marriages. But many scholars argue otherwise. They say Jesus wasn't insisting that adultery is the only grounds for divorce. In fact, Jesus forgave an adulterous woman in a moving symbol of what a husband could do instead of divorcing his wife (John 8:4–11). And Paul made a case for abandonment as grounds for divorce (1 Corinthians 7:15).

So the topic is more complicated than it sounds in the Sermon on the Mount. For this reason, many scholars say that Jesus was giving the counterpoint—exaggerated for effect—to the prevailing, male-friendly view of divorce: that it was acceptable for a man to divorce his wife for just about anything. The woman, however, couldn't divorce her husband, though exceptions were later made in certain cases, such as repeated beatings, failure to support the wife, or refusal to have sex with her.

RABBI MARRIAGE COUNSELORS

For guidance about divorce, the Jews looked to the law of Moses. This law says that a man can write his wife a certificate of divorce if she is "displeasing to him because he finds something indecent about her" (Deuteronomy 24:1 NIV).

advised gouging out the eyeballs. He was exaggerating, though a few unfortunate Christians throughout history took him literally. His point may have been that the pain of gouging out our eyes is nothing compared to the pain we'll experience from adultery. So we should go to great lengths to avoid committing adultery.

Swearing an oath. Jesus wasn't talking about profanity or about swearing "to tell the truth, the whole truth, and nothing but the truth." Some people in his day made promises a bit like the modern variation, "I swear on my mother's grave." But they would invoke God's name instead. Some Jewish scholars in the Pharisee branch of the religion ruled that the only oath that was binding was an oath invoking God's name. So people wanting a loophole out of their promise could say something like, "I swear by heaven," which was a bit like making a promise while crossing their fingers. Jesus said that God's people should skip this dance of the semantics. Instead, they should become trustworthy people who mean what they say: "Just say a simple, 'Yes, I will,' or 'No, I won't' " (Matthew 5:37).

Retaliation. The old Jewish law—"eye for eye" and "tooth for tooth" (Deuteronomy 19:21)—was intended to provide for fair justice, to make sure there was no overdoing it or underdoing it. Jesus told his followers to let go of their desire to get even, probably because he knew that revenge can consume a person. And if a Roman soldier ordered a follower of Jesus to carry something for a mile—as Roman soldiers could do, later forcing a man named Simon of

Rabbis debated what that meant.

Followers of Rabbi Shammai (about 50 BC–AD 30) said *indecent* (from a Hebrew word that can also be translated as *indecency* or *nakedness*) means adultery. But followers of Rabbi Hillel (about 70 BC–AD 10) pointed to the earlier phrase "displeasing to him" and insisted that this allows divorce for anything that displeases a husband, including

- talking with a stranger;
- burning a meal;
- failing to heal quickly from a dog bite; or
- not looking as attractive as another woman.

Rabbi Jesus seemed to offer a third option: Instead of looking for a way to bury your marriage, look for a way to revive it.

Jesus said that God allowed divorce "only as a concession to your hard hearts" (Matthew 19:8). Hard-hearted enough to hurt a spouse. And hard-hearted enough to withhold forgiveness when it's needed most.

But hard-heartedness that ends in divorce is not what God wants for his people.

A LETTER OF DIVORCE
Jewish law says that a man who wants to divorce his wife has to put it in writing—and then give her the letter.

The Bible doesn't say how to phrase the letter, but rabbis in the past offered suggestions. Here are two:

- "Behold, you are free [to be married] to any man!"
- "Let this be to you from me a writ of divorce, a letter of release and a decree of dismissal, to permit you to be married to any man you desire."

Cyrene to carry Jesus' cross—that person shouldn't resist. Instead, the draftee should offer even more help if it's needed, earning a reputation as a helper, not a grumbler and resister. And if someone backhanded them on the right cheek—more of an insult than an assault—Jesus didn't want his followers to retaliate with a counterinsult that could inflame the argument. He advised them to endure the rudeness and walk away.

WHAT CRIMINALS COULD EXPECT

Jesus preached a gospel of second chances—of compassion and forgiveness incredibly out of sync with Jewish and Roman laws at the time.

"If someone slaps you on the right cheek," Jesus said in the Sermon on the Mount, "offer the other cheek also." In the next breath he added, "Love your enemies! Pray for those who persecute you!" (Matthew 5:39, 44).

This was not the reality in Israel.

Whether they were standing before Jewish elders in a synagogue or before Roman officials in a palace, reality for convicted criminals spun around the three r's: retaliation, reparation, and revenge. That's what they could expect.

The poorer they were and the lower on the social ladder, the worse their punishment. That's because the people passing judgment were usually the wealthy elite—and they favored their own kind. Ancient records show that this happened among the Romans and the Jews, even though the Jews had a law against it: "Do not twist justice in legal matters by favoring the poor or being partial to the rich and powerful. Always judge people fairly" (Leviticus 19:15).

JEWISH JUSTICE

Though Rome ruled, they generally deferred to local authorities, allowing the conquered nations to settle their own legal disputes. Roman administrators usually stepped in only for serious cases that threatened the peace and stability of the empire—cases such as murder, robbery, and insurrection.

In Israel, the synagogue elders exercised full jurisdiction over civil and religious matters, deciding which punishment fit the crime. Old Testament laws about restitution and punishment applied. For instance, a person convicted of stealing and slaughtering a single ox had to make restitution with five head of cattle (Exodus 22:1).

Jewish elders could also order a criminal beaten or banned from the synagogue. Some crimes—such as murder, adultery, and blasphemy—called for execution. But there is some evidence that Romans in the Jewish homeland may have reserved the right to final judgment in capital offenses, at least for a time. That's apparently why the Jewish high council, known as the Sanhedrin, took Jesus to Pilate, the Roman governor, and asked him to pass the death sentence. Historians debate the matter, because the Jews occasionally executed people without Roman permission.

ROMAN JUSTICE

Prosecuting attorneys didn't exist. So it was up to a private individual or group—usually the offended party—to bring a complaint to the Roman official in charge of the region.

False charges were a bad idea. To protect against abuses of the legal system, those who brought fraudulent charges could end up suffering the punishment they had intended for the accused.

In Jesus' time, the Roman legal system wasn't consistent throughout the empire. Justice varied from one province to the next. Roman governors had the authority to act on the

Hating enemies. "You have heard the law that says, 'Love your neighbor' and hate your enemy,'" Jesus said (Matthew 5:43). Actually, there's no law in the Bible telling Jews to hate their enemies. But there are songs about it: "O LORD, shouldn't I hate those who hate you? Shouldn't I despise those who oppose you? Yes, I hate them with total hatred, for your enemies are my enemies" (Psalm 139:21–22). The monklike community of Jews that produced the

emperor's behalf. In dishing out judgment, they had a free hand. They could choose to rely on precedents from past Roman cases, or not.

Civil disputes were often tried by a judge or a jury. Qualifications for jury duty: male, over 25 years of age, with property valued at no less than 7,500 denarii. One denarius was a typical day's wage for a common laborer. To translate that for today, if we assume a daily wage of $58, based on the minimum wage of $7.25 an hour, we would need assets totaling at least $435,000 before we could serve on a jury.

Criminal cases were often heard by the regional governor—a man who commonly held the Roman title of *proconsul.*

Whether standing in front of a judge or a jury, people on trial usually had to answer questions about their status in society before they could testify. The lower the rank, the worse it would typically go for that person. For example, wealthy Roman citizens generally were not tortured. And when the rich were sentenced to execution (many were merely exiled instead), they were killed as painlessly as possible. The poor, on the other hand, could expect beatings before their execution.

Bribes were expected. Luke confirms this when he reports that Governor Felix held Paul in custody for two years, hoping all the while that Paul would pay him off (Acts 24:26). Wealthy litigants could quickly breeze through a trial by sending gifts to judges, lawyers (including the opposing lawyer), jurors, or witnesses.

Given realities like these, Jesus' advice to turn the other cheek might have struck a chord of common sense with the crowds of people lashed to the bottom rung of the social ladder.

ROMAN CRIMES AND FINES

CRIME	PUNISHMENT
Cutting down another person's trees	Fine of 25 coins per tree (currency not stated)
Breaking bone of free person/slave	Fine of 300/150 coins
Killing another's animal or slave	If crime is admitted, pay owner value of lost property. If contested and found guilty, pay double.
Violent intent causing loss of limb	Amputation of limb, unless defendant settles with victim
Giving a drug to another person, resulting in that person's death	Taking the same drug
Lying under oath	Execution by being thrown from a cliff
Arson with malicious intent	Execution by burning

famous Dead Sea Scrolls said much the same. These Jews, called Essenes, meaning "pious ones," lived at Jesus' time about 14 miles (23 km) from Jerusalem, near the Dead Sea. In *Rule of the Community*, a book of regulations the Essenes observed, everyone was instructed to "hate the sons of darkness," generally considered to be the Roman occupiers. Jesus, however, had come to change the world for the better. He didn't want to further alienate the enemies of God. He wanted to win them over to God's side. Kindness does that more effectively than a club.

"Don't do your good deeds publicly, to be admired by others" (Matthew 6:1). Some religious leaders of Jesus' day were experts at tooting their own horns, "blowing trumpets in the synagogues and streets to call attention to their acts" (Matthew 6:2). They'd make a big show of giving to charity, praying in public, and fasting.

Like Muslims today, many Jews of the day prayed at set times in the morning, afternoon, and evening. Some Jews apparently timed their prayers so they'd be in public places where they could show off how religious they were by offering long-winded speeches to God. Jesus said to pray privately and to keep the prayers short and simple. Then he gave an example: The Lord's Prayer, which probably took less than 30 seconds.

Jews, by law, had to fast only one day a year: Yom Kippur. That was the national day of repentance, also known as the Day of Atonement. But some Pharisees fasted "twice a week" (Luke 18:12), skipping meals on Mondays and Thursdays. And they'd dress the part: ragged clothes of mourning, unwashed bodies—making it obvious they were fasting. Jesus said this was a great way to get attention from other people. But he added that those who want God's attention should be discreet about their fasting. After all, fasting was supposed to be a deep and personal spiritual experience: an expression of heartache, regret, or devotion to God. Not a photo op.

"I tell you not to worry about everyday life—whether you have enough food and drink, or enough clothes to wear" (Matthew 6:25). That seems like callous advice, especially given the fiscally struggling farmers and shepherds who were probably in the crowd. One springtime of drought and their gardens and pastures could shrivel into a wasteland—decimating the crops that would have provided food for the winter, and starving the livestock that would have produced meat, clothing, and four-legged currency for trade at the market.

Yet many Bible experts say Jesus wasn't telling people to repress their legitimate concerns. Everyone needs food, clothing, and shelter. And we should be concerned about these needs—at least concerned enough to work hard to provide for ourselves and our family. But not so concerned that we obsess, worry, stockpile, and hoard. "Don't store up treasures here on earth," Jesus had just finished saying before launching into his message about worry. "Wherever your treasure is, there the desires of your heart will also be. . . . You cannot

PLANTS IN JESUS' LAND

"Look at the lilies of the field," Jesus said to people worried about where they would find money for clothing. "They don't work or make their clothing, yet Solomon in all his glory was not dressed as beautifully as they are. And if God cares so wonderfully for wildflowers that are here today and thrown into the fire tomorrow, he will certainly care for you" (Matthew 6:28–30).

When Jesus spoke these words on a Galilean hillside, the crowd may have been standing in a field laced in wildflowers. Dozens of varieties blanket modern Israel in the spring, including scarlet anemones, red corn poppies, and white and yellow chamomiles.

The Bible names 128 plants. In Israel today, there are about 2,400 plant species—though many were imported in recent centuries and didn't exist there in Bible times. One example is the eucalyptus tree, which now dominates the Israeli landscape. Native to Australia, they were introduced to Israel by the British in the 1920s to provide shade for soldiers and to draw water from mosquito-infested swamps.

SOURCES OF FOOD, CLOTHING, SHELTER

Many plants were important sources of food and clothing, as they are today: barley and wheat for bread, bean-like lentils for soup, cotton for cloth, and flax for linen.

Vegetables and fruits included apricots, cucumbers, dates, figs, grapes, melons, onions, pomegranates, and olives eaten or crushed to produce cooking oil or a dip for bread.

Trees and shrubs included
- the acacia tree, used to build the Ark of the Covenant that held the 10 Commandments;
- cedars of Lebanon (in what was once northern Israel) along with cypress—both used in building the Jerusalem Temple;
- thorny shrubs, which Roman soldiers may have used to produce a mock crown for Jesus; and
- oak and tamarisk.

MUSTARD SEED

There are many kinds of mustard plants with tiny seeds that are crushed to make seasoning. Black mustard (Brassica nigra) grew along the Sea of Galilee and may be the kind of mustard plant Jesus spoke of: "If you had faith even as small as a mustard seed, you could say to this mountain, 'Move from here to there,' and it would move. Nothing would be impossible" (Matthew 17:20). The seed is about two millimeters or less in size—about a sixteenth of an inch. In Jesus' time, these seeds weren't used for seasoning as much as they were used for crushing into cooking oil and for medicine (pungent mustard poultices). In Israel, this shrub generally grows two to five feet high (less than two meters).

serve both God and money" (Matthew 6:19, 21, 24).

We should learn to trust God for the needs we can't meet on our own. That's perhaps what Jesus was saying. We might prefer to depend on our own strength and resources, but in the end we really do depend on God. One Jewish rabbi in ancient times put it something like this in his commentary on the Old Testament book of Deuteronomy: "No matter how rich a king is or how much he owns, only God can send him the rain he needs to go on living" (Sifre on Deuteronomy, 42.1.5 AUTHOR'S PARAPHRASE).

Whether we like it or not, in God we trust. Jesus knew that accepting this fact of life can take the edge off worry. "Can all your worries add a single moment to your life?" he asked the crowd (Matthew 6:27). Quite the contrary, according to a 12-year study of 1,663 men published in the May 2007 issue of *Psychological Science*. Men who found themselves in the top 50 percent of the group when it came to neurosis testing were more likely to die during the study. For every five low-worry men who died during that study, seven high-worry men died.

"Do not judge others. . . . The standard you use in judging is the standard by which you will be judged" (Matthew 7:1–2).

Jesus wasn't saying that good Christians should keep their mouths shut whenever they see someone doing something wrong or hurtful. After all, Jesus and his disciples spoke out against warped ideas about God and against religious teachings that exploited and hurt people.

In his short message about judging others, Jesus was making several points that track with other ancient Jewish teachings—some from his own century. One Jewish saying from the time goes something like this: "The way you dish out judgment is the way people will dish it up for you." In other words, if you tend to be harsh, people will tend to treat you harshly. If you tend to be compassionate, people will be more likely to give you the benefit of the doubt.

One rabbi from Jesus' century, Hillel, suggested, "Do not judge your neighbor until you have been in his situation."

When Jesus told people not to criticize the speck in someone's eye when they had a plank in their own, he was again teaching a common idea, using a metaphor from his carpentry experience. His point was a bit like our "Practice what you preach." Isocrates, a Greek writer from about 300 years before Jesus, put it this way: "Do nothing in your actions that you condemn in your words."

"Do to others whatever you would like them to do to you" (Matthew 7:12).

This is the Golden Rule. But it's not unique to Jesus, though he's the one who made it famous. Many others in his century and earlier said much the same thing:

- "Let us show our generosity in the same manner we would want it shown to us" (Roman official Seneca, 4 BC–AD 65).
- "What you consider hateful, don't do it to your neighbor" (Rabbi Hillel, about 70 BC–10 AD).
- "Do not do to others what you would not want others to do to you" (Chinese philosopher Confucius, 400s BC).

PETER'S HOUSE CHURCH

Hovering above the ruins of what was probably Peter's house in Capernaum is a memorial that looks more like a UFO than a chapel. This octagon-shaped chapel was built by Franciscans in 1990, placed several feet above the ruins. It has a window in the floor, allowing tourists to see the ruins below. Many Bible experts are convinced that Peter lived in the house that once stood here and that he hosted Jesus as his guest. Among the clues suggesting this is the fact that sometime during the first century, Christians turned the home into a house church. Graffiti scratched into the plaster walls in several languages—including Aramaic (the language of Jesus) and Latin (the language of the Romans)—bore the words *Jesus, Lord, Christ,* and *Peter.* Also, a Spanish pilgrim, the Lady Egeria, visiting the site in the AD 380s, described the "House of Simon, called Peter," reporting that it had been turned into a church, with the original walls still standing. Later, in the mid-400s, this house that stood just a few yards from the shoreline of the Sea of Galilee was expanded into an octagon-shaped church. This church was destroyed in the 600s, probably by Arab invaders.

CAPERNAUM, HEADQUARTERS OF JESUS

This ancient fishing town and trading hub, nestled on gently rolling ridges along the Sea of Galilee, was Jesus' base of operation during his ministry, perhaps for several reasons:

- Nearly half of his disciples may have called it home: fishermen Peter and his brother Andrew; tax collector Matthew; and fishermen James and his brother John.
- It was probably a busy border town rather than a quiet fishing village, as previously thought. Located just inside Galilee's eastern border, on a branch of the trade route called *Via Maris* (Latin for "Way of the Sea"), the city maintained a customs station that taxed products coming and going. A Roman centurion commanded a small garrison of soldiers there. Population may have been 1,500 or more.
- The city was located near Jesus' boyhood home of Nazareth, about 20 miles away (32 km), which is a day's walk.

About 30 yards (27 meters) from Peter's house are the ruins of the city synagogue. Under the floor of a partially restored synagogue from the fourth century are the foundation stones of the first-century synagogue that the Bible says a Roman centurion helped fund. Here, too, is where Jesus so astonished people with his teachings and healing that "news about Jesus spread quickly throughout the entire region of Galilee" (Mark 1:28).

THE LORD'S PRAYER

Our Father which art in heaven, Hallowed be thy name.
Thy kingdom come. Thy will be done in earth, as it is in heaven.
MATTHEW 6:9–10 KJV

There's one thing troubling about the most famous prayer in the Bible—the 30-second masterpiece that Jesus created on the spur of the moment to teach his disciples how to pray.

Luke's Gospel says the disciples had asked for the lesson: "Lord, teach us to pray" (Luke 11:1). Then Luke reports a condensed, 15-second version of the prayer. Matthew's Gospel preserves a longer version of the prayer and sets the scene during the Sermon on the Mount.

What's troubling to some Christians today is that Jesus' example of what prayer should be—a conversation with God—has become an example of what prayer should not be: mindless repetition. Many Christians today recite the Lord's Prayer in every worship service. It's a ritual. And it's so familiar that some Christians try to fly this prayer to heaven on automatic pilot.

Prayer at its best, Jesus practiced and preached, comes from the heart. It doesn't come from snapping synapses that automatically retrieve memorized words and feed them to the mouth without bothering to ask our thoughts on the matter.

Yet when we do pause to think about the words in this short prayer, they become a wonderful guide to the art of conversation with God.

— HOW NOT TO PRAY

It was a strange question the disciples asked Jesus. They knew how to pray. They were Jews. The Jewish religion was a praying religion. Like Jews and Christians today, the Jewish people of Jesus' time prayed both spontaneous prayers and written prayers.

Jewish historian Josephus, writing in Jesus' century, said the Jews offered sacrifices and prayed twice a day: "in the morning and about the ninth hour [3:00 p.m.]" (*Antiquities of the Jews* 14.4.3). Many prayed three times a day.

Yet there was plenty of holier-than-thou self-promotion going on during those prayer times. Some Jews—especially some religious leaders—wanted others to see how religious they were. So, thinking more like real estate agents than religion scholars, they focused on location, location, location. Their daily to-do list might have included three lines:

- 9:00 a.m.—pick up bread, pray in front of busy baker's shop
- Noon—stretch legs, pray at busiest city gate
- 3:00 p.m.—go to synagogue, pray in front of crowd

HOW JEWS PRAYED IN JESUS' DAY

Jews had their own version of the Lord's Prayer—one that was especially important to them and that played a key role in their prayer lives and in their worship services.

It was a collection of prayers called *Amidah*, Hebrew for "standing." Jews stood while they recited these prayers at the customary prayer times each day.

Some called the prayers by their ancient name, *Shemoneh Esrei*, Hebrew for "eight plus ten." This refers to the original 18 prayers, though some Jews added a nineteenth prayer in about AD 100. The collection includes three prayers of praise, followed by 13 requests and then three prayers of thanks.

Here's a prayer from each of these three sections:

PRAISE

"You are holy and your name is holy, and your holy ones praise you every day. Blessed are you, my Lord, the God who is holy."

REQUEST

"Forgive us, our Father, for we have sinned; pardon us, our King, for we have rebelled; for you are the one who pardons and forgives. Blessed are you, Lord, the gracious one who abundantly forgives."

THANKS

"We thank you, for it is you alone who is my Lord our God and the God of our fathers, forever and ever. You are the Rock and Shield of our salvation, you alone, from generation to generation. We thank you and tell of your praise, for our lives are in your hands and our souls are trusting in you. Every day your miracles are with us: Your wonders and favors are at all times, evening, morning, and afternoon. O Good One, your compassions are never exhausted and your kindnesses are continual. We put our hope in you."

Jesus had a word to describe these prayerful people: hypocrites. And he had advice for his disciples about this kind of self-promotion:

Prayer tip 1. "When you pray, don't be like the hypocrites who love to pray publicly on street corners and in the synagogues where everyone can see them. I tell you the truth, that is all the reward they will ever get" (Matthew 6:5).

Jesus said to pray in private. He often slipped away from the disciples to pray. Sometimes "before daybreak" (Mark 1:35). Sometimes late in the day, retreating "up into the hills by himself to pray" (Mark 6:46).

That's not to say Jesus argued against praying in public. He prayed in front of the disciples, the crowds who followed him, and the worshippers in synagogue services. But his prayers weren't to draw attention to himself.

Prayer tip 2. "When you pray, don't babble on and on as people of other religions do. They think their prayers are answered merely by repeating their words again and again" (Matthew 6:7).

The most famous Bible example of babbling prayer was when the prophet Elijah took on 850 prophets of Canaanite gods. It was a battle of the gods, to see whose god could send fire from heaven to burn up a sacrificed bull. Team Baal prayed all day, dancing and cutting themselves, trying to wake up their chief god, Baal. They got nothing. Elijah's turn. He prayed a 30-second prayer, and the fire fell.

No need for long-winded prayers, droning chants, or carefully constructed arguments about why God should give us what we want. "Your Father knows exactly what you need even before you ask him!" (Matthew 6:8).

With that in mind, Jesus recommended prayer that is short, simple, and straight from the heart.

DID JESUS BORROW THE LORD'S PRAYER?

Several lines in the Lord's Prayer sound remarkably like other prayers that Jews were praying at the time.

The most obvious parallel shows up in the way Jesus started his prayer. He seemed to pull from one particular Jewish prayer that was—and still is—recited in worship services: the "Holy Prayer." Jews call it the Kaddish, meaning "holy." When we look closely at this prayer, it seems obvious why Jesus chose to build on it.

Here are the opening lines, alongside the opening lines of the Lord's Prayer.

HOLY PRAYER (KADDISH)	LORD'S PRAYER
Holy and honored is his great name	Our Father in heaven, may your name be kept holy.
in all the earth, which he created according to his will.	May your will be done on earth, as it is in heaven.
May he set up his kingdom in your lifetime.	May your Kingdom come soon.

What may have attracted Jesus to the Holy Prayer is the very next line: "May his salvation blossom and his Anointed near."

The "Anointed" and the "Anointed One" are names the Jewish people used for the Messiah. This Holy Prayer of the Jews not only praised the holiness of God; it asked for God to send the Messiah to save them.

Hidden within the opening lines of the Lord's Prayer, it seems, is a clue that God has already started to answer the prayer. The Messiah has come—"in your life-time." And he has brought with him the Good News of how to find salvation and become citizens of God's kingdom.

LEARNING FROM THE LORD'S PRAYER

Bible experts see a wealth of insight in the short prayer that Jesus offered as a model for his disciples. "Pray like this," Jesus said.

"Our Father in heaven." God's only Son didn't have a monopoly on the word *Father* when it came time to address God. In prayer, Jews often called God their heavenly Father.

- "The LORD is like a father to his children, tender and compassionate to those who fear him" (Psalm 103:13).
- "Surely you are still our Father! Even if Abraham and Jacob would disown us, LORD, you would still be our Father. You are our Redeemer from ages past" (Isaiah 63:16).

What's unique about Jesus calling God "Father" is that Jesus had an intimate relationship with him: the intimacy between a loving father and son. Jesus seemed to invite his followers to share in that intimate connection—to talk with God as people who are part of the family, as God's other sons and daughters.

"May your name be kept holy." The first half of Jesus' prayer is actually a prayer for God. Jesus wasn't talking about God's name alone, but about God himself, whose holy name reflects his character. In our day, it's a bit like saying, "His name opens doors," or "His name is mud." It's not the name we're talking about, it's the person.

Many Jews in ancient times, as today, considered God's name so holy that they wouldn't even speak it when they read it in the Bible. God revealed his name to Moses at the burning bush: "I AM WHO I AM" (Exodus 3:14). In Hebrew, this name is represented by four letters: YHWH, usually spelled Yahweh (YAH-way). But when Jews come to that name in their Bible, out of respect they generally inserted another word: *Adonai*, meaning "my Lord."

When Jesus prayed, "May your name be kept holy," he may have had in mind something God had said about the sinful Jewish nation: "They brought shame on my holy name" (Ezekiel 36:20). If so, Jesus was saying he wanted people to respect God's holiness.

"May your kingdom come soon." Respect wasn't enough. Jesus wanted more for God. This phrase reads like a plea for God to carry out his plan to defeat sin once and for all and to reign over everyone, not just the willing few of the current age, but the willing all of the ages to come.

"May your will be done on earth, as it is in heaven." Jesus was admitting that God's kingdom hadn't come in its fullness, because not everyone was doing God's will. Jesus was asking for that kingdom to come because he wanted everyone in the world to worship the Lord as their one and only God—as is already done in heaven.

"Give us today the food we need." This begins the second half of the prayer—the part concerned about human needs. One word in this phrase hasn't shown up anywhere else in ancient Greek writing. It's a word that describes food—or "bread," a metaphor for food. Bible experts suggest at least three possibilities. Bread for today, as in

- "Give us this day our daily bread" (Matthew 6:11 KJV);
- tomorrow; or
- survival.

No matter which bread Jesus had in mind, he was saying that we depend on God for our survival—like the Hebrews of the Exodus who needed their daily manna: bread from heaven.

"Forgive us our sins, as we have forgiven those who sin against us." An older version of the prayer asks for forgiveness from "our trespasses." *Trespass* means "overstepping the boundary," which is sin. In William Shakespeare's day, when the King James Version of the Bible was translated, *trespass* was a polite way of saying *sin*.

Jesus said we should not only ask God to forgive us, but also cultivate a spirit of forgiveness toward others.

A lot hangs on that second phrase. In what some Christians hope is hyperbole—exaggeration to get the point across—Jesus later added a PS: "If you forgive those who sin against you, your heavenly Father will forgive you. But if you refuse to forgive others, your Father will not forgive your sins" (Matthew 6:14–15).

There's a similar verse in the Apocrypha, a collection of ancient Jewish writings inserted between the Old and New Testaments in many Christian Bibles, especially those of Catholics and Eastern Orthodox religions. It comes from a book written about 200 years before Jesus: "Forgive your neighbor the wrong he has done, and then your sins will be pardoned when you pray" (Sirach 28:2 NRSV).

"Don't let us yield to temptation, but rescue us from the evil one." Jesus may have adapted this line from a similar prayer in the Talmud, a collection of ancient Jewish writings passed along by word of mouth before being written down in about AD 200. Among the prayers that Jews said each morning and evening, this one begins: "Don't lead us into the power of temptation and sin, or let the tug of evil drag us down" (Talmud, *Berakhot* 60b, author's paraphrase).

The Greek word for *temptation* is the same for a spiritual "test." Many Bible experts prefer the second word in this prayer because God doesn't tempt people: "Do not say, 'God is tempting me.' . . . He never tempts anyone else. Temptation comes from our own desires, which entice us and drag us away" (James 1:13–14).

Jesus, it seems, was teaching us to pray that God wouldn't put us through difficult times that test our faith. Hard times like Job faced, including health, family, and financial problems. A prayer request like this would reflect not only our weakness and our fear of failing the test, but also our confidence in his ability to spare us the hardship—or to see us safely through. That's why we go to God for help.

Jesus prayed a similar prayer the night of his arrest, hours before his execution on the cross: "My Father! If it is possible, let this cup of suffering be taken away from me. Yet I want your will to be done, not mine" (Matthew 26:39).

"For yours is the kingdom and the power and the glory forever. Amen." Jesus probably didn't say this. It's not in the oldest copies of the prayer or in the oldest Bible commentaries. That's why most versions of the Bible today omit it.

It does show up, however, in the *Didache*—the oldest Christian manual of worship rituals. Written by the AD 200s, the *Didache* instructs Christians to say the Lord's Prayer three times a day.

A NEW TAKE ON THE LORD'S PRAYER

Given what many Bible experts see in the background to the Lord's Prayer, a paraphrase that reflects these insights could read:

Father in heaven, I want everyone in the world to worship you as their one and only God.

Please make this happen soon, so that everyone will live as you want them to live, just as those in heaven live.

Give us the food we need.

Forgive us when we sin. And help us forgive those who sin against us.

Don't put us through spiritual tests, for we're afraid we'll fail and do what Satan wants. Save us from that.

You have the power to do all of this and more. What an awesome God you are.

JESUS ON FASTING

"When you fast, don't make it obvious."
MATTHEW 6:16

Many Christians never fast as part of their religion.

A fast is when someone decides to temporarily stop some, or all, eating and drinking. Though some people do this as a way to express their sorrow, repentance, or deep desire for God to answer their prayers, many Christians don't see the point.

To them, fasting is Jewish, not Christian. They consider it one of many practices made obsolete with the coming of Christ and the beginning of the new covenant—God's new way of working with people.

Though the Old Covenant orders Jewish people to fast on the Day of Atonement (Yom Kippur) to express sorrow for sins they've committed in the past year, there's no such commandment in the New Testament. Not from Jesus. Not from the apostle Paul. Not from anyone.

Once, when Jewish leaders cornered Jesus and asked him why his disciples never fasted, Jesus not only said it wasn't necessary. He said it was inappropriate. He said it would be like refusing to eat at a wedding feast that the host had worked hard to prepare.

What's surprising about Jesus' response is that he fasted. So did his disciples, most likely. After all, Jesus did advise them that when they fasted they should keep it a secret instead of flaunting it as some people did to show how religious they were.

So why didn't Jesus tell that to the Jewish leaders?

Some scholars say he was preparing Jews for a day in the near future when fasting would no longer be necessary.

THE EVOLUTION OF FASTING

Jewish people started fasting at the time they became a nation.

They were camped at the base of Mount Sinai in Egypt sometime in the 1400s or 1200s BC—Bible scholars debate which century. Refugees headed home to what is now Israel; they spent about a year camped there while God gave Moses not only the 10 Commandments but hundreds of other laws that organized Israel into a nation of 12 tribes.

These laws included a calendar of sacred days, one of which was the Day of Atonement—a national day of repentance and forgiveness: "The tenth day of the seventh month is the Great Day of Forgiveness. It is a solemn day of worship; everyone must go without eating to show sorrow for their sins" (Leviticus 23:27 CEV).

This was the only day of the year when all healthy Jews were supposed to fast. The frail were exempt. This was also the only day of the year when the high priest was allowed to go into the holiest room at the worship center, where Jews kept their most sacred object, the Ark of the Covenant. The ark was a gold-covered chest that held the 10 Commandments engraved in stone. The Jews considered this room the earthly throne of God. So when the priest went inside, he was approaching God.

In time, the Jews began fasting on other occasions—often when they wanted to approach God in prayer with a concern, such as a personal or a national crisis.

Once, during a civil war pitting the doomed tribe of Benjamin against all the other tribes of Israel, the coalition tribes sought God's direction by bringing him an offering and by fasting all day (Judges 20:26).

Decades later, after Philistine invaders slaughtered King Saul and most of his sons, a group of Jews retrieved their bodies "and they fasted for seven days" (1 Samuel 31:13). It was an expression of their grief.

The degree of fasting in Israel varied, and fasting was prohibited for people in poor health:

Mild fast. A bit like giving up something for Lent, Jews would sometimes enter into a partial fast. During three weeks of mourning, the prophet Daniel "had eaten no rich food. No meat or wine crossed my lips, and I used no fragrant lotions" (Daniel 10:3).

Partial fast. Normally, Jews drank water during a fast. But they'd give up everything else: all food, wine, and juices. When King David learned that the son born of his affair with Bathsheba was sick, "he went without food and lay all night on the bare ground" (2 Samuel 12:16). This continued until the child died a week later.

Total fast. Usually for a short time and during a personal or a national crisis, Jews abstained from all food and liquid, including water. They would also skip pleasures such as sex, bathing, and anointing their skin with fragrant oil— the ancient version of deodorant. Queen Esther gave these instructions before going to see the Persian king to ask for his help in stopping a Jewish holocaust: "Go and gather together all the Jews of Susa [the capital city] and fast for me. Do not eat or drink for three days, night or day" (Esther 4:16).

By the time of Jesus, the Jewish people had established traditions of fasting on selected days of the year. These extra fast days commemorated pivotal moments in their history—such as the day when Babylonian invaders from what is now Iraq destroyed the 400-year-old Temple Solomon had built in Jerusalem.

Some branches of the Jewish religion, including the rule-obsessed Pharisees, fasted two days each week. This extra fasting was portrayed as a mark of piety—above and beyond the call of religious duty.

Most fasted on Mondays and Thursdays. It's uncertain why they picked those days.

Some guess it was because these were considered good days to appeal to God. That's because Jewish tradition says that Moses climbed Mount Sinai on the fifth day of the week, Thursday, to receive the 10 Commandments. And he came back down with them on the second day of the week, Monday. So by fasting from sunup to sundown on those days, they apparently felt they were following the example of Moses—and perhaps making themselves holy enough to approach God.

Others guess the Jews selected Mondays and Thursdays because these were the busiest days of the week: market days and trial days at the Temple. That made them an ideal time to flaunt piety by dressing the part of a person on a fast.

FASTING FOR SHOW

Jesus wasn't a fan of fellow Jews who wore their religious practices like a peacock's tail.

"When you fast, don't put on a sad face like the hypocrites," Jesus said. "They make their faces look sad to show people they are fasting. I tell you the truth, those hypocrites already have their full reward. So when you fast, comb your hair and wash your face. Then people will not know that you are fasting, but your Father, whom you cannot see, will see you. Your Father sees what is done in secret, and he will reward you" (Matthew 6:16–18 NCV).

There's a funny play on words here.

WHEN JEWS SKIP FOOD

There's only one day a year when the Bible says Jews should fast: the Day of Atonement. "You must go without eating to show sorrow for your sins" (Leviticus 16:29, CEV).

This is the day each year, in September or October, when Jews reflect on their

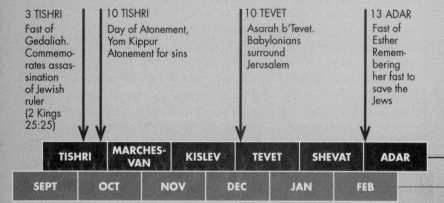

3 TISHRI
Fast of Gedaliah. Commemorates assassination of Jewish ruler (2 Kings 25:25)

10 TISHRI
Day of Atonement, Yom Kippur Atonement for sins

10 TEVET
Asarah b'Tevet. Babylonians surround Jerusalem

13 ADAR
Fast of Esther Remembering her fast to save the Jews

TISHRI	MARCHES-VAN	KISLEV	TEVET	SHEVAT	ADAR
SEPT	OCT	NOV	DEC	JAN	FEB

When Jesus talked about hypocrites putting on a sad face, he used a word that means "hide." Here's the wordplay: These hypocrites "hide to be seen." They hid their true face behind the mask of a sad expression—or in their case, beneath a layer of dirty ashes. Some people signaled that they were fasting or mourning by putting ashes on their head and face. It was like the custom today of wearing a black armband.

Fasting in secret wasn't a new idea. It shows up in ancient Jewish writings such as the *Testament of Joseph*, written sometime between the Old and New Testaments.

During a seven-year fast, Jacob's son Joseph reportedly said, "I appeared to the Egyptians as one living the easy life. That's because those who fast for God's sake instead of for people's attention are rewarded with a healthy appearance. When my master was away from home, I drank no wine. And I skipped my meals for three days, taking the food to the poor and sick" (*Testament of Joseph* 1:29–30 AUTHOR'S PARAPHRASE).

JESUS CRITICIZED FOR NOT FASTING

The Gospels of Matthew, Mark, and Luke tell the story of a group of Jews asking Jesus why his disciples didn't fast. After all, the Pharisees fasted. And so did the disciples of John the Baptist.

Anything but predictable, Jesus pointed his reply in a direction that still puzzles Bible experts.

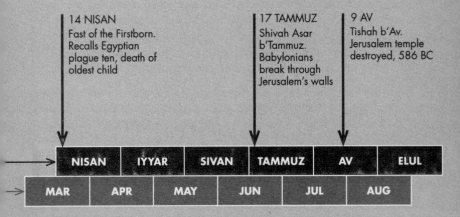

sins and seek God's forgiveness. In time, Jews started adding other days of fasting to commemorate events in their nation's history.

Major fasts in red, observed from sundown to sundown. Others observed from dawn to dusk.

14 NISAN
Fast of the Firstborn. Recalls Egyptian plague ten, death of oldest child

17 TAMMUZ
Shivah Asar b'Tammuz. Babylonians break through Jerusalem's walls

9 AV
Tishah b'Av. Jerusalem temple destroyed, 586 BC

NISAN	IYYAR	SIVAN	TAMMUZ	AV	ELUL

MAR	APR	MAY	JUN	JUL	AUG

He could have said the disciples fasted but that they chose to do it privately. Jesus fasted during his temptation in the desert badlands, where he "became very hungry" (Matthew 4:2). And he was probably fasting in Samaria when his disciples pleaded with him to eat and he replied, "I have a kind of food you know nothing about" (John 4:32). Also, he and his disciples probably kept the traditional Jewish fast days—especially the only one required in their Bible: the Day of Atonement.

But instead of reporting any of this, Jesus seemed to imply that it was inappropriate to focus so much on fasting—and that attitudes toward fasting would be changing soon.

He did this with three short comparisons.

Wedding. You don't fast during a wedding celebration. Apparently portraying himself as the groom, Jesus said that "someday the groom will be taken away from them [his disciples], and then they will fast" (Mark 2:20).

Clothing. You don't patch an old cloth with new cloth that hasn't been washed. Once the new cloth shrinks, it will pull away from the old cloth and make the rip worse. The old and new are incompatible (see Luke 5:36).

Wine. You don't put new wine in old, brittle wineskins. As the new wine continues to ferment, producing gases that stretch the sealed container, the old wineskins can't expand to contain it. The old can't handle the new (see Luke 5:37).

Many Bible experts say that the implication of the last two analogies is that the Jewish traditions were about to change. The old covenant, or agreement, that God had with the Jews was about to be replaced by a new covenant. When that happened, fasting as a required ritual in the quest for righteousness would become as obsolete as the sacrificial system. Jews stopped sacrificing in AD 70 after the Roman army destroyed the Jerusalem Temple, the only place Jews were allowed to offer sacrifices to God.

Jesus was setting up a new system, many Bible experts say. And the point of his comparisons was that his message couldn't be contained in Judaism. To try to force Christianity into Judaism—to require all Christians to be Jews—could have damaged both the Jewish religion and the Christian message. The apostle Paul would later fight that battle, resisting attempts by Jewish Christians to impose Jewish law and tradition on all Christian converts.

CHRISTIAN FASTING

Surprisingly, for many, the first known manual of Christian behavior orders believers to fast.

The manual, probably written in the AD 100s, was called *Didache*, Greek for "teaching." It tells Christians to "fast on behalf of those who persecute you" (*Didache* 1:3). That sounds Christian enough, paraphrasing Jesus: "Pray for those who persecute you!" (Matthew 5:44).

But there's also a Pharisee-sounding rule. It orders Christian converts who are preparing for baptism to fast two days every week: on Tuesday and Friday. Church leaders said they picked those days so Christians wouldn't be confused with "the hypocrites"—Pharisees who fasted on Mondays and Thursdays.

Many Bible scholars say the writers of this manual missed the point Jesus was making: The hypocrisy of the Jews was in publicizing their fasting to make themselves look spiritually superior to others.

Initially, it seems, the Christians who fasted were new converts getting ready for their baptism, which generally took place on Easter. Some historians speculate that this fasting on Fridays helped jump-start the tradition of fasting on Good Friday, to mark the crucifixion of Jesus. Historians add that this most likely evolved into the tradition of giving up something for Lent, a 40-day fast that leads to Easter. The 40 days commemorate Jesus' fast during his desert temptation.

It's a mystery where writers of the *Didache* came up with the idea that Christians should fast.

Though the New Testament doesn't retire the practice entirely—apparently leaving it up to the Holy Spirit to provide individual guidance on when and how a person should fast—it does warn Christians not to use fasting or any other kind of self-deprivation as a technique for coercing God or for trying to overpower sin in their lives—as if a human could manhandle sin.

For either of these, fasting is portrayed as unnecessary and ineffective.

"Don't let anyone condemn you by insisting on pious self-denial," Paul wrote to Christians in Colossae, a city in what is now Turkey. "These rules may seem wise because they require strong devotion, pious self-denial, and severe bodily discipline. But they provide no help in conquering a person's evil desires" (Colossians 2:18, 23).

In today's era of the new covenant, when God's laws are written on the human heart, many New Testament experts say that fasting is a matter between the individual and God, and not a spiritual discipline that any individual or group should impose on another.

JESUS AND DISCIPLES BREAK SABBATH RULES

*"The Sabbath was made to serve us;
we weren't made to serve the Sabbath."*
Mark 2:27 THE MESSAGE

One law in the Bible has produced more than a thousand laws, which many Jews still observe.

"You have six days each week for your ordinary work, but the seventh day is a Sabbath day of rest dedicated to the LORD your God" (Exodus 20:9–10).

It's commandment number four from the Bible's famous 10.

God's intent, it seems, was to give people a day for rest and worship.

Moses explained it this way to the Jewish refugees he was leading home to Israel: "In six days the LORD made the heavens, the earth, the sea, and everything in them; but on the seventh day he rested" (Exodus 20:11).

That's not to say God needed a day off. But Moses used this slice of the Creation story to help justify the law: If God took a day off from creating things, people should take a day off, too.

For Jews, Sunday was the first day of the week. Day seven started at sundown on Friday and continued until sundown on Saturday. During those 24 hours, Jews weren't supposed to work.

But what is work?

One person's work can be another person's relaxation—fishing, for example.

In the writings of Moses only two examples of work are forbidden on the Sabbath:

Don't gather firewood. After someone reported a Jewish refugee loading up on firewood during the Exodus, "the whole community took the man outside the camp and stoned him to death" (Numbers 15:36).

Don't build a fire. "You must not even light a fire in any of your homes on the Sabbath" (Exodus 35:3). The Sabbath was ladies' day off, too. No cooking. Food prep was done ahead of time.

That's it—the only examples of forbidden work.

It was clear to most Jews, though, that they should avoid other kinds of work, too. But what, exactly? And what exceptions were allowed in unusual circumstances?

Enter the Jewish scholars: scribes, Pharisees, and rabbis.

Centuries before Jesus, Jews began to offer their educated interpretation of exactly what constituted work and how they should spend their Sabbath. This spawned hundreds of laws, which one rabbi described in this way:

The rules about the Sabbath. . .are as mountains hanging by a hair, for Scripture is scanty and the rules many.

HAGIGAH 1:8

Ever growing, these teachings about the Sabbath got passed along by word of mouth until Jewish leaders collected and preserved them in a religion encyclopedia of Jewish history and commentary known as the Mishnah, compiled by about AD 200.

Long before either the Mishnah or the ministry of Jesus, some Jews started to practice these emerging teachings. Practice evolved into tradition. And this tradition, for some, took on the authority of sacred Scripture.

As far as many Jewish experts were concerned, breaking any one of these man-made laws was no different than breaking God's law. In other words, these experts were saying that when it came to interpreting the Bible, "It's my way or the highway."

Jesus took the highway.

WHEN THE SABBATH BECAME SUNDAY

It seems unlikely that one of Jesus' disciples stood up in a church meeting one day and said, "Hey, I have a great idea. Let's switch the Sabbath to Sunday, in honor of Jesus' resurrection."

There's no solid evidence that Christians started meeting on Sunday during the apostles' lifetime. There are just hints, such as Paul's asking the Corinthians to put away some money for an offering on Sundays, "the first day of each week" (1 Corinthians 16:2).

More likely, Christians continued worshipping on the Sabbath as Jesus had done. In the decades that followed, some probably started meeting on Sunday as well. This wasn't a substitute day of rest. More likely, it was a brief time together to take Communion, sing, pray, and then go back to work.

Only in AD 321 did Sunday become an official day of rest—a declaration made not by a church leader but by the Roman emperor Constantine, who had legalized Christianity.

Later in that century, church leaders such as Ambrose and Chrysostom began teaching that Sunday was the new Christian Sabbath—a day of rest and worship.

BUILDING A WALL TO PROTECT THE LAW

Imagine the Sabbath as a private getaway at the end of a busy week. Many Jews do. In Jesus' time, as today, observant Jews thought of the Sabbath as a day of utter relaxation. It was a day of joy, too—happy time spent with family, close friends, and God.

Jews wanted to protect that day and the law on which it was built. In a sense, they built a wall around it. Jewish scholars didn't want their fellow Jews coming within a whisper or even a thought of working on the Sabbath. And that worry gave rise to a pair of Sabbath laws:

"Don't talk about work you need to do in the morning."

"Don't think about work or stressful concerns."

One of the oldest collections of Sabbath laws dates to about a century before Jesus. It's from the famous Dead Sea Scrolls, a 2,000-year-old library hidden in caves near the Dead Sea and discovered in the 1940s and '50s. These scrolls belonged to a group of isolationist Jews called Essenes. The Essenes apparently stashed their scrolls in caves just before the Roman army annihilated their village in AD 68, while crushing a nationwide Jewish uprising.

One particular scroll preserves some of their Sabbath laws. It's called the *Damascus Document* because it mentions the city of Damascus a lot. This scroll reveals that the Essenes were hard-core Sabbath observers who made the imposing Sabbath laws of Pharisees look like Sabbath Lite.

Compare:

Pharisees to the rescue. If a person fell into a well—or even if an animal fell in—Pharisees allowed for a Sabbath rescue. "Which of you doesn't work on the Sabbath?" Jesus asked a group of Pharisees. "If your son or your cow falls into a pit, don't you rush to get him out?" (Luke 14:5).

Essenes on holiday. Essenes, however, would have waited a day. "If any person falls into a well, you will not rescue that person with a ladder or a rope or any other device" (*Damascus Document* 11:16–17).

─ DEAD SEA SABBATH LAWS ──────────────

The Essenes lived at Qumran, a small community in the Judean badlands 14 miles (23 km) east of Jerusalem.

Like monks, they isolated themselves from other Jews because they said the Jerusalem priesthood was a fraud—and had been ever since the Jews won their freedom from Syria in 152 BC. One of the Jewish rebel leaders celebrated by naming himself the high priest, though Jewish law said he didn't qualify. So the Essenes left Jerusalem to wait for the Messiah to come and set things right.

Here's a sampling of Essene Sabbath laws, some of which the Pharisees would have declared too harsh. Don't:
- talk about work or about anything you have to do the next day;
- walk outside the village more than a quarter of a mile—
  Pharisees could walk twice as far, more than half a mile;
- draw water from a well or scoop water into a cup;
- drink outside the village;
- wear perfume (the ancient version of deodorant);
- help an animal give birth;
- fast from eating food, because the Sabbath should be a joyful day;
- ask a non-Jew to do your work for you;
- carry anything to or from your house; and
- rest near a Gentile.

Sabbath was considered a Jews-only observance. A couple of centuries after Jesus, Rabbi Simeon ben Laqish put it in writing. He said that any Gentile who observes the Sabbath "deserves death."

FORBIDDEN ON THE SABBATH TODAY

Orthodox Jews refrain from the following Sabbath day activities:

- talking on the telephone;
- driving or riding in any kind of vehicle;
- carrying anything outside the home, including chewing gum in the mouth;
- shopping;
- cooking (food is prepared ahead of time and can be kept warm as long as no one touches the temperature settings on the Sabbath);
- mowing or gardening; and
- doing laundry.
- turning on or off anything that uses electricity, including lights, television, computer, radio, air conditioners, and alarm clocks (fridge light is unscrewed);
- carrying out business dealings;
- writing;

THIRTY-NINE CATEGORIES OF LAWS

From the single law—don't work on the Sabbath—Jewish scholars developed 39 categories of forbidden Sabbath work, mostly agricultural since that's the culture in which the prohibitions developed.

They fit into four general groups.

Producing food
- Sowing
- Plowing
- Reaping (cutting grain, picking other crops)
- Tying sheaves (putting stalks of grain into bundles)
- Threshing (beating grain kernels loose from the stalks)
- Winnowing (sifting grain from loose flakes of chaff)
- Sorting (putting like crops together)
- Grinding (grain into flour)
- Sifting (impurities from flour)
- Kneading (mixing flour with yeast and water into dough)
- Baking

Construction
- Building
- Demolishing
- Putting out a fire
- Starting a fire
- Putting on the finishing touches
- Carrying something to or from a house

Making clothing
- Shearing wool
- Cleaning
- Combing
- Dyeing
- Spinning
- Stretching threads
- Making loops
- Weaving threads
- Separating threads
- Tying a knot
- Untying a knot
- Sewing
- Tearing in preparation to sew

Making leather goods
- Trapping
- Slaughtering
- Skinning
- Salting meat to preserve it
- Tanning (curing hides in the sun)
- Scraping (removing hair)
- Cutting leather into pieces
- Writing (onto leather scrolls)
- Erasing

Within each of these 39 categories, a litany of laws developed over the years—hundreds of them.

LOOPHOLE AROUND THE SABBATH LAWS

Some of the ancient Sabbath laws became impractical, so Jewish scholars created what they declared kosher loopholes.

For example, an observant Jew today can't carry anything outside the house on the Sabbath. Not chewing gum in the mouth. Not money in a pocket. Not even a key to lock the home while they're worshipping at the synagogue, though it is permissible to make the key into something they can wear, like a tie bar.

They can carry things inside the house. But that limitation is a problem when sharing a Sabbath meal with other Jewish families.

Rabbis solved this problem by allowing Jews to declare a neighborhood or even an entire city an eruv, a collection of homes joined into one.

Step 1: The Jewish community designates an area with marked boundaries, such as a city wall, a fence, or a wire.

Step 2: The community shares food that is stored in all the houses of the eruv. Often, one person simply passes out matzo, crackerlike unleavened bread that doesn't have to be replaced often. This symbolizes that all the Jews in the community share their food and live as one happy family.

JESUS DEBATES THE SCHOLARS: EATING

Pharisees criticized Jesus for what they considered his breach of Sabbath laws on two fronts.

- He allowed his disciples to pick a snack of grain while walking through a field on the Sabbath.
- He practiced medicine by healing people on the Sabbath.

Matthew, Mark, and Luke all report the first clash. And all four Gospels, including John, report clashes over Jesus' healing people on the Sabbath.

As for the grain snack, Pharisees insisted it broke several of the 39 prohibited categories of work: reaping, threshing, and winnowing. And then there was the matter of carrying food in their mouths while walking. That was also a no-no.

Jesus offered a trio of rebuttals.

Hungry David. When David was on the run from Saul, he and his hungry men stopped at the worship center on the Sabbath, the day that sacred bread was put in the Temple for the priests. David ate the bread and no one criticized him for it. By implication, Jesus was asking his critics, "Why are you interpreting the law so rigidly when you have historical precedent for cutting us some slack?"

Priests work on the Sabbath. They offered sacrifices and led in worship services. And no one criticized them for it. "I tell you," Jesus said, "that there is something here greater than the temple" (Matthew 12:6 CEV). Scholars don't agree on what Jesus meant by that. Perhaps he was talking about himself or about the Kingdom of God that he was ushering in. Either way, he was saying that what he was doing was even more important than what the priests were doing.

Compassion trumps ritual. "You would not have condemned my innocent disciples if you knew the meaning of this Scripture: 'I want you to show mercy, not offer sacrifices' " (Matthew 12:7). Jesus was drawing from Hosea 6:6, a prophecy that urged the Jewish nation 700 years earlier to stop mistreating people and then offering insincere sacrifices as if observing these rituals gave them a free pass to treat people like dirt. God values love above ritual.

JESUS DEBATES THE SCHOLARS: HEALING

The Pharisees also hated to see Jesus heal people on the Sabbath.

Treating people didn't fit into any of the 39 prohibited categories. But some rabbis in ancient times taught that it was wrong to treat sick people on the Sabbath if lives weren't at risk. And because the Sabbath was supposed to be a joyful day, a few rabbis added that it was inappropriate to visit the sick—or even to pray for them.

Again, Jesus offered three rebuttals.

Circumcision is allowed—why not healing? Jewish boys were circumcised on the eighth day of life—even if that day fell on the Sabbath. The ritual ushered them into the covenant community of God's Chosen People. Jesus called this a healing of sorts. And he asked the Jewish scholars that if it was okay to heal this part of the body on the Sabbath, why "are you angry with me because I healed a man's whole body on the sabbath?" (John 7:23 NRSV).

Two rabbis a generation later agreed with Jesus, sounding almost as if they were quoting him:

> *If we suspend the Sabbath ban on work because of one part of the body, isn't it logical that we do the same for a person's entire body?*
> RABBI ELIEZER (ABOUT AD 90)

> *If circumcision, which affects only one of 248 parts of the human body, can suspend the Sabbath, how much more important is it that the whole body suspend the Sabbath.*
> RABBI ELEAZAR BEN AZARIAH (ABOUT AD 100)

You'd free a trapped animal—why not a human trapped by illness? Even the strict Pharisees said it was perfectly acceptable to help a sheep or any other animal out of a well or a pit on the Sabbath. "How much more valuable is a person than a sheep!" Jesus argued (Matthew 12:12).

The Sabbath is a day to do good deeds. Teaching in a synagogue, Jesus called up a man with a deformed hand.

"Does the law permit good deeds on the Sabbath, or is it a day for doing evil?" Jesus asked his critics. "Is this a day to save life or to destroy it?" (Mark 3:4).

His critics stood silent. Angry that they didn't show a trace of compassion for this man, Jesus instantly healed him.

The critics—Pharisees and Jews who supported Herod's dynasty—immediately began plotting to kill Jesus.

WHEN TO ATTACK THE JEWS

Armies invading Israel in Bible times discovered that the Sabbath was the best day to attack a Jewish city.

Many Jews wouldn't fight back. It was their day off.

Among the most famous Jewish defeats on the Sabbath:

701 BC. In perhaps the oldest reference to the Sabbath outside the Bible, Assyrian king Sennacherib, from what is now Iraq, wrote in wedge-shaped cuneiform script that he had captured Lachish, near Jerusalem, on Jewish king Hezekiah's "seventh time." Scholars suggest he meant the seventh day of the week.

597 BC. Babylonian records say their invasion force from what is now Iraq captured Jerusalem "on the second day of the month of Adar." That was March 16 on our calendar, the Sabbath.

588 BC. The Babylonians returned for an encore invasion, launching a new assault on Jerusalem on January 15, the Sabbath.

586 BC. After a long siege, the Babylonians broke through Jerusalem's wall on the ninth day of the fourth month of Jewish king Zedekiah's eleventh year. The Sabbath.

168 BC. When Syrians hoping to wipe out the Jewish religion attacked Israel on the Sabbath, Jewish soldiers refused to "profane the sabbath day" by fighting. Instead, they insisted, "Let us all die in our innocence" (1 Maccabees 2:34, 37). They did.

During the freedom fight that followed this massacre, Jewish guerrilla leaders decided they had to fight on the Sabbath to avoid annihilation. They won their independence. The Jews later continued this practice of fighting on the Sabbath when they revolted against Rome in AD 66 and when they fought their Arab neighbors in modern times.

JESUS' FAVORITE TEACHING METHOD: PARABLES

*In his public ministry he never
taught without using parables.*

MARK 4:34

Looking for the most authentic teachings of Jesus?
Even the more skeptical Bible scholars—those who question the authenticity of anything and everything in the Bible—point to Jesus' parables.

These experts say that stories such as the parables of the Good Samaritan and the Prodigal Son are Jesus' teachings that suffered least from two corrupting influences:

- the fractured memory of the Gospel writers; and
- add-on comments by well-meaning scribes who later made copies of the Gospels and couldn't resist inserting their own insights.

What made these parables so tamperproof?

Stories are easy to remember. We might not recall much of a sermon or a lecture, but good stories stick in the cobwebs of our memory like juicy flies in a spider's trap.

Bible experts say there are several clues that Jesus' parables are genuine.

They track with his preaching. The parables sum up his core ideas about how people should live as citizens of God's kingdom.

They clash with the values of Jewish leaders. Many of his parables criticized the teaching and behavior of Jewish leaders in power. This would have angered those leaders. And it certainly did, according to the four Gospel writers and several Roman historians from the first century.

They draw their images from Jesus' slice of history. Had the stories been added later, the scenes wouldn't track so well with what archaeology and literature from the first century reveal about life in Galilee during Jesus' day.

People before Jesus seldom used parables. Though a few notables, such as Plato and Aristotle, used parables before Jesus, there's no evidence that anyone used them a lot. One-third of Jesus' New Testament teachings are parables.

People after Jesus seldom used parables. Hardly any parables show up in ancient Christian writings outside the Gospels—not in the rest of the New Testament or in books written later by church leaders. This suggests that no one did parables like Jesus—before him or after him. They were his trademark.

HOW TO SPOT A PARABLE

Bible scholars get into yelling matches over this. They can't seem to agree on how to define a parable.

The old standby is that a parable is an earthly story with a heavenly meaning. That certainly works with many parables, such as the most famous: the fictional story of a Samaritan man helping a robbery victim after a couple of Jewish leaders refused to lift a finger. That's a story set on earth. But it teaches a spiritual lesson by giving a practical example of what it means to "love your neighbor."

But what about this story, also widely considered a parable: "The Kingdom of Heaven is like the yeast a woman used in making bread. Even though she put only a little yeast in three measures of flour, it permeated every part of the dough" (Matthew 13:33).

Where's the story? And where on earth is the heavenly meaning? This two-line snippet sounds more like a riddle than a parable.

A comparison, sometimes. Not all of Jesus' parables are stories complete with a plot, hero, and villain. Some are similes—a short sentence or two that compares something in the physical world to something in the spiritual world.

"What is the Kingdom of God like? How can I illustrate it? It is like a tiny mustard seed that a man planted in a garden; it grows and becomes a tree, and the birds make nests in its branches" (Luke 13:18–19).

Using word pictures from planet Earth, Jesus managed to give his listeners a peek into the spiritual dimension. God's kingdom will start small, like a tiny mustard seed or a small plug of yeast—or a lone rabbi and his 12 disciples.

Hidden meaning, sometimes. Many parables hide their meaning from all but the teacher's closest followers. That was to help keep the teacher from getting in trouble with the authorities.

The Greek philosopher Plato used this approach 400 years before Jesus, with good reason. His mentor was Socrates—a philosopher whose ideas so offended the sensibilities of some good citizens that he was arrested, tried, and sentenced to execute himself by drinking poisonous hemlock. Afterward, when Plato taught in public, he sometimes remained cryptic. But alone with his devoted students, he let down his guard and explained himself more fully.

Jesus did the same. He said so when his disciples asked why he taught with parables: "You are permitted to understand the secrets of the Kingdom of Heaven, but others are not. To those who listen to my teaching, more understanding will be given" (Matthew 13:11–12). So after Jesus taught some of the more perplexing parables to the crowds, "when he was alone with his disciples, he explained everything to them" (Mark 4:34).

Clear meaning, sometimes. On the other hand, many parables were clear enough for even Jesus' most violent enemies to understand. In one such parable, Jesus told a story about evil tenant farmers who refused to obey the landowner—going so far as to murder the landowner's son.

"When the leading priests and Pharisees heard this parable, they realized he was telling the story against them—they were the wicked farmers" (Matthew 21:45).

Both types of parables, Jesus said, fulfilled prophecy.

- Parables easy to understand fulfilled a psalm: "I will speak to you in parables. I will explain things hidden since the creation of the world" (Matthew 13:35).

- Parables reserved for devoted followers of Jesus fulfilled a prediction from Isaiah: "When you hear what I say, you will not understand. . . . For the hearts of these people are hardened, and their ears cannot hear" (Matthew 13:14–15).

A story, usually. Most of Jesus' parables spin around a story, a word picture that most of his listeners could conjure up in their mind's eye. The scenes were from their time and place in history.

Many of his parables dealt with farming: workers in a vineyard, a farmer spreading seed, and a farmer's question about what to do with weeds in a wheat field. Galilee, where Jesus taught, was known for its fertile farmland. The Jewish historian Josephus, from Jesus' century, said there were only two large cities in the region. The rest was countryside and small farming communities.

A spiritual meaning, always. The stories Jesus told pulled double duty. They were never just stories. The farmer throwing seed into his field wasn't just a story about agriculture. From this mental image, listeners were supposed to make the connection to the spiritual message of how the Kingdom of God grows—with Christians spreading the teachings of Jesus like seeds scattered in a field. In fact, most of Jesus' parables are about God's Kingdom: what it's like and how God's people are supposed to live as citizens of that Kingdom.

One main meaning, often. Parables usually have one big idea pushing them. So say most Bible scholars—as least for the past 100 years.

But for about 1,900 years before that, most scholars searched for hidden messages in every fleeting detail. They treated the parables as allegories—with every element symbolizing something else.

There is some of that going on in many of Jesus' parables. In the story of the Prodigal Son, for example, the father represents God patiently waiting for his lost children to come home. But some early scholars took the symbolism overboard, sometimes using the technique to manufacture ammunition for a war of ideas they were waging with others in the church.

Take, for example, the parable about mixing yeast into "three measures of flour" (Luke 13:21). Here's what some early church leaders said the three scoops of flour represented:

- Three major sections of the Bible: law, prophets, and Gospels— uniting the sacred writings of Jews and Christians (Hilary Poitiers, about AD 315–367)

- Jews, Greeks, and Samaritans—uniting all races (Theodore of Mopsuestia, about AD 350–429)
- Three passions of the soul: reason that produces good judgment; anger so we can hate evil; and desire so we can aspire to live a good life (Jerome, about AD 347–420)

Symbolism in the details, sometimes. There are times when details in a parable represent something else. Jesus made that clear when he explained to his disciples the parable about a farmer whose enemy planted weeds among the farmer's wheat. In the parable, Jesus said the farmer decided not to pull the weeds, for fear of damaging the wheat. In the early stages of growth, it's nearly impossible to tell the difference between the wheat and the weeds, or darnel ryegrass with poisonous seeds. The farmer would separate the two at harvesttime.

The disciples didn't understand the point of the story. So Jesus explained.

"The Son of Man is the farmer who plants the good seed. The field is the world, and the good seed represents the people of the Kingdom. The weeds are the people who belong to the evil one. The enemy who planted the weeds among the wheat is the devil. The harvest is the end of the world, and the harvesters are the angels. Just as the weeds are sorted out and burned in the fire, so it will be at the end of the world. The Son of Man will send his angels, and they will remove from his Kingdom everything that causes sin and all who do evil" (Matthew 13:37–41).

Big surprise in little package, often. Many of Jesus' parables come to us as wisdom in a box, gift wrapped—and waiting to blow up in our faces like a balloon loaded with flour.

Jesus tells a simple story. But it's rigged. He may have rigged it to blow up the moment he finished his last sentence. Other times, he let the listeners take the story home, where it would blow up once they figured out what the story meant.

It's the story's meaning that's volatile.

Jesus may have gotten the idea for explosive stories from the prophet Nathan. The prophet used this kind of parable to prod King David into repenting of his adultery with Bathsheba. David had a harem of at least seven wives, yet he stole the only wife of one of his soldiers who was away at war, fighting for king and country.

If Nathan had confronted David directly, the king could have raised his defenses in reflex—refusing to give the matter any thought. But Nathan arranged for the king to think first and decide later about how to respond. Nathan told a story about a rich man who owned vast herds but who stole the one and only lamb of a poor man—and then slaughtered the pet lamb for a meal.

Livid, David said a man like that deserved to die.

"You are that man!" Nathan answered (2 Samuel 12:7).

It was just a short story—a word picture wrapped in a tiny package. But it packed a wallop of a surprise that changed David's life. He repented right away. And God forgave him.

That's what Jesus did with many of his parables. He confronted his listeners with their sinful behavior or their wrongly preconceived notions, giving them a chance to think first and act later.

PARABLES OF JESUS

The Gospel writers report about 40 to 65 parables of Jesus. The numbers vary because scholars vary—they can't agree on which stories and sayings qualify as parables. This is a short list of 42 parables that most would agree are parables.

John's Gospel is a no-show because it doesn't report any of Jesus' parables, though many argue that John includes at least two: the Good Shepherd (John 10:1–18) and the True Vine (John 15:1–8).

PARABLE	MATTHEW	MARK	LUKE
Lamp hidden under basket	5:14–16	4:21–22	8:16; 11:33–36
Praying for food, getting bad things	7:9–11		11:11–13
Wise, foolish builders	7:24–27		6:46–49
No fasting at wedding banquet	9:15	2:19–20	5:33–39
New cloth sewn on old cloth	9:16	2:21	5:36
New wine in old wineskins	9:17	2:22	5:37–38
Farmer planting in four soils	13:3–8, 18–23	4:3–8, 14–20	8:5–8, 11–15
Separating weeds from wheat	13:24–30, 36–43		
Mustard seed becomes big plant	13:31–32	4:30–32	13:18–19
Yeast in bread	13:33		13:20–21
Hidden treasure found in field	13:44		
Selling everything for a valuable pearl	13:45–46		
Fishing net in water	13:47–50		
Homeowner with gems	13:52		
Searching for lost sheep	18:12–14		15:4–7
Ungrateful creditor	18:23–25		
Vineyard workers getting a day's pay	20:1–16		
Two sons who won't work	21:28–32		
Tenant farmers who murder	21:33–44	12:1–11	20:9–18
Invitation to a wedding banquet	22:2–14		14:15–24
Blooming fig tree	24:32–35	13:28–31	21:29–33
As unexpected as a thief at night	24:42–44		12:39–40
Good servant, bad servant	24:45–51		12:42–48
Ten bridesmaids waiting for wedding	25:1–13		
Three servants with investment money	25:14–30		19:12–27
Separating sheep from goats	25:31–46		
How seed grows secretly		4:26–29	
Servants watching for master's return		13:34–37	12:35–40
Lender who writes off two loans			7:41–43
Good Samaritan			10:30–37
Friend in need at midnight			11:5–8
Fool who dies rich			12:16–21
Fig tree without figs			13:6–9
Taking a humble seat at a banquet			14:7–14
Cost of constructing a building			14:28–30
Cost of war			14:31–33
Lost coin			15:8–10
Lost (prodigal) son			15:11–32
Shrewd business manager			16:1–8
Rich man and Lazarus in afterlife			16:19–31
Servant treating master with respect			17:7–10
Persistent widow and unfair judge			18:2–8
Prayers of Pharisee and tax collector			18:9–14

TIPS FOR UNDERSTANDING A PARABLE

Figuring out what a parable means isn't an exact science. But we get a little help from the times when Jesus explained the meaning to his confused disciples. There are other guidelines that Bible scholars recommend as well.

Look for code words. Many figures of speech were well-known symbols in the Old Testament and other Jewish writings.

God is often described as a ruler, judge, landowner, or parent. That helps identify him as the father in the parable of the Prodigal Son and the landowner in the story of the tenant farmers who killed the landowner's son.

Jewish people often appear as servants, children, a vine, or a flock. Judgment Day was often described as a harvest, as seen in the parable about separating grain stalks from weeds. And God's Kingdom was often described as a bountiful feast or a joyful wedding.

Compare the retelling in other Gospels. One Gospel writer might have added a detail that another skipped.

In Luke 14, Jesus tells a parable about a rich man who prepared a huge feast, but the invited guests made excuses for not coming. So the man invited the poor, the crippled, and the blind—anyone and everyone. Matthew 22 tells much the same parable, identifying it as a wedding feast.

Read together, these two parables seem to say that the Jews—God's chosen people—were the ones first invited into the wedding banquet (God's Kingdom). But they by and large refused (as seen later in the crucifixion of God's Son). So God would invite others (the rest of the world) to come and enjoy the celebration (heaven).

Pay attention to other parables or teachings nearby. The Gospel writers sometimes arranged the parables by topic. Luke 15, for example, is a chapter about finding something that's lost. And Luke stacks the chapter with three parables on the topic: lost sheep, lost coin, and lost (prodigal) son.

The context helps us understand the point of the three parables. Jesus used these stories to answer the complaint of Jewish scholars, who said he shouldn't be associating with "tax collectors and other notorious sinners. . .even eating with them!" (Luke 15:1–2). But Jesus was saying that these sinners were lost, and he was on a mission to find them—because God was waiting for them with a broken heart. That was the point of the parable about the father waiting for his prodigal son to come home.

Pay attention to the end of the parable. The key to a parable often lies in the last few words.

That's how the Jewish leaders figured out they were the evil farmers in the story of the tenant farmers who killed the landowner's son. In the story, the landowner rents his vineyard to several farmers. But at harvest time, they refuse to give him his share of the crops. Instead, they kill his servants who are sent to collect. Finally, the patient landowner gives them one more chance, sending his own son. But the farmers murder him, too.

Jesus asked the Jewish leaders what they thought the landowner would do to the farmers.

"He will put the wicked men to a horrible death," they answered, "and lease the vineyard to others who will give him his share of the crop after each harvest" (Matthew 21:41).

Jesus responded by wrapping up his parable with a quote from the Psalms—one that the Jewish leaders knew well: "The stone that the builders rejected has now become the cornerstone." To make sure they got the message, he added a comment: "The Kingdom of God will be taken away from you and given to a nation that will produce the proper fruit" (Matthew 21:42–43).

These leaders of the Jewish nation were the "builders" who had rejected God's plan for their nation. And they were the evil farmers destined to lose their land because of it.

Within a couple of decades, Christianity became a predominantly non-Jewish movement. And within about 40 years, the Jews were a people without a homeland—banned from their Holy City of Jerusalem for rebelling against Rome.

PLATO'S PARABLE OF LIFE IN A CAVE

About 400 years before Jesus, the Greek philosopher Plato created a parable to make a point.

His point: We can learn very little through our senses, but a great deal through open-minded reason.

PARABLES OF THE RABBIS

Though historians have collected about 2,000 ancient parables from Jewish teachers, no one seemed to wield them as often as Jesus—or as skillfully.

Yet some of the rabbis' parables sound very much like those of Jesus.

Compare Jesus' parable about wisdom to a rabbi's parable published a couple of centuries later in the Mishnah, a collection of sacred Jewish writings.

"[A wise person] builds a house on solid rock. Though the rain comes in torrents and the floodwaters rise and the winds beat against that house, it won't collapse because it is built on bedrock. . . . [A foolish person] builds a house on sand. When the rains and floods come and the winds beat against that house, it will collapse with a mighty crash." JESUS, MATTHEW 7:24–27

"What can we say about a man whose wisdom outweighs his good deeds? He is like a tree with many branches and few roots. The wind will easily uproot the tree, knocking it over. What can we say about a man whose good deeds outweigh his wisdom? He is like a tree with few branches but many roots. No wind in the world can move it."

SAYINGS OF THE JEWISH FATHERS
(HEBREW: PIRQE AVOT 3:27, AUTHOR'S PARAPHRASE)

His parable: *Allegory of the Cave.*

Plato painted a word picture of prisoners chained their entire lives below ground in a cave, unable even to turn their heads. All they could see were shadows of themselves and others projected in front of them on the cave wall. The words they heard, as far as they could tell, came from the shadow figures.

Released one bright day, these prisoners made the painful, eye-squinting ascent from the cave to discover that everything they thought they knew was just a shadow of reality. Their upward journey out of the cave illustrated how reason allows us to see what we otherwise never would have imagined.

PARABLE OF A FARMER PLANTING SEEDS

*"A farmer went out to plant some seeds.
As he scattered them across his field, some seeds fell
on a footpath, and the birds came and ate them."*
MATTHEW 13:3–4

Though Bible experts might not admit it out loud, many of them wish Jesus had done a better job of explaining this particular parable—the parable about a farmer scattering seeds onto four types of soil: packed, rocky, weedy, and good-to-grow.

Bible scholars aren't known for scratching their heads in confusion over a Bible passage. That would make them look, well, confused. And people think of them as experts. But with this particular parable, many of them seem as confused as the rest of us.

Here's the clue. If we could scoop their scholarly insights about this parable into a bucket and then scoop their disagreements into another bucket, we'd have two buckets we wouldn't want to drop on our toes.

After telling the parable to a crowd, Jesus privately explained its symbolism to his disciples. He said that the seed was the message about God's Kingdom, and the four soil types were four groups of people who would hear the message and respond in four different ways.

But what's the point? That's where the confusion peaks.

Is this the "Parable of the Farmer," intended to reveal the persistent nature of God or Jesus, symbolized by the farmer? Or is it the "Parable of the Four Soils," intended to focus on the diverse kinds of people who hear the message?

And by identifying only one type of soil as good, was Jesus trying to show who would and wouldn't make it into God's Kingdom? Or was he trying to encourage his disciples, to assure them that even though many would reject their message, some would accept it—and God's Kingdom would grow?

A little background on farming in Jesus' day can help us plow through questions like these.

PLANTING THE PARABLE

Jesus didn't say what kind of seeds the farmer planted. But the fact that the farmer "scattered them across his field" instead of planting them in rows suggests one of Galilee's biggest crops: wheat. Or it might have been the drought-resistant barley, or maybe flax, whose stems provided fiber for linen.

If wheat, the farmer was planting near the end of fall—starting around November. The sirocco winds of summer, blowing in hot and hard from Africa's

Sahara Desert, had faded away, replaced by cool, moist sea breezes from the Mediterranean.

Early rains of fall, arriving months before the main rains of winter, had softened the sunbaked ground. This cued the farmer to yoke up his oxen and break out the wooden plow tipped with a metal blade.

Historians estimate that each family in Jesus' hometown of Nazareth owned an average of roughly five acres. But in Roman times, people measured land by the jugerum, about a third of an acre. That's the area a farmer is said to have been able to plow in a single day with a team of oxen. It's a little more than half a football field. So in Nazareth, plowing would have involved about three weeks of hard labor.

It's unclear if most land in Galilee belonged to individual farmers or if they leased it from rich landowners and paid them back with a share of the crops. There was plenty of tenant farming going on throughout Israel. Jews had divided Galilee among themselves after they won their independence from Syrian occupiers about 200 years before Jesus. But in time, family farms grew smaller as they were divided among sons and grandsons. Some men sold their inheritance and took up other trades in villages.

If the farmer in Jesus' story followed the advice of Pliny, the first-century Roman author of *Natural History*, he fertilized the ground before plowing—perhaps by penning his sheep in the field. "When it comes to methods of fertilizing a field, the only point that is universally agreed upon," Pliny wrote, "is that we must never sow without first spreading manure on the ground."

When it came time to throw seeds on the plowed field, the farmer would walk the field broadcasting seeds with a sweeping motion of his arm, from left to right—or right to left if he was a lefty. Pliny said there was a trick to spreading the seed evenly. He said that farmers should match the distance of each step they took with the distance that their arm swept from side to side while tossing the seeds in an arcing spray.

For the average field, Pliny recommended a little more than a bushel (3.5 decaliters) of wheat seeds per jugerum—five modii, which is about five pecks (four pecks to a bushel). More seed if the soil was rich.

Afterward, some farmers plowed the ground again to bury the seeds.

In the parable, the seed fell onto four different kinds of soil—and suffered four different fates:

- **Some seeds fell on a footpath.**
- Birds ate them.
- **Some seeds fell on shallow soil with underlying rock.**
- The seeds sprouted quickly because the soil was shallow and warm. But because the plants didn't have deep roots, they wilted under the hot sun and died.
- **Some seeds fell among thorns.**

- The thorns choked the life out of the tender plants.
- Some seeds fell on fertile soil.
- They produced a crop that was 30, 60, and even 100 times as much as had been planted.

DECODING THE PARABLE

Jesus decoded the parable for his disciples when he met with them privately. The decoding appears in Matthew 13:18–23; Mark 4:14–20; and Luke 8:11–15.

Seed. It symbolizes "the message about the Kingdom." This is the "message" or Good News Jesus is delivering about what God's spiritual Kingdom is like and how people on earth can start living now as citizens of that eternal Kingdom.

Packed dirt of a footpath. It represents "those who hear the message about the kingdom and don't understand it. Then the evil one comes and snatches away the seed that was planted in their hearts."

The "evil one" in Jesus' parable is Satan. He shows up in other ancient Jewish writing as a bird. In the *Apocalypse of Abraham*, probably written during Jesus' century or the next, Satan is described as a bird harassing Abraham. And in another book written about a century before Jesus, Satan appears as an enemy prince who sent "birds to devour the seed which was sown in the land, in order to destroy the land. . . . Before the farmers could plow their seed underground, the birds plucked it from the surface" (*Jubilees* 11:11).

Rocky ground. It symbolizes people "who hear the message and immediately receive it with joy. But because they don't have deep roots, they don't last long. They fall away as soon as they have problems or are persecuted for believing God's word" (Matthew 13:20–21).

This is similar to a line from a Jewish book written a couple of centuries before Jesus: "The children of the ungodly put out few branches; they are unhealthy roots on sheer rock" (Sirach 40:15).

Thorny ground. This soil represents people "who hear God's word, but all too quickly the message is crowded out by the worries of this life and the lure of wealth, so no fruit is produced" (Matthew 13:22).

Fertile ground. This refers to people "who truly hear and understand God's word and produce a harvest of thirty, sixty, or even a hundred times as much as had been planted!" (Matthew 13:23).

Bible experts debate the projected yield of the harvest. Some say it's wildly excessive; that Jesus used exaggeration to illustrate the incredible growth of God's Kingdom. Others use different methods of calculation to show that the yield is perfectly normal.

For example, some say the yield refers to the number of grains in a single head of wheat—30, 60, or 100. A normal head of wheat contains about 30 to 65 grains. Pliny confirms that wheat branching into two heads could produce 100 grains.

Other Bible experts say the yield refers to how much grain the farmer got back compared to how much he used in the planting. It's estimated that given the absence of pesticides, irrigation, and animal control, every bushel of wheat planted in Jesus' day yielded about seven bushels. So if this were the mental picture that came to mind when Jesus told the parable, 30 to 100 bushels for every bushel planted would have been phenomenal.

Farmer. Jesus didn't decode the farmer. But in context, the farmer could symbolize God, Jesus, or even Jesus' followers who would later carry out his assignment of taking the message of salvation to everyone.

Many of the first listeners, however, probably considered the farmer a symbol of God—the main character in many of Jesus' parables. At least one Jewish book written late in Jesus' century compared God to a farmer: "For I sow my law in you, and it will produce fruit in you" (2 Esdras 9:31).

Another book also thought to have been written late in the first century portrays Jesus as a farmer who reaps an end-time harvest of souls: "And the congregation of the chosen and holy will be sown, and all these chosen ones will stand before him on that day" (1 Enoch 62:8).

BIBLE AGRICULTURAL ED: WHEAT—FROM THE FIELD TO THE FEAST

Twenty thousand years before Jesus, Galileans gathered up wild grain. So says Smithsonian Institution archaeobotanist Dolores R. Piperno, who led a research team that found grain among the ruins of an ancient community near the Sea of Galilee.

It would take another 10,000 years, most scientists say, for people to start planting wheat and beating the grain into flour for bread.

Once cultivation started, farmers learned to match wheat and other crops to the best-suited soil and terrain. In the fertile northland of Galilee, where most of Israel's rain falls—about 30 inches (76 cm) each year—wheat became the main crop. It produced about half of what the people ate each day.

HARVESTING THE PARABLE'S MESSAGE

Scholars sifting through the sack of details stuffed into this parable can't seem to settle on one major grain of truth. Instead, they point out that Jesus talked about several kinds of soil producing various results. So, perhaps, they say, Jesus intended his listeners to harvest several grains of truth. Here are some they suggest:

Spread God's message about salvation everywhere. The farmer spread the seed everywhere there was even the slightest hope of producing a harvest. He wasn't stingy with his seed, concentrating only on the most fertile soil. This suggests it might not be the best idea to go after the biggest evangelical bang for the buck, writing off the inner city for the suburbs, as an example. Wherever there's soil—people—there should be seed—God's Word.

Expect disappointments—and amazing successes. Three out of four soils in the parable produced nothing but rejection, false hope, and disappointment.

Many people rejected Jesus' message about the faith it takes to become a citizen of God's Kingdom. Jesus knew this would happen, and he gave his followers a strategy for dealing with this discouraging reality: "If any place refuses to welcome you or listen to you, shake its dust from your feet as you leave to show that you have abandoned those people to their fate" (Mark 6:11).

Failure, however, isn't the final word. A prophet 700 years before Jesus said as much in a similar metaphor comparing God's Word to seed: "The rain and snow... cause the grain to grow, producing seed for the farmer and bread for the hungry. It is the same with my word. I send it out, and it always produces fruit. It will accomplish all I want it to, and it will prosper everywhere I send it" (Isaiah 55:10–11).

Though three out of four soils disappoint, one soil more than compensates—producing an astonishing harvest beyond anyone's wildest dreams.

The only seeds that count are the ones that grow. In some "once-saved, always-saved" theological circles, two of the soils represent people who could make it into God's Kingdom. The rocky soil and the thorny circle symbolize people who accept Jesus' message, but who later allow hard times to silence the message. Yet many Christians would insist that these people are spiritually safe and secure forever because they accepted Jesus.

This particular parable, however, seems to add support to Christians who argue otherwise—that people have the freedom of choice to discard their faith.

In this parable, the first three soils represent people who bring nothing to God's harvest. They are useless to God's Kingdom. The only people who contribute anything to the harvest are those with crops alive and growing in the farmer's field. These are people who choose to become disciples of Jesus and who choose to remain disciples of Jesus.

Granted, there are Bible passages that seem to support Christians on both sides of this debate.

Eternal security: "My sheep listen to my voice; I know them, and they follow me. I give them eternal life, and they will never perish. No one can snatch them away from me" (John 10:27–28).

Freedom to discard the faith: "Many will turn away from me.... But the one who endures to the end will be saved" (Matthew 24:10, 13).

However, if the parable of the farmer contains one central grain of truth, many scholars insist it is this: Our salvation depends on living a life of fruitful obedience to God.

A Christian book thought to have been written a few decades after Jesus agrees. And it does so in the form of a farming analogy much like Jesus' parable: "The farmer sows many seeds and seedlings in the ground, but not all that have been sown will grow, and not all that were planted will take root. Likewise, those souls that have been sown in the world will not all be saved" (2 Esdras 8:41).

Yet the task of Jesus' followers throughout the ages has been to plant the seeds of the Gospel message everywhere they can.

PARABLE OF THE GOOD SAMARITAN

"There was once a man traveling from Jerusalem to Jericho.
On the way he was attacked by robbers. . . . A Samaritan
traveling the road came on him. When he saw the man's condition,
his heart went out to him. He gave him first aid."
LUKE 10:30, 33–34 THE MESSAGE

Luke was the only writer in the Bible who thought this parable—perhaps Jesus' most famous of all—was a story worth telling.

There are probably a couple of reasons the parable caught Luke's eye—assuming he wrote the anonymous Gospel that early church leaders named after him because they insisted he was the author.

Luke was a physician. The Good Samaritan did a doctor's duty, treating a patient.

Luke was an outsider. He was a Gentile in the Christian religious movement started by Jews. Samaritans were outsiders in their own country, surrounded by Jews who hated them for their race and their religion—calling the Samaritans half-breeds and heretics.

Jews in the parable act with disdain in spite of their divine mandate: "Love your neighbor as yourself" (Leviticus 19:18). Jews didn't think the Samaritans on their doorstep qualified as neighbors. Consider the following Samaritan bashing from Jewish Bible scholars a century or two before Jesus' ministry began.

Two nations I hate, and the third isn't even worthy of being called a
nation:
* ***those who live on Mount Seir*** *[ancient Edom, part of modern*
  Jordan];
* ***the Philistines*** *[central coast, including the modern Palestinian*
  Gaza Strip]; and
* ***the fools who live in Shechem*** *[also known as Sychar, main city*
  of the Samaritans].
                              SIRACH 50:25–26, ABOUT 200 BC

Those who eat the food of Samaritans are like those who eat pig [Jewish
law prohibits eating pork].
                              SHEVI'IT 8:10,
PASSED ON ORALLY BEFORE BEING WRITTEN ABOUT AD 200

If you do good, know who you're helping. . . . Help God's people, but don't help a sinner. . . . God hates sinners.

SIRACH 12:1, 4, 6

Everyone who wants to join the congregation of the chosen must pledge to live according to the rule of the community. . . . To love all the children of light and to hate all the children of darkness.

DEAD SEA SCROLL *MANUAL OF DISCIPLINE*
FOR JEWS IN THE DESERT COMMUNITY OF QUMRAN,
1QS 1:15, WRITTEN ABOUT 100 BC

Jews had about as much love for Samaritans as many Israelis today have for the Palestinians. And the idea of a Samaritan helping a fallen Jew made about as much sense as a suicide bomber ripping off his explosive jacket so he could administer CPR to an Israeli who had collapsed in a Tel Aviv café.

Jesus had a radical point to make; at least it was radical as far as most Jews were concerned: Neighborliness knows no bounds. Not geographical, racial, or spiritual. So Jesus crafted a parable about a man who obeyed one of God's greatest laws, but who came from a noncountry, a hated race, and a warped religion.

BAD BOYS OF THE BADLANDS

A question sparked the parable. It came from a biblical scholar, an expert in Jewish law.

"Teacher," the scholar asked, "what should I do to inherit eternal life?" (Luke 10:25).

"What does the law of Moses say?" Jesus replied.

The scholar quoted a pair of laws that, when linked together, were known in Jewish circles as "the greatest law."

" 'You must love the LORD your God with all your heart, all your soul, all your strength, and all your mind.' And, 'Love your neighbor as yourself.' "

Part one of this greatest law—"love the Lord"—comes from Deuteronomy 6:5, an excerpt of a prayer the Jews recited each day. Part two—"love your neighbor"—comes from Leviticus 19:18.

When Jesus told the scholar he had answered correctly, the man asked a follow-up question: "Who is my neighbor?"

Conventional Jewish wisdom would have answered, "Your fellow Jews, and anyone else who worships the only true God."

But Jesus was unconventional.

Intending to radically broaden the definition of "neighbor," Jesus created a word picture—a story that the scholar could see in his mind's eye.

The setting was the 17-mile upward walk from Jericho to Jerusalem—a more than half-mile ascent from the Jordan River Valley 800 feet (244 meters) below sea level to Jerusalem in the Judean hills 2,500 feet (762 meters) above sea level.

This was a well-traveled but dangerous stretch of badlands that looks a bit like a rock family reunion of Mars, the Grand Canyon's little brother, and the South Dakota Badlands. Travelers would make their way along hillside trails, ravines, and dry riverbeds called wadis (WAH-dees). It was best to travel in groups because bandits would sometimes hole up in caves that honeycombed the area and wait for an easy mark to show up.

In Jesus' parable, an easy mark did show, a Jewish man headed down to Jericho. Bandits beat him, robbed him of everything including his clothes, and then left him for dead.

READING BETWEEN THE LINES

For the first 1,900 years of Christianity, most Bible experts taught that the main truth behind the parable of the Good Samaritan had nothing to do with being neighborly and compassionate.

Instead, they said the story was an allegory loaded with code words that reveal a deeper meaning: tracing the fall and salvation of humanity.

Scholars interpreted the code words in various ways. But many early Christian scholars offered the following code key:

- **Jewish man assaulted by bandits on a trip from Jerusalem to Jericho.** The man represents Adam and all of fallen humanity. Adam means "humanity."
- **Jerusalem.** Garden of Eden. Because the traveler was on a downhill trip to Jericho, the journey represented Adam's descent from the Garden of Eden into the sin-contaminated world.
- **Jericho.** The sinful world.
- **Bandits.** Hostile powers, such as Satan and his demons, along with false teachers.
- **Clothes stripped away.** Humanity's loss of the "robe of obedience."
- **Victim's wounds.** Disobedience.
- **Victim is left "half dead."** Humanity's disobedience requires the death penalty.
- **Jewish priest and Temple assistant.** The Jewish law, unable to save humanity.
- **Samaritan.** Jesus, humanity's Savior.
- **Bandages.** The teachings of Jesus.
- **Donkey that carried the injured man.** The body of Jesus that bore the brunt of humanity's sin, as prophesied: "It was our pains he carried— our disfigurements, all the things wrong with us" (Isaiah 53:4 THE MESSAGE).
- **Innkeeper.** Leader of the church.
- **The inn.** The church, which welcomes everyone.
- **The promised return of the Samaritan.** The Second Coming of Jesus.

BAD BOYS OF THE TEMPLE

Two Jewish religious leaders came upon the injured man—first a priest and later a Temple assistant, someone who helped maintain the Jerusalem worship center.

Surprisingly, the two marched right past their "neighbor" like they were power walking with downtown rush-hour crowds past homeless strangers lying on the sidewalk.

As the scholar listened to this parable, he might have wondered why these godly men ignored such a great commandment. Perhaps two possibilities came to mind:

- The holy men feared the bandits might still be nearby, so they hurried off; or
- the holy men didn't want to get spiritually defiled by touching a corpse.

It took a week to cleanse such ritual defilement: "All those who touch a dead human body will be ceremonially unclean for seven days. They must purify themselves on the third and seventh days with the water of purification; then they will be purified" (Numbers 19:11–12).

During the week of cleansing, Temple personnel wouldn't have been able to worship in the Temple. But in the case of the priest, that didn't seem much of a problem. He was likely headed out of Jerusalem. The original language specifies the direction: "down." As far as the Jews were concerned, every direction away from Jerusalem was "down," because the city sits on the crest of a ridge in the Judean hills. That's why the Jews would say they were going "up" to Jerusalem, whether they were coming from the north, south, east, or west.

Aside from the defilement problem, the scholar listening to Jesus' parable may have known about a debated loophole in that law. Eliezer, a respected rabbi who lived in Jesus' century, argued that even a high priest who came upon an unattended body "should defile himself" and bury the corpse (*Nazir* 7:1). How much more, Eliezer probably would have argued, should a regular priest or a priest's assistant have been willing to bury the body.

UNLIKELY HERO FROM THE HEARTLAND

The Jews and Samaritans had hated each other for about 400 years by the time Jesus crafted this parable.

Both groups worshipped God, revered the laws of Moses, and considered themselves God's chosen people descended from Abraham.

Samaritans presented themselves as survivors of the lost northern tribes of Israel, a nation wiped off the political map in 722 BC by Assyrian invaders from what is now Iraq. Samaritans lived in the heart of the land of Israel, in Samaria, and worshipped at Mount Gerizim, where they said Abel had built humanity's first altar and where Abraham had offered to sacrifice Isaac. It was at this mountain that the Bible says Joshua, after conquering much of the Promised Land, gathered the Jews to renew their covenant with God.

The Jews presented themselves as the remnant of the southern tribe of Judah, the Israelite nation with the only legitimate king (descended from David) and the only legitimate worship center, a temple they said God ordered built in Jerusalem.

Jews treated Samaritans as

- an impure race of Israelite leftovers from the Assyrian war, who intermarried with Assyrian settlers; and
- religious heretics who revered only the books of Moses, which they had edited to fit their beliefs—especially their choice of Mount Gerizim as a worship center instead of Jerusalem.

The first known hostility between the two groups shows up in the book of Ezra. The Samaritans joined other groups in the region trying unsuccessfully to stop the Jews from rebuilding Jerusalem. Babylonian invaders from what is now Iraq had leveled the city in 586 BC, exiling the southland Jews from their homeland. A century later, the Jews were returning home and rebuilding—in spite of the unwelcome response of the Samaritans.

Three centuries after that, in 128 BC, the Jews invaded Samaria and destroyed the Samaritan temple on Mount Gerizim. Then, about 20 years later, the Jews finished the job, destroying the main Samaritan city, located at the base of the mountain: Shechem, known in Jesus' time as Sychar.

Hatred between the two groups continued into Roman times. In 63 BC, Romans ordered the Jews to stop persecuting the Samaritans. Then Herod the Great launched an extensive rebuilding program in Samaria, from 37 to 4 BC.

This support from Rome gave fresh boldness to the Samaritans, who began to harass the Jews. They defiled the Jerusalem Temple during Passover celebrations in AD 6–9, scattering bones in the courtyard. And in AD 52—about 20 years after Jesus' ministry—they slaughtered a group of Jewish pilgrims from Galilee at the Samaritan border town of En-Gannim (modern Janin).

Jews and Romans both retaliated, the Romans with such cruelty that Rome fired Pilate, the regional governor. Decades later, around AD 67, the Romans massacred 11,600 Samaritans on Mount Gerizim while crushing a Jewish revolt.

With such longstanding animosity between Samaritans and Jews, the scholar listening to Jesus' parable would have been jarred by the twist in the plot. A Samaritan not only stopped to help the injured Jew, but also nursed the man's wounds with wine (which disinfected) and oil (which softened and protected the skin, promoting healing). He took the man to an inn, stayed with him that night, and then gave the innkeeper two silver coins—enough to cover room and board for about two weeks. He also promised to pay more on his return visit if the tab ran higher.

"Now which of these three would you say was a neighbor to the man who was attacked by bandits?" Jesus asked the scholar.

"The one who showed him mercy."

"Yes," Jesus replied. "Now go and do the same."

Some Bible experts today wonder whether Jesus created this story out of the blue, or if he spun it around a teaching that any Jewish scholar would have known—a prophecy criticizing heartless priests and praising mercy over rigid obedience to rules: "Israel, what should I do with you? . . . I want faithful love more than I want animal sacrifices. . . . The priests are like robbers waiting to attack people; they murder people on the road to Shechem and do wicked things" (Hosea 6:4, 6, 9 NCV).

Either way, Jesus clearly made the point that anyone who is in need and within our reach of help is our neighbor. When in doubt about what to do, the parable implies, we should do the kind thing.

PARABLE OF THE LOST SON

"A man had two sons. The younger son told his father,
'I want my share of your estate now before you die.'
So his father agreed to divide his wealth. . . . A few days later
this younger son packed all his belongings and moved to a
distant land, and there he wasted all his money in wild living."
LUKE 15:11–13

Jesus kept bad company.

Like a light in the darkness attracting bugs, Jesus drew to himself the ugliest of humanity—spiritual lowlifes, prostitutes, the demon-possessed, and Jewish tax collectors who collaborated with Roman occupiers by bidding for the right to impose taxes on their own neighbors.

Top Jewish priests and scholars didn't approve. As far as they were concerned, a rabbi was known by the company he kept. Good rabbis kept good company.

At first thought, it's easy to understand their pious criticism: "This man is friendly with sinners. He even eats with them" (Luke 15:2 CEV).

After all, don't we advise our families and friends to avoid trashy people, arguing that it's easier for lowlifes to drag us down than it is for us to pull them up?

And wouldn't it be a rare church that would tolerate its pastor drafting Sunday's sermon at a table in the local bar, in an effort to stay focused on the church's target audience? And if that pastor accepted an invitation to eat a meal with the community's harem of friendly prostitutes or exotic dancers, wouldn't that be considered something other than a smart career move?

The top Jewish scholars were right. We can know a rabbi by the company he keeps. Jesus' audience revealed a lot about him and his mission. He had come to defy gravity—to lift up the spiritual bottom dwellers. And to help his critics understand why he was risking his reputation to do this, he told three short parables:

The Lost Sheep. A shepherd with a flock of 100 sheep went searching for the one that turned up missing. Then he celebrated when he found the lost sheep.

The Lost Coin. A woman with 10 silver coins lost one and then hunted frantically for it. When she found it, she threw a party.

The Lost Son. A young man cashed in his family inheritance and left home to squander it. When he came home, bankrupt, his father was so happy to see him alive and safe that he threw a party.

Jesus had come to find the lost sheep, the lost treasure, the lost son—all of which biblical scholars say are symbols of lost souls. Instead of criticizing Jesus for this, the religious leaders should have thrown him a party.

LEAVING THE NEST, LOADED

It's a bizarre story. The very idea of a son asking for his inheritance before his father had died. That was as insensitive in Bible times as it would be today.

It's like saying, "Dad, don't take this personally, but from a cash flow point of view, I wish you were dead. Could I please have my inheritance now so I don't have to go on living with such terrible thoughts?"

The Jews had laws about how to dish out the inheritance. Some show up in the Jewish Bible, which Christians know as the Old Testament. And some show up in the teachings of rabbis—either written before Jesus' time or passed along by word of mouth and finally recorded by about AD 200 in a collection of sacred laws called the Mishnah.

According to scripture, the younger son in the parable would have inherited a third of his father's holdings. The oldest son would have gotten a double share (Deuteronomy 21:17). And he would have been put in charge of the extended family, or clan.

But none of this would have happened until the father died or became incapacitated.

Consider Jewish financial advice popular in Jesus' day:

> As long as you live, don't give anyone power over you—not your son, wife, brother, or friend. Don't give anyone your property. . . . It's better that your children have to come to you for help than for you to go to them. . . . When you come to the end of your life, and you know that death is near, go ahead and distribute your inheritance.
>
> SIRACH 33:20, 22, 24, ABOUT 200 BC

> If a father deeds his property to go to his son after the father dies, then the father can't sell it since it's deeded to the son, and the son can't sell it since it's still in the possession of the father.
>
> MISHNAH, BAVA BATRA 8:7

Though the rabbis typically advised fathers not to distribute their holdings until death came knocking at the door, they at least allowed a man to divide his holdings ahead of time—as long as the sons didn't take possession of the property until the father died. In the meantime, the property belonged to joint tenants: father and son.

In such a case, "if the father sells his property," the Mishnah says, "it is sold only until he dies [and then it reverts back to the son]. If the son sells the property, the buyer has no claim until the father dies."

As far as the rabbi scholars in Jesus' audience were concerned, this parable started out with a double-barreled shocker: The son asked for his inheritance, and the father gave it to him.

Somehow, the son turned his property into cash. Jesus' audience may have figured that the son allowed his father to buy him out, giving him cash while keeping the property in the family.

THE WILD SPREE

"This younger son packed all his belongings and moved to a distant land, and there he wasted all his money in wild living" (Luke 15:13). Life on the wild side included "prostitutes" (Luke 15:30). And probably lots of wine and food.

Wasteful spending is how the story got its traditional name, the parable of the Prodigal Son. *Prodigal* means "lavishly wasteful."

At this point in the story, some scholars in Jesus' audience may have associated the wild son with Jesus himself, whom they had criticized earlier as "a glutton and a drunkard" (Luke 7:34), and who was known to have associated with at least one woman "who had lived a sinful life" (Luke 7:37 NIV).

Money gone, the prodigal suddenly found himself without friends and in the middle of a drought that had scorched the land and dried up the job market. The only work he could find was tending hogs—livestock that the Jews considered ritually unclean: "Don't eat pork. . . . Don't even touch a dead pig!" (Deuteronomy 14:8 CEV).

Rabbis hated the idea of a Jewish pig farmer: "Cursed is the man who raises pigs" (Talmud, *Baba Kamma* 82b). But the starving young Jew had little choice. In time, his stomach began growling for the seed pods he fed the pigs. These were probably dried carobs (*Ceratonia siliqua*), which look a bit like pea pods on steroids. Grown throughout the Middle East, they provided fodder for livestock and nourishment for the desperately poor.

Writing a few centuries after the time of Jesus, one rabbi historian said, "When the Israelites are reduced to carob pods, then they repent" (Rabbi Acha, about AD 320).

That's exactly what happened to the prodigal: "He said to himself, 'At home even the hired servants have food enough to spare, and here I am dying of hunger! I will go home to my father and say, "Father, I have sinned against both heaven and you, and I am no longer worthy of being called your son. Please take me on as a hired servant" ' " (Luke 15:17–19).

CARATS GROWING ON TREES

Beans inside the pods hanging from carob trees—pods that the starving prodigal was tempted to eat—are so consistent in size that the Greeks used them to measure gems. The English word *carat* comes from the Greek word for carob: *keration*. The weight of a carat is 0.2 grams, a tenth of a dime.

THE WELCOME HOME

What follows is the most touching line of the story. "While he was still a long way off, his father saw him coming" (Luke 15:20).

It's as if the father—every day, all day—kept an eye on the road, waiting, hoping, and praying to see his lost boy crest the horizon.

No "Shame on you!"

No "I told you so!"

No "What'd you do with all the money that I spent my life working for?"

The father "ran to his son, embraced him, and kissed him" (Luke 15:20).

Suddenly, in the midst of a drought, the father was swimming in joy.

He cloaked his son in a robe and dressed him in sandals, perhaps as symbols of the young man's restored authority as a full member of the family instead of as a servant. The young man got a ring, too—perhaps a signet ring engraved with the family seal, which would allow him to sign contracts in his father's name.

The boy had partied away his inheritance. But now it was time for his father to show him what a real party was like, with family and friends who would always be there for him. Of course, every party needs a party pooper, and this one was no exception: the prodigal's big brother.

Walking back from a hard day's work in the fields, he heard the music, saw the dancing, and smelled the beef on the barbie. When he learned that the party was for his little brother, he couldn't believe it. Livid, he refused to join the celebration—even after his father begged him.

"All these years I've slaved for you," the older son complained. "And in all that time you never gave me even one young goat for a feast with my friends" (Luke 15:29).

That seems like a valid complaint. The father was honoring the dishonorable, though he had never bothered to honor the honorable. It was as if the father were rewarding sin.

Yet it was nothing of the kind. The older son would enjoy a wonderful reward for his years of devotion.

"Look, dear son," his father said. "Everything I have is yours. We had to celebrate this happy day. For your brother was dead and has come back to life! He was lost, but now he is found!" (Luke 15:31–32).

THE POINT

Most Bible experts today agree that this parable, reported only in the Gospel of Luke, contains more symbolism than most. Each main character seems to represent someone.

The lost son represents the tax collectors, prostitutes, and other sinners Jesus was teaching, trying to point them home, to God.

The father is God, eagerly waiting for his lost children to find their way home.

The older brother is the scholarly audience, the Pharisees and teachers of the Jewish law. They treated the returning lost sons and daughters with contempt, as if those once-lost souls were unwelcome in the eternal home God had built for them.

Because of the symbolism attached to these three characters, Bible experts today debate which character has the starring role, and whether the parable should be called

- the parable of the lost son;
- the parable of the loving father; or
- the parable of the resentful brother.

The title probably wouldn't matter to Jesus, as long as people get the message. He told the parable to defend his right to minister among the spiritually sick. He had explained earlier to his scholarly critics, "Healthy people don't need a doctor—sick people do. I have come to call not those who think they are righteous, but those who know they are sinners and need to repent" (Luke 5:31–32).

Yet most Jewish intellectuals remained unconvinced that healed souls and the return of long-lost sons and daughters were momentous events worth celebrating.

KOSHER On the Jewish Menu	NON-KOSHER Off the Jewish Menu
WATER ANIMALS	
Fish with scales and fins: salmon, bass, tuna, grouper, flounder, halibut, perch	**Fish without scales and fins:** catfish, octopus, sturgeon, dolphin, shark **Shellfish:** lobster, shrimp, crab, oyster, clam
LAND ANIMALS	
Animals with split hooves and that chew the cud*: cattle, oxen, sheep, goat, deer, gazelle, antelope, giraffe	**All other mammals:** pig, camel, rabbit, horse, donkey, lion, dog, rat, monkey, hippopotamus, elephant, bat
FLYING ANIMALS, FOWL	
Most birds: chicken, turkey, duck, goose, quail, pheasant, partridge, dove, pigeon, grouse	**Scavenger birds and birds of prey:** vulture, buzzard, eagle, hawk, falcon, owl, stork, seagull
INSECTS, REPTILES, AMPHIBIANS	
Winged insects that walk on the ground and can jump: grasshopper, locust, cricket	**Winged insects that walk on the ground but don't jump:** ant, beetle, butterfly **All reptiles:** snake, crocodile, lizard **All amphibians:** frog, toad, salamander

PARABLE OF THE SHEEP AND GOATS

*"When the Son of Man comes in his glory...
all the nations will be gathered in his presence,
and he will separate the people as a shepherd
separates the sheep from the goats."*
MATTHEW 25:31–32

It's Judgment Day in one of the last parables Jesus told. In two or three days, he would be hanging from a cross.

His disciples knew his death was imminent; he had told them so. And they had tried talking him out of going to Jerusalem, where he said he would die. But he went anyway. His disciples followed at the urging of Thomas: "Let's go, too—and die with Jesus" (John 11:16).

In Jerusalem, Jesus debated the Jewish scholars and preached to crowds at the Temple. Then he retreated down Jerusalem's eastern hillside, descending into the narrow Kidron Valley before climbing up the ridge of hills called the Mount of Olives. There, overlooking the city, he sat down.

Jesus had been talking about the decimation of Jerusalem, which prompted his 12 disciples to ask when this would happen and when Jesus would come back after his death. "What sign will signal your return and the end of the world?" (Matthew 24:3).

As usual, Jesus' response included parables—five of them this time. Four of the parables urged people to stay prepared for Jesus' return

- like a homeowner expecting a thief in the night;
- like a faithful servant taking good care of the estate while the owner is away;
- like bridesmaids loaded with plenty of lamp oil as they wait for the groom; and
- like servants wisely investing the money their master has entrusted to them.

The fifth parable, preserved in Matthew 25:31–46, isn't about being prepared. It's about what will happen to those who are prepared and those who aren't.

CODED PARABLE

Most of Jesus' parables have at least a touch of symbolism. The parable of the sheep and the goats has more than its fair share.

Jesus says the Son of Man will return in glory, accompanied by angels. All nations will assemble before him for judgment, and he will separate the godly people from the ungodly as easily as a shepherd separates sheep and goats. Godly people are those who show compassion for the needy. Their reward: eternal life. Ungodly people ignore the needy. Their sentence: eternal punishment.

Son of Man. This was Jesus' favorite way of referring to himself. The history of this title suggests that Jesus used it because it pointed both to his humanity and his divinity.

Humanity: About 600 years earlier, God used this title for the prophet Ezekiel—as a way of reminding the prophet that he was only human.

Divinity: For the prophet Daniel, the title seemed to point to the Second Coming of Jesus. Daniel had a vision he described this way: "I saw someone like a son of man coming with the clouds of heaven. . . . He was given authority, honor, and sovereignty over all the nations of the world, so that people of every race and nation and language would obey him. His rule is eternal—it will never end. His kingdom will never be destroyed" (Daniel 7:13–14).

In his last known parable, Jesus promised to return in glory as a king who would judge the nations. (For more about Son of Man, see "Christ: Not Jesus' Favorite Title," page 285.)

All the nations. In ancient Jewish writing, this phrase often refers to the nations outside Israel—the Gentiles. But in this case, most Bible experts say that Jesus probably intended for his disciples to picture all the people of the world—Jews and Gentiles, past and present.

Raising the dead for Judgment Day was a common Jewish teaching before and after Jesus' ministry: "Then the Most High will say to the nations that have been raised from the dead, 'Look now, and understand whom you have denied, whom you have not served, whose commandments you have despised' " (2 Esdras 7:37 NRSV, probably written late in the first century AD).

Sheep. Throughout the Bible and in other revered Jewish writings, sheep symbolize God's people. The book of 1 Enoch—probably written about a century before the time of Jesus and referred to in Jude 1:14—describes God as "Lord of the sheep."

In a Judgment Day vision, the prophet says he saw the sheep "all white, and their wool was abundant and clean. . . . And the Lord of the sheep rejoiced with great joy because they were all good" (1 Enoch 90:32–33).

Goats. In this parable, goats symbolize godless people. Why Jesus chose goats as the bad guys is up for debate. Perhaps he had in mind the scapegoat the Jews killed on the annual Day of Atonement (also known as Yom Kippur). This goat was released into the wilderness, symbolically carrying away the sins of the nation.

Or maybe Jesus was working from a perspective of value, with sheep more valued than goats because of the coat of wool they produced each year. Perhaps, too, Jesus was working the shepherd angle, knowing that sheep are generally more obedient than goats.

Right hand, left hand. "He will place the sheep at his right hand and the goats at his left" (Matthew 25:33). Those on his right were rewarded with eternal life. Those on his left were punished.

A generation before Jesus, a poet named Virgil (70–19 BC) wrote the epic tale of Aeneas, the Trojan said to have founded Rome and proclaimed its divine mission to civilize the world. In this and other Greek writings, the road to the right led to the heavenly Elysian fields, while the road to the left led to Tartarus, the place of torment:

> *Night rushes down, and headlong drives the day:*
> *It is here, in different paths, the way divides;*
> *The right to Pluto's golden palace guides;*
> *The left to that unhappy region tends,*
> *Which to the depth of Tartarus descends;*
> *The seat of night profound, and punished fiends.*
>
> AENEID, BOOK 6, 540–43, AUTHOR'S PARAPHRASE

A Jewish story, probably written in Jesus' century, tells of Judgment Day, with an angel on the judge's right side writing the good deeds of people and an angel on the left recording the sins:

> *The wondrous man who sat on the throne judged and sentenced the souls. There were two angels beside him. The one on the right wrote down the righteousness and the one on the left the wickedness.*
>
> TESTAMENT OF ABRAHAM

My brothers and sisters. This phrase is the key to unlocking the parable. The phrase is a tag Jesus gave to needy people in his story:
- the hungry needing food;
- the thirsty needing a drink;
- the stranger needing hospitality;
- the naked needing clothes;
- the sick needing care; and
- the imprisoned needing visitors.

The king judging the nations said he took it personally when his subjects helped the needy. "I tell you the truth, when you did it to one of the least of these my brothers and sisters, you were doing it to me!" (Matthew 25:40). He said he also took it personally when people ignored the needy. "When you refused to help the least of these my brothers and sisters, you were refusing to help me" (Matthew 25:45).

But who are "my brothers and sisters"? Bible experts aren't sure.

There are several theories, but the most popular, for many Bible readers, would come as quite a surprise.

Needy Christians. Most Bible experts today say this is who Jesus had in mind. Jesus didn't call everyone his brothers and sisters. These are terms he reserved for his followers.

"Jesus asked, 'Who is my mother? Who are my brothers?' Then he pointed to his disciples and said, 'Look, these are my mother and brothers. Anyone who does the will of my Father in heaven is my brother and sister and mother!' " (Matthew 12:48–50).

All needy people. In a quick read, it might seem as if Jesus is talking about all needy people. Some Christian charities quote this passage as a mandate to help the poor.

Jesus certainly cared about the needy. They were his target audience: "The blind see, the lame walk, the lepers are cured, the deaf hear, the dead are raised to life, and the Good News is being preached to the poor" (Matthew 11:5).

The Old Testament writers continually urge God's people to help the needy, especially the most vulnerable: orphans, widows, and refugees.

The New Testament writers do the same: "Whenever we have the opportunity, we should do good to everyone—especially to those in the family of faith" (Galatians 6:10).

Kingdom. Godly people "inherit the Kingdom prepared for [them] from the creation of the world" (Matthew 25:34). Whatever or wherever this Kingdom is—and many Christians identify it as heaven—it's a place where "good people will go to live forever" (Matthew 25:46 NCV).

The fire that burns forever. Those who reject the Kingdom end up in a place "prepared for the devil and his demons." It's a place they go "into eternal punishment" (Matthew 25:41, 46).

The prophet Daniel, writing 500 years before Jesus' ministry, was the first Bible writer to reveal that people would have a choice between eternal reward and eternal punishment. He quoted a celestial being, a "man dressed in linen clothing," whose voice "roared like a vast multitude" (Daniel 10:5–6).

"Everyone whose name is written in God's book will be saved. Many people who have already died will live again. Some of them will wake up to have life forever, but some will wake up to find shame and disgrace forever. The wise people will shine like the brightness of the sky. Those who teach others to live right will shine like stars forever and ever" (Daniel 12:1–3 NCV).

Many Christians say this place of eternal torment is hell—where sinners literally burn forever.

Many Bible scholars, however, say that Christians shouldn't be so quick to interpret the Bible's descriptions of hell literally—for several reasons:

Hell *is a figurative word*. In the original language, the word is *Gehenna*. It's the name of a valley on Jerusalem's south side. This is where Jews once sacrificed humans to idols—a sin that reaped the whirlwind of God's judgment when invaders wiped Israel off the political map. Afterward, *Gehenna* developed into a symbol of judgment, much like the date 9/11 has come to symbolize terrorism.

Eternal torture serves no redemptive value. When God punishes people in the Bible, it is a corrective—to help them or to make them an example that will steer others away from danger.

Fire destroys. Perhaps it's the destruction of sinners—not the suffering—that will last forever.

"They will go away." Maybe the eternal punishment of sinners is God granting them their wish. In life, they had wanted nothing to do with him. And in everlasting life, they get what they wanted: eternal separation from God.

GENEROUS JEWS

God urged the Jews to help people in need. The Jewish Bible is full of the evidence: laws, proverbs, and pleas from the prophets.

Law. "When you harvest the grapes in your vineyard, don't pick the vines a second time. Leave what is left for foreigners, orphans, and widows. Remember that you were slaves in Egypt; that is why I am commanding you to do this" (Deuteronomy 24:21–22 NCV).

Proverb. "Whoever gives to the poor will lack nothing, but those who close their eyes to poverty will be cursed" (Proverbs 28:27).

Prophet. "For the many crimes of Israel, I will punish them. . . . They walk on poor people as if they were dirt" (Amos 2:6–7 NCV).

SAVED BY GOOD DEEDS?

Is helping needy people the way to make it into heaven?

Some people read this parable that way.

If they're right, maybe the apostle Paul got salvation wrong: "God saved you by his grace when you believed. And you can't take credit for this; it is a gift from God. Salvation is not a reward for the good things we have done" (Ephesians 2:8–9).

And maybe James—who early church leaders said was Jesus' brother—got it right: "Faith by itself isn't enough. Unless it produces good deeds, it is dead and useless" (James 2:17).

Most Bible experts today say that the words of Jesus, Paul, and James don't clash.

The scholars say that our eternal destiny isn't determined by our portfolio of good works. Instead, they say, our nature as Christians will determine our lifestyle. Christians, by nature, help people in need—whether the needy are sinners or saints.

A ROMAN SOLDIER ASKS JESUS FOR HELP

When Jesus returned to Capernaum,
a Roman officer came and pleaded with him,
"Lord, my young servant lies in bed,
paralyzed and in terrible pain."
MATTHEW 8:5–6

For a rabbi who would later tell his followers to "go and make disciples of all the nations" (Matthew 28:19), Jesus seemed stuck in the mud of Jewish Galilee.

Most of his miracles and teachings took place on this county-sized plug of turf—among the Jews. What little contact he had with non-Jews sometimes seemed like an intrusion. They'd interrupt his work among the Jews by hunting him down and asking for favors.

On occasion, it seemed as if Jesus couldn't have cared less about the Gentiles. When he was traveling in what is now southern Lebanon, a Gentile woman pleaded with him to heal her demon-possessed daughter.

Jesus gave her the silent treatment: "not even a word" (Matthew 15:23).

She kept begging, nagging, pestering—until Jesus' disciples, fed up with it, asked him to send her away. Only then did Jesus say anything to her—and what he said sounds a lot like, "Get lost!" Not a great thing for a good shepherd to say to a sheep.

"I was sent only to help God's lost sheep," Jesus told her, "the people of Israel."

"Lord, help me!"

"It isn't right to take food from the children and throw it to the dogs," replied Jesus, famed for his compassion.

"That's true, Lord," the woman answered, "but even dogs are allowed to eat the scraps that fall beneath their master's table."

"Dear woman," Jesus said, finally allowing his true feelings to flow, "your faith is great. Your request is granted."

Why Jesus pushed this desperate woman so far is anyone's guess. Perhaps he wanted to show his disciples how far her faith was willing to go.

Before Jesus met this woman, he had already met another Gentile who had hunted him down and asked for a favor. The Gentile was a Roman soldier. If that soldier was any indication, Jesus already knew by the time he met the woman how far a Gentile's faith could go. He knew it could outlast the faith of any Jew he had ever met.

AN ARMY OF ROMAN PEACEKEEPERS

"Roman peace," as the Rome-based empire called its occupation of other countries, was enforced in Jesus' day by an army scattered throughout the empire.

Tacitus, the first-century Roman historian, reported that no legions were stationed in what is now Israel. Though Rome posted small units throughout Israel, the closest full legions were in neighboring Syria and Egypt. Tacitus placed the empire's 25 legions as follows:

   8: France and Germany, along the Rhine River
   6: Germany, along the Danube River
   4: Syria
   3: Spain
   2: Egypt
   2: Africa

The entire Roman army was made up of about 150,000 soldiers organized into 25 legions, with each legion divided into cohorts, which were divided into centuria.

   Legion: 6,000 soldiers (10 cohorts)
   Cohort: 600 soldiers (6 centuria)
   Centuria: 100 soldiers

These numbers suggest that the centurion who approached Jesus was one of 1,500 centurions, each of whom commanded about 100 soldiers. Numbers varied from time to time, with centurions sometimes commanding only about 80 men. Soldiers served 20 years before retiring.

THE SOLDIER BEHIND THE REQUEST

By Jewish standards, both the woman and the soldier who came to Jesus were outsiders. They weren't among God's Chosen People. They were among God's Not Chosen People.

But the lines of Chosen and Not Chosen began to blur the day Jesus finished his Sermon on the Mount and headed back to his ministry headquarters in Capernaum.

Along the way, the Roman officer met him and told him about his sick servant. Luke's version of the story says the officer "sent some respected Jewish elders to ask him to come and heal his slave" (Luke 7:3). Perhaps both versions are correct, with the soldier sending the elders ahead of him.

Read together, the two versions throw some light on this soldier.

He was compassionate. He went out of his way to help his servant, going so far as to humble himself before Rabbi Jesus, asking a favor when soldiers more often barked out orders that people had to obey or die trying.

The soldier's "young servant" was lying in bed, "paralyzed and in terrible pain" (Matthew 8:6). Some speculate the boy had polio, a contagious viral infection that can produce these symptoms and that was common in Jesus' day. But the boy could have been suffering from any number of problems, including nerves damaged by injury or disease.

He was a motivated soldier. The Greek language identifies the soldier as a centurion, commander of 100 men. Centurions typically started out at the bottom of the army, as legionnaires recruited from the lower ranks of society.

Upper-class Romans, on the other hand, usually advanced directly to the rank above centurion: tribune, commander of a cohort, 600 men and their six centurions.

He was relatively rich. A centurion's pay was at least 15 times more than the soldiers he commanded—60 times more in some cases.

Legionnaires at the time drew a meager 225 denarii a year. That was less than the going rate for a common laborer, who earned a denarius a day—or more than 300 denarii a year, with time off for the Sabbath and other special days. For a centurion, the pay ranged from a low of 3,750 denarii to a high of 15,000.

He was a friend to the Jews. "He loves the Jewish people and even built a synagogue for us," the Jewish elders told Jesus (Luke 7:5).

That could suggest the soldier was a "God-fearer," at least a partial convert to the Jewish faith. Many Gentiles worshipped God but stopped short of observing the two most extreme Jewish laws: circumcision and eating only kosher food. On the other hand, the soldier may have been no more than a benefactor, who respected the Jewish religion but didn't worship with the Jews.

Archaeological evidence supports two parts of this story. There's new evidence of a Roman outpost at Capernaum, including houses with Roman-style baths. Though Rome didn't station any of its 6,000-man legions in Israel, it did

---

HEALING FROM A DISTANCE

Jesus wasn't the only first-century Galilean rabbi on record to promise healing from a distance:

> Once, the son of Rabbi Gamaliel became sick with a fever. He sent two scholars to Rabbi Hanina ben Dosa to ask him to pray for the boy.
>
> Rabbi Hanina went to an upper room and prayed. When he came down he told the scholars, "Go, the fever has left him."
>
> "Are you a prophet?" they asked.
>
> "I am neither a prophet nor the son of a prophet," the rabbi answered. "But I have been blessed in this way. If my prayer flows fluently from my lips, I know that God has accepted my request. But if my prayer falters, then I know that he has rejected my request."
>
> The scholars made note of the time. When they returned to Gamaliel and reported Hanina's words and the time he spoke them, Gamaliel answered, "By heaven! That's exactly what happened. At that very moment the fever left my son and he asked for a drink of water."
>
> MISHNAH, BERAKOTH 34B

The difference between Rabbi Hanina and Rabbi Jesus is that Hanina prayed for healing, but Jesus did the healing himself.

scatter units throughout the land. Some were stationed in Jerusalem, at a garrison overlooking the Temple. Others were stationed in Rome's regional headquarters, the seaport city of Caesarea. And it would have made sense to station some at Capernaum, a border town and customs stop along an international trade route.

There are also ruins of a Capernaum synagogue, which archaeologists have partly restored. Though this synagogue dates to about 300 years after Jesus, it sits on what archaeologists say was probably the same black stone foundation used for the synagogue in Jesus' day.

He understood Jewish sensitivities about non-Jews. When Jesus offered to go to the soldier's house and heal the servant, the soldier politely declined. He apparently knew that many Jews considered the houses of non-Jews to be ritually unclean.

So if a rabbi or any other Jew went inside, they would have to undergo cleaning rituals—including a bath—before they could worship God again.

Though the Jewish Bible says no such thing, early Jewish scholars made what they considered a logical leap of faith after reading passages such as Ezra's call for Jews to give up "the unclean ways of their non-Jewish neighbors in order to worship the LORD, the God of Israel" (Ezra 6:21 NCV).

One Jewish scholar from Roman times put it this way: "The homes of Gentiles are unclean" (Mishnah, *Ohalot* 18.7).

He had incredible faith in Jesus' ability to heal. Anti-Gentile teachings in mind, the soldier offered an incredible alternative: "Lord, I am not worthy to have you come into my home. Just say the word from where you are, and my servant will be healed. I know this because I am under the authority of my superior officers, and I have authority over my soldiers. I only need to say, 'Go,' and they go, or 'Come,' and they come. And if I say to my slaves, 'Do this,' they do it" (Matthew 8:8–9).

MIRACLE MILE

Jesus was on his way home to Capernaum when he met the Roman soldier. Jesus had just finished the Sermon on the Mount. If ancient tradition is right, the sermon took place on a hillside now called Mount of the Beatitudes, about a mile (1.6 km) west of Capernaum.

Jewish leaders from Capernaum credit the soldier with building their synagogue, the foundation of which probably lies beneath the ruins of a synagogue built about three centuries later.

New archaeological evidence—Roman-style homes—substantiates the Bible's claim that Rome had stationed soldiers at Capernaum, a border town and customs stop along an international trade route.

JESUS REACTS

Turning to the people around him—Jews mostly, if not exclusively—Jesus said, "I tell you the truth, I haven't seen faith like this in all Israel!" (Matthew 8:10).

In the fuller quote, which Luke skips, Jesus adds, "Many Gentiles will come from all over the world—from east and west—and sit down with Abraham, Isaac, and Jacob at the feast in the Kingdom of Heaven" (Matthew 8:11).

The prophet Isaiah had said as much 700 years earlier:

- "In Jerusalem, the LORD of Heaven's Armies will spread a wonderful feast for all the people of the world" (Isaiah 25:6).
- "You are my servant. . . . You will do more than restore the people of Israel to me. I will make you a light to the Gentiles, and you will bring my salvation to the ends of the earth" (Isaiah 49:3, 6).
- "Don't let foreigners who commit themselves to the LORD say, 'The LORD will never let me be part of his people.' . . . "I will bring others, too, besides my people Israel" (Isaiah 56:3, 8).

Jesus was confirming Old Testament predictions that Gentiles would one day worship God and join his Kingdom. But Jesus added that many Jews, on the other hand, wouldn't make the cut.

That would have come as a shock to many in the crowd—the very idea that God would choose the Not Chosen over the Chosen.

There's a trace of wordplay in the way Jesus phrased his message. Many Jewish writers trash-talked their Roman occupiers, calling them nasty names, including "sons of darkness," in contrast to the Jewish people, called "sons of light."

Jesus essentially said that many sons of the kingdom of light would become sons of the kingdom of darkness: "The sons of the kingdom will be cast out into outer darkness. There will be weeping and gnashing of teeth" (Matthew 8:12 NKJV).

From that day on—a day marked by the faith of a lone Gentile soldier—the beginning of the end had come for the Age of the Chosen. With the Messiah's arrival, as prophets had predicted, all who chose God would be chosen by God.

Jesus healed the soldier's servant that very hour.

JESUS STOPS A STORM

Suddenly a windstorm struck the lake.
Waves started splashing into the boat, and it was about to sink. . . .
Jesus got up and ordered the wind and the waves to be quiet.
The wind stopped, and everything was calm.
MARK 4:37, 39 CEV

Keeping it short and sweet, Matthew, Mark, and Luke each report the miracle of Jesus calming a storm on the Sea of Galilee—condensing it to a snippet of a story we can read in 30 seconds.

Why so short?

For the first time in history, someone shows up who's able to do more than talk about the weather. And he gets a 30-second spot. About half a dozen verses.

Yet when we see how the disciples reacted, the snippet makes sense.

They didn't say a word to Jesus.

After all, what do you say to a man who talks to the wind? Probably nothing, until you get over the shock that the wind is listening.

STORM CHASING

None of the Gospels says exactly where Jesus and the disciples set sail on the freshwater lake, or what town they were headed for. All three say the men were sailing toward the region of the Gerasenes, a plain on the lake's eastern shore. And they all report that the boat crossed the lake "to the other side."

The first-century Jewish historian Josephus said the Jews divided the Sea of Galilee with an imaginary line, starting where the Jordan River enters the lake at the north and ending where the Jordan exits in the south. That line separated one side of the lake from "the other side."

Capernaum, Jesus' ministry headquarters, lies on the opposite side of the lake from the Gerasenes. And in Matthew's account, the fishing village of Capernaum was Jesus' last reported location. Mark places Jesus somewhere by the lakeshore, telling parables. Luke also reports that Jesus was teaching parables to a large crowd that had gathered.

Exhausted from the day's work, presumably in the vicinity of Capernaum, Jesus said to his disciples, "Let's cross to the other side of the lake" (Mark 4:35). Once on board, Jesus quickly fell asleep "at the back of the boat with his head on a cushion."

Some historians say the cushion is a hint that this wasn't a typical fishing boat, because fishermen didn't take cushions for napping on the job. Beside 13 men would have been crowded in a fishing boat.

During a drought in 1986 that shrunk the Sea of Galilee, archaeologists uncovered the remains of an ancient fishing boat buried in mud along the lake's northwestern shore. Dubbed "the Jesus boat," because it was carbon-dated to around Jesus' time and contained coins from AD 29 and 30, it would have seated about 10 men. It measured about 25 feet long and 7 feet wide (8 x 2 m).

Jesus may have hired a larger transport boat for his journey to the Gerasenes. Josephus says that rentals were available. He says the contracts called for boats to be returned undamaged except in the case of unavoidable problems, such as a surprise storm. Even the contracts recognized the lake's long history of sudden storms.

RX FOR GALILEE'S SUDDEN STORMS

How could professional fishermen get caught in a killer storm on the one and only lake they had fished all their lives?

At least four of Jesus' disciples had worked as fishermen: brothers James and John and brothers Peter and Andrew. Yet they managed to get themselves and the rest of their group swept into a cyclone of a storm.

And—shades of *Gilligan's Island*—they apparently did it on what should have been about a three-hour tour. It's about a six-mile (10 km) row from Capernaum to the Gerasene lakeside village of Gergesa, also known as Kursi.

In fairness to the fishermen, they had two excellent excuses:

- The bizarre lay of the land places the Sea of Galilee in the perfect spot for the perfect storm, driven by sudden daytime winds that no one could predict.
- Most fishermen worked in the calm of the night.

The lake sits like a shallow mixing bowl 686 feet (209 meters) below sea level. It measures only about 50 yards (46 meters) deep at its deepest, seven miles (11 km) wide at its widest, and 13 miles (21 km) long. But just beyond its banks on the east, west, and north, hills soar up to half a mile above the lake's surface.

Sparks setting off explosive storms blow in from 26 miles (42 km) to the west: the Mediterranean Sea. Cool sea breezes fight their way toward the lake, pouring down the steep ravines. Lake breezes and thermal updrafts above the lake surface usually manage to fight back the sea breezes until early afternoon. But by about 2:00 p.m., the sea breezes often break through onto the northwestern shore.

If the mixture of clashing temperature and wind speed is right, three spinning wind curls develop, according to a study reported in the *Journal of Physical Oceanography* in 2002. The largest spins counterclockwise over the center of the lake. The two smaller ones spin clockwise above the north and south parts of the lake.

This action, combined with rising heat from the sunbaked land nearby, can stir up intense, sudden windstorms, churning the smooth lake into choppy seven-foot (two meter) waves—high enough to flip a small fishing boat or a transport vessel.

As evening approaches and the land cools, the winds usually die down in time for fishermen to work the night shift.

BEYOND STORM CHASERS

We have storm chasers today who follow the wind to watch and learn. Jesus kicked it up a notch. He was a storm soother—the only one on record with witnesses to document his power.

Ancient Jewish writings do, however, tell stories of others who said they knew how to stop a storm:

Beat it with a club. "Seafarers told me that the wave that sinks a ship appears with a white fringe of fire at its crest. The way to make it stop is to beat it with a club engraved with these words: 'I am that I am, Yah, the Lord of Hosts, Amen, Amen, Selah' " (Mishnah, *Bava Batra* 73a). That was a rabbi passing along advice eventually written down by about AD 200. Some Jewish scholars speculate these words were an allegory criticizing the political problems of the day.

Pray it away. Two stories in ancient Jewish writing tell of prayer power stopping a storm. In one story, a Jewish boy stopped the storm with his prayers after the prayers of non-Jews failed (Mishnah, *Berakoth* 9:1).

In another, Rabbi Gamaliel, traveling by ship, said he saw a huge wave coming at him. He figured it was punishment for a recent bad judgment he had made in a case, so he quickly confessed that his motives were right: "Lord of the universe, you know that my decision wasn't intended to bring honor to myself or to my family, but to you so that the strife in Israel wouldn't grow worse." In that moment, as the story goes, "the raging sea subsided" (Mishnah, *Bava Metzia* 59b).

Jump overboard. Remember Jonah?

Name it and claim it. The power, that is. Antiochus IV Epiphanes, a Syrian invader who ruled Israel in the 100s BC, thought himself invincible and believed with "superhuman arrogance that he could command the waves of the sea" (2 Maccabees 9:8). At least until God struck him with a bowel disorder that left him smelling so bad no one could stand to carry him on a litter. He couldn't even stand the smell himself.

In all of known history, Jesus is the only one who exhibited the power to control the weather.

"He rebuked the wind and said to the waves, 'Silence! Be still!' Suddenly the wind stopped, and there was a great calm" (Mark 4:39).

WALKING ON WATER—OR ICE

There's another story of Jesus stopping the wind on the Sea of Galilee.

He had sent the disciples ahead to Bethsaida, by boat, while he stayed on land to pray. At 3:00 a.m., he could see they were in trouble, struggling against the wind and waves. So he went to them, "walking on the water. . . . Then he climbed into the boat, and the wind stopped" (Mark 6:49, 51).

Oceanographer Doron Nof of Florida State University said a rare combination of a cold snap and the unusual water conditions in the Sea of Galilee could have created slabs of floating ice.

He said there are salty springs along the west shore. Salt water is heavier than freshwater, so he said it could have created a layer of salt water just below the surface of the lake. The freshwater trapped above it could have frozen more quickly than the rest of the lake. Two cold days below freezing could have been just enough to create some ice floes.

With Jesus walking on the ice floes that dipped slightly below the surface, it could have looked like he was walking on water.

There are lots of problems with this theory. One is that Matthew reports the boat was "far away from land" (Matthew 14:24). Literally, "many *stadia*." A *stadia* is about 200 yards (183 meters). That's well beyond the range of the shoreline springs.

Also, when Peter tried walking on the water but sank, Jesus criticized him for his lack of faith, not for leaving his ice skates back in Capernaum.

JESUS FEEDS 5,000

Jesus took the five loaves and two fish,
looked up toward heaven, and blessed them. . . .
A total of 5,000 men and their families were fed.
MARK 6:41, 44

This is the only miracle of Jesus reported in all four Gospels. And this miracle may have been four times bigger than any one of the Gospels revealed. Jesus may have fed not just 5,000 hungry souls, but perhaps 20,000.

"About 5,000 men were fed that day, in addition to all the women and children!" (Matthew 14:21). All four Gospels agree that the "5,000" count refers to only the men. If each man on average had a woman and a couple of kids with him, that's 20,000 people.

But a later story reported in Matthew and Mark tells of Jesus feeding "about 4,000 people" (Mark 8:9). Some Bible experts say this second miracle may be another witness's account of the first miracle. After all, the scholars say, it would be easy to see how one person might estimate a crowd at 4,000 while another might estimate it at 5,000 or more.

Even assuming the smaller numbers of 4,000 to 5,000, a crowd like that would have emptied both of the fishing villages in the area where Jesus ministered: Capernaum and Bethsaida. These next-door neighbors, less than four miles (6 km) apart, were home to an estimated 2,000 to 3,000 souls each, and perhaps fewer.

However many people Jesus fed with what amounts to a couple of fish sandwiches, this particular miracle whetted the crowd's appetite for more.

Here's one possible reason. As this miracle unfolded, they saw Moses in Jesus. They saw the Exodus Israelites in themselves, stranded in a "remote place" (Mark 6:35). They saw manna in the miraculously multiplied bread from heaven. And they saw quail in the fish they ate.

It was an Exodus déjà vu—with a new Moses leading them back to the paradise lost. Jesus, they concluded, was the Messiah they had been waiting for—the God-sent deliverer who had come to drive out the Romans and restore the Promised Land to its former glory. That's probably why "they were ready to force him to be their king" (John 6:15).

Jesus slipped away, however, leaving them to digest the miracle—and to discover its real meaning.

MIRACLE ON LOCATION

Ancient tradition is a lot clearer than the Bible about where this miracle took place.

By the late AD 300s, after Roman emperor Constantine legalized Christianity, pilgrims began descending on Israel to walk in the footsteps of Jesus. One visitor was a woman named Egeria—probably a Spanish nun, or perhaps French. Those are educated guesses based on clues in an extensive letter she wrote home to her "sisters."

She said that Galilean locals placed the miracle of Jesus feeding the 5,000 at what is now Tabgha, about two and a half miles (four km) west of Capernaum.

Egeria described the site:

Above the lake there is also a field of grass with a lot of hay and several palm trees. Beside the field lie the Seven Springs, each of which produces a huge supply of water. In the field where the Lord fed the people. . .the stone on which the Lord placed the bread has been made into an altar. Visitors take small pieces of rock from the stone for their welfare, and it benefits everyone who does.

Luke, on the other hand, says that when Jesus performed the miracle, he and the disciples were headed "toward the town of Bethsaida" (Luke 9:10). This was a fishing village and the childhood home of Philip, along with brothers Peter and Andrew.

Lost for centuries, the village has recently been identified by some archaeologists as et-Tel ("the Mound"), less than 4 miles (6 km) east of Capernaum. The ruins lie about one and a half miles inland—too far for a fishing village, some say. And it's on the east side of the Jordan River, which puts it in the Roman district of Gaulanitis, though John writes of "Bethsaida in Galilee" (John 12:21).

Lake clay at et-Tel shows that the village was once right on the water. Perhaps the lake today is smaller than it was in Jesus' time. Or maybe Jordan River sediment filled the area. As for the meandering river itself, it may have shifted west of the village, which would have put the village in Galilee before the shift. Archaeologists excavating the site say it was occupied in Jesus' day and that a major earthquake known to have devastated the area in AD 363 may have helped cut Bethsaida off from the shoreline.

Stirring the pot with even more confusion, Mark reports that Jesus and the disciples got in a boat and sailed to Bethsaida *after* the miracle, not before.

If Mark, Luke, and the pilgrim Egeria are all right, perhaps Jesus started somewhere west of Tabgha—such as in Magdala, hometown of Mary Magdalene. Walking toward Bethsaida, Jesus could have stopped in the fields and rolling hills of Tabgha to feed the crowd. Then afterward, he and the disciples could have boarded a boat to finish their trip to Bethsaida.

Many Bible experts, however, say that Jesus probably performed the miracle near Bethsaida. Wherever it took place, crowds had followed Jesus there. He spent much of the day teaching them and healing their sick.

FAST FOOD

"Late in the afternoon the twelve disciples came to him and said, 'Send the crowds away to the nearby villages and farms, so they can find food and lodging for the night. There is nothing to eat here in this remote place' " (Luke 9:12).

"You feed them," Jesus replied. John's report says Jesus turned to Philip, who had grown up in Bethsaida, and asked where they could buy some bread.

"Six months' wages would not buy enough bread for each of them to get a little," Philip answered (John 6:7 NRSV). According to the original language, Philip actually said "200 denarii," not "six months' wages." A denarius was a day's wage for a common worker. At the going rate for bread, 200 denarii would have bought about 2,400 loaves—enough for about half a loaf per person if there were only 4,000 to 5,000 in the crowd. The loaves probably looked like today's pita bread.

Andrew, another native of Bethsaida, told Jesus, "There's a young boy here with five barley loaves and two fish. But what good is that with this huge crowd?" (John 6:9).

Barley was considered poor man's wheat. Philo, a Roman historian who lived in Jesus' time, writes that barley was best suited for animals "and poor people." Not as tasty as wheat, barley was much cheaper. For the price of a sack of wheat, a person could have bought two or three sacks of barley.

But this particular barley bread may have had more to do with timing than money. Mark said the crowds sat on "green grass," which suggests it was still springtime, before the summer heat baked the countryside brown. Barley was harvested in early spring, as early as March. That was two to four months before the wheat harvest.

The fish were probably dried, salted, or pickled—common methods of preserving them as a meal for the road. There are several kinds of delicious fish in the Sea of Galilee. But one of the local favorites is a mild-tasting variety named after the lake's most famous fisherman: Saint Peter's Fish (*Tilapia galilea*).

Jesus blessed the food. It was common to look to the sky when praying a blessing. A common mealtime prayer over bread went like this:

You are blessed, oh Lord our God, king of the universe and the one who brings us bread from the earth.

MISHNA, BERAKH 6:1

Jesus broke the bread and fish and gave it to the disciples to distribute among the people. "They all ate as much as they wanted" (John 6:11). And there were 12 baskets of leftovers, perhaps with each disciple walking among the crowd collecting what was left.

DIGESTING THE MIRACLE

There was more going on than a miraculous feeding—at least as far as Bible-savvy Jews were concerned.

Many of them recognized it right away, which may be why they wanted to crown Jesus king of the Jews.

Jews saw in the details of this miracle scenes not only from the most notable event in their nation's history, the Exodus. They saw light at the end of the tunnel, a way out of their Roman oppression.

Moses himself had promised that one day God would send another prophet like him: "God will raise up for you a prophet like me from among your fellow Israelites" (Deuteronomy 18:15).

Jews in Jesus' day connected this promise to predictions of a coming messiah-prophet who would save Israel from their newest oppressor, the Romans.

"When the people saw him do this miraculous sign, they exclaimed, 'Surely, he is the Prophet we have been expecting!' " (John 6:14).

It was easy for the Jews to see the links to the past by comparing this miracle of Jesus with similar miracles in the time of Moses:

MOSES AND JEWS WALKING TO PROMISED LAND	JESUS AND JEWS WALKING IN PROMISED LAND
Oppressed by Egyptians	Oppressed by Romans
Traveling in remote part of Sinai	Traveling in remote part of Galilee
Food problem: "Even if we caught all the fish in the sea, would that be enough?" (Numbers 11:22).	Food problem: "Even if we worked for months, we wouldn't have enough money to feed them!" (John 6:7).
Manna rained from heaven, and the Jews made it into bread.	From five loaves of bread, Jesus produced enough to feed thousands.
A storm-blown flock of quail provided the Jews with all the meat they could eat.	From two fish, Jesus fed the people all they could eat and then some.

Stomachs full, many Jews recognized the links to the future as well.

Feast. "The LORD of Heaven's Armies will spread a wonderful feast for all the people of the world. It will be a delicious banquet" (Isaiah 25:6).

Free food and peace. "If you don't have any money, come, eat what you want! . . . When you are set free, you will celebrate and travel home in peace. Mountains and hills will sing as you pass by, and trees will clap" (Isaiah 55:1, 12 CEV).

This is what many Jews expected life to be like after the Messiah came—political utopia. But by leaving the scene of the miracle, Jesus declared himself more than a politician. And this meal was more than a picnic.

"I tell you the truth," Jesus explained the next day, "Moses didn't give you bread from heaven. My Father did. And now he offers you the true bread from heaven. The true bread of God is the one who comes down from heaven and gives life to the world. . . . I am the bread of life! Your ancestors ate manna in the wilderness, but they all died. Anyone who eats the bread from heaven, however, will never die" (John 6:32–33; 48–50).

Jesus presented himself not only as a new and improved Moses, he presented himself as the Son of God who would lead his followers through the spiritual desert and into the Promised Land of eternal life.

For most Jews, that proved a little too hard to swallow.

BARLEY BREAD MIRACLE 800 BC

Jesus wasn't the first Jew in the Bible to silence a mass of growling stomachs with a few loaves of barley.

The prophet Elisha did it, too, more than 800 years before Jesus.

During a drought, a man brought Elisha a small sack of grain and 20 loaves of barley. Elisha told him to feed it to the people.

"What?" the man asked. "Feed a hundred people with only this?"

"Give it to the people so they can eat," Elisha answered. "For this is what the LORD says: Everyone will eat, and there will even be some left over!" (2 Kings 4:43).

They did. There was. And centuries later, many Christians would see in this story a foreshadowing of Jesus' greater miracle.

JESUS SHINES AT THE TRANSFIGURATION

Jesus' appearance was transformed, and his clothes became dazzling white, far whiter than any earthly bleach could ever make them. Then Elijah and Moses appeared and began talking with Jesus.

MARK 9:2–4

What exactly did Jesus morph into on the Mount of Transfiguration? Matthew, Mark, and Luke all say that Jesus changed into what sounds like a being of light. The term they used for this transformation was the Greek word from which we get *metamorphosis—metamorphoo.*

In our physical world, perhaps the closest parallel is what happens when an earthbound caterpillar morphs into a soaring butterfly.

The Bible and other ancient Jewish and Christian writings often describe celestial beings as glowing, and as passing along their glow to humans who come into contact with them:

- "When Moses came down Mount Sinai. . .he wasn't aware that his face had become radiant because he had spoken to the LORD. . . . He covered his face with a veil" (Exodus 34:29, 33).
- "I looked up and saw a man dressed in linen clothing. . . . His face flashed like lightning" (Daniel 10:5–6).
- "An angel of the Lord came down from heaven. . . . His face shone like lightning, and his clothing was as white as snow" (Matthew 28:2–3).
- "There will be no night there—no need for lamps or sun—for the Lord God will shine" (Revelation 22:5).
- "Those who lead many to righteousness will shine like the stars forever" (Daniel 12:3).

Examples like these, alongside clues that follow in the brief story of the Transfiguration, have led many Bible experts to speculate that Jesus momentarily reverted to the heavenly form he left when he came to earth—and the form to which he would return after his work on earth was finished.

THREE MEN WITH NO GRAVES

Crucifixion day was approaching—perhaps just months or weeks away. So Jesus had stopped beating around the bush about his imminent death. There was no more time to gradually prepare his disciples for what was coming. He bluntly told them that he "must suffer many terrible things" and that "he would be killed, but three days later he would rise from the dead" (Mark 8:31).

Jesus took his closest friends—Peter along with brothers James and John—"up on a mountain to pray" (Luke 9:28).

What happened next reads like a prequel to Jesus' prayer in the Garden of Gethsemane on the night of his arrest. Both times, Jesus took these same disciples with him to pray. Both times, they fell asleep. But this first time was unique, too.

"When they woke up, they saw Jesus' glory and the two men standing with him" (Luke 9:32). The men were Moses and Elijah, glowing with celestial glory. In a double-barreled blast from the past—at least 1,200 and 800 years, respectively—the two ancients talked with Jesus "about his exodus from this world, which was about to be fulfilled in Jerusalem" (Luke 9:31).

The question is, why these two men?

The short answer is: God knows, but the Bible doesn't say.

Yet it's hard for most Bible scholars, curious by nature, to warm up to silence. So they read between the lines, searching for clues and then offering their educated guesses.

Cheating death. One theory says they were the two perfect candidates for a return performance, at least in the eyes of many Jews. Neither man had died—not in a normal way, at least. Elijah had flown to heaven in a whirlwind escorted by chariots of fire. And the vague phrasing of Moses' death, alone on Mount Nebo, followed by his burial by God, suggested to some Jewish scholars in ancient times that he hadn't actually died at all. That put Moses and Elijah on common ground with Jesus: No grave would hold them.

Stamp of approval. Jesus once said, "I did not come to abolish the law of Moses or the writings of the prophets. No, I came to accomplish their purpose" (Matthew 5:17). Perhaps Moses represented the Jewish law and Elijah the teachings of the prophets. If so, their appearance with Jesus would have shown their support for his ministry—which would take the Jewish religion to the next level.

Fulfilling the prophecy of Elijah's return. Jews expected Elijah to come back announcing the arrival of the Messiah. The last of the classical Jewish prophets said so: "I am sending you the prophet Elijah before the great and dreadful day of the LORD arrives" (Malachi 4:5). Jesus later told his disciples that John the Baptist fulfilled this symbolic prophecy. Yet it seems that Elijah topped it off by showing up in glorified person.

Fulfilling the prophecy of Moses' return. Many Jews expected Moses to come back, too. One ancient Jewish book quoted God as saying, "Moses, I swear to you, as you devoted your life to their service in this world, so too in the time to come when I bring Elijah, the prophet, to them, the two of you will come together" (Midrash, *Deuteronomy Rabbah* 3:17).

Fulfilling an end-times prophecy. One Jewish book thought to have been written in Jesus' century offered this sign of the end times: "Whoever remains after all that I have foretold to you. . .shall see those who were taken up, who from their birth having not tasted death" (2 Esdras 6:24–26).

THE NEW MOSES

In this story, as in several others, the Gospel writers subtly compare Jesus to Moses. Bible experts say they did this to present Jesus as the new Moses—the provider of a new law, this time written on the heart instead of on stone. It would serve as a new covenant between God and humanity, and a new path to salvation.

It's hard to miss the parallels:

	MOSES	JESUS
Entourage on the mountain	"The LORD instructed Moses: 'Come up here to me, and bring along Aaron, Nadab, Abihu' " (Exodus 24:1).	"Jesus took Peter, James, and John, and led them up a high mountain" (Mark 9:2).
The shining	"Moses came down from Mount Sinai. . . . But he did not know that his face was shining" (Exodus 34:29 NCV).	"While they watched, Jesus' appearance was changed; his face became bright like the sun" (Matthew 17:2 NCV).
God in a cloud	"Moses climbed up the mountain, and the cloud covered it. . . . On the seventh day the LORD called to Moses from inside the cloud" (Exodus 24:15–16).	"A cloud overshadowed them. . . . Then a voice from the cloud said, 'This is my Son' " (Luke 9:34–35).

TERROR ON THE MOUNTAIN

No sooner were the disciples up from their nap than they were back on the ground.

Instead of waking to see Jesus praying, they saw him shimmering with light—along with two others they somehow discovered were Moses and Elijah, perhaps from the conversation. Suddenly, a cloud rolled in and covered them all. A voice from inside the cloud identified itself as coming from the Father of Jesus: God Almighty. God had appeared in clouds before, at the dedication of the Jerusalem Temple, on Mount Sinai, and while leading the Exodus Israelites in a pillar of cloud. One prophet said that when the Messiah comes, "God will bring back the ancient pillar of cloud" (Isaiah 4:5 THE MESSAGE).

Terrified, the disciples "fell face down on the ground" (Matthew 17:6). With good reason. They probably remembered

- what God had told Moses: "No one may see me and live" (Exodus 33:20); and
- what the Israelites had told Moses: "Don't let God speak directly to us, or we will die!" (Exodus 20:19).

Jesus calmed the disciples with the same words that Moses used to calm the Israelites: "Don't be afraid" (Matthew 17:7).

Not having a clue how to respond, Peter blurted out, "Master, it's wonderful for us to be here! Let's make three shelters as memorials—one for you, one for Moses, and one for Elijah" (Luke 9:33).

Jesus declined. Not surprisingly, though, once Rome legalized Christianity in the AD 300s, Christians carried out Peter's plan. They built three churches on Mount Tabor. The oldest tradition about the Transfiguration says it was there that the miracle took place.

Jesus told the disciples not to tell anyone about what they had seen until he rose from the dead. "So they kept it to themselves, but they often asked each other what he meant by 'rising from the dead' " (Mark 9:10).

Only after the Resurrection—an idea the disciples couldn't seem to grasp—did the story make sense. Only then would they understand that Jesus really is the Son of God and that eternal life is real.

JESUS AND THE TAX MAN ZACCHAEUS

Jesus entered Jericho and made his way through the town. There was a man there named Zacchaeus. He was the chief tax collector in the region, and he had become very rich.

LUKE 19:1–2

Zacchaeus was a wee little man. A wee little man was he."
Short as a rat's twitch, he had to scramble up a sycamore tree to catch sight of Jesus passing through Jericho. The hometown crowd wasn't in the least inclined to open a path for Zacchaeus, though he was probably one of the richest businessmen in the city.

People hated him because he was also as crooked as a rat's twitch.

A tax collector, Zacchaeus had gotten rich by overassessing the property values of his neighbors and then bagging and banking the excess taxes he collected. It was a "pick your own salary" job, by picking the pockets of your neighbors.

Jesus was nearing the end of his years of ministry, on his way to Jerusalem one last time, a day's walk away. Jews throughout Israel had heard of Jesus, the unusual rabbi who drew crowds like a hero, taught confidently without citing the authority of other rabbis, and healed the sick without medicine. Anyone with a speck of curiosity wanted to see him—the godly and the godless alike.

Zacchaeus was the latter.

Fortunately for him, that's just the kind of person Jesus was looking for.

TAX BRACKET FOR THE POOR: 35 PERCENT

Jews got double-dipped in taxes. Romans skimmed off an estimated 25 percent of a Jew's income each year. The Jewish Temple in Jerusalem required another 10 percent—the tithe—along with a silver half-shekel (about a day's salary) for Temple maintenance.

Romans assessed taxes in three main ways:

Land tax. This was the biggie. Each year, Roman representatives collected an estimated 20 to 25 percent of a farmer's harvest. City folks, like those in Jerusalem, paid a house tax and a city sales tax instead. Many of the rich and well connected were exempted from this tax.

Per-person tax. Also once a year, Jewish men ages 14–65 paid a tax equal to a day's wages: a silver denarius. It's possible they had to pay for their wives as well.

Customs toll booth tax. Seaports, gate entrances into cities, and crossroads along international trade routes were among the spots where tax collectors like Matthew set up booths. As merchants and farmers passed by, the tax collector, with an armed guard, assessed the value of the merchandise—often overassessing. Then he collected the tax, ranging from 2 to 5 percent of the assessed value. People paid these tolls at various locations along the way to their destination.

Zacchaeus, as a chief tax collector in Jericho, probably managed several customs

— HOW TO TREAT A TAX MAN ON THE TAKE —

Jericho crowds swarmed Jesus, walking alongside him excited and noisy. But with a single string of words, Jesus likely managed to stun them into momentary silence.

"Zacchaeus!" he said. "Quick, come down! I must be a guest in your home today" (Luke 19:5).

Of all the people in Jericho that Jesus could have honored with his presence, he chose the equivalent of the town bully, the banker weasel, and the placekicker who lost the big game—all rolled into one stinker of a human.

"Everyone who saw the incident was indignant and grumped, 'What business does he have getting cozy with this crook?' " (Luke 19:7 THE MESSAGE).

Zacchaeus, on the flip side, was delighted—and probably shocked. He knew all too well what most rabbis taught about him and his tax colleagues: They were extortionists, collaborators with the occupying Roman army, and as ritually unclean as a corpse on the dinner table.

No respected rabbi would exchange words with such a raw sinner, let alone share lodging and a meal with him. Doing so would signal that the rabbi condoned the tax man's exploitation of his countrymen.

The Jewish Bible, which Christians call the Old Testament, doesn't demean tax collectors. But revered Jewish scholars interpreting that Bible certainly did. They said so in ancient writings that many Jews hold dear:

> **It's okay to lie to the tax man**
> *"It's perfectly acceptable to tell murderers, robbers, or tax collectors that the money you have is for a temple offering, or that you're a member of the king's family and exempt from taxes."*
>
> MISHNAH, NEDARIM 3:4

booths throughout the lucrative Jericho region. Romans typically subcontracted this regional job to the local highest bidder, who paid the Romans his bid in advance. Then he hired men to work the booths for him and collect the taxes. They kept part of what they collected as their salary. Zacchaeus got the rest.

This was a setup ripe for rip-off.

A tax collector's salary depended on how much he took in. And he alone had the power to assess the value of the merchandise. The higher he assessed it, the more money he made. Many tax collectors got rich, climbing the social ladder on the backs of their neighbors.

Toilet tax. The son of one tax collector in Jesus' day became emperor of Rome: Vespasian (AD 9–79). He remembered the family trade when he needed money. Once, he ordered an unpopular tax on public toilets. When his son Titus scolded him about the tax, Vespasian held a coin up to his son's nose.

"Does it stink?" Vespasian asked.

"No," Titus answered.

"Well, it comes from the toilet."

Wherever the money came from, it was money nonetheless. At least as far as tax collectors were concerned.

Avoid letting tax men into your house

"If a tax collector goes inside a house, everything in the house becomes ritually unclean and needs to go through purification rituals."

MISHNAH, *TOHOROTH* 7:6

Let tax men keep their dirty change

"Don't take change back from the wallet of a tax collector. And don't accept any charitable contributions from them, either."

TALMUD, *BABA METZIA* 10:1

As viewed by his own people, Zacchaeus was the ultimate outcast. And his story shows up in a Bible book nicknamed "Gospel of the Outcasts," partly because it highlights the compassion Jesus had for people like Zacchaeus.

JESUS ON TAXES AND TAX MEN

Jesus knew that many tax collectors were corrupt. On occasion he said so (see Matthew 5:46). Yet he considered taxes and crooked tax men relatively minor problems compared to organized religion and the Jewish leaders of his day:

- "Show me the coin used for the tax. . . . Whose picture and title are stamped on it?" "Caesar's," they replied. "Well, then," he said, "give to Caesar what belongs to Caesar, and give to God what belongs to God" (Matthew 22:19–21).
- To Jewish scholars asking if Jews should pay Roman taxes
- "I tell you the truth, corrupt tax collectors and prostitutes will get into the Kingdom of God before you do" (Matthew 21:31).
- To Jewish priests and other religious leaders
- "Follow me and be my disciple" (Luke 5:27).
- To Matthew, operating a tax collector's booth

TAX REFUND

Sometime during Jesus' overnight visit, Zacchaeus had a radical change of heart. Money dropped from his top priority.

This is reflected in a promise he made to Jesus: "I will give half my wealth to the poor, Lord, and if I have cheated people on their taxes, I will give them back four times as much!" (Luke 19:8).

Zacchaeus must have had quite a wad of money to donate 50 percent of his assets to charity. Rabbis in ancient times recommended that people give away no more than 20 percent of their holdings. To give more would be to risk bankruptcy, at least for most folks. And then the overly generous person might become a burden to society.

On top of Zacchaeus' extreme donation, he offered an outrageously generous restitution to anyone he cheated—about four times what Jewish law required.

Law: "Suppose you cheat in a deal. . .or you steal or commit fraud. . . . You must make restitution by paying the full price plus an additional 20 percent to the person you have harmed" (Leviticus 6:2, 5).

Zacchaeus: "I will now pay back four times as much to everyone I have ever cheated" (Luke 19:8 CEV).

So if he cheated someone out of 100 coins, instead of paying back 120 coins, he promised to pay back 400.

Zacchaeus decided to use the payback rate for the serious crime of sheep rustling. In an agricultural economy, stolen livestock could mean the difference between a family's life and death. "If you steal a sheep and slaughter it or sell it, you must replace it with four sheep" (Exodus 22:1 CEV).

Jesus recognized the promise as genuine. So he replied, "Salvation has come to this home today" (Luke 19:9).

It wasn't Zacchaeus' vow that produced salvation. It was salvation that produced the vow. Contact with Jesus changed the tax collector. The tin man found a heart.

This short story ends with a one-liner that doubles as a mission statement for Jesus: "The Son of Man came to seek and save those who are lost" (Luke 19:10).

A day earlier, the crowd figured Jesus had made a foolish choice—and was probably not such a great rabbi after all.

We can only imagine what they thought the next day, when the tax collector started delivering their refunds.

TAX MEN IN THE PECKING ORDER

Many tax collectors enjoyed life near the top of the social pecking order.

Like other prosperous businessmen, they were members of the equestrian class—one notch below senators. That's if they were Roman citizens in good standing and they had a net worth equal to that of a multimillionaire today.

Their worth had to measure at least 400,000 sesterces, which was equal to 1,600,000 denarii. A single denarius was a day's salary for a working-class man. So they needed assets equal to more than 4,000 years of a working man's salary.

There's no indication that Zacchaeus was a citizen of Rome, or that he had that much money.

Also among the Roman business class were bankers, exporters, and builders awarded lucrative contracts—such as contracts for building aqueducts and arenas.

The name *equestrian* came from Rome's earlier days, when most members of this class came from the Roman cavalry and when senators were prohibited from engaging in trade or business.

Romans dressed in the uniform of their rank. Equestrians wore white togas with a narrow purple strip. Senators wore togas with a wide purple strip. The emperor wore a purple robe.

THE SECRET OF ETERNAL LIFE

Let me reveal to you a wonderful secret. . . .
We will all be transformed! . . . For our dying bodies
must be transformed into bodies that will never die.

1 CORINTHIANS 15:51, 53

Christianity without eternal life is bean soup without beans. You can't have one without the other.

If someone turned up solid evidence that Jesus stayed dead and that the New Testament teachings about eternal life are fiction, Christianity would go belly-up.

The apostle Paul said as much:

If there is no resurrection of the dead, then Christ has not been raised either. And if Christ has not been raised, then all our preaching is useless, and your faith is useless.

1 CORINTHIANS 15:13–14

BODY OR SPIRIT—WHICH ONE IS ETERNAL?

Christians argue about what form humans will take in the next life.

Each side loads its argument with ammo from the Bible, even though the Bible seems to give itself some wiggle room.

Physical body. Some Christians insist we'll have physical bodies. The Bible repeatedly says we'll have bodies in the afterlife: "We will put on heavenly bodies; we will not be spirits without bodies" (2 Corinthians 5:3).

Spiritual body. Others say we'll live as spirit entities in a spiritual dimension. They say the Bible's descriptions of the afterlife are symbolic and are presented in physical terms because we physics-bound humans have no frame of reference to understand the spiritual dimension.

Combo body: physical and spiritual. Still others speculate that we'll have the best of both worlds—perhaps like the resurrected body of Jesus.

He could suddenly appear and disappear. "Two of Jesus' followers were walking to the village of Emmaus. . . . Jesus himself suddenly came and began walking with them. . . . Suddenly, their eyes were opened, and they recognized him. And at that moment he disappeared!" (Luke 24:13, 15, 31).

He could pass through the walls of a locked house. "The disciples were meeting behind locked doors because they were afraid of the Jewish leaders. Suddenly, Jesus was standing there among them!" (John 20:19).

He could eat. "The whole group was startled and frightened [at Jesus' suddenly appearing], thinking they were seeing a ghost! 'Why are you frightened?' he asked. . . . 'Touch me and make sure that I am not a ghost, because ghosts don't have bodies, as you see that I do.' . . . Then he asked them, 'Do you have anything here to eat?' They gave him a piece of broiled fish, and he ate it as they watched" (Luke 24:37–39, 41–43).

He could levitate. " 'You will receive power when the Holy Spirit comes upon you. And you will be my witnesses, telling people about me everywhere.' . . . After saying this, he [Jesus] was taken up into a cloud while they were watching" (Acts 1:8–9).

When a person gets "saved," eternal life is what they get saved for. They're spared the punishment for their sins: "The payment for sin is death" (Romans 6:23 NCV). Once saved, instead of punishment they get the ultimate reward: "the free gift of life forever."

That's salvation.

What does it take to receive this gift of salvation?

The apostle Paul puts it this way: "Say the welcoming word to God—'Jesus is my Master'—embracing, body and soul, God's work of doing in us what he did in raising Jesus from the dead. That's it. You're not 'doing' anything; you're simply calling out to God, trusting him to do it for you. That's salvation" (Romans 10:9 THE MESSAGE).

WHAT IS THE KINGDOM OF GOD?

It's not just heaven. It's more. And it's not just then, in the future. It's now, too.

When we read the phrase "Kingdom of God" we can substitute it with "eternal life" and come away with the right idea. That's what many Bible experts say.

All four Gospels—Matthew, Mark, Luke, and John—talk about the "Kingdom of God." Matthew added a variation, "Kingdom of Heaven," perhaps to help people quickly see how it related to them, because many Jews and Christians alike believed they would one day live in heaven.

But "Kingdom of God" may not be the best translation for us today.

We see the word *kingdom* and think of a territory with borders. But the word literally means reign, authority, or rule. God's rule, or spiritual kingdom, extends to everyone devoted to him—in heaven and on earth.

The Jews who copied the famous Dead Sea Scrolls, and who lived in an isolated community near the Dead Sea shoreline, taught that God's Kingdom was an earthly one. They wrote end-time prophecies about God sending his angels to defeat evil once and for all and then setting up a utopian kingdom on earth.

The Pharisees—rule keepers to the max—taught that they could usher in the Kingdom of God through their strict obedience to Jewish laws and rituals.

Jesus disagreed with both groups. As far as he was concerned, God's Kingdom wasn't limited to some future era on earth. Nor could worship rituals flip the switch and power up God's Kingdom. It was already here, at least in part. It was identified by people devoted to God and living in a way that honored him. Their lives exhibited mercy, forgiveness, justice, and concern for the poor and powerless.

Though God's Kingdom had come only in part—because not everyone served God—it will one day come in fullness, when Jesus returns. "At the name of Jesus every knee should bow, in heaven and on earth and under the earth, and every tongue confess that Jesus Christ is Lord, to the glory of God the Father" (Philippians 2:10–11).

THE EVOLUTION OF ETERNAL LIFE

Many critics of the Bible say that religious people in ages past gradually developed the idea of eternal life.

They say the idea didn't blossom until the time of Jesus—halfway through what is now the 4,000-year history of the Jewish people.

Those critics actually have a leg to stand on, shaky though many Christians would say it is.

As far as the Bible reports, Israel's most famous heroes of the faith served God without the promise of eternal life. Israel began in about 2100 BC, with God promising to make Abraham's family into a great nation. Abraham and the Jewish heroes who followed—people such as Moses, David, Solomon, and Isaiah—devoted their lives to God with no known promise of eternal life.

The idea of a resurrection into eternal life didn't seem to show up in the Bible until an angel introduced it to the prophet Daniel in the 500s BC. Describing the end times, the angel said, "Many of those whose bodies lie dead and buried will rise up, some to everlasting life and some to shame and everlasting disgrace" (Daniel 12:2).

Until then, and a few centuries beyond, when the idea finally began to sink in, Jews seemed to have had more theories about the afterlife than a casket has bones. Here are a few of the more notable, implied in various stories, poems, and prophecies of the Old Testament and the Apocrypha, which are Jewish writings from between the times of the Old and New Testaments.

Death is the end of existence.
- "The dead cannot praise you; they cannot raise their voices in praise. Those who go down to the grave can no longer hope in your faithfulness" (Isaiah 38:18).

Death is eternal sleep.
- "Death is better than a life of misery, and eternal sleep than chronic sickness" (Sirach 30:17). In ancient Jewish poetry, the second line often repeats the first. In this case, "death" in line one is the parallel of "eternal sleep" in line two. And "misery" in line one refers to "chronic sickness" in line two.

All that lives on is the memory.
- "His memory will not disappear, and his name will live through all generations" (Sirach 39:9).

Bodies decay, but spirits of the righteous and unrighteous live on in Sheol, a mysterious place of the dead.
- "The LORD will hand you and the army of Israel over to the Philistines tomorrow, and you and your sons will be here with me" (1 Samuel 28:19). Speaking is the spirit of the dead Samuel—"an old man wrapped in a robe." He was talking to King Saul through a medium.
- "Earth opened its mouth and in one gulp swallowed them down, the men and their families. . . . And that was the end of them, pitched alive into Sheol" (Numbers 16:32–33 THE MESSAGE).

Bodies can be resurrected, but it's unknown for what or for how long.
- "After my body has decayed, yet in my body I will see God! I

will see him for myself. Yes, I will see him with my own eyes. I am overwhelmed at the thought!" (Job 19:26–27).

- "Those who die in the LORD will live; their bodies will rise again! Those who sleep in the earth will rise up and sing for joy! For your life-giving light will fall like dew on your people in the place of the dead!" (Isaiah 26:19).
  There's something beyond this life, but no one knows what.
- "Enoch lived 365 years, walking in close fellowship with God. Then one day he disappeared, because God took him" (Genesis 5:23–24).
- "Elijah was carried by a whirlwind into heaven" (2 Kings 2:11).

By the time of Jesus, there was still some diversity among the Jews about what to make of eternal life. But many top scholars taught that God's people would live forever.

Some historians speculate that those Jewish scholars adapted the idea from Greek philosophers, such as Plato (ca. 428–348 BC), who said the soul was immortal and separate from the body. Plato said that after a person dies, his or her soul is freed and returns to its natural element—whatever that is. Plato didn't say.

Writing in a collection of books called *Antiquities of the Jews*, a first-century historian named Josephus—a Jew by race and a Roman by citizenship—described what the three main Jewish groups taught about eternal life:

Pharisees: "They believe that souls have immortal strength. And they believe that after this life, the souls of people will be rewarded or punished, based on whether they obeyed God's laws or disobeyed. Those who disobeyed will be sentenced to eternal life in prison. But those who have obeyed God will receive the power to revive and live again." Though this sounds like reincarnation, scholars say it probably wasn't Josephus' intent—just his awkward phrasing.

Sadducees: "The doctrine of the Sadducees is this: That souls die with the bodies." The New Testament confirms the clash between Pharisees and Sadducees: "Sadducees say there is no resurrection or angels or spirits, but the Pharisees believe in all of these" (Acts 23:8). Some New Testament profs try to drum this distinction into the brains of their students with a memory tool about Sadducees not believing in life after death: "That is why they are Sad-you-see."

Essenes: "The doctrine of the Essenes is this. . . . They teach that souls live forever, and that righteous people should work hard for the rewards waiting for them." Jews warmed up to the idea of eternal life even more after Romans crushed the Jewish uprising in AD 70 and destroyed Jerusalem and the Temple. That's because the Sadducees, closely tied to the priesthood, lost influence when the Temple fell and the priesthood became obsolete.

JESUS ON ETERNAL LIFE

In the entire Bible, the person who seems best equipped to enlighten humans about eternal life is the Eternal Being himself: God the Son.

John puts Jesus at the beginning of time. Describing Jesus as the "Word," (*Logos* in Greek)—a scholar's term in ancient times referring to the mysterious power behind the universe—John writes, "In the beginning the Word already existed. The Word was with God, and the Word was God" (John 1:1).

Jesus kicked that up a notch. He placed himself at both the beginning and the end of human history: "I am the Alpha and the Omega, the First and the Last, the Beginning and the End" (Revelation 22:13).

Jesus answered these questions about eternal life:

What is eternal life?

It's literally "life of the age." That's shorthand for "life of the age to come." In other words, it's salvation. It's God's declaration that we're not guilty of sin and that we don't deserve the death penalty. Instead, we get to enjoy life forever.

"Everyone who has faith in him will have eternal life and never really die. . . . No one who has faith in God's Son will be condemned" (John 3:16, 18 CEV).

Why does God offer us eternal life?

He loves us. "God loved the world so much that he gave his one and only Son, so that everyone who believes in him will not perish but have eternal life. God sent his Son into the world not to judge the world, but to save the world" (John 3:16–17).

How can we know we have God's gift of eternal life?

It's a done deal if we trust what Jesus taught and try to live accordingly.

- "Anyone who believes in me will live, even after dying. Everyone who lives in me and believes in me will never ever die" (John 11:25–26).

BORN AGAIN, TO LIVE FOREVER

Entering into eternal life—which begins the moment we take the leap of faith and put our trust in Jesus—is such a remarkable experience that Jesus compared it to the miracle of birth.

"I tell you the truth, unless you are born again, you cannot see the Kingdom of God" (John 3:3). Some translate "born again" as "born from above."

Bible experts debate what Jesus meant when he connected "born again" with "being born of the water and the Spirit" (John 3:5). In that second phrase, it's not clear if he was talking about

- physical birth after the water breaks, followed by spiritual birth;
- water baptism followed by the Holy Spirit's guidance; or
- a single spiritual experience predicted nearly 600 years earlier: "I'll pour pure water over you and scrub you clean. . . . I'll put my Spirit in you and make it possible for you to do what I tell you and live by my commands" (Ezekiel 36:25, 27 THE MESSAGE).

Whatever Jesus meant, the new life he was talking about is one that he said would never end. Even after the physical body dies, the life of those people who put their faith in him will go on and on.

PATH TO SALVATION

For those who like the step-by-step approach to getting saved, the apostle Paul worked up a concise road map.

It shows up in a letter he wrote to Christians in Rome, to introduce himself and his beliefs to a group of people he hoped to meet soon.

- "Everyone has sinned and fallen short of God's glorious standard" (Romans 3:23 NCV).
- "The wages of sin is death" (Romans 6:23).
- "God showed his great love for us by sending Christ to die for us while we were still sinners" (Romans 5:8).
- "It is by believing in your heart that you are made right with God, and it is by confessing with your mouth that you are saved" (Romans 10:10).

Three words for a dead man. "Lazarus, come out!" That's all Jesus needed to say to wake the dead. It also awakened the Jewish leaders to his dramatic power, which they feared he might use to launch a revolution against Rome. Their solution? Kill him.

- "Anyone here who believes what I am saying right now and aligns himself with the Father, who has in fact put me in charge, has at this very moment the real, lasting life and is no longer condemned to be an outsider. This person has taken a giant step from the world of the dead to the world of the living" (John 5:24 THE MESSAGE).
- "Whoever accepts and trusts the Son gets in on everything, life complete and forever! . . . The person who avoids and distrusts the Son is in the dark and doesn't see life. All he experiences of God is darkness" (John 3:36 THE MESSAGE).
- " 'Teacher, what should I do to inherit eternal life?' Jesus replied, 'What does the law of Moses say? How do you read it?' The man answered, '"You must love the LORD your God with all your heart, all your soul, all your strength, and all your mind." And, "Love your neighbor as yourself." '
- 'Right!' Jesus told him. 'Do this and you will live!'" (Luke 10:25–28).

What will eternal life be like?

It's forever, and it's not like life as we know it. "Marriage is for people here on earth. But in the age to come, those worthy of being raised from the dead will neither marry nor be given in marriage. And they will never die again. In this respect they will be like angels. They are children of God and children of the resurrection" (Luke 20:34–36).

JESUS RESURRECTS LAZARUS

"Lazarus's sickness will not end in death.
No, it happened for the glory of God so that the
Son of God will receive glory from this."

JOHN 11:4

Jesus wouldn't have done very well as a doctor working in the emergency room. Not if the way he treated Lazarus is any indication.

Located at least a day's walk away from Lazarus, Jesus got terrible news from a messenger: Lazarus was dreadfully sick and probably dying.

This was no typical patient in need of a healing miracle—Jesus' forte— this was a friend of Jesus, and the brother of two sisters who had treated Jesus kindly: Mary and Martha.

Jesus could have rushed to Lazarus' home in Bethany, a suburb of Jerusalem. Better yet, he could have healed him long-distance, just as he had done for the servant of a Roman soldier in the fishing village of Capernaum.

Instead, Jesus waited for his patient to die.

If a doctor did that today—putting his patient along with the family and friends through needless misery—we wouldn't call him the Son of God. We'd have other names for him. And we'd put them in writing, in a malpractice suit.

This was no isolated incident. There was a pattern at work here.

Remember the story of the man born blind? Disciples asked Jesus why the man had to suffer like that—if it was because of sin. His answer: "This happened so the power of God could be seen in him" (John 9:3). That reply is almost identical to the explanation Jesus gave for letting Lazarus die.

Like the blind man, Lazarus would become a living parable—even in death. The drama of his story would give the followers of Jesus insights about God that words alone could never convey.

For those who would stand with Jesus by Lazarus' tomb, seeing was believing. Believing was faith. And faith opened the door to life everlasting: "Your faith has saved you; go in peace" (Luke 7:50).

JOURNEY TO JERUSALEM

It was a dangerous house call.

Jesus' disciples figured as much, and they tried to talk him out of going. Only about two or three months earlier, during the mid-December festival honoring the Temple's rededication—a festival today called Hanukah—Jerusalem Jews had "picked up stones to kill him" (John 10:31). But Jesus slipped away.

Seeing Jesus' resolve to go back anyhow, Thomas said to his fellow disciples, perhaps cynically: "Let's go, too—and die with Jesus" (John 11:16).

It's a mystery where Jesus was at the time.

The Bible places him "beyond the Jordan River near the place where John was first baptizing" (John 10:40). That's probably a reference to "Bethany, an area east of the Jordan River, where John was baptizing" (John 1:28). John had baptized Jesus there two or three years earlier. This Bethany isn't the same one where Lazarus lived, but another area by the same name, and not necessarily a village.

If this distant Bethany rested across the river from Jericho, it could have been just a day's walk to Lazarus' village on the outskirts of Jerusalem. Lazarus' sleepy little hometown was nestled on the eastern slopes of a ridge called the Mount of Olives. That put the village about a mile and a half (2.5 km) east of Jerusalem.

Given one day's travel between the two places, the timeline might have looked like this:

- Day 1: Messenger leaves to find Jesus; Lazarus dies that day and is buried.
- Day 2: Messenger finds Jesus early, but Jesus decides to wait before leaving.
- Day 3: Jesus waits a second day.
- Day 4: Jesus arrives at Lazarus' hometown.

Some Bible experts speculate that Jesus was much farther away—about 80 miles (130 km) north of Jerusalem and east of the Sea of Galilee in the region of Batanea, called Bashan in Old Testament times. If Jesus had been there, it would have taken him four days, traveling the typical 20 miles (32 km) a day, to reach Jerusalem. That means Jesus could have left Batanea the same day Lazarus died.

Some scholars like this theory for several reasons. It fits the timing of Jesus' travel. The names of Batanea and Bethany sound similar in Greek, as they do in English. Jews lived in the area, including some Essenes, an isolationist group that some say influenced John the Baptist. And first-century Jewish historian Josephus, along with the ancient Greek edition of the Old Testament, referred to Batanea as "beyond the Jordan."

Counterpoint: There's no indication John baptized people that far north. He ministered and was eventually executed in the region of Perea, which was ruled by Herod Antipas.

HOW TO BURY A JEW

Jews didn't embalm their dead. They buried them right away. Usually the day they died. In the hot climate of a desert region, they had to; bodies decomposed quickly.

Wash the body. Loved ones would strip the corpse and gently wash it, sometimes pouring scented oil over the skin to help mask the odor during the upcoming days when mourners would visit the tomb.

Dress the body. In Jesus' day, some Jews dressed the corpse in a robe, much as we dress corpses today.

Wrap the body in cloth strips. Others simply wrapped part of the body in strips of cloth. They also used strips of cloth to gently tie the feet together at the ankles and the arms to the torso.

Scent the body with spices. Wrapped into the strips of cloth were scented spices and oils—anything that would help hide the odor. Some preferred scents: balm, myrrh, aloe, and spikenard. Even common kitchen spices such as cinnamon and dill could help mask the smell of death.

Cover the face. About the size of a napkin, a separate cloth was draped over the face to hide it during decomposition. Some used this also to secure the jaw, tying the jaw closed. Others used separate strips of cloth to secure the jaw.

Wrap the body in a shroud. Like the famous Shroud of Turin, a long strip of cloth as wide as the body and twice the length covered the corpse, front and back. Half the single bolt of cloth would lie under the body. The rest would be brought up over the head and stretched down to the feet to cover the front.

Close the tomb. After about a week of mourning, survivors would seal the tomb. The flesh decomposed in a year or two.

Return to put bones in a container. After the flesh was gone, someone would enter the tomb, gather up the bones, and place them in a limestone casket called an ossuary. Bones of the entire family rested in this burial box.

JESUS GETS ANGRY

By the time Jesus arrived at the Jerusalem suburb, Lazarus was dead by any ancient standard and well beyond resuscitation.

Day three was the cutoff, the point of no return. Until then, rabbis taught, the body might revive:

> The soul hovers over its former body for three days, hoping to re-enter it. But as soon as the body begins to change appearance [through decomposition], the soul leaves.
> LEVITICUS RABBAH 18:1 (JEWISH COMMENTARY ON LEVITICUS)

> Mourning isn't complete until at least the third day. For three days the soul returns to the grave, thinking it will return to the body. But when it sees the color of the face change, it goes away.
> GENESIS RABBAH 100:64A

We go out to the cemetery and examine the dead within three days. . . .
One man was found alive, and he lived for another 25 years. Another
was found alive and he fathered five children.

TALMUD, SEMAHOT 8, RULE 1

But Lazarus had been dead four days by the time Jesus arrived.

In Western culture today, the deepest mourning comes first, before the burial. But in the heat of ancient Israel, it was just the reverse. The day of death was the day of burial. Mourning followed, as the reality of the loved one's death set in.

Rabbis in ancient times suggested three stages of mourning. Their advice survives in a collection of writings revered among the Jews, the Talmud:

- **Sobbing.** The first three days were for the deepest mourning. Loved ones could sob and scream their grief. Those able to afford it would hire professional mourners.
- **Sadness.** The next seven days were for continued mourning, often less intense and more pensive.
- **Remembrance.** During the last 20 days of a 30-day mourning period, loved ones sometimes expressed their sorrow by continuing to refrain from bathing, grooming their hair, or wearing clean clothes.

When Jesus arrived on day four, many family friends were still hovering near Lazarus' sisters, Mary and Martha. Confronted by the grieving sisters, who had hosted him on visits past—feeding him and anointing him with oil—Jesus did two things that perplex Bible experts.

He wept. And he got angry.

Scholars debate why.

They look for clues in the events that led to Jesus' reaction.

Event 1. Martha, meeting Jesus outside the village, lamented that if Jesus had been there sooner, Lazarus would not have died. Jesus assured her that Lazarus would rise again. But Martha misunderstood, saying she believed Lazarus would rise again someday. Jesus tried to help her see that someday was today, because "the resurrection and the life" was standing right in front of her.

Event 2. Mary arrived weeping, with an entourage of grieving friends.

Reaction. "When Jesus saw her weeping and saw the other people wailing with her, a deep anger welled up within him, and he was deeply troubled" (John 11:33). It was then that "Jesus wept." Some scholars say a more accurate translation would be "Jesus burst into tears."

Some mourners watching Jesus speculated that he wept because he loved Lazarus. Others weren't so sure, saying if he loved Lazarus so much, he should have healed him like he had healed others.

In the original language, "deep anger" could imply an outburst, perhaps accompanied by a grunt or a groan. The word used to describe his anger could also describe a furious, snorting warhorse in battle. The ancient Greek edition of the Old Testament used the same word to describe a livid king who would "vent his anger against the people" (Daniel 11:30).

Most scholars today tend to line up behind one of two theories about why Jesus reacted the way he did.

Theory 1: He was angry at the people's lack of faith. Jesus had already raised two people from the dead: the daughter of a synagogue leader named Jairus, and the son of a widow in the village of Nain. In addition, he had just finished telling Martha, "I am the resurrection and the life. Anyone who believes in me will live, even after dying" (John 11:25). And yet these mourners were grieving "like people who have no hope" (1 Thessalonians 4:13).

Theory 2: He was angry about the pain death causes. Surrounded by grieving people he knew well and loved dearly, he felt their pain. He was angry that they had to go through this, just as many of us get angry over the death of someone we love. Conquering death was why Jesus came. He felt passionately about the heartache it caused. And like a warhorse about to engage in battle, his anger flared as he charged toward his two targets: Lazarus first, and the Crucifixion a short time later, within weeks.

DEAD MAN WALKING

Jesus asked to see Lazarus' tomb. A grave in the dirt was all some people could afford. But Lazarus rested in a tomb, probably a small cave chiseled into the face of a limestone hillside. Abandoned quarries in the area were often converted into cemeteries.

Tomb entrances were usually sealed by flat Frisbee-shaped stones that rolled left and right. When Jesus asked some of the men to open Lazarus' tomb, Martha tried to stop him: "Lord, he has been dead for four days. The smell will be terrible" (John 11:39).

Jesus wasn't concerned about what the people would smell, but about what they would see: "Didn't I tell you that you would see God's glory if you believe?" (John 11:40).

Magicians trying to work wonders often mumbled long-winded, secret incantations. But Jesus spoke just three words, loud and clear. After thanking God for hearing what sounds like it must have been a previous prayer, Jesus woke the dead: "Lazarus, come out!" (John 11:43).

Had Lazarus been wrapped like many non-Jewish cultures wrapped their dead, he would have had a tough time doing as he was told. Many cultures wrapped corpses mummy-style, so they couldn't come back from the dead even if they wanted to. But many Jews at this time often dressed the bodies in nice clothes, as we do today. Then they gently bound the feet at the ankles and the arms at the side. A napkin-sized cloth often covered the face and bound the jaw closed.

"The dead man came out, his hands and feet bound in graveclothes, his face wrapped in a head cloth. Jesus told them, 'Unwrap him and let him go!' " (John 11:44).

The Jewish leaders in Jerusalem soon got word of this. They feared that miracles this dramatic, performed so close to the Jewish capital, could convince many that Jesus was the Messiah—and that now was the time to drive out the Romans and restore Israel to independence and glory.

The Jewish leaders worried that such a war of independence would end in disaster, with the destruction of the Temple. About 40 years later, that's exactly what happened. In AD 70 Rome crushed a Jewish revolt, leveling not only the Temple but also much of Jerusalem.

The high priest, Caiaphas, called a meeting of the high council. Item one and only on the agenda: what to do with a would-be messiah who could raise the dead.

Their final solution? Kill him.

"It's better for you that one man should die for the people than for the whole nation to be destroyed," Caiaphas explained (John 11:50).

Little did Caiaphas know he was helping fulfill prophecy. Dying for the people was exactly what Jesus had come to do, just as prophets had predicted: "He was wounded and crushed because of our sins. . . . The LORD gave him the punishment we deserved" (Isaiah 53:5–6 CEV).

JEWISH LEADERS PLOT TO KILL JESUS

Jesus entered the Temple and began to drive out the people buying and selling animals for sacrifices. He knocked over the tables of the money changers and the chairs of those selling doves. . . . When the leading priests and teachers of religious law heard what Jesus had done, they began planning how to kill him.

MARK 11:15, 18

Jesus had a knack for making enemies in high places.

It was inevitable, given his mission: "The Spirit of the LORD is upon me, for he has anointed me to bring Good News to the poor. He has sent me to proclaim that captives will be released. . .that the oppressed will be set free" (Luke 4:18).

There was only one way for Jesus to defend the down and out. He had to take on the high and mighty. Uppity insiders ran the system that oppressed the powerless. They wrote the laws to their own advantage. They enforced the laws. And they punished folks who didn't comply.

Among the Jewish community in Jesus' day, no one was higher than the high priest. He ran the Sanhedrin, a council of about 70 men who ruled the Jewish nation. It was Congress and the Supreme Court rolled into one, or Parliament and the Supreme Court.

Josephus, a Jewish historian from that century, had this to say about the high priest: "He knew how to get money" (*Antiquities of the Jews* 20.9.2).

His techniques, as reported by Josephus:

Bribes. With well-placed investments, he bought friends among the social elite.

Forced tithing. He sent "wicked servants" to farms at harvesttime. There they stole tithes that the farmers were supposed to take to the Temple so priests on duty could share it as their salary. Essentially, the high priest confiscated the income from the lower priests. It's a bit like a company president today taking a monster salary and leaving his grunts to fight for the leftovers.

Beatings. "He beat people who refused to give him the tithes." Result: Some of the priests starved to death.

Jesus refused to condone exploitation by Jewish leaders. He also objected to their oppressive teachings that demanded more of the people than God ever intended. Jesus practiced what he preached, breaking their self-serving rules.

He had to die, Jewish leaders agreed.

Oddly, the Gospel writers don't agree on what prompted that decision.

Four writers offer four possible motives:
- healing a man on the Sabbath;
- raising Lazarus from the dead;
- chasing merchants from the Temple courtyard; or
- showing up to teach in Jerusalem two days before Passover.

This assortment of possibilities has scholars scrambling to figure out what really prompted the Jewish leaders to target Jesus.

MOTIVE 1: HEALING ON THE SABBATH

Early in his ministry, Jesus walked into a synagogue on the Sabbath, and there he saw a man with a deformed hand.

"Hold out your hand," Jesus said. Then he healed it.

A group of Jewish Bible scholars called Pharisees were watching. They weren't happy.

"The Pharisees called a meeting to plot how to kill Jesus" (Matthew 12:14).

The problem was that Jesus had broken one of their sacred rules.

In all of the Jewish Bible, the Old Testament, there's not one word prohibiting Jews from treating sick people on the Sabbath. But there were such laws in the ancient equivalent of a church manual, an assortment of man-made laws to help people know how to apply Bible teachings to everyday life. Rabbis and other Jewish scholars had created these laws as commentary on the Bible.

Some Jewish groups, like the Sadducees, agreed with Jesus that these laws weren't binding. Sadducees observed only the laws of Moses recorded in the first five books of the Bible.

But other Jewish groups, especially the Pharisees, observed the extra laws. Rather than admit that the laws were man-made, many Pharisees argued that God gave them to Moses for the Jews to pass along by word of mouth from generation to generation. Called the Oral Law, many of these rules are preserved in the Mishnah, a vast collection of laws and commentary that the Jews started putting into writing by about AD 200.

Here's a clue about how vast these extra laws had become. Consider one written law of Moses: "The seventh day is a Sabbath day of rest dedicated to the LORD your God" (Exodus 20:10). It spawned more than a thousand oral laws. These add-on laws told Jews exactly what they should and shouldn't do on the Sabbath.

Healing people, for example, was considered work—a no-no on the Sabbath. The only exception: if the sick person's life was on the line. One rabbi expressed the exception this way:

> If someone has a pain in the throat on the Sabbath, you may drop medicine in the patient's mouth. But that's only because it might be a matter of life and death. If someone is at risk of dying, treating the patient takes a higher priority than the Sabbath.

MISHNAH, YOMA 8:6

JEWISH GROUP   **KNOW YOUR JEWS**

	WHO THEY WERE	UNIQUE BELIEFS	INFLUENCE	OBJECTIONS TO JESUS	MEMBERS
PHARISEES	Rule-obsessed scholars, they taught that Jews should not only observe the laws in the Bible but the unwritten laws passed down by tradition.	Resurrection of the dead. Eternal life. The Messiah will overthrow Rome.	Wide influence among Jews trying to please God.	He didn't obey their unwritten laws. He said he was God's Son.	Teachers (Rabbis) Writers Lawyers (Scribes)
SADDUCEES	Jewish scholars tied to the priesthood, they taught that Jews needed to observe only the laws in their Bible.	No afterlife. No angels or spirits.	Wide influence regarding the Temple. Probably controlled the top council led by the high priest.	His popularity might spark a revolution. He predicted the Temple's destruction.	Priests Temple workers Rich rulers Land barons Rich merchants
ESSENES	Monklike Jews descended from priests, they lived in isolated communities waiting for the Messiah. They were more obsessed with rules than even the Pharisees. They produced the famous Dead Sea Scrolls.	Temple priests were frauds. Jewish rebels in the 100s BC replaced the genuine Temple priesthood (ancestors of the Essenes) with cronies. God will send two messiahs, one a priest and one a king.	Very little. Some say John the Baptist, son of a priest, joined them for a time.	Isolated, they may have known nothing about Jesus.	Descendants of priests
ZEALOTS	Revolutionaries, they fought for Jewish independence from Rome, sometimes using terror techniques, including murder.		They launched the Jewish revolt of AD 66. Rome crushed the Jews and destroyed Jerusalem and the Temple, which has never been rebuilt.	He was a false messiah because he refused to lead a revolt against Rome.	Jews upset with the Roman occupation Sicarii ("dagger," their favorite weapon). Extreme zealots, they terrorized and murdered people cooperating with Rome.
HERODIANS	Probably Sadducees, for the most part; they supported the Romans and their appointed leaders, the dynasty of King Herod the Great.		Mainly in political matters.	He claimed to be King of the Jews, which threatened Herod's dynasty.	Friends and palace officials of Herod's ruling descendants

A man with a deformed hand wasn't in danger of dying. So the Pharisees argued that Jesus should have waited a day to heal him.

These extra laws worked like a museum's knee-high barrier, keeping people at arm's length from a priceless vase. Step over the barrier and you get in trouble with museum officials who fear you might break the vase. Step over the line marked by the add-on laws and Jews got in trouble with Pharisees, who feared someone might break the super-sacred written law.

Jesus objected to add-on laws, especially when they made life tougher for people. "The Sabbath was made to serve us," Jesus said. "We weren't made to serve the Sabbath" (Mark 2:27 THE MESSAGE).

It's not recorded in the New Testament, but given Jesus' tendency to quote the Jewish Bible to make a point, he might have referred the Pharisees to the story of King Jeroboam. A prophet healed the king's paralyzed hand on a holy day when work was forbidden: "The man of God prayed to the LORD, and the king's hand was restored and he could move it again" (1 Kings 13:6).

MOTIVE 2: RAISING THE DEAD

Sometime near the end of Jesus' ministry, he raised Lazarus from the dead. He did it right under the noses of the Jewish leaders—in Bethany, less than two miles (3 km) from the Jerusalem Temple where the high priest and others ran the Jewish nation.

Their reaction: "The leading priests and Pharisees called the high council together. 'What are we going to do?' they asked each other. 'This man certainly performs many miraculous signs. If we allow him to go on like this, soon everyone will believe in him. Then the Roman army will come and destroy both our Temple and our nation' " (John 11:47-48).

The council feared that miracles this remarkable might lead people to mistake Jesus for the promised Messiah and rally behind him in a doomed revolt against Rome.

But it was the Jewish leaders who made the mistakes—two big ones:

Jesus was the promised Messiah. Why they rejected Jesus in spite of the astonishing proof—his miracles of healing the sick and raising the dead, along with his fulfilling of prophecies about the Messiah—serves as a testimony to the lure of power. Collaborators with the Roman occupiers, the Jewish leaders served at the pleasure of Rome. Even high priests were hired and fired by Rome. Caiaphas, the high priest of the moment, held his position for 18 years—longer than any other high priest in that century. Some didn't last a year.

Jesus wasn't the kind of messiah they expected. Conventional wisdom said the Messiah would be a warrior like David and that the Messiah's kingdom would be a Jewish kingdom on earth. When the Jews later accused Jesus of being a rebel leader who wanted to free Israel, Jesus said they got that wrong.

"My Kingdom is not an earthly kingdom. If it were, my followers would fight to keep me from being handed over to the Jewish leaders" (John 18:36).

MOTIVE 3: DISTURBING THE PEACE

Storming through the Temple courtyard on the Monday before his Friday crucifixion, Jesus flipped the merchants' tables. He scattered their money and drove off Jews who were buying and selling live animals to sacrifice at the Temple.

"When the leading priests and teachers of religious law heard what Jesus had done, they began planning how to kill him" (Mark 11:18).

Priests ran the Temple ministry. They were angry that Jesus dared to intrude on their turf.

Besides, the merchants were providing convenience-store services to the worshippers. Pilgrims coming to the Temple for worship didn't need to bring their own sacrificial animals. They could buy a priest-approved kosher sacrifice right there at the Temple. And men needing to pay their temple dues—an annual half-shekel temple tax—could get their Roman coins and other foreign currency exchanged for the only currency approved by the Temple priests: silver coins from Tyre, a city in what is now Lebanon. These coins were high quality. And they made a subtle statement: "We're not Romans."

What provoked Jesus to get so angry?

The biggest clue appears in what he said afterward: "The Scriptures declare, 'My Temple will be called a house of prayer for all nations,' but you have turned it into a den of thieves" (Mark 11:17).

Bible experts don't agree why Jesus scattered the people. Here are four of the most popular theories:

Protect the Gentile worship area. The Temple sanctuary building, which only priests could enter, was protected by three walled courtyards.

- *Jewish men.* Just outside the entrance into the Temple sanctuary was the courtyard of Jewish men. No women allowed.
- *Jewish women.* Beyond that was the courtyard of Jewish women. No Gentiles allowed.
- *Gentiles.* Beyond that was the sprawling courtyard of the Gentiles where anyone was allowed, including gawkers, mockers, and hawkers.

This outer courtyard was as close to the sacred Temple as Gentiles could get. So the courtyard was their sacred sanctuary for worshipping God. Signs etched in stone and painted blood red warned that any Gentiles entering Jewish sections of the Temple compound could expect execution. Temple guards patrolled the perimeter.

Problem with the theory. Evidence from history suggests that merchants worked only in one relatively small area of the massive courtyard: the red-roofed Royal Stoa along the south wall.

Maintain the purity of the Temple. Jesus wasn't concerned about only the Gentiles. He was upset that business had wormed its way inside the sacred Temple complex.

One prophet spoke of a coming day when business deals would be handled somewhere else: "At that time there will not be any buyers or sellers in the Temple of the Lord All-Powerful" (Zechariah 14:21 NCV).

Problem with the theory. There's no indication that the Jews considered the outer courtyard sacred. And even if they did, the business being conducted was for the benefit of worshippers. Also, why would Jesus purify a worship center he knew was doomed? "These great buildings. . .will be completely demolished," he said, referring to the Temple. "Not one stone will be left on top of another!" (Mark 13:2). Roman soldiers fulfilled that prediction about 40 years later, in AD 70.

Get rid of people exploiting worshippers. Jesus' criticism that the Jews had turned God's place of prayer into a "den of thieves" could suggest price gouging. For the convenience of on-site currency exchange and a livestock market, worshippers paid a convenience premium. And it's possible that priests charged the merchants a fee for the right to conduct business on Temple property—especially given Josephus' report that the high priest knew how to shake the shekel tree.

Problem with the theory. Jesus didn't chase out just the merchants. He ran off their customers, too.

Announce that God has finally rejected the temple system of worship. The Jews had perverted the temple worship system God had given them, so God was about to shut the system down.

They had perverted it in at least two ways. Jesus hinted at both in his one-line criticism.

1. "My Temple will be called a house of prayer for all nations."

The Jews built their worship around a caste system, with foreigners as outcasts, relegated to the outside courtyard. Gentiles couldn't get near the altar, located inside the courtyard of Jewish men.

It's as if the Jews insisted on ignoring one of their most famous prophets from 700 years earlier: "I [God] will also bless the foreigners who commit themselves to the LORD. . . . I will bring them to my holy mountain of Jerusalem. . . . My Temple will be called a house of prayer for all nations" (Isaiah 56:6–7).

2. "You have turned it into a den of thieves."

By "den of thieves," Jesus didn't mean that's where Jewish culprits were doing their thieving. He meant it was their den—their safe house.

The Temple was no longer a holy place. It had become a hole-in-the-wall hideout where the Jews felt safe, secure, and forgiven—in spite of all the nasty stuff they did outside the Temple. They figured they could sin their way through each year and then come to the Temple at Passover or some other annual festival, offer a sacrifice, and then walk away clean as a snowflake.

One prophet had warned against harboring a false sense of security in the Temple: "Do you really think you can steal, murder, commit adultery, lie. . .and then come here and stand before me in my Temple and chant, 'We are safe!'— only to go right back to all those evils again? Don't you yourselves admit that this Temple, which bears my name, has become a den of thieves?" (Jeremiah 7:9–11).

Problem with the theory. Just because Jesus quoted Isaiah and Jeremiah doesn't mean he felt limited to their context. He could have meant something entirely different.

ANOTHER JESUS AT THE TEMPLE

Jesus Christ wasn't the only Jesus on record in the first century to predict the collapse of the Temple, Jerusalem, and the Jewish nation.

About 30 years after Jesus Christ, and four years before the Jews revolted against Rome in AD 66, a farmer named Jesus walked the streets of Jerusalem belting out a terrifying prediction. It was a prophecy he lived to see fulfilled.

Here are excerpts of his story, as reported by the first-century historian Josephus:

Jesus began yelling: "A voice cries out from the East, a voice from the West, a voice from the four winds. It's a voice against Jerusalem, the holy temple, and the entire Jewish race!"

Day and night he continued yelling this, all over the city. Some of the city leaders had him beaten severely. But he had nothing to say for himself or to the men who beat him.

Yet afterward he continued his chanting through town until the city rulers—fearing his message came from God, as it proved to be—took him to Roman governor Albinus. The governor had Jesus beaten until his bones were showing. Yet he said nothing to defend himself and he shed no tears. Instead, with every stroke of the whip he repeated in a dreadfully mournful tone, "Woe, woe to Jerusalem. . . ."

Jesus continued this lament for seven years and five months. . .until after the revolt. When the Romans returned and surrounded Jerusalem, he walked around the outside wall crying out as loud as he could: 'Woe, woe to the city again, and to the people, and to the holy temple!' Just as he added, "Woe, woe to myself also," a stone from one of the Roman catapults killed him instantly.

WARS OF THE JEWS (BOOK 6, CHAPTER 5, SECTION 3)

MOTIVE 4:
SHOWING UP WITH WARPED IDEAS

After cleaning house at the Temple, Jesus followed up by teaching the crowds massed around him.

"When Jesus had finished. . .he said to his disciples, 'As you know, Passover begins in two days, and the Son of Man will be handed over to be crucified.' At that same time the leading priests and elders were meeting at the residence of Caiaphas, the high priest, plotting how to capture Jesus secretly and kill him. 'But not during the Passover celebration,' they agreed, 'or the people may riot' " (Matthew 26:1–5). Luke 22 reports the same thing.

Passover was the most popular Jewish festival of the year. It commemorated the Exodus—the release of the Jewish people from Egyptian slavery during the time of Moses. The name comes from the last of the 10 plagues, when the angel of death "passed over" the Jews and killed the oldest child in each Egyptian family. That tragedy prompted Egypt's pharaoh to release the Jews—something the earlier nine plagues of frogs, locusts, and other miseries had failed to do.

In Jesus' day, Jewish pilgrims came to Jerusalem by the hundreds of thousands to worship at the Temple and to pray for a messiah to free them from Roman oppression. Greater Jerusalem was home to an estimated 100,000 souls, give or take a few tens of thousands; estimates vary. During Passover week, the number of souls in Jerusalem exploded to anywhere from double to ten times the population—up to a million. Estimates vary that wildly.

With so many Jews in town, most of them fed up with a century of Roman occupation, there was always potential for an uprising. Governor Pilate brought extra Roman soldiers to town to help maintain peace. Caiaphas, appointed by the Romans, had a vested interest in peace as well. He didn't want any trouble. He wanted a strategy for quietly arresting Jesus and shutting him up forever.

Bible experts debate which day Caiaphas called this final strategy session. Matthew says it was two days before Passover. But there's confusion about which day Passover began that year, sunset Thursday or sunset Friday. Many scholars say that Matthew was talking about Jesus' celebration of the Passover meal with his disciples, better known as the Last Supper. They ate that meal on Thursday evening, hours before Jesus' arrest. If so, Caiaphas plotted the arrest of Jesus on Tuesday.

He need not have bothered. Thursday night, one of Jesus' disciples, Judas, would agree to lead the Temple police to a place where they could arrest Jesus privately, away from adoring crowds.

The four accounts of the Jewish leaders plotting to kill Jesus don't necessarily clash. It's not as if one Gospel writer got it right while the others should have checked their sources. Instead, the reports suggest that the Jewish leaders had been plotting exit strategies for Jesus throughout his ministry.

They had no idea that the most degrading exit they could arrange would only make his comeback seem all the more wonderful.

A SHADY LADY POURS PERFUME ON JESUS

A Pharisee invited Jesus to have dinner with him. . . .
When a sinful woman in that town found out that Jesus
was there, she bought an expensive bottle of perfume. . . .
The woman kissed his feet and poured the perfume on them.
LUKE 7:36–38 CEV

Pharisees—the Bible scholars of Jesus' day—didn't often invite Jesus home for a meal. One Pharisee, however, did. What happened during that meal might help explain why other Pharisees pulled the welcome mat out from under Jesus.

Law keepers to the max, Pharisees taught that they could make heaven on earth if enough people would follow their example by obeying all the Jewish laws and shunning all appearance of evil. God's Kingdom would come, they said, if people started living like citizens of God's Kingdom.

Trouble was, their idea of Kingdom citizens didn't look anything like the Kingdom citizens Jesus had in mind.

For a Pharisee, Kingdom people were holy birds of a feather who flocked together. They set an example for the rest of the world to aspire to—like diners at a five-star restaurant on display before starving souls peering through the window.

For Jesus, Kingdom citizens invited the hungry inside.

Citizens of God's Kingdom shouldn't isolate themselves, Jesus taught. "You are the light of the world—like a city on a hilltop that cannot be hidden. No one lights a lamp and then puts it under a basket. Instead, a lamp is placed on a stand, where it gives light to everyone in the house. In the same way, let your good deeds shine out for all to see, so that everyone will praise your heavenly Father" (Matthew 5:14–16).

The trouble with light in a dark world is that it draws bugs.

When Jesus came to the Pharisee's house, bugs fluttered in. One in particular was no social butterfly.

PARTY CRASHER

The woman who crashed the dinner party of Simon the Pharisee was no lady. Not by the Pharisees' standards. Bible experts translate the word describing her in a variety of ways: "sinner," "immoral woman," "town harlot."

This woman had done something terribly wrong. And because Jewish women weren't allowed to run businesses or own property, it's a fair guess that she committed some kind of sexual sin—perhaps adultery or prostitution.

What's not a fair guess is that she was Mary Magdalene. That theory got started hundreds of years after Jesus. But most scholars today dismiss the idea for at least two reasons:

The timing makes no sense. If this woman had been Mary Magdalene, Luke could have used this story as the perfect opportunity to introduce her. Instead, he introduced her and several other female supporters of Jesus immediately after this story—as if none of them had anything to do with the story. When Luke did introduce Mary Magdalene, he said Jesus exorcized her of seven demons. But he said nothing about her being a prostitute or about her anointing Jesus with perfume.

A politician's wife probably wouldn't have traveled with an ex-prostitute. One of the women who financially supported Jesus and traveled with his entourage was Joanna. She was the wife of Chuza, a business manager for Herod Antipas, ruler of Galilee. If Joanna had been traveling in the company of a former prostitute, or a woman with any kind of a bad reputation, it probably wouldn't have generated confidence in her husband's ability to manage anything, including his wife.

Some scholars speculate that the mystery woman may have been Mary of Bethany, the sister of Martha. All three of the other Gospels tell similar stories that place the event in Bethany. John's Gospel is the only one that identifies the woman as Martha's sister: "Mary took a twelve-ounce jar of expensive perfume made from essence of nard, and she anointed Jesus' feet with it, wiping his feet with her hair" (John 12:3).

There are a few differences in the four versions of the story—enough that many Bible experts suspect the writers were describing two or more events. Yet, since early Christian times, many other experts say the differences are easily explained and that all four Gospels are probably talking about the same event.

There are two main differences in the stories.

Feet or head. John agrees with Luke that the woman poured perfume on Jesus' feet. But Matthew and Mark say she poured it over his head.

Possible solution. Twelve ounces (a third of a liter) was enough to pour over both.

Simon's home or Lazarus' home. Matthew, Mark, and Luke all place the dinner in the home of a man named Simon. John—the only one to identify the woman as Mary—places the dinner in the home of Lazarus, the brother of Mary and Martha.

Possible solution. Simon and Lazarus may have been neighbors who hosted Jesus together. And there may have been some confusion over where the banquet took place. If that's what happened, Mary of Bethany would not have been a party crasher. She would have been an invited guest.

Whoever the woman was and whatever her sin, she crossed the line.

Even if she was someone other than Mary, the fact that she walked into the Pharisee's house uninvited wouldn't have been the problem, say some Bible experts. Otherwise, the Pharisee would have promptly ordered her out. Parties like this, honoring a famous rabbi, were often open-door events. Gallery gawkers were welcome—to watch the invited guests, listen and learn from the conversation, and envy the host.

HOOKERS IN THE HOLY LAND

Given all the fiery words that Roman and Jewish leaders vented over prostitution in Jesus' time, it's a wonder nobody outlawed the profession.

It was legal in the Roman Empire. It was legal in the Jewish homeland.

Laws of adultery didn't apply. Roman law preserved in the *Justinian Code* declared that married men who had sex with prostitutes were not guilty of adultery, as long as they paid for the services. And prostitutes committed no adultery unless they were married.

Prostitutes included

- **destitute women** trying to survive—prostitution wasn't a preferred career path;
- **captives**—citizens of defeated cities or travelers kidnapped by pirates and then sold at auction;
- **children abandoned at birth** and raised as investments to work the brothels; and
- **barmaids and waitresses** multitasking at inns, which often doubled as brothels.

"Disgraceful debauchery" is how Diodorus Siculus described prostitution in *Historical Library*, a 40-volume collection of books he wrote in the first century BC.

"In dealing with brothels," writes Dio Chrysostom in one of his surviving speeches from the first century, "we must certainly not give in to the argument that there are two sides to this profession. We must sternly forbid prostitution and insist that no one, rich or poor, be allowed to practice this trade. . .which the entire world condemns as shameful and brutal. . . . We must not allow people to exploit helpless women or children captured in war or bought as slaves and expose them to shameful practices conducted in dirty booths all over the city."

"Let her be stoned." That's the punishment recommended by Philo, a first-century Jewish historian, writing in *The Special Laws III*. "She has filled the souls of men and women with lust, polluting the beauty of the immortal mind and worshipping the beauty of the body that will soon die. . . . She sells herself to anyone who comes by, as if her beauty were just another product on sale at the market."

Surprisingly, even Moses stopped short of outlawing prostitution, though Jewish law did include some restrictions:

- "Priests may not marry a woman defiled by prostitution" (Leviticus 21:7).
- "If a priest's daughter defiles herself by becoming a prostitute, she also defiles her father's holiness, and she must be burned to death" (Leviticus 21:9).
- "You must not bring to the house of the LORD your God any offering from the earnings of a prostitute" (Deuteronomy 23:18).

Rabbis joined with many Romans in condemning prostitution as evil. Yet even the rabbis didn't usually treat prostitution as a crime like adultery, which was a capital offense.

In Luke's version of the story, which focuses on the Pharisee's reaction, the woman crossed the line when she stepped out of the shadows and into the spotlight. Jesus crossed the line, too, by letting her proceed. At least that's what the Pharisee said to himself. "If this man were a prophet," Simon thought, "he would know what kind of woman is touching him. She's a sinner!" (Luke 7:39).

HOW TO WELCOME GUESTS

When we invite guests into our home, we generally welcome them with a warm handshake. We take their coat, if they have one, invite them to sit, and offer them something to eat or drink.

The customs were different in Jesus' day.

Kiss. Instead of a handshake, a kiss on the cheek was the common welcome—a touch of modern Europe in the ancient Middle East.

Water for dusty feet. Most roads were dirt paths. And the most common mode of transportation was walking in sandals. On dry days—of which there were many in Israel—each step exploded into a tiny dust ball encrusting the feet. Though it wasn't required, many hosts offered water for guests to wash their feet. Some would even have one of their servants do the washing—a bit like an in-house shoe-shine boy, with water and a towel instead of polish and a brush.

Oil for the head. For special guests, some hosts would offer oil for the hair, to cool the head from the blazing sun. Usually it was unscented olive oil—inexpensive and locally grown.

Jesus' host, Simon the Pharisee, offered him none of these.

SHADY LADY BRINGS HER OWN BOTTLE

"While he [Jesus] was eating, a woman came in with a beautiful alabaster jar of expensive perfume made from essence of nard" (Mark 14:3).

Nard had an earthy, cypresslike smell with a sky-high price. Premium nard was made of oil extracted from the roots and stems of the spikenard plant, native to India's Himalaya mountains. Merchants importing it to Israel by caravan had to travel nearly two years each way, some 2,500 miles (4,000 kilometers). The delivery fee was enormous: almost a year's salary for a 12-ounce flask (a third of a liter). In Roman currency, it cost 300 denarii. Employers at the time hired laborers at a denarius a day.

Whether or not the woman started pouring the perfume on Jesus' feet and eventually worked her way to his head, she probably would have preferred to pour it all on his head. If she started at his feet, she may have done so because of the way he was reclining around the knee-high dinner table. People usually reclined on their side, with their head near the table and their feet extended behind them.

When a host poured oil of any kind on a guest—let alone something as extravagant as nard—it served as a wonderful expression of hospitality. Some Arab tribes still welcome guests this way.

In Jesus' day, it wasn't just an attempt to sooth a guest's hot, dry scalp from the desert sun and the arid afternoon winds common in Israel. Nor was it merely a gift of fragrance a century before people in the region started bathing with soap.

There was nobility to it—and sanctity:

- Israel's kings were anointed with oil at their coronation and were sometimes referred to as God's "anointed one." *Messiah* literally means "Anointed One."
- Priests were anointed at their ordination.
- Holy objects such as the Temple altar and the lamp stands were anointed during ceremonies dedicating them for sacred use.

Oil poured on a guest sent a powerful message: You are special.

In telling the story, Luke paints a word picture rippling with emotion:

There's compassion. Readers feel compassion for this woman, because she was crying. Her tears fell on Jesus' feet, and she quickly brushed them off with her hair and then kissed his feet.

There's shock. The woman empties her jar of "expensive perfume" onto Jesus. A year's salary poured out in seconds.

There's anger. Readers get upset with the Pharisee for judging the woman so harshly.

Surprisingly, Jesus expressed no anger toward this particular Pharisee, though he sometimes got upset at the callousness of others. That might suggest he considered the man a friend, like Lazarus. Instead of condemning the Pharisee, Jesus taught him just as he patiently taught many others—with a parable.

"A man loaned money to two people—500 pieces of silver to one and 50 pieces to the other. But neither of them could repay him, so he kindly forgave them both, canceling their debts. Who do you suppose loved him more after that?" (Luke 7:41–42).

The coins were Roman denarii. So the difference in money for the average Jew working six days a week and earning a denarius a day would have been about two months' salary compared to almost two years' salary.

Jesus then brought the parable home.

"Look at this woman kneeling here. When I entered your home, you didn't offer me water to wash the dust from my feet, but she has washed them with her tears and wiped them with her hair. You didn't greet me with a kiss, but from the time I first came in, she has not stopped kissing my feet. You neglected the courtesy of olive oil to anoint my head, but she has anointed my feet with rare perfume. I tell you, her sins—and they are many—have been forgiven, so she has shown me much love. But a person who is forgiven little shows only little love" (Luke 7:43–47).

Law-abiding Pharisees considered themselves holier than most people and in need of very little forgiveness. But this woman, who had apparently met

Jesus earlier and was anointing him in gratitude for what he had done for her, knew the extent of the spiritual debt she had been forgiven.

Luke doesn't tell us how Simon reacted. But when Jesus assured the woman that her sins were forgiven, Simon's friends mumbled, "Who does he think he is, forgiving sins!" (Luke 7:49 THE MESSAGE). Only God could forgive sins.

Jesus knew who he was.

"I am the Son of God. . . . The Father set me apart and sent me into the world. Don't believe me unless I carry out my Father's work. But if I do his work, believe in the evidence of the miraculous works I have done, even if you don't believe me. Then you will know and understand that the Father is in me, and I am in the Father" (John 10:36–38).

Unfortunately, most Pharisees trusted their ancient traditions more than they trusted their own eyes. We can only hope Simon was an exception.

THE FIRST PALM SUNDAY

News that Jesus was on the way to Jerusalem swept through the city. A large crowd of Passover visitors took palm branches and went down the road to meet him.

JOHN 12:12–13

J esus had two great Sundays in a row. But the week between was a killer. This savage week takes up a disproportionate amount of space in all four of the Gospel stories about Jesus—anywhere from a fourth of Mark to almost half of John.

Since Roman times, Christians have called the week between Palm Sunday and Easter "Passion Week." *Passion* is an outdated word. It's from the Latin *passio*, meaning "suffering," as in Suffering Week.

Some call it Holy Week instead. But to many people, that hardly seems fitting. This is the week Jesus got arrested, tried overnight, and nailed to a cross by nine o'clock the next morning.

What's holy about that?

He died for our sins, some would answer.

His blood washed away our sins, just as the blood of sacrificial animals in Old Testament times purified God's people: "I have given you the blood on the altar to purify you, making you right with the LORD. It is the blood, given in exchange for a life, that makes purification possible" (Leviticus 17:11).

Since the beginning of human history, the Bible says sin has been a capital offense. At first, God gave animals as substitutes to die in our place. Then, the New Testament writers say, God gave his Son as the final sacrifice for all people and for all time.

The sacrificial system was about to end.

The beginning of the end came on a Sunday, when Jesus rode into Jerusalem to the cheers of a crowd. They welcomed him as the king God had sent to save them. They expected salvation for a lifetime in the kingdom of Israel. But Jesus brought salvation for an eternity in the Kingdom of God.

THE RIDE

Jesus approached Jerusalem from the east on a Sunday. He was loaded with prophecies awaiting fulfillment. They didn't have to wait long.

Jesus traveled the typical route from Jericho, a day-long climb from the Jordan River Valley along a winding dirt trail that eventually rose up and over a ridge called the Mount of Olives and into Jerusalem.

Before cresting the Mount of Olives, where travelers caught their first glimpse of Jerusalem, Jesus had to pass the villages of Bethany and Bethphage

RESURRECTION COUNTDOWN

DATE	EVENT	MATTHEW	MARK	LUKE	JOHN
Friday, March 27, AD 33	Jesus arrives in Bethany				12:1
Saturday	Dinner with Lazarus, Martha, Mary	26:6–7			12:2
	A woman anoints Jesus with scented oil	21:1–11	14:3	7:36–38	12:3
Sunday (Palm Sunday)	Jesus rides into Jerusalem as crowds cheer	21:12	11:1–11	19:28–40	12:12–20
Monday	Jesus chases merchants from the Temple	21:23–25:46	11:15–16		
Tuesday	Jesus teaches at the Temple	26:14–16	11:27–13:37	20:1–21:4	
Wednesday	Judas arranges to betray Jesus*	26:17–30	14:10–11		
Thursday	Jesus eats the Last Supper with his disciples	26:36–56	14:12–25	22:7–20	13:1–38
	Jews arrest Jesus in the Garden of Gethsemane	26:57–27:61	14:32–52	22:39–53	18:1–14
Friday	Jesus is tried overnight; crucified at 9 a.m.; dead by 3 p.m.; buried before sunset	27:62–66	14:53–15:47	22:54–23:56	18:19–19:42
Saturday (Sabbath)	Romans post guards at tomb	28:1–15			
Sunday (Easter)	Jesus rises from the dead	28:1–20	16:1–20	24:1–49	20:1–29

* The Bible doesn't reveal the exact day, but many scholars guess Wednesday.

on the slopes of the Mount of Olives. Bethany was less than 2 miles (3 km) from Jerusalem. The exact site of neighboring Bethphage remains a mystery.

Many Jews expected God's Messiah to come from the east, just as Jesus did. Describing the Messiah as "king over all the earth," one prophet said, "His feet will stand on the Mount of Olives, east of Jerusalem" (Zechariah 14:4). The prophet went on to describe end-time scenes from what some scholars say will be Jesus' Second Coming.

Fully aware of other prophecies about the Messiah's coming, Jesus arranged to bring them to life.

He apparently rented a donkey, because all the disciples had to do was untie it and bring it to Jesus. Matthew reported two donkeys: a mother "with its colt beside it" (Matthew 21:2).

Some Bible experts say Matthew got it wrong. They say Matthew was trying too hard to squeeze the story into an Old Testament prophecy and that he didn't understand the genre in which the prophecy was written: Hebrew poetry. In fact, some scholars say that Jesus probably walked the entire way to Jerusalem and that all the Gospel writers added the donkey story because it fit so neatly into a prediction from 500 years earlier: "Rejoice, O people of Zion! Shout in triumph, O people of Jerusalem! Look, your king is coming to you. He is righteous and victorious, yet he is humble, riding on a donkey—riding on a donkey's colt" (Zechariah 9:9).

Matthew, some scholars speculate, added the second donkey because he incorrectly thought Zechariah was talking about two donkeys. Zechariah wasn't; there's just one donkey in the prophecy. Instead of rhyming, Hebrew poetry repeats ideas. It's called parallelism, which is one of the unique features of Hebrew poetry. "People of Zion" and "people of Jerusalem" are the same people. "Riding on a donkey" and "riding on a donkey's colt" is one ride on one critter.

Bible experts rallying to Matthew's defense argue that there may have been two donkeys: a mother and her unbroken colt. If so, Jesus may have ridden on the colt and took the mother along to calm the colt in the cheering crowd. Some artists, however, show a young colt tagging alongside its mother carrying Jesus.

Why a donkey instead of a horse? The answer lies in prophecy mingled with Jewish tradition.

For Jews who knew their Bible, the donkey represented

- **Royalty.** During crown prince Solomon's short jaunt across town for his coronation, "Solomon rode on David's mule" (1 Kings 1:38 CEV).
- **Messiah.** In an early prophecy about the tribe of Judah, from which Jesus' family descended, Jacob told about "the coming of the one. . .whom all nations will honor. He ties his foal to

a grapevine, the colt of his donkey to a choice vine" (Genesis 49:10–11). Again, this is poetry—with one donkey.

- **Peace.** Zechariah's prediction about a humble king riding on a donkey emphasizes peace. It does so in a follow-up verse that contrasts the donkey in verse 9 with a warhorse: "I will remove the battle chariots from Israel and the warhorses from Jerusalem. I will destroy all the weapons used in battle, and your king will bring peace to the nations" (Zechariah 9:10).

For Jesus, the donkey carried more than just him. It carried the message about who he was.

THE GLORY

Jesus had spent two nights in Bethany, arriving on Friday and eating on Saturday with Mary, Martha, and their brother, Lazarus, whom Jesus had raised from the dead, perhaps just a few weeks earlier.

By Sunday morning, word had reached Jerusalem that Jesus was on the outskirts of town, coming to celebrate Passover. Once he and his disciples crested the Mount of Olives, people in Jerusalem on the next ridge would have seen him. Many knew of his miracles, especially his resurrection of Lazarus. As he rode down the slope into the Kidron Valley, a large crowd in Jerusalem rushed down the ridge to meet him.

"Many in the crowd spread their garments on the road ahead of him, and others spread leafy branches they had cut in the fields. Jesus was in the center of the procession, and the people all around him were shouting, 'Praise God! Blessings on the one who comes in the name of the LORD! Blessings on the coming Kingdom of our ancestor David! Praise God in highest heaven!' " (Mark 11:8–10).

This wasn't how Jews welcomed a celebrity. This is how they welcomed a king whom they believed was their messiah, a savior sent from God.

That much is clear in their actions and their words.

A carpet of cloaks. This wasn't the first time Jews carpeted the ground with their clothes. About 900 years earlier, a group of Jewish soldiers did the same when they learned that a prophet had just anointed their commander, Jehu, as the next king. Before joining Jehu in a coup that ended King Ahab's dynasty, "they quickly spread out their cloaks on the bare steps and blew the ram's horn, shouting, 'Jehu is king!' " (2 Kings 9:13).

Waving palm branches. It was like waving the Jewish flag right under the noses of the occupying forces of Rome.

Some 200 years earlier, the Jews had driven off their Syrian occupiers. In a victory procession, the Jews entered Jerusalem "with praise and palm branches... because a great enemy had been crushed and removed from Israel" (1 Maccabees 13:51).

The Jews would also drive out the Roman occupiers in AD 66—temporarily, at least. During the four years of freedom that followed, while Rome organized a crushing counterstrike, Jews minted their own coins—decorated in palm branches.

Even in the Roman world, waving palm branches was a sign of victory. Suetonius, a first-century Roman historian writing a history of the emperors, tells of Caligula fighting a gladiator who was armed with only a wooden sword. When the gladiator fell on purpose to make the emperor look good, Caligula "stabbed him with a real dagger and then danced around with a palm branch, as victors do" (*Life of Caligula*, 32).

The chant. The crowd chanted lyrics from a psalm of hope that Jewish pilgrims in Jerusalem often recited at Passover. During the week of celebration, worshippers recited six psalms: 113–118. But in this particular moment they rallied around the last line of a song inspired by an exciting scene of deliverance:

"This is the LORD's doing, and it is wonderful to see. This is the day the LORD has made. We will rejoice and be glad in it. Please, LORD, please save us. Please, LORD, please give us success. Bless the one who comes in the name of the LORD" (Psalm 118:23–26).

Some scholars say that Psalm 118 probably commemorates King David's return to Jerusalem after a victory in battle. David was the first Jewish leader to secure Israel's national boundaries.

Though the psalm doesn't mention David, the crowd does. David was Israel's most respected king and the ancestor from whom they expected the Messiah to descend.

Taken together, the blended quotes in this chant expressed the crowd's exuberant belief: The Messiah has finally come.

Pharisees watching this procession connected the dots right away.

"Teacher," they yelled to Jesus, "get your disciples under control!" (Luke 19:39 THE MESSAGE).

"If they kept quiet," Jesus answered, "the stones along the road would burst into cheers!" (Luke 19:40).

That was a very Jewish response, and the Pharisees may have connected those dots, too—all the way back to the prophet Isaiah. In a prophecy about a day yet to come, when God would save his people, Isaiah described the uncontainable joy: "The mountains and hills will burst into song, and the trees of the field will clap their hands!" (Isaiah 55:12).

That day of salvation had come.

SIGNS OF THE END TIMES

"What sign will signal your return and the end of the world?"
MATTHEW 24:3

S eems like a simple enough question the disciples asked Jesus. But given his convoluted answer, you'd think a five-year-old had just asked Daddy where babies come from.

Shining stars of Bible scholarship who have studied Jesus' answer are left scratching their heads and arguing with each other over what on earth he was talking about.

Some say Jesus got it wrong. After all, he did give his disciples a truckload of signs about when the world would end—and then he said, "This generation will not pass from the scene before all these things take place" (Mark 13:30).

That was about 50 generations ago, measuring 40 years to a generation. C. S. Lewis, a widely respected Christian writer of the 1900s, describes that single sentence as "the most embarrassing verse in the Bible." Other Bible experts, however, offer theories that don't make it look embarrassing at all.

Scholars don't see eye to eye on much of anything about the answer Jesus offered his disciples. But they do agree on a name for it: the Olivet Discourse. It's a speech, or discourse. And Jesus did his talking on the Mount of Olives.

Had Jesus made this speech at a modern-day press conference, reporters would have pummeled him with follow-up questions. Instead, as far as the Gospels of Matthew, Mark, and Luke report, all Jesus got was the equivalent of a five-year-old's dumbfounded "Huh?"

There's a reason the disciples asked the question in the first place.

Jesus had already told them he would be leaving and coming back later. And he told them humanity was headed to the end of the world as they knew it, followed by Judgment Day. Now, walking out of Jerusalem's majestic Temple complex—the only Jewish temple in the world—Jesus announced that it would be leveled.

"When will all this happen?" the disciples asked.

Jesus answered with vague clues that Bible experts say could fit timelines in Jesus' century, or millenniums afterward.

Worse, after offering all these clues, Jesus admitted, "No one knows the day or hour when these things will happen, not even the angels in heaven or the Son himself. Only the Father knows" (Mark 13:32).

We're left hanging with follow-up questions like this:

"So if you can't give us a day, a decade, a century, or a millennium, what's the point of the signs?"

As with most Bible prophecies, the point of Jesus' speech is clear: Be ready.

But the point of the signs and exactly what they're pointing to are a matter of speculation. Fortunately for us, Bible scholars love to speculate. They figure one day they might strike gold.

KISS THE TEMPLE GOOD-BYE

In a thousand years of Jewish history up to the time of Jesus, the Jews had worshipped at only three temples in Jerusalem.

Temple 1. Solomon finished the first Temple in about 960 BC. Exquisitely crafted, it lasted nearly 400 years—until Babylonian invaders from what is now Iraq tore it down in 586 BC.

Temple 2. Jews returning from exile in Babylon finished the second Temple in 515 BC. It lasted almost 500 years, at which time Herod the Great remodeled and expanded it.

Temple 3. Famed for his building projects, Herod began renovating the Temple in about 20 BC—a job that extended for more than 80 years, until AD 64. The last and largest Jewish Temple ever built, it survived a measly six years

---

HOME COOKING DURING A SIEGE

When the Roman army surrounded Jerusalem, a starving mother trapped inside killed, cooked, and ate her own breastfeeding child.

This horrifying story survives in a book about the Jewish war with Rome. The author was the Jewish historian Josephus, a traitor who joined the Romans to save his own skin and who advised them during the half-year siege of Jerusalem:

Her name was Mary. . . . She did an unnatural thing. She held up her son who had been breastfeeding and said, "Oh unfortunate child, who am I saving you for in this war, this famine, this rebellion? If the famine doesn't kill us, the Romans will, or the rebels. The best we can hope for is slavery. So come and be my meal." . . . She killed her son. Then she roasted him, ate half of him, and hid the other half for later.

Rebels smelled the meat and threatened to cut Mary's throat if she didn't show them her food. She said she saved an excellent portion for them, and brought out what was left of her son. "This is my own son. I cooked him myself. Come and eat. I've already eaten." . . . . The men left, trembling—more terrified than they had ever been before. . . . When word got out about this, people considered their fellow Jews who had already died as lucky, for they hadn't lived long enough to see such misery.

WARS OF THE JEWS 6.3.4

Similar stories appear in the Old Testament from Babylon's siege of Jerusalem in 586 BC.

In 2 Kings 6, two women agreed to kill and eat their two children, sharing the meat. But after eating the first child, the mother of the second child reneged on her promise.

In the book of Lamentations, a survivor of the Babylonian siege complains to God: "Tenderhearted women have cooked their own children. They have eaten them to survive the siege" (Lamentations 4:10).

before the Romans leveled it.

Jesus predicted it would happen.

His prediction is what sparked his speech about signs of the end times on earth.

"As Jesus was leaving the Temple that day, one of his disciples said, 'Teacher, look at these magnificent buildings! Look at the impressive stones in the walls.' Jesus replied, 'Yes, look at these great buildings. But they will be completely demolished. Not one stone will be left on top of another!' " (Mark 13:1–2).

The prophet Daniel had said the same thing about 500 years before Jesus—seemingly adding a prediction that the Messiah would be killed first: "The Anointed One will be killed, appearing to have accomplished nothing, and a ruler will arise whose armies will destroy the city and the Temple" (Daniel 9:26).

Herod's doomed Temple was majestic and expansive. The king started his renovation by doubling the size of the Jerusalem hilltop on which the Temple sat, to about 525 yards by 330 yards (480 meters by 302 meters). He brought in fill dirt, held in place by a huge retaining wall. Part of that wall survives today: the famous Western Wall—also called the Wailing Wall—where the Jews come to pray. This wall is all that remains of the Jewish Temple, and for this reason, it is the most sacred Jewish site on earth.

Josephus, a first-century Jewish historian who was also a Roman citizen, described Jerusalem's landmark this way:

Massive panels of gold covered much of the outside. When the morning sun rose over the Mount of Olives and struck the golden temple, it reflected fiery rays that forced everyone to look away—as if it were the sun. Other parts of the temple walls were built of shimmering white limestone. Travelers headed toward the city and catching their first sight of the temple in the distance thought Jerusalem was a mountain covered in snow.

WARS OF THE JEWS 5.5.6

About 33 years after Jesus' crucifixion, the Jews revolted against Rome. The year was AD 66. Jews drove out the Roman garrison stationed in Jerusalem. Then they chased off Roman reinforcements sent from neighboring Syria.

Emperor Nero assigned General Vespasian to recapture the Jewish homeland. With an army of about 60,000, Vespasian overran northern Israel by AD 68. That summer Nero killed himself. Vespasian became emperor, and the general's son—Titus—took over the fight for Israel. Titus surrounded Jerusalem in the spring of AD 70. By early summer, Titus' soldiers had broken through the city walls. They slaughtered the starving Jews inside—at least 600,000 souls, according to Tacitus, a Roman historian of that century. Josephus estimated that 1.1 million Jews died. Scholars today estimate Romans killed 100,000 and enslaved another 100,000.

Many Jews made a desperate last stand at the Temple. According to Dio Chrysostom, another Roman historian of the first century, some Jewish defenders considered it such an honor to die defending the Temple that they refused to surrender. Instead, they fell on Roman swords, jumped into fires, and even killed each other.

After the battle, the Romans began dismantling the city walls. By mid-August, they had destroyed the Temple, too. Archaeologists say that a burn scar shaped like an arch and seared into bedrock on the Temple hilltop confirms Roman reports that soldiers set fire to the complex. Perhaps fired by wood burning inside the sanctuary and the attached supply buildings, the limestone arch toppled over and branded itself onto the rock. If a fire burns hot enough, it can crumble limestone into powder.

It would take the Jewish nation nearly 2,000 years to rise from the ashes—declaring itself a sovereign nation again in 1948. As for the Temple, it's history. Sitting in its place on the Temple hilltop for the past 600 years has been a gold-topped Muslim shrine called the Dome of the Rock—Jerusalem's new distinguishing landmark.

— THE ART OF READING END-TIMES SIGNS ——

Sitting on the Mount of Olives with a panoramic view of Jerusalem in front of him, Jesus predicted not only the end of the city—but of all creation as well. "Heaven and earth will disappear" (Luke 21:33).

Don't worry. It already happened. Jesus was speaking symbolically. We missed everything—from the Second Coming to Judgment Day.

That's what some respected Bible scholars insist.

"All that the church hoped for in the second coming of Christ is already given in its present experience of Christ through the Spirit." Those are the words of the late C. H. Dodd, a Welsh New Testament scholar in the 1900s who directed the translation of the *New English Bible*. According to Dodd, Jesus taught that God's kingdom had already come and that we are already experiencing eternal life.

A little evidence:

- **The Kingdom came.** After the Pharisees asked Jesus when God's Kingdom would come, Jesus answered, "The Kingdom of God can't be detected by visible signs. You won't be able to say, 'Here it is!' or 'It's over there!' For the Kingdom of God is already among you" (Luke 17:20–21). (For more about the Kingdom of God, see "What Is the Kingdom of God?" page 201.)
- **Eternal life starts now.** "Those who listen to my message and believe in God who sent me have eternal life. They will never be condemned for their sins, but they have already passed from death into life" (John 5:24).

Dodd's take on the end times represents one of many ways to interpret Jesus' predictions.

There are three main approaches:

Theory 1: Jesus' predictions have already come true. Bible scholars call Dodd's approach "realized eschatology." But in plain English it means that the events Jesus predicted for the end times have already happened—they've been "realized." *Eschatology* comes from the Greek word *eschatos*, which means "last."

According to Dodd's way of understanding, when Jesus predicted a time of tribulation, he may have been talking about Rome's devastating counterstrike against the rebellious Jews. The war against Rome ended in the destruction of Jerusalem and the collapse of the Jewish nation.

The fall of Jerusalem and the Jewish nation, some say, may have been the Second Coming and Judgment Day wrapped in one—with Jesus returning to punish the sinful.

Not all Bible experts read Jesus' predictions that way.

Theory 2: Jesus' predictions are coming true today. Some scholars say that Jesus' predictions are being fulfilled today—that the church has been living in the time of tribulation Jesus described: "Nation will go to war against nation, and kingdom against kingdom. There will be earthquakes in many parts of the world, as well as famines. . . . A brother will betray his brother to death, a father will betray his own child, and children will rebel against their parents and cause them to be killed" (Mark 13:8, 12).

Theory 3: Some of Jesus' predictions have come true; others are yet to come. Many Bible experts say that some of Jesus' predictions may have been fulfilled when Jerusalem fell but that other predictions don't match history. So they must point to the future.

This third approach probably has the biggest block of fans.

SIGNPOSTS TO OBLIVION

Called the Little Apocalypse, Jesus' teaching about signs of the end times is reported in three Gospels: Matthew 24, Mark 13, and Luke 21. Most Bible experts say that Mark's version came first and that Matthew and Luke use it as a main source.

Here are a few of the signposts Jesus said would point to the end of time as we know it.

"Wars and threats of wars" (Mark 13:7). Jesus started with something familiar. Jewish writers for centuries had warned that hard times would come before the end times:

When you see that some of the predicted signs have occurred, then you will know that it is the very time when the Most High is about to visit the world that he has made. So when there shall appear in the world

*earthquakes, tumult of peoples, intrigues of nations, wavering of leaders,
confusion of princes, then you will know that it was of these that the Most
High spoke from the days that were of old.*

2 ESDRAS 9:1–4,
A JEWISH BOOK PROBABLY WRITTEN SHORTLY
AFTER ROMANS DESTROYED JERUSALEM IN AD 70

"The Good News must first be preached to all nations" (Mark 13:10).
Christians fulfilled this prediction in Jesus' century, according to many Bible
experts. "All nations," they say, refers to the world of the disciples—mainly the
Roman Empire that covered most of the land around the Mediterranean Sea.

Jesus' prediction tracks with the last known request he made of his disciples—
an assignment known today as the Great Commission: "Go and make disciples
of all the nations, baptizing them in the name of the Father and the Son and
the Holy Spirit. Teach these new disciples to obey all the commands I have
given you. And be sure of this: I am with you always, even to the end of the age"
(Matthew 28:19–20).

Christian writers in the AD 100s and 200s said that Jesus' disciples died
honoring his last request; most were martyred. Thomas was apparently martyred in India, after starting churches that still claim him as founding pastor.
Matthew is said to have died in Ethiopia, John in Turkey, and Thaddaeus (also
known as Judas, son of James) in Iran.

**"The day is coming when you will see what Daniel the prophet spoke
about—the sacrilegious object that causes desecration standing in the Holy
Place. . . . Then those in Judea must flee to the hills"** (Matthew 24:15–16).

The prophet Daniel put it this way: "His army will take over the Temple
fortress, pollute the sanctuary, put a stop to the daily sacrifices, and set up the
sacrilegious object that causes desecration" (Daniel 11:31).

Bible experts have suggested several possible fulfillments of this prophecy:

- *Syrian invaders.* In the 100s BC, Antiochus IV Epiphanes
  conquered the Jewish homeland and outlawed the Jewish
  religion. At the Jerusalem Temple, he reportedly sacrificed a pig,
  an animal the Jews considered ritually unclean. This would have
  contaminated the holy site. The Jews revolted and won their
  freedom.
- *Roman Emperor Caligula.* He ordered a statue of himself erected
  at the Temple. He was assassinated in AD 41, before anyone
  carried out the order.
- *Jewish rebels.* During the last stages of the Jewish war against
  Rome, which ended with the Temple's destruction in AD 70,
  Jewish rebels called Zealots retreated into the Temple sanctuary
  where only priests were allowed.

- *Roman General Titus.* One of the favorite theories is that after the Romans conquered Jerusalem, General Titus set up his military standards in the most sacred room of the Temple, where the Jews had once kept the ark containing the 10 Commandments. The standards were poles with insignias on them. Jews considered them idolatrous because they included pictures of the emperor, whom the Romans worshipped as a god. God had instructed that only the high priest could enter this most sacred room, and only on one day each year: Yom Kippur, the Day of Atonement set aside for the entire nation to repent of sin.

Luke's version of Jesus' prediction seems to add support to this theory. Luke told the Judeans to run for the hills "when you see Jerusalem surrounded by armies, then you will know that the time of its destruction has arrived" (Luke 21:20).

Christians living in Jerusalem at the time remembered Jesus' warning—and took his advice. So said Eusebius, a church leader living in Palestine during the early AD 300s. Writing his book *Church History*, Eusebius said the Christian fugitives escaped east of the Jordan River, to a town in Perea, in present-day Jordan.

Jesus warned that fleeing in winter or on the Sabbath would be difficult.

Traveling on the Sabbath would mean abandoning traditional Jewish beliefs about resting on this sacred day. Traveling in winter meant crossing dry gullies called wadis (WAH-dees) that winter rains might churn into thrashing rivers.

The Jewish war stretched over several winters. Josephus reports that one large group of refugees got trapped between the Roman army and the swift-flowing Jordan River, flooded by heavy rain. Fifteen thousand refugees died in the battle.

"There will be strange signs in the sun, moon, and stars" (Luke 21:25). Centuries earlier, Jewish prophets had spoken of similar signs. Mark's version of Jesus' prediction quotes two, Isaiah and Joel. "The sun will be darkened, the moon will give no light, the stars will fall from the sky, and the powers in the heavens will be shaken" (Mark 13:24–25).

This doesn't necessarily mean the end of the universe, some scholars say. Jesus may have been using a metaphor—a symbolic way of saying that Judgment Day will be such a monumental event that even the sky will stand silent before the Lord.

For a more literal connection, at least to ancient history, Josephus reported strange events in the sky before the Jews rebelled against Rome:

There was a star resembling a sword that hung above the city, along with a comet. . . . And when Jerusalem was crowded with pilgrims celebrating Passover, a bright light from the sky illuminated the temple altar and

sanctuary at the ninth hour of the night [possibly 3:00 a.m.]. For half an
hour, the place seemed as bright as day.

WARS OF THE JEWS 6.5.3

**"Then everyone will see the Son of Man coming on the clouds with
great power and glory"** (Mark 13:26). Though some Bible experts say they
don't necessarily see a future Second Coming here, many do.

Part of the reason some see a Second Coming is because Jesus seemed to
draw this sign out of a vision reported by the prophet Daniel: "As my vision
continued that night, I saw someone like a son of man coming with the clouds
of heaven. He approached the Ancient One and was led into his presence. He
was given authority, honor, and sovereignty over all the nations of the world,
so that people of every race and nation and language would obey him. His rule
is eternal—it will never end. His kingdom will never be destroyed" (Daniel
7:13–14).

Another reason is because of what angels told the disciples as they watched
Jesus leave planet Earth, ascending into the clouds: "Someday he will return
from heaven in the same way you saw him go!" (Acts 1:11).

**"I tell you the truth, this generation will not pass from the scene before
all these things take place"** (Mark 13:30). Jesus got this one wrong, some Bible
experts say.

His mistake only confirms what he told his disciples moments later: "No
one knows the day or hour when these things will happen, not even the angels
in heaven or the Son himself. Only the Father knows" (Mark 13:32).

The trouble is, if Jesus missed it, he didn't miss it by just a day or an hour.
He missed it by millenniums.

Since the time he misspoke—if that's what it was—we humans have gone
from catapulting boulders at stone walls to launching satellites at comets.

Assuming Jesus got it right, here are a few theories about what it was he got
right:

- Jesus was talking about the fall of the Jerusalem Temple. The
  Romans destroyed it about 37 years later. So Jesus came back
  symbolically in judgment.
- He was talking about a future "sacrilegious object that causes
  desecration" and a time of tribulation to follow. The generation
  that experiences these will be the generation that sees the Son of
  Man coming in the clouds.
- The Greek word for "generation" can also mean "race," as in the
  Jewish people. Jesus may have been saying the Jews would live
  to see his predictions come true.

The big surprise for many students of the Bible is that Jesus wasn't really
trying to answer the "when" question.

Most scholars say that if he had really wanted to do that, he'd have done a better job. He wouldn't have been so vague. And he wouldn't have given himself 2,000 years or more of wiggle room.

In fact, many scholars say the date isn't set in celestial concrete. Jesus hinted that the end depends on God's grace and humanity's response: "Unless the Lord shortens that time of calamity, not a single person will survive. But for the sake of his chosen ones he has shortened those days" (Mark 13:20).

The apostle Peter later added this explanation to Christians confused about why Jesus was taking so long to come back: "The Lord isn't slow about keeping his promises, as some people think he is. In fact, God is patient, because he wants everyone to turn from sin and no one to be lost. The day of the Lord's return will surprise us like a thief" (2 Peter 3:9–10 CEV).

Scholars may argue about the point of Jesus' speech, just as the Christians who took the warnings literally during the AD 60s and fled Jerusalem may have sang praises for his predictions that saved them. But whatever else Jesus intended to say, he made one point clear: "You also must be ready all the time, for the Son of Man will come when least expected" (Matthew 24:44).

THE END ISN'T NEAR—IT'S HERE

We've been living in the end times for almost 2,000 years, some Bible experts say.

As the theory goes—and it's just one of many—the end times began with the departure of Jesus.

Consider a few parallels between the end times that Jesus predicted and the end of Jesus' time on earth—the Crucifixion.

END-TIME TOPIC	END-TIME SIGNS	END OF JESUS
Darkness	"Right after that time of suffering, 'The sun will become dark' " (Mark 13:24 CEV).	"About noon the sky turned dark and stayed that way until around three o'clock" (Mark 15:33 CEV).
Temple	"The time is coming when all these things [the Temple complex] will be completely demolished" (Luke 21:6).	"The curtain in the sanctuary of the Temple was torn in two, from top to bottom" (Mark 15:38).
Arrested	"You will be handed over to the local councils and beaten in the synagogues" (Mark 13:9).	"Judas Iscariot. . .went to talk to the leading priests to offer to hand Jesus over to them" (Mark 14:10 NCV).
Beaten	"You will be. . .beaten" (Mark 13:9).	"Pilate. . .ordered Jesus flogged with a lead-tipped whip" (Mark 15:15).

THE LAST SUPPER

Jesus took some bread, gave thanks, broke it,
and gave it to the apostles, saying, "This is my body,
which I am giving for you. Do this to remember me."
LUKE 22:19 NCV

Some rituals change our lives. Marriage, for example. One swap of "I dos" and we can be "I do-ing" till we die.

On the evening of his arrest, Jesus instituted a ritual that turned more than a thousand years of Jewish tradition in a new direction. It's a ritual that pointed God's people away from the hundreds of Jewish laws written on leather scrolls and toward laws written on the heart.

The new ritual shouldn't have come as a surprise. God had given the Jews 600 years' advance notice:

"The day is coming," says the LORD, "when I will make a new covenant with the people of Israel and Judah. This covenant will not be like the one I made with their ancestors when I took them by the hand and brought them out of the land of Egypt. They broke that covenant. . . . But this is the new covenant I will make with the people of Israel on that day," says the LORD. "I will put my instructions deep within them, and I will write them on their hearts" (Jeremiah 31:31–33).

The old agreement, based on the 10 Commandments and the hundreds of laws that grew out of them, was sealed in blood—the blood of animals sacrificed for the sins of the nation: "Then Moses took the blood from the basins and splattered it over the people, declaring, 'Look, this blood confirms the covenant the LORD has made with you' " (Exodus 24:8).

The new agreement, based on God's love for people, was also sealed in blood—the blood of Jesus sacrificed for the sins of the world: "This is my blood, which confirms the covenant between God and his people. It is poured out as a sacrifice for many" (Mark 14:24).

Jesus said this at a meal now known as the Last Supper. This was the last meal he ate with his disciples before the Crucifixion the next morning.

The ritual that came from this meal goes by many names, most of which come from the Bible:

- **Lord's Supper.** "They worshipped together at the Temple each day, met in homes for the Lord's Supper, and shared their meals with great joy and generosity" (Acts 2:46).
- **Communion.** "The cup of blessing which we bless, is it not the communion of the blood of Christ? The bread which we break, is it not the communion of the body of Christ?" (1 Corinthians 10:16 NKJV).

- **Eucharist** (Greek for "thanks"). "He took a cup of wine and gave thanks to God for it" (Mark 14:23).
- **Table of the Lord.** "You cannot eat at the Lord's Table and at the table of demons, too" (1 Corinthians 10:21).
- **Mass** (Latin *missa*, for "dismissed"). Early Christians used this word from Rome's preferred language to conclude the ritual: *Ite, missa est.* "Go, you are dismissed."

PASSOVER: NEW AND IMPROVED?

Invite Bible experts to a banquet and ask them if the Last Supper was a Passover meal—or as Jews call it in Hebrew, the *Seder* (SAY-dur).

You'll end up with a food fight. At least figuratively.

There's quite a debate among scholars about the Last Supper. At the center of the storm is the Gospel of John. In the story of Jesus' last two days alive, it's the odd book out, apparently clashing with Matthew, Mark, and Luke.

These first three Gospels say that Jesus ate the Last Supper as a Passover meal on Thursday night. Jews ate a Passover meal once a year each spring to commemorate the Exodus: God freeing the Jews from slavery in Egypt.

John, however, skips details of the Last Supper. Even more confusing, he says that the Friday crucifixion of Jesus took place "on the day of preparation for the Passover" (John 19:14). In other words, Passover wasn't Thursday night. It was Friday night. According to John, the "day of preparation for Passover" was daytime on Friday. Sundown marked the beginning of Saturday, the Jewish Sabbath—and Passover, it seems, if John is correct.

So was Passover on Thursday night, as Matthew, Mark, and Luke imply? Or Friday night, as John implies?

Scholars serve up a buffet of theories to explain the apparent discrepancy.

Early Passover. Jesus knew he would be dead on Passover, so he celebrated it a day early with his disciples.

Redefine "day of preparation." When John said that Jesus died on Preparation Day, he was talking about preparation for the Sabbath, not Passover. Sabbath begins at sunset on Friday. The Gospel writers consistently use "day of preparation" to refer to the Sabbath. So does the first-century Jewish historian Josephus.

Two days of Passover meals. Priests couldn't possibly sacrifice enough lambs in a single day to accommodate the hundreds of thousands of pilgrims who had come for Passover. So they spread the celebration meal over two days.

Following the Dead Sea calendar. Instead of following the lunar calendar, Jesus followed the solar calendar used by the Jews who preserved the Dead Sea Scrolls at the nearby community of Qumran.

Bible experts debate these theories, but not the setting. Jewish pilgrims had swarmed into Jerusalem for a two-in-one festival: the one-day festival of

Passover and the weeklong Festival of Unleavened Bread (made without yeast), which began on the same day as Passover. Both festivals commemorated the Exodus.

"Go and prepare the Passover meal, so we can eat it together," Jesus told his disciples. "As soon as you enter Jerusalem, a man carrying a pitcher of water will meet you. Follow him. At the house he enters, say to the owner, 'The Teacher asks: Where is the guest room where I can eat the Passover meal with my disciples?' He will take you upstairs to a large room that is already set up. That is where you should prepare our meal" (Luke 22:8–12).

Some archaeologists have recently said that the group probably ate at a site now marked by Jerusalem's Church of the Apostles, part of the Crusader-era Church of Saint Mary. The Church of the Apostles, archaeologists say, seems to have been built over the ruins of a first-century worship center commemorating the Last Supper and doubling as Christianity's headquarters for a time. Experts speculate that Christians built it after the Romans destroyed Jerusalem in AD 70. Persian invaders destroyed the church in AD 614, and Crusaders built another in its place four centuries later.

Three kinds of food have been on the menu since the first Passover in Moses' time: lamb, bitter herbs, and unleavened bread.

"On this night they must roast the lamb over a fire. They must eat it with bitter herbs and bread made without yeast" (Exodus 12:8 NCV).

Passover lamb. At the first Passover, some blood of this lamb marked the outside door—a signal for the angel of death to pass over the house. The blood of the lamb saved God's people, which is why some New Testament writers later describe Jesus as a sacrificial lamb: "the precious blood of Christ, the sinless, spotless Lamb of God" (1 Peter 1:19).

In Jesus' day, the Jews sacrificed the lamb at the Temple, burned the fat on the altar as an offering to God, and then took the meat as the main course for the Passover meal.

Bitter herbs. Horseradish or lettuce is often served today. The bitter taste, rabbis taught, was intended to remind the Jews of the bitterness of their slavery.

Flat bread. Matzo bread, which looks like large crackers, reminds the Jews that their ancestors fled Egypt in a hurry. They took supplies but didn't have time to wait for bread dough to rise. They hurriedly mixed the bread, baked or fried it, and hit the road.

In the centuries after Moses, an order of service emerged: with singing and essentially toasting God with four cups of grape juice or wine diluted three parts water to one part wine. If the wine hadn't been diluted, the toaster would have been toasted by the fourth cup.

Bible experts speculate that the third cup of wine in this meal is the one that Jesus said represented his blood that would be poured out in a few hours. It's the cup raised after the meal of lamb, bread, and bitter herbs.

"Then they sang a hymn and went out to the Mount of Olives" (Mark 14:26). The fourth and final cup usually followed a hymn from Psalms 113–118, a collection of songs the Jews call the *Hallel* (Hebrew for "praise").

The closing words of the final praise song seem oddly coincidental—or perhaps intentionally pointing toward what was about to happen over the coming weekend. If this was the last song Jesus sang before he faced the horrors ahead, its words must have seemed to him a gift from heaven—a reminder of what his sacrifice would mean to the world:

> *The stone the masons discarded as flawed*
> *is now the capstone [which finishes the job]!*
> *This is GOD's work.*
> *We rub our eyes—we can hardly believe it!*
> *This is the very day God acted—*
> *let's celebrate and be festive!*
> *Salvation now, GOD. Salvation now!*
> *Oh yes, GOD—a free and full life!*
>
> PSALM 118:22–25 THE MESSAGE

Jesus had earlier quoted some of these very words when he predicted his execution and the effect it would have on humanity (see Mark 12:10).

ON THE MENU

For the Passover meal in Moses' time, the Jews ate roasted lamb, yeast-free bread, and bitter herbs. But over the centuries, they added more food and symbolism to what was already a richly symbolic meal:

Bitter herbs (often romaine lettuce or horseradish). They symbolized the bitterness of slavery.

Mixed nuts and fruit (chopped nuts, apples, sweet wine). Mortar the slaves used to build Egyptian cities.

Veggies with saltwater dip (parsley, celery, or boiled potatoes). Tears of the slaves.

Roasted meat (lamb, goat, chicken, or beets for vegetarians). The Passover lamb the slaves ate hours before Egypt's king freed them.

Boiled egg. The Passover sacrifice the Jews offered after reaching Israel and building the Temple in Jerusalem. Mourners ate eggs, so in a double metaphor the eggs also represented mourning over the Temple the Romans destroyed in AD 70.

Yeast-free bread. The rush for the Jews to leave Egypt; they didn't have time to let bread dough rise.

Wine (diluted, or grape juice). Drinking four cups of wine marks various points in the Passover service and symbolizes four promises of God's deliverance: "I will free you. . .rescue you. . .redeem you. . .claim you as my own people" (Exodus 6:6–7).

TWO RITUALS WITH PLENTY IN COMMON

Some Bible experts say they see no solid evidence that the Last Supper was a Passover meal. There's no mention of roasted lamb, for example—the meal's main course. But others point to intriguing parallels between the two meals.

SOMETHING IN COMMON	PASSOVER MEAL	LAST SUPPER
More than a meal— it's a memory	"This is a day to remember. Each year, from generation to generation, you must celebrate it [Passover] as a special festival to the LORD" (Exodus 12:14).	"Do this to remember me" (Luke 22:19).
Commemorating freedom	*From slavery in Egypt:* "Celebrate the Passover each year in the early spring. . .for that was the month in which the LORD your God brought you out of Egypt" (Deuteronomy 16:1).	*From slavery to sin:* "My blood. . .is poured out as a sacrifice to forgive the sins of many" (Matthew 26:28).
Selective menu	"Roast the [lamb's] meat over a fire and eat it along with bitter salad greens and bread made without yeast" (Exodus 12:8).	"Jesus took some bread. . . and he took a cup of wine" (Mark 14:22–23).
Bread: symbol of suffering	"Eat this bread—the bread of suffering—so that as long as you live you will remember the day you departed from Egypt" (Deuteronomy 16:3).	"Jesus took some bread, gave thanks, broke it, and gave it to the apostles, saying, 'This is my body, which I am giving for you' " (Luke 22:19 NCV).
Blood: symbol of salvation	"Take some of the blood [of the sacrificed lamb] and smear it on the sides and top of the doorframes. . . . On that night I will pass through the land of Egypt and strike down every firstborn son. . . . When I see the blood, I will pass over you" (Exodus 12:7, 12–13).	"This is my blood. . . . It is poured out as a sacrifice to forgive the sins of many" (Matthew 26:28).

CANNIBALS AT COMMUNION?

In the years after Jesus, Christians would get blamed for some nasty behavior—including cannibalism. That charge grew out of rumors that the Christians were eating human flesh and drinking human blood during the ritual of Communion.

In a sense, some might argue, they were guilty as charged.

Some early church leaders in the century after Jesus agreed with many Roman Catholics and Eastern Orthodox Christians today. These church leaders taught that during the ritual of Communion, the bread and wine miraculously become the actual body and blood of Jesus.

Other early church leaders, along with most Protestants today, argued that the bread and juice only represented the body and blood of Jesus.

Catholics and Orthodox Christians make their point by quoting Jesus: "This is my body. . . . This is my blood" (Mark 14:22–24). Not, "This is a metaphor."

They also cite early church leaders who agreed with them. Writing in the early AD 100s, Bishop Ignatius of Antioch in Syria warned Christians against a rising heresy that said Jesus wasn't actually human—that he was a divine spirit who only looked human. "Stay away from heretics like this," he wrote. "They don't take Communion or pray because they say the bread is not really the flesh of our Savior Jesus Christ, who suffered for our sins" (*Letter of Ignatius to Christians in Smyrna*, chapter 7).

Protestants also argue their case by citing Bible references and church tradition. They also add some logic.

Jesus was using a metaphor, they insist, just as clearly as Moses was using a metaphor when he instituted the Passover meal. "Eat this bread—the bread of suffering—so that as long as you live you will remember the day you departed from Egypt" (Deuteronomy 16:3). When Jews ate the Passover meal, they didn't teach that they were eating the actual bread that their enslaved ancestors had eaten. Also, if someone had walked in on the Last Supper during the ritual and asked the disciples where the body of Jesus was, they would have pointed to Jesus, not to the bread.

About two decades after Jesus, when Paul gave Christians instructions on how to conduct a Communion service, he addressed his comments to "anyone who eats this bread or drinks this cup" (1 Corinthians 11:27). If he believed Christians were eating the literal flesh of Jesus, Protestants ask, why did he call it bread?

Also, the first church manual—the *Didache* (Greek: "teaching")—probably written in the early AD 100s—says nothing about the bread and wine transforming into flesh and blood.

Jesus didn't seem concerned about what the disciples were putting into their mouths, whether it was bread and wine or flesh and blood. Instead, he seemed concerned about the same thing God was concerned about when he instituted the Passover ritual. Jesus wanted them to remember this pivotal moment in history. So he gave them a physical tool—a memory device they could see, touch, smell, and taste.

What was the pivotal moment he wanted them to remember?

The apostle Paul puts it this way: "What you must solemnly realize is that every time you eat this bread and every time you drink this cup, you reenact in your words and actions the death of the Master. You will be drawn back to this meal again and again until the Master returns" (1 Corinthians 11:26 THE MESSAGE).

Jesus wanted us to remember that he died for us.

The ritual wasn't for his sake, but for ours. It would become a reminder of the effect that Christ's death had on us: "At one time you all had your backs turned to God. . . . But now, by giving himself completely at the Cross, actually dying for you, Christ brought you over to God's side and put your lives together, whole and holy in his presence. You don't walk away from a gift like that!" (Colossians 1:21–23 THE MESSAGE).

Bible experts debate how the death of Jesus brings us to God, partly because the Bible doesn't explain it clearly. The Bible just says it's a fact. Take it or leave it.

Paul says take it.

LOW-DOWN JOB

In a shocker, the Gospel of John skips the Last Supper. It preserves nothing about Jesus starting the ritual of Communion—perhaps because John had read those accounts in the earlier Gospels. For his account of Jesus' life and ministry, written later, he decided to tell a story the others missed: the story of Jesus washing the feet of the disciples.

Not only did revered rabbis not wash the feet of other people, but even Jewish slaves didn't usually do it—the chore was beneath them.

In this dusty land with unpaved trails, people generally washed their own feet when they got to where they were going. Rabbis taught that the Jewish host could allow their non-Jewish slaves to wash the feet of a guest, but they shouldn't order their Jewish servants to do it.

The rabbis were big on humility, to a degree. Rabbi Yehuda ha-Nasi, who lived in what is now Israel during the AD 100s, "was said to be so humble that he would do anything for others except relinquish his superior position when it came time to sit at a table." Dignitaries were seated by rank.

Emperor Caligula was big on humility, too—the humility of others. He once forced senators to humble themselves before him, according to the Roman historian Suetonius. "He ordered some of the highest ranking senators to strip down to their togas and run beside his chariot and to wait on him at dinner time, standing with napkin in hand" (Life of Caligula 26.2).

Jesus humbled himself willingly, stripping down to the clothing of a slave and washing the feet of his disciples. Then he urged his disciples to follow his example—to serve others rather than expecting others to serve them. "I have given you an example to follow. Do as I have done to you" (John 13:15).

JESUS PRAYS
ONE LAST PRAYER

Jesus went with them to the olive grove called Gethsemane,
and he said, "Sit here while I go over there to pray." . . .
He went on a little farther and bowed with his face to the ground,
praying, "My Father! If it is possible, let this cup of suffering be
taken away from me. Yet I want your will to be done, not mine."
MATTHEW 26:36, 39

A s Jesus walked to the olive grove where he knew he would be arrested, we might wonder if he silently quoted a psalm:

Though I walk through the valley of the shadow of death,
I will fear no evil;
For You are with me;
Your rod and Your staff, they comfort me.

PSALM 23:4 NKJV

Jesus literally walked through a dark valley—the Kidron Valley. It was nighttime. His walk to Gethsemane was just under a mile (1.5 km). That's if the ancient traditions about the site of the Last Supper and the prayer in Gethsemane are right.

Jesus and his disciples left Mount Zion, the ridge on which Jerusalem rested, and descended into the narrow Kidron Valley. Many called the valley Brook Kidron, because of the stream that flowed there after a rain.

The group then trudged a little ways up the western slope of the Mount of Olives—only about 100 yards (90 meters). They were still near the base of the ridge, only about a sixth of the way to the top. That's where tradition says Jesus stopped to pray.

As he waited for his arrest, he prayed a prayer so emotional, so painful, and so human that some church leaders in ancient times insisted that it couldn't have happened that way.

The "offensive" verses describe Jesus praying intensely enough that he sweated huge drops—like blood—and that he needed an angel to comfort him. These verses are missing from some ancient copies of the Bible, and scholars today aren't sure which version of the story is right.

With or without those verses, however, all four Gospels make it clear that Jesus agonized over what was about to happen to him.

A QUIET PLACE TO PRAY

Jewish pilgrims visiting Jerusalem for Passover generally stayed in the greater Jerusalem area, which included the 2-mile-long (3 km) ridge of hills called the Mount of Olives. There were too many visitors for everyone to stay inside the walled part of the city. Estimates range from hundreds of thousands to about one million—from double Jerusalem's population to ten times the number.

Jesus often met with his disciples on the Mount of Olives, to teach them or to pray. Piecing together all four versions of the story—in Matthew, Mark, Luke, and John—it seems that Jesus and his disciples went to a garden area called Gethsemane. Bible experts say that name is probably a composite word, *gat semanim*, which is Hebrew for "oil press."

If that's correct, Jesus may have retreated to an olive grove on the ridge named for its main crop. There was probably an olive press near the grove, from which the garden took its name. This would have made it easier to transport olives and press them into olive oil.

Because olives aren't harvested until fall, the grove would have been a quiet and restful place at Passover time in the spring.

The Roman Catholic Church of All Nations, built from 1919 to 1924 with contributions from many countries, commemorates the site and preserves a little grove of old olive trees. They're probably not the original trees from Jesus' day. Roman writers say that General Titus had all the trees in the area cut down to build catapults and other weapons for use in laying siege to Jerusalem in AD 70.

Across the street from the church is a small cave where the disciples may have slept while Jesus prayed. There are several reasons many Bible experts say Jesus and his disciples probably stayed there:

- **Protection.** The cave offered warmth from the chilly springtime evenings and water from a cistern.
- **Possible site of oil press.** It has a notch in the wall like those used to insert the tip of a wooden beam. Farmers rested bags of olives under the beam and then loaded the beam with weight to crush the olives into oil.
- **Ancient letter.** The first Christian pilgrim on record—a woman named Egeria—wrote a letter about her Holy Land travels during the AD 300s, shortly after Rome legalized Christianity. She said pilgrims go "into Gethsemane" with candles "so they can see."
- **Church leader.** Theodosius, in the AD 500s, said Gethsemane was in a cave.

HOW TO COMPLAIN TO GOD IN PRAYER

On the night the Jews arrested Jesus for the trial and execution that quickly followed, Jesus pleaded with God in prayer: "Don't make me suffer by having me drink from this cup" (Matthew 26:39 CEV).

This was more than a request. It was a complaint, a way of saying, "This feels like a terrible plan. Can't you think of something better?"

God allows people to pray like that—freely, honestly, even bluntly. And many people of the Bible did just that.

- *My friends won't really listen, all because of you, and so you must be the one to prove them wrong. . . . You, God, are the reason I am insulted and spit on.*

  A NOT-SO-PATIENT JOB,
  ACCUSED BY HIS FRIENDS OF SINNING,
  WHICH THEY SAID BROUGHT ON ALL HIS TROUBLES
  (JOB 17:4, 6 CEV)

- *You can't be serious! You can't condone evil! So why don't you do something about this? Why are you silent now? This outrage! Evil men swallow up the righteous and you stand around and watch!*

  THE PROPHET HABAKKUK,
  AFTER HEARING THAT GOD WOULD PUNISH THE JEWS
  BY SENDING INVADERS FROM THE PAGAN NATION OF BABYLON
  (HABAKKUK 1:13 THE MESSAGE)

- *Long enough, God—you've ignored me long enough. I've looked at the back of your head long enough. Long enough I've carried this ton of trouble, lived with a stomach full of pain.*

  JEWISH SONGWRITER,
  SINGING THE BLUES
  (PSALM 13:1–2 THE MESSAGE)

— JESUS: TOO HUMAN FOR COMFORT

In Jesus' day, people had a hard time thinking of him as God. But in the generations that followed, many Christians would have a hard time thinking of him as human.

Some of those Christians—even in the early church—had a whopper of a problem with the Gospels' report of what happened during Jesus' prayer time at Gethsemane.

Jesus told his disciples, "Sit here while I go and pray." Then he left with his three best friends, Peter, James, and John. "He became deeply troubled and distressed. He told them, 'My soul is crushed with grief to the point of death. Stay here and keep watch with me.' He went on a little farther and fell to the ground. He prayed that, if it were possible, the awful hour awaiting him might pass him by. 'Abba, Father,' he cried out, 'everything is possible for you. Please take this cup of suffering away from me. Yet I want your will to be done, not mine' " (Mark 14:32–36).

Up to that time, there's no record of any Jew calling God "Abba." Some scholars say it's an intimate term, like *Daddy* or *Papa*. Others say it's the word a son would call his father in Aramaic, a language the Jews learned centuries earlier when the Babylonians and Persians dominated the Middle East. Yet even that makes the word uniquely personal. Jesus called God his father. Christians later followed his example.

All of this paints an emotional scene. Luke—a master at using words to paint pictures for the mind's eye—kicks it up a notch:

> *Then an angel from heaven appeared and strengthened him. He prayed more fervently, and he was in such agony of spirit that his sweat fell to the ground like great drops of blood.*
>
> LUKE 22:43–44

Jesus wasn't sweating blood. He was sweating huge, steady drops—like thick drops of blood from a wound. He was so upset that an angel came to comfort him. In other words, he was so human that he needed help from above to calm him down. That's more human than some church leaders could handle.

These are the two verses that got deleted from some ancient copies of Luke. Or perhaps they got added to the other copies. Scholars can't agree which.

Some scholars insist that these two verses feel like an intrusion—that they don't track with the comparatively unemotional feel in the rest of Luke's Gethsemane story. As the theory goes, the low level of emotion in most of Luke's story about Jesus in Gethsemane feels like a polite report from an unbiased stoic. But these two verses feel like a punch in the kisser by a ticked-off Rocky Balboa.

Other scholars agree, adding that this is the very reason we should consider the description authentic. Who would have the nerve to add something like this to the story, they ask—something that seems to diminish the deity of Jesus?

Another reason some Bible experts consider the verses authentic is that Luke uses similes—which is what he did when he said Jesus' sweat fell "like great drops of blood." Luke uses another simile when he describes the baptism of Jesus, saying the Holy Spirit descended "like a dove" (Luke 3:22).

If there was any tweaking of the story, many scholars say, it's more likely the verses got tweaked out of the Bible, perhaps by Gnostic Christians. This was a large and influential group in the early centuries. They taught that Jesus wasn't really human but that he only appeared human and pretended to suffer. Later Christians slapped this movement with a "heresy" ticket.

With or without Luke's two unsettling verses, many would agree there's still plenty of humanity on display in Jesus. He got up to check on his disciples to make sure they were praying for him—not once, but four times according to Matthew. Only then did Jesus give up and tell them to go ahead and sleep.

Fully human, his divinity showed up, too. Instead of submitting to his own will, he yielded to his Father's will. He knew what was at stake for humanity: salvation.

ONE CUP OF TROUBLE, TO GO

Jesus used a metaphor when he prayed for God to "take this cup of suffering away from me" (Mark 14:36).

A person who had to "drink from the cup" was headed into a world of hurt—to use a metaphor from today.

And when someone advised that unfortunate soul to go ahead and do what had to be done—to drink from the cup—it was like saying to "bite the bullet," "just do it," or "deal with it."

JESUS ARRESTED

*Jesus was arrested and led away
to the house of the high priest.*

LUKE 22:54 CEV

Bible critics love the story of Jesus' arrest and trial before the top Jewish leaders. It's that full of holes and clashing facts. Or so it seems after you read all four versions of the story.

Matthew, Mark, Luke, and John all tell the tale. But they can't seem to agree on some of the important details—like who, when, and where.

Who tried the case? John says that Annas and his son-in-law Caiaphas did, calling them both the high priest—which is quite a puzzle because there could be only one high priest at a time. Luke says the high council conducted the trial. About 70 Jewish scholars and priests made up this council, known as the Sanhedrin. Matthew and Mark say that the high priest and the high council together tried Jesus.

When was the trial? Luke says the Jewish leaders gathered at daybreak. But John says that's when the trial ended, "in the early hours of the morning" (John 18:28). Matthew and Mark say it extended throughout the night, while Peter waited outside by a fire in the high priest's courtyard.

Where did the Jews conduct the trial? Matthew, Mark, and Luke agree that the Jews tried Jesus in the home of Caiaphas. But John says that Jesus was shuffled between the homes of Annas and Caiaphas. Yet all four Gospels, John included, place Peter in a single courtyard awaiting the outcome. It was as if Caiaphas had a father-in-law's suite added to his house. Or maybe they shared a duplex. At least that's what Christians can expect to hear from Bible critics offering the benefit of their creative problem solving.

Bible experts drawing on insights from ancient history offer a few solutions of their own.

WHAT GOT INTO JUDAS?

After Judas had spent perhaps three years traveling with Jesus and witnessing his dramatic miracles—healing the sick, walking on water, and raising the dead—what on earth would provoke him to betray Jesus into the hands of people determined to kill him?

Nothing on earth, perhaps.

Luke and John both say that "Satan entered into Judas Iscariot" (Luke 22:3; see also John 13:27). After that, Judas "went to the leading priests and captains of the Temple guard to discuss the best way to betray Jesus to them. They were delighted, and they promised to give him money. So he agreed and began looking for an opportunity to betray Jesus so they could arrest him when the crowds weren't around" (Luke 22:4–6).

That opportunity came during the Last Supper, when Judas discovered that the next stop on the agenda was a nearby olive grove for a nighttime prayer. He left the meal early to report this to the Jewish leaders.

Besides demon possession, two other possible motives for Judas' betrayal are just guesses. Gospel writers didn't seem to know the motive, which may be why they simply attributed it to the work of the devil.

Hunger for freedom. One popular theory is that Judas wanted to force Jesus into declaring himself Israel's Messiah—to provoke a Jewish war of independence that would drive out the Romans.

Hunger for money. Judas was the group's treasurer. "He was a thief, and since he was in charge of the disciples' money, he often stole some for himself" (John 12:6). Jewish leaders agreed to reward Judas with 30 silver coins, probably shekels—the currency Jews used to pay their annual Temple taxes. That would have tallied to about 12 ounces of silver, or $120 on today's market when silver sells for $10 an ounce.

There's a flaw in this theory: Judas gave the money back. When he found out the next morning that the Jews had sentenced Jesus to death, he rushed back to the Temple and protested, "I have betrayed an innocent man" (Matthew 27:4). Then he threw the money down and went out and hanged himself. The priests later used the money to buy a potter's field for a cemetery.

This scene was predicted 500 years earlier: "They counted out for my wages thirty pieces of silver. And the LORD said to me, 'Throw it to the potter'—this magnificent sum at which they valued me! So I took the thirty coins and threw them to the potter in the Temple of the LORD" (Zechariah 11:12–13).

Some scholars wonder whether Judas chose suicide by hanging because of a Jewish law found preserved on one of the famous Dead Sea Scrolls. The law is estimated to have been written about the time of Jesus' birth:

"If a spy betrays his own people. . .you should execute him by hanging him from a tree" (*Temple Scroll* 64:7–8).

JESUS UNDER ARREST

While Jesus prayed in the olive grove, Judas walked to meet him, followed by a group of Temple police reinforced by a detachment of Roman soldiers.

Normally, Roman soldiers lived on their base at the coastal city of Caesarea, about 55 miles (85 km) away. A Roman-style town built by Herod the Great, this city named after Caesar served as the Roman capital of the Jewish homeland. Soldiers had come to Jerusalem for crowd control during the springtime Passover festival—and to offer a show of force in case the Jews decided this would be a good time to revolt.

The arresting officers marched to Jesus in the dark of night, though they may have had some light from a nearly full moon. Passover at this time in Jewish history was celebrated on the first full moon after the vernal equinox, the first day of spring. The group also carried torches and lanterns. Torches may have been made from sap-soaked wood chips or oil-soaked rags stuffed into a metal cage at the end of a stick. The lanterns may have been household olive oil lamps carried inside clay pots.

Judas identified Jesus for the police by using a prearranged code: a kiss on the cheek. Like a handshake in Western cultures today, it was a traditional greeting—and still is in many Middle Eastern and European cultures.

This particular kiss, however, gave way to a phrase commemorating the worst kind of betrayal: the kiss of death, given by a supposed friend. Not since Delilah smooched her boyfriend Samson into a nap and then gave him a haircut had the Bible seen a friend-turned-betrayer as despicable as Judas. Both villains cashed in on a friendship by cashing in a friend.

A Jew once wrote a song about that:

> I would be able to take it
> if one who hates me were putting me to shame.
> I could hide from him.
> It is not one who hates me
> who has put himself up against me.
> But it is you, a man like myself,
> one who has gone with me,
> my close friend.

PSALM 55:12–13 NLV

BALLAD OF THE BAD HIGH PRIESTS

Jewish balladeers in ancient times sang the blues about low-life high priests. One ballad names Annas from Jesus' story—and moans over the very technique that Annas and his son-in-law Caiaphas used to arrest Jesus: secret plots.

Bad news for me, the family of Boethus.
    Bad news for me, their beating sticks!
Bad news for me, the family of Annas.
    Bad news for me, their secret tricks!
Bad news for me, the family of Kantheros.
    Bad news for me, their laws!
Bad news for me, the family of Ishmael.
    Bad news for me, their fisted paws!
For they are the high priests with an army of cronies:
    Sons as temple treasurers collect the cash.
    Sons-in-laws as temple police guard the stash.
    Servants quiet dissenters with a club and a lash.

BABYLONIAN TALMUD, PESAHIM 57A, AUTHOR'S PARAPHRASE

Jesus' dozen disciples were armed, barely: "Look, Lord, we have two swords among us" (Luke 22:38). Peter carried one, for when the police started to arrest Jesus, Peter unleashed it and sliced off the right ear of the high priest's slave.

"Put away your sword," Jesus told him, healing the slave immediately. "Those who use the sword will die by the sword. Don't you realize that I could ask my Father for thousands of angels to protect us, and he would send them instantly? But if I did, how would the Scriptures be fulfilled that describe what must happen now?" (Matthew 26:52–54).

Moments later, all the disciples deserted Jesus and ran off.

TRIAL BY JEW

Here's where the details tangle into a knotty mess—where the four Gospel writers leave their readers wondering who tried Jesus, at what time, and where.

The short answer that many scholars suggest: There were probably three Jewish trials. Overnight, Annas interrogated him first, followed by Caiaphas and part of the high council, all of whom found Jesus guilty of dishonoring God. Then around daybreak the rest of the council showed up, heard the findings, and concurred with the death sentence.

John alone reports that the arresting officers took Jesus first to "Annas, the father-in-law of Caiaphas, the high priest at that time" (John 18:13). By that time, around AD 33, Annas was retired. His stretch as high priest had ended nearly 20 years earlier (AD 6–15). Yet scholars say there were two good reasons to continue calling him the high priest:

- **Out of respect.** It was much like people today calling retired public officials by their title: president, senator, judge.
- **Out of practical reality.** He was the patriarch of a dynasty of high priests. His five sons and his son-in-law Caiaphas served in a nearly unbroken chain as high priests for many years. When Annas spoke—even as a retiree—people listened.

The arresting officers who took Jesus first to Annas and then to Caiaphas may not have had far to travel. The two priests may have shared the same palace complex reserved for the high priest.

After Jesus reached Caiaphas, the Jewish leaders scurried around trying to find people to testify against Jesus. Even at this late hour, perhaps after midnight, many came forward. Some lied. Some told the truth, quoting Jesus' prediction that he would destroy the Temple and then rebuild it in three days—a prediction Jesus intended as a metaphor about his death and resurrection.

But none of the complaints were serious enough for Caiaphas, who wanted Jesus dead. In utter frustration he asked Jesus, "Are you the Messiah?" (Mark 14:61).

Jesus sealed his fate with the answer: "I am."

That's the answer God gave when Moses asked to know God's name: "I

Who I Am. Say this to the people of Israel: I Am has sent me to you" (Exodus 3:14).

In case Caiaphas didn't make that connection, Jesus seemed to offer a little help: "You will see the Son of Man seated in the place of power at God's right hand and coming on the clouds of heaven" (Mark 14:62).

This bold statement draws from two Old Testament prophecies, both of which refer to a messiah with near-divine privileges:

- **Stepping on the clouds.** "I saw someone like a son of man coming with the clouds of heaven. He approached the Ancient One and was led into his presence. He was given authority, honor, and sovereignty over all the nations of the world, so that people of every race and nation and language would obey him. His rule is eternal—it will never end. His kingdom will never be destroyed" (Daniel 7:13–14).

- **Seated beside God.** "The LORD said to my Lord, 'Sit in the place of honor at my right hand until I humble your enemies, making them a footstool under your feet.' The LORD will extend your powerful kingdom from Jerusalem; you will rule over your enemies" (Psalm 110:1–2).

Caiaphas ripped his clothes. It was a common way of expressing deep anger or grief. "You have all heard his blasphemy," Caiaphas said. "What is your verdict?"

"Guilty!" they all cried. "He deserves to die!" (Mark 14:64).

WAS THE TRIAL ILLEGAL?

Had there been an appeals court in Jesus' day, his case may have qualified for a retrial.

The Jewish council that tried him seems to have broken several laws in the process. That's according to rules of procedure preserved in the Mishnah (*Sanhedrin* 4:1; 5:2), a collection of Jewish laws passed along by word of mouth and finally written down by about AD 200 or earlier.

- Trials weren't allowed on the day before Sabbath or the day before a festival such as Passover.
- The trial was supposed to be held on the Temple grounds—not in the house of one of the judges.
- Death-penalty cases had to be tried in daylight.
- Conviction required confirmation at least one day later, giving the council time to sleep on the matter.
- Capital cases were supposed to start with reasons for acquittal, not with reasons for conviction.

Yet another document in the ancient Jewish literature identifies Jesus of the New Testament by name and says the high council gave defense witnesses plenty of time to step forward:

Jesus was hanged on Passover Eve. Forty days before the execution a messenger began making this announcement throughout the town: "Jesus is being led out for stoning, because he has practiced sorcery and led Israel away from God's law. Whosoever has anything to say in his defense, let him come and speak." Since no one came to Jesus' defense, he was hanged on Passover Eve.

TALMUD, BARAITHA, *SANHEDRIN* 43A,
PROBABLY WRITTEN BY AD 200

Hanging probably refers to the common execution method of the day: hanging on a cross. That's where Jesus would find himself by 9:00 a.m.

PETER CHICKENS OUT, ROOSTER CROWS

A church marks the site of the worst day in Peter's life. And it bears a name commemorating his cowardice: Church of Gallicantu (Latin: "Rooster Crowing").

Jesus had warned Peter that before the rooster crowed in the morning, Peter would have denied knowing him three times.

The Church of Gallicantu is built on the site where one ancient tradition says this happened—at the home of Caiaphas. While Jewish leaders tried Jesus inside, Peter waited outside in the courtyard with another follower of Jesus, perhaps John.

People who were huddled around the charcoal fire outside repeatedly asked Peter if he was a disciple of Jesus. Peter denied it. Three times. After his third denial, "immediately a rooster crowed" (John 18:27).

Some Bible experts say this crowing may have been a Roman trumpet signal at 3:00 a.m., marking the end of the third three-hour watch of the night. The Romans called the signal the "cock crow." But most scholars say the noise more likely came from an actual rooster. The rooster may have crowed at the approaching dawn or for any number of reasons—to announce his territory or in response to a hen cackling as she laid an egg. Like dogs, roosters make noise for lots of reasons.

PETER'S NORTHERN ACCENT

There's a reason Peter got cornered into denying Jesus three times—why once wasn't enough.

The reason was his Galilean twang. He had the same accent Jesus did. Yet while hanging out in the courtyard of the high priest, Peter refused to admit he was one of Jesus' disciples.

"You must be one of them; we can tell by your Galilean accent" (Matthew 26:73). What did the accent sound like?

Northerners from Galilee had trouble pronouncing a hard *h* and perhaps other guttural sounds produced in or near the throat—like the *ch* in "Loch Ness" and the *g* in "go fish."

Some English dialects today drop the hard *h*. In parts of England, happy carpenters could be singing, "If I 'ad a 'ammer, I'd 'ammer in the morning."

One of Israel's famous judges used this knowledge of accents to identify Jews from a tribe that refused to help him during wartime: Ephraim, north of Jerusalem. Whenever he suspected a man came from Ephraim, he ordered him to pronounce the word *Shibboleth*. "If he was from Ephraim, he would say 'Sibboleth'" (Judges 12:6). When that happened, phonetics became fatal.

There's another ancient story about the Galilean accent. It shows up in the Talmud, a collection of Jewish tradition, laws, and commentary.

As the story goes, a Galilean asked for `amar, which is wool. But the southern Jew to whom he was talking replied:

> You stupid Galilean. Do you mean a donkey (*ham r*), wine (*hamar*), wool (`amar), or a lamb (*immar*)?
>
> BABYLONIAN TALMUD, *ERUBIN* 53B

From an *h*-dropping Galilean, all four of those words could sound alike. Here's what New York City rabbinic student and freelance linguist Steg Belsky says they're supposed to sound like:

Donkey, *ham r*:
- **hhah-MAWR** (*MAW* rhymes with "saw"; then add the "R" sound)

Wine, *hamar*:
- **hhah-MAHR** (*MAH* rhymes with "Open your mouth and say Ahhh")

Wool, `amar:
- **ah-MAHR** (`ah sounds like Homer Simpson gargling, according to Belsky, who apparently watches cartoons in his spare time)

Lamb, *immar*:
- **im-MAHR**

Peter's accent was so strong that if he had eaten out in Jerusalem, he might have ordered some red donkey with his lamb chops and a little extra wool for his wine dip.

JESUS ON TRIAL BEFORE PILATE

*"The entire council took Jesus to Pilate, the Roman governor.
They began to state their case: 'This man has been leading our
people astray by telling them. . .he is the Messiah, a king.' "*
LUKE 23:1–2

Not one trial, but five. That's what Jesus endured, by some accounts.
The trials began around midnight. And they ended by about nine
o'clock the next morning on what became the last day of his humanity.

SAINT PILATE

Some Christians not only respect Pilate for his reluctance to crucify Jesus, they pray to him.

He's considered a saint in both the Ethiopian Church and the Coptic Church, the main church in Egypt. Legends embraced by these churches say that Pilate eventually converted to Christianity and died a martyr.

Roman historians from Pilate's century paint a different picture. Philo (20 BC–AD 50) describes him with a long string of unsaintly words: "He was incredibly inflexible, doggedly stubborn, and coldly unmerciful. . . . His governing methods included corruption, insulting people, taking whatever he wanted, violence, executions without trial, outright murder, and monstrous inhumanity that never wavered."

Tiberius Caesar appointed Pilate as the fifth governor of Judea, a territory in what is now southern Israel. Pilate served for a decade, from about AD 26 to 36. He seems to have worn several administrative hats in this relatively small province off the beaten trail:

- **Governor.** Matthew, Mark, and Luke all describe Pilate's authority with a generic word that means Pilate governed the province.
- **Procurator.** Tacitus (about AD 56–117), a Roman historian, said Pilate was a procurator. Romans gave this title to a region's CFO, chief financial officer. But the title also doubled as a word meaning "governor."
- **Prefect.** An ancient stone monument honoring Pilate describes him as "prefect of Judea." Romans gave this title to administrative officials in charge of a region's finances, military, and judicial system. Prefects had the power to sentence people to death.

Recommending Pilate for this job was none other than Sejanus—the emperor's number one man, emperor-in-waiting, and a Jew-buster who might have felt more appreciated in Nazi Germany in the 1940s.

Tiberius executed him in AD 31 for plotting a takeover. Afterward, Tiberius killed many of Sejanus' associates. Though Pilate survived this purge, he knew he stood on shaky ground with Tiberius two years later, when Jesus came to trial. So when the Jewish leaders threatened to declare Pilate "no friend of Caesar" for refusing to execute a rebel leader, Pilate's survival instinct kicked in. He did what was politically expedient, sentencing Jesus to death.

Pilate had a right to fear the Jews. Three years later, Jewish leaders lodged a complaint about him after he ordered Roman troops to slaughter an unarmed gathering, which Pilate said he thought was plotting a revolt. Recalled to Rome, Pilate was never heard from again. Many historians guess that the emperor ordered him to commit suicide—a common practice among administrators who disgraced the empire.

Many scholars plot the date on the calendar: Friday, April 3, AD 33.

With justice running on fast-forward, the Jewish leaders rushed Jesus to the home of Annas, the retired high priest. That was trial one, or at least an interrogation. Next, they took him to Annas' son-in-law Caiaphas, the current high priest, who had assembled part of the high council. By around daybreak—5:30 a.m., long before Daylight Saving Time added an hour—the rest of the high council showed up and concurred with the findings of Caiaphas. Jesus had dishonored God and deserved to die.

Three trials down. Two to go.

Only Roman officials could legally sentence someone to death. In the Jewish region of Judea, that official was Pilate, the governor. But when Pilate found out Jesus was from Galilee, he passed him off to the Galilean ruler visiting Jerusalem for Passover, Herod Antipas, son of Herod the Great. Jesus refused to talk to Herod. So Herod bounced him back to Pilate.

What's surprising is that Pilate, a Roman with a documented distaste for Jews, was the only one interested in sparing Jesus. The Jewish leaders weren't. And the Jewish Galilean ruler couldn't have cared less. Yet Pilate tried several maneuverings to free Jesus.

The intriguing question is why? What did Pilate—an outsider famous for infamy—see in Jesus?

── JESUS, REBEL KING AND TAX DODGER ──

Caiaphas and other Jewish leaders tweaked the charges against Jesus. They must have realized that Pilate wouldn't sentence Jesus to death for something as harmless as breaking a religious rule: for disrespecting the Jewish God.

They exaggerated a little. They said Jesus claimed to be the Messiah, which was true. But they added their own interpretation of what Jesus meant by taking that title, which was not true. They portrayed him as a rebel king of the Jews who intended to lead a revolt against Rome.

To prove their point, they said that Jesus had urged the Jews "not to pay their taxes to the Roman government" (Luke 23:2). As though they had succeeded months earlier with their trick question, "Is it right to pay taxes to Caesar or not?" (Matthew 22:17).

"Whose picture and title are stamped on it?" Jesus had asked. "Caesar's," they replied. "Well, then," Jesus answered, "give to Caesar what belongs to Caesar, and give to God what belongs to God" (Matthew 22:20–21).

It's unclear exactly when and where the Jews leveled these charges against Jesus.

Pilate might have stayed with a contingent of Roman soldiers at a fortress complex overlooking the sprawling Temple: Antonia Fortress, named after Mark Antony. But many historians say it's more likely he stayed at Herod's palace, at the other end of town and a short walk from Caiaphas' home.

John says that Caiaphas' trial ended "in the early hours of the morning" (John 18:28). So the Jews may have taken Jesus to Pilate before or shortly after the sun rose at about 5:30 a.m. Many Roman rulers like Pilate judged cases that early, according to Roman politician and writer Seneca (4 BC–AD 65). Some ended their workday by late morning.

Mark says the trial was over before "nine o'clock in the morning" (Mark 15:25), the time Mark says Jesus was crucified. Luke seems to agree. He reports that Jesus spoke to the criminals hanging on crosses beside him in the morning, adding that at noon, "darkness fell across the whole land until three o'clock" (Luke 23:44). John, however, says that Pilate didn't sentence Jesus until "about noon" (John 19:14).

Many Bible experts say the best way to settle the discrepancy is to keep in mind that the people didn't have clocks. They estimated the time, occasionally rounding to the nearest third-hour watch of the day: nine o'clock, noon, three o'clock, six o'clock. What may have seemed closer to 9:00 a.m. for one witness may have seemed closer to noon for another.

— POINTED QUESTIONS FOR JESUS —

Pilate wasn't about to rubber-stamp the Jewish sentence.

"Are you the king of the Jews?" he asked Jesus.

Matthew, Mark, and Luke all report only the short, vague answer Jesus gave, which essentially means, "Those are your words, not mine." But John takes the conversation further, reporting that Jesus said, "My Kingdom is not an earthly kingdom. If it were, my followers would fight to keep me from being handed over to the Jewish leaders. But my Kingdom is not of this world" (John 18:36).

"Not guilty." That was Pilate's finding. The king of an invisible world posed no threat to Rome.

"Not good enough." That was the reaction of the Jewish leaders.

The order of events that followed isn't clear. But at some point, Pilate found

ESCAPE CLAUSE

A line that should have gotten Jesus off the hook worked a generation later for some of his relatives, according to church historian Hegesippus, writing in the AD 100s.

Charged with leading a rebel movement against Rome, Jesus defended himself before Pilate by saying, "My Kingdom is not an earthly kingdom" (John 18:36). With that, Pilate was ready to release him as no threat to Rome. But the Jewish leaders insisted otherwise.

About 50 years later, the Roman emperor Domitian arrested the grandchildren of Jesus' brother Jude. Domitian, said to have worried that Jesus would return, asked the Jewish men about the Messiah and his Kingdom. Hegesippus reported that the men assured Domitian that the Kingdom of Jesus was not of this world.

Domitian released them as no threat to his kingdom on planet Earth.

out that Jesus was Galilean. And he knew that Galilee's ruler, Herod Antipas, was in town for Passover. So he passed the hot potato over to Herod.

Pilate owed him.

Herod was one of several Jewish rulers who had gotten Pilate in trouble with the emperor years earlier, when Pilate first came to Judea. Roman historians say that Pilate erected in Jerusalem some golden shields engraved with the names of Roman emperors. The Jews considered these idolatrous. After hearing the Jewish objections, the emperor overruled Pilate and ordered him to get the shields out of the city. So the governor made a bad first impression with his boss—and Herod had helped.

Herod, who had earlier beheaded John the Baptist, knew about the miracles Jesus had done. So he didn't consider Jesus a political hot potato—more like a magic act. Jesus refused to perform. He said nothing to Herod, whom he had once described as a "fox" (Luke 13:32)—not a compliment.

Jesus may have considered the silent treatment a way of fulfilling a prophecy: "He was led like a lamb to the slaughter. And as a sheep is silent before the shearers, he did not open his mouth. Unjustly condemned, he was led away" (Isaiah 53:7–8).

Herod entertained himself by dressing Jesus up like a king, making fun of him, and then returning him to Pilate dressed in the kingly costume. Pilate loved the joke. "Herod and Pilate, who had been enemies before, became friends that day" (Luke 23:12).

Pilate reported his finding to the Jews. "You brought this man to me, accusing him of leading a revolt. I have examined him thoroughly on this point in your presence and find him innocent. Herod came to the same conclusion and sent him back to us. Nothing this man has done calls for the death penalty. So I will have him flogged, and then I will release him" (Luke 23:14–16).

There were three degrees of Roman beatings. From mildest to harshest they were, in Latin, *fustigatio*, *flagella*, and *verberatio*. Pilate was referring to a mild beating. That was a relative slap on the wrist compared to a *verberatio*, from which we get the word *vibrate*—as in a beating that will rattle your bones. The Roman historian Josephus says that those vicious beatings—a prerequisite for crucifixion—could expose intestines and bones.

The Jewish leaders insisted on nothing less than death for Jesus.

Pilate tried another strategy. Ancient Roman history confirms that Roman officials often showed mercy during local festival days, releasing selected prisoners. It was a way of trying to placate the locals. Pilate gave the Jews a no-brainer of a choice. He would release either Jesus, who had hurt no one, or Barabbas, "a revolutionary who had committed murder in an uprising" (Mark 15:7).

Some Jewish revolutionaries were ancient terrorists called Sicarii. The name comes from *sicae*, Latin for "dagger." These "dagger men" hid knives under their robes. Then they'd mix into crowds at festivals such as Passover, stab to death Jews who sympathized with Rome, and then quickly blend back into the crowd.

"Kill Jesus!" the Jews cried. "Give us Barabbas!" (Luke 23:18 CEV).

PILATE'S RELUCTANT SENTENCE

Pilate did not want to execute Jesus. The question is why not?

Many Bible experts say the answer is fear. Pilate feared Jesus for two reasons.

Jesus claimed to be the Son of God. It didn't take long for Pilate to realize Jesus was no threat to the empire. Then, in the process of declaring him not guilty, Pilate discovered that Jesus might be some kind of a god.

This happened when the Jewish leaders reacted to Pilate's declaration, saying, "By our law he ought to die because he called himself the Son of God" (John 19:7).

Pilate's reaction? "When Pilate heard this, he was more frightened than ever" (John 19:8). This suggests that he had been frightened before, perhaps recognizing from his interrogations of Jesus that this was no ordinary man.

Pilate's first question of Jesus after the Jews leveled this new charge?

"Where are you from?" (John 19:9). As if Jesus might be from the realm of the gods.

Jesus all but confirmed that this was exactly where he came from. When Pilate prodded Jesus to answer him, saying he had the power to crucify him, Jesus replied, "You would have no power over me at all unless it were given to you from above" (John 19:11).

Pilate's cage rattled, he again tried to free Jesus.

Pilate's wife had a nightmare about Jesus. In the early morning hours of this trial, while Pilate's wife was still asleep, she had a dream so vivid and disturbing that she interrupted the trial to warn her husband.

"As Pilate was sitting on the judgment seat, his wife sent him this message: 'Leave that innocent man alone. I suffered through a terrible nightmare about him last night'" (Matthew 27:19).

In ancient times, people thought of dreams as a gateway to the spirit world—as a way for gods to communicate to people. God often communicated to prophets and others through dreams. Many people wanting guidance from their favorite deity would go to a temple or shrine dedicated to the god and sleep there, hoping to learn something in a dream.

The wife of Julius Caesar had a nightmare about her husband the night before the senate swarmed him with knives, according to Roman historian Cassius Dio, writing in the AD 100s. "The night before he was slain, his wife dreamed that their house had fallen in ruins and that her husband had been wounded by some men and he had taken refuge within her" (*Roman History* 44:17.1).

It was after hearing of his wife's dream that Pilate gave the Jews a choice between freeing Barabbas or Jesus.

Though it may have been fear of the spirit world that drove Pilate to protect Jesus, fear of consequences in the political world led Pilate to kill him.

"If you release this man, you are no 'friend of Caesar,' " someone in the Jewish mob yelled. "Anyone who declares himself a king is a rebel against Caesar" (John 19:12).

In other words, "If you're for Jesus, you're against Caesar."

Scholars who say Jesus died in about AD 33 speculate that Pilate was already on shaky ground with the Caesar: Tiberius. The Roman official who had recommended Pilate for the job of governing Judea, Sejanus, was executed during an attempted coup in AD 31, along with many of his allies. Jews told Pilate, "If you release this man, you are no 'friend of Caesar' " (John 19:12).

Pilate let his political reality settle the case.

"Pilate saw that he wasn't getting anywhere and that a riot was developing. So he sent for a bowl of water and washed his hands before the crowd, saying, 'I am innocent of this man's blood. The responsibility is yours!' " (Matthew 27:24).

Irony as thick as a crossbeam, innocent Pilate killed innocent Jesus while the guilty watched.

ROMAN CRIMES TO DIE FOR

Jews had the 10 Commandments, basic rules of life on which their hundreds of other laws were based. Romans had the 10 Tables—written in about 450 BC, expanded to 12 Tables, tweaked as needed over the centuries, and kept in force for nearly 1,000 years. Capital offenses ranged from stealing crops to writing offensive poetry:

- Anyone who publically insults someone with a loud voice, or writes a poem to insult someone, or otherwise destroys someone's reputation should be clubbed to death.
- Anyone who uses incantations and magic to stop someone else's crops from growing should be sacrificed to Ceres [Roman goddess of grain].
- Any adult who cuts or steals someone else's crops should be sacrificed to Ceres and hanged.
- You are within your legal right to kill someone who is stealing from you at night.
- You are within your legal right to kill someone who is stealing from you during the day, only if the thief has a weapon. Otherwise, call out for help.
- Anyone found guilty of lying during a trial should be thrown from the Tarpeian Rock [a cliff now about 50 feet (15 meters) high, perhaps higher in ancient times].
- Anyone who purposely burns a building or a pile of grain beside a building should be tied, beaten, and burned at the stake.
- Any judge found guilty of taking a bribe to decide a case should be executed.
- Any Roman who has stirred up a war against the country or has handed over a fellow Roman to an enemy is guilty of treason and should die.

JESUS EXECUTED AND BURIED

They brought Jesus to a place called Golgotha (which means "Place of the Skull").... Then the soldiers nailed him to the cross.

MARK 15:22, 24

The big question is why did Jesus have to die?

- **Why Romans said he had to die: insurrection.** Jesus called himself a king. But Jewish leaders assured the Roman governor, Pilate, "We have no king but Caesar" (John 19:15).
- **Why Jews said he had to die: self-preservation.** Jesus might spark a revolt. Caiaphas, the high priest, put it this way: "If we allow him to go on like this, soon everyone will believe in him. Then the Roman army will come and destroy both our Temple and our nation" (John 11:48).

But the hardball question is why did God say he had to die?

God isn't famous for explaining himself. Yet the Bible does offer a few clues.

Sin is a capital offense. It has been from the beginning. God told Adam that if he broke the one and only law—eating forbidden fruit—"you are sure to die" (Genesis 2:17). The apostle Paul added, "The wages of sin is death" (Romans 6:23).

Life is in the blood. God said this when he set up the system of animal sacrifices. "Life is in the blood, and I have given you the blood of animals to sacrifice in place of your own" (Leviticus 17:11 CEV).

Jesus' death fulfilled the death penalty requirement for everyone. "Our High Priest offered himself to God as a single sacrifice for sins, good for all time.... When sins have been forgiven, there is no need to offer any more sacrifices" (Hebrews 10:12, 18).

Jesus' death set the stage for the Resurrection. It took the Resurrection to finally convince Jesus' disciples that he was God's Son. The Resurrection was so convincing that in the years that followed most of the disciples willingly died as martyrs. After seeing Jesus risen from the dead and hearing him promise the same future for them, they died expecting that "everyone who believes in him will not perish but have eternal life" (John 3:16).

BEFORE THE NAILS

Soldiers had already beaten Jesus once. It was Pilate's futile attempt to convince the Jewish leaders to let him free Jesus. That was a mild thrashing compared to the bone-rattling beating that would precede the Crucifixion.

The beating. Stripped and tied to a post, Jesus was beaten with a weapo[n] some gladiators used in the arena: a whip loaded with perhaps half a dozen lea[ther] lashes or more—each lash embedded with chunks of bone, leather, or hooks.

The point was to tear up the victim. Romans hoped the gore would discourage onlookers from breaking the law. Writers who witnessed crucifixions in Jesus' day said they saw lashes rip open skin and muscle, exposing the victim's bones and intestines. Some victims never made it to the cross; they died at the beating.

The mockery. Next, Roman soldiers humiliated Jesus, dressing him in a fake royal robe, handing him a stick for a scepter, and jamming a wreath of thorns onto his head as a crown.

The walk. Like other crucifixion victims, Jesus had to carry his cross to the execution site. It's not clear what he carried—the entire cross or just the crossbeam, assuming the vertical poles stayed planted in the ground for each new victim. By some estimates, the crossbeams alone weighed about 30–40 pounds (13–18 kg). That's about the weight of four or five standard two-by-four boards eight feet long (5 cm x 10 cm, 2.5 meters long).

It's unknown how far Jesus walked. Tourists following the Via Dolorosa (Way of Suffering) in Jerusalem today—from the Monastery of Flagellation to the Church of the Holy Sepulchre—cover about one-third of a mile, some 500 meters. Though the actual route follows modern streets and may be nothing like the direction Jesus traveled, the distance is probably about right. The monastery is built in the vicinity of the Antonia Fortress, the highest point in the city and the building from which Roman soldiers kept watch over the Temple courtyard. Some speculate that Pilate stayed in this fortress when he came to Jerusalem from his home in Caesarea. But most Bible experts say it's more likely Pilate chose to stay in the palace of the former king of the Jews, Herod the Great. If so, this may have been where soldiers tormented Jesus and prepared him for execution.

Both sites are roughly the same distance from the Church of the Holy Sepulchre, which is built over what most scholars say was Jesus' execution and burial site.

The Bible says Jesus died at Golgotha, a Hebrew word that means "place of the skull." In Latin, the language of Rome, it was called Calvary, which means "skull." Scholars can only guess why it earned that name. Three guesses:

- It was on a hill with a cliff face eroded to look a little like a skull. There is a hill like this near the Garden Tomb.
- It produced skulls as birds picked the flesh away.
- It produced skulls, and a nearby cemetery kept them.

Most experts prefer the third guess for several reasons.

The Church of the Holy Sepulchre, said to mark both sites—the execution and burial of Jesus—was built in the AD 300s, shortly after Rome legalized Christianity. So the tradition is ancient.

Archaeologists say the sites were both outside the walled city in Jesus'

ROMANS DESCRIBE CRUCIFIXION

For folks wondering if the Bible writers made up the story of Jesus' crucifixion—and if the Romans really used crucifixion at all—Roman writers from Jesus' time confirm both facts:

Jesus crucified

- "There was a wise man who was called Jesus, a good man. . . . Pilate condemned him to be crucified."
  JOSEPHUS (ABOUT AD 37–101), ANTIQUITIES OF THE JEWS 18.3.3

- "Christ suffered the ultimate penalty at the hands of procurator Pontius Pilate when Tiberius was emperor of Rome."
  TACITUS (ABOUT AD 55–120), ANNALS OF IMPERIAL ROME 15.44

Crucifixion horror

- "He was whipped until his bones showed."
  JOSEPHUS, WARS OF THE JEWS 6.5.3

- "Each criminal who goes to execution must carry his own cross on his back."
  PLUTARCH (ABOUT AD 46–120), SERA 554

- "Sixteen men. . .were paraded out, chained together by the foot and neck, each carrying his own cross. The executioners added this grim public spectacle to the punishment as an extra deterrent to anyone thinking about committing the same crime."
  CHARITON (ABOUT 25 BC–AD 50), CHAEREAS AND CALLIRHOE 4.2.7

- "Some hang their victims upside down. Some impale them through the private parts. Others stretch out their arms onto forked poles."
  SENECA (ABOUT 4 BC–65 AD), TO MARCIA ON CONSOLATION 20.3

- "Is there such a thing as a person who would actually prefer wasting away in pain on a cross—dying limb by limb one drop of blood at a time—rather than dying quickly? Would any human being willingly choose to be fastened to that cursed tree, especially after the beating that left him deathly weak, deformed, swelling with vicious welts on shoulders and chest, and struggling to draw every last, agonizing breath? Anyone facing such a death would plead to die rather than mount the cross."
  SENECA, EPISTULAE MORALES (MORAL LETTERS) 101.14

time. And Jewish law required that executions take place outside the city.

Archaeologists also say the church sits over a used-up rock quarry that had been converted to a cemetery and garden in Jesus' day. John reports, "The place of crucifixion was near a garden, where there was a new tomb, never used before" (John 19:41). Depleted rock quarries were excellent spots for tombs because people could chisel into the cliff face of the quarry.

Cyril of Jerusalem, writing in about AD 350, says, "It was a garden where he [Jesus] was crucified. For though it has now been most highly adorned with royal gifts, yet formerly it was a garden, and the signs and the remnants of this remain" (*Catechesis* 14.5).

However far Jesus needed to carry his cross, it was too far. He collapsed, perhaps mainly because of his two beatings. Soldiers pulled someone out of the crowd to finish the job: Simon of Cyrene, a city in what is now Libya. He may have been a Jew visiting Jerusalem for the Passover festival, because Cyrene was home to a large community of Jews at the time.

TIME TO DIE

An iron nail driven through the heel bone of a man crucified in Jesus' century survives as grim evidence that the Romans did, in fact, crucify people in the area.

The victim's name was Jehohanan, the Hebrew version of "John." He died in his 20s, sometime between AD 7 and 70—before or during the Jewish revolt against Rome. Jehohanan's burial site was discovered in 1968 in the Kidron Valley, between Jerusalem and the Mount of Olives.

Romans nailed Jesus to the cross, Gospel writers report. If they followed the technique used with Jehohanan, they drove the nail through a chunk of wood first and then through the feet of Jesus. The wood acted like a lock washer, keeping victims from pulling loose by popping the nails through their flesh and bones.

In Jehohanan's case, Romans may have nailed the feet separately along the right and left sides of the vertical stake. Or they could have turned both feet to the side and used one nail to pin both feet to the front. There's no apparent nail scraping on the bones of Jehohanan's hands or arms. This suggests the Romans tied his arms to the cross.

As for Jesus, "soldiers nailed him to the cross" (Mark 15:24). The Romans didn't follow a how-to manual for fastening victims to a cross. They tied some, which prolonged the dying. They nailed some. They accessorized with ropes and nails for others, customizing death to the tools on hand and placing victims in various positions. The Roman historian Seneca wrote of people "sitting on a cross," referring to a chunk of wood added to the vertical pole. This seat prolonged the torture by relieving pressure on the chest muscles and making it easier to breathe.

If the vertical stake was permanently positioned in the ground, the Romans may have nailed Jesus' hands to the crossbeam and then used forked poles to raise it to the top of the vertical stake. Then they nailed Jesus' feet to the vertical stake.

Gospel stories tell of people offering Jesus wine at least a couple of times, perhaps more. Matthew and Mark each describe two instances: "wine mixed with bitter gall," followed by "sour wine" (Matthew 27:34, 48); and "wine drugged with myrrh," followed by "sour wine" from a bystander (Mark 15:23, 36).

The story reads as if compassion and taunting were both at work here. Myrrh, like frankincense, was a bitter-tasting painkiller. Ancient Jewish writings say that a group of Jerusalem women offered crucifixion victims wine mixed with frankincense. But in Jesus' case, it looks as if the soldiers were giving it to him. "Sour wine" was a cheap kind, popular among soldiers and common folks. A bystander offered this to Jesus, apparently to comfort him. But Luke adds that "soldiers mocked him. . .by offering him a drink of sour wine" (Luke 23:36).

The Romans nailed Jesus to the cross by morning, sometime between 9:00 a.m. and noon. Mark says 9:00 a.m.; John says noon. But in an era before clocks, witnesses estimated the time and may have rounded to what they thought was the nearest three-hour watch of the day. Roman soldiers stood guard in three-hour watches: 6:00 a.m., 9:00 a.m., noon, and so on.

Crucified beside Jesus were two men described by the same Greek word used earlier for Barabbas. Some scholars translate it "revolutionaries"; others use "bandits" or simply "criminals." One of the men confessed that he was a sinner. But Jesus assured him, "Today you will be with me in paradise" (Luke 23:43), using a word the Jews used to refer to a place of eternal bliss—heaven, as Christians call it. Another Jewish writer in Jesus' century used the word this way: "It is for you that paradise is opened, the tree of life is planted, the age to come is prepared, plenty is provided" (2 Esdras 8:52 NRSV).

"By this time it was noon, and darkness fell across the whole land until three o'clock" (Luke 23:44). This wasn't a total solar eclipse. Those last no more than seven and a half minutes. More likely, thick clouds darkened the sky. For the followers of Jesus, this darkness would have seemed appropriate—a symbol of mourning over the death of someone deeply revered, or of God's judgment on the Jewish leaders who not only failed to recognize the Messiah, but also orchestrated his execution.

"At about three o'clock, Jesus called out with a loud voice, 'Eli, Eli, lema sabachthani?' which means 'My God, my God, why have you abandoned me?' " (Matthew 27:46). Some bystanders heard his first two words and thought he was calling Elijah, a prophet the Jews taught would come back to introduce the Messiah.

Bible experts offer two main theories about why Jesus said God abandoned him.

- **Sin.** One theory says Jesus had taken on the sins of the world. In response, God had to turn his back on the sins Jesus carried. So the spiritual connection between divine Father and divine Son was momentarily broken.
- **Prophecy.** A second theory says Jesus was teaching with his last breaths, pointing his followers to a psalm that predicted what he had just suffered:

My God, my God, why have you abandoned me? . . . Everyone who sees me
mocks me. . . . My life is poured out like water. . . . They have pierced my
hands and feet. . . . They divide my garments among themselves and throw
dice for my clothing.

PSALM 22:1, 7, 14, 16, 18

Offered wine one last time by a bystander, Jesus tasted it and cried out, "It is finished!" (John 19:30). "Father, I entrust my spirit into your hands!" (Luke 23:46).

He died.

Death was confirmed by a lance piercing his chest, releasing "blood and water" (John 19:34). The "water" may have been serous fluid that cushions and lubricates the layers of tissue lining the body cavities. Or it may have been blood serum. When someone dies, his blood separates into two forms: clear liquid and red, solid blood cells used in clotting.

Jewish leaders considered this a shameful death—appropriate for the crime. Jesus had claimed that God sent him, but crucifixion suggested that God had cursed him. Criminals executed in Bible times could be "hung on a tree. . .for anyone who is hung is cursed in the sight of God" (Deuteronomy 21:22–23).

The Roman soldiers didn't seem to agree that Jesus was cursed. After Jesus died, an earthquake in this quake-prone region shook Jerusalem so violently that the curtain inside the Temple ripped from top to bottom. This curtain was huge, thick as a hand and 60 feet wide by 30 feet long (18 x 9 meters). "The Roman officer and the other soldiers at the crucifixion were terrified by the earthquake and all that had happened. They said, 'This man truly was the Son of God!' " (Matthew 27:54).

Some Bible experts say that God sent a message with that earthquake. The curtain that got ripped was probably the most sacred one in the Temple. It blocked the entrance into the Temple's holiest room—the Most Holy Place. Only the high priest could go into this room, and only once a year: on the Day of Atonement (Yom Kippur), a national day of repentance. To atone for the sins of all the people, the priest went inside the room and sprinkled blood on the gold-covered chest that contained the 10 Commandments. This chest was the Ark of the Covenant, sometimes described as God's footstool on planet Earth. The room was considered his earthly home.

God's message, according to some scholars, was this:

- **The age of temple sacrifices was over.** The ultimate sacrifice had just been made. About 40 years later, the Romans would crush a Jewish rebellion and destroy the Temple—which has never been rebuilt.
- **God is freely accessible to everyone.** There's no need to come with a sacrifice for our sins or with a high priest to speak on our behalf.

PROPHECIES JESUS FULFILLED IN DYING

Jesus knew his Bible, and especially the prophecies that referred to him as the Messiah. The Gospel writers report that even in dying, Jesus said and did things to fulfill some of those prophecies. Jesus apparently wanted his disciples to make the connections and to use those connections in sermons and debates they would face in the coming years.

PREDICTION	FULFILLMENT
"They have pierced my hands and feet" (Psalm 22:16).	"Soldiers nailed him to the cross" (Mark 15:24).
"Everyone who sees me mocks me" (Psalm 22:7).	"The leading priests, the teachers of religious law, and the elders also mocked Jesus. "He saved others," they scoffed, "but he can't save himself!" (Matthew 27:41–42).
"They divide my garments among themselves and throw dice for my clothing" (Psalm 22:18).	"Soldiers gambled for his clothes by throwing dice" (Luke 23:34).
"If only one person would show some pity. . . . But instead. . .they offer me sour wine for my thirst" (Psalm 69:20–21).	"Jesus. . .said, 'I am thirsty.' A jar of sour wine was sitting there, so they soaked a sponge in it, put it on a hyssop branch, and held it up to his lips" (John 19:28–29).
"My life is poured out like water" (Psalm 22:14).	"One of the soldiers. . .pierced his side with a spear, and immediately blood and water flowed out" (John 19:34).
"The LORD protects the bones of the righteous; not one of them is broken!" (Psalm 34:20).	"The soldiers came and broke the legs of the two men crucified with Jesus [to speed death]. But when they came to Jesus, they saw that he was already dead, so they didn't break his legs" (John 19:32–33).
The cry of a righteous man suffering: "My God, my God, why have you abandoned me?" (Psalm 22:1).	The cry of Jesus dying: "My God, my God, why have you abandoned me?" (Mark 15:34).
"I entrust my spirit into your hand" (Psalm 31:5).	"Jesus shouted, 'Father, I entrust my spirit into your hands!' " (Luke 23:46).
"He was buried like a criminal; he was put in a rich man's grave" (Isaiah 53:9).	"Joseph, a rich man. . .went to Pilate and asked for Jesus' body. . . . He placed it in his own new tomb" (Matthew 27:57–58, 60).

A Christian writer sums it up this way, illustrating his point by referring to Israel's first worship center, a tent called the Tabernacle: "Christ has now become the High Priest. . . . He has entered that greater, more perfect Tabernacle in heaven, which was not made by human hands and is not part of this created world. With his own blood—not the blood of goats and calves—he entered the Most Holy Place once for all time and secured our redemption forever" (Hebrews 9:11–12).

DEAD AND BURIED

As a deterrent, Romans sometimes left bodies rotting on the cross—to the delight of hungry birds. Roman historians report that soldiers sometimes stood guard day and night to make sure no one took the corpses for burial. But in times of peace, the Romans often deferred to local customs.

The Jews practiced same-day burials. Even in the case of an executed criminal, their law said, "You must bury the body that same day" (Deuteronomy 21:23).

Josephus reported that the Romans complied with this law. "Even criminals who have been sentenced to crucifixion are taken down and buried before sunset" (*Wars of the Jews* 4.5.2).

Surprisingly, a member of the Jewish high council that had condemned Jesus to death asked the Roman governor, Pilate, for Jesus' body. The man was Joseph from the village of Arimathea. "He had not agreed with the decision and actions of the other religious leaders" (Luke 23:51). Assisting him was another council member, Nicodemus.

They took Jesus' body to Joseph's newly cut tomb. With Sabbath fast approaching at sundown, there was apparently no time to fully prepare Jesus' body for burial. But they wrapped the corpse with about 75 pounds (37 kg) of spices to help mask the smell of decay. They probably expected to come back after the Sabbath, in the daylight of Sunday, to wash and fully prepare the body for burial.

They were in for a surprise.

JESUS BACK FROM THE DEAD

*"You are looking for Jesus of Nazareth, who was crucified.
He isn't here! He is risen from the dead!"*
MARK 16:6

From our side of the empty tomb, it's all too easy to bad-mouth the disciples for doubting the Resurrection until it looked them in the eye.

After all, Jesus had told them exactly what was going to happen.

Jesus tried the direct approach. "Listen, we're going up to Jerusalem, where all the predictions of the prophets concerning the Son of Man will come true. He will be handed over to the Romans, and he will be mocked, treated shamefully, and spit upon. They will flog him with a whip and kill him, but on the third day he will rise again" (Luke 18:31–33).

Jesus tried the symbolic approach. "Destroy this temple, and in three days I will raise it up" (John 2:19).

Jesus tried the mysterious approach. "As they went back down the mountain [after the Transfiguration], he told them [disciples Peter, James, and John] not to tell anyone what they had seen until the Son of Man had risen from the dead" (Mark 9:9).

Jesus had even demonstrated his resurrection skill set by bringing back to life at least three people: the daughter of a synagogue leader named Jairus, the son of a widow, and Lazarus.

Yet on day three after the Crucifixion, when Jesus showed up freshly undead, "the whole group was startled and frightened, thinking they were seeing a ghost!" (Luke 24:37).

What part of "on the third day he will rise again" did they not understand? That's what many of us want to know.

Maybe they were thinking the same thing Martha had thought about her brother Lazarus when Jesus assured her, "Your brother will rise again" (John 11:23).

Martha answered, "He will rise when everyone else rises, at the last day."

"I am the resurrection and the life," Jesus told Martha.

But even then, Martha couldn't imagine the resurrection Jesus had in mind. Not until she saw it with her own eyes. It may have been much the same for the disciples, huddled in a locked room while the body of their Messiah lay on a slab.

RESURRECTION TIMELINE

Gospel writers don't give us a precise timeline of Resurrection weekend. But piecing together reports from all four Gospels, and presuming the events revolved around Passover beginning on Friday, April 3 of AD 33, one possible timeline could look like this.

Friday
- 3 p.m., Jesus dies
- Pilate grants Joseph of Arimathea permission to bury Jesus
- 6 p.m., sunset, Jesus in tomb

Saturday
- Jewish leaders convince Pilate to seal and guard Jesus' tomb
- 6 p.m., sunset, when Sabbath ends, women buy burial spices

Sunday
- Before sunrise, Jesus rises from the dead; terrified guards flee
- 5:30 a.m., sunrise, several women go to Jesus' tomb
- Angels tell the women Jesus has risen
- The women report the news to the disciples
- Peter and James confirm that the tomb is empty
- Jesus greets Mary Magdalene
- Mary tells the disciples, "I have seen the Lord!"
- Jewish leaders bribe guards to say the disciples stole Jesus' body
- Afternoon, Jesus walks to Emmaus with two followers, and then eats with them
- Evening, Jesus appears to the disciples

— MYSTERY OF THE RESURRECTION ──────

Wouldn't it be wonderful if this pivotal moment in Christian history were crystal clear, easy to understand, and written into the public record so everyone knew it really happened?

But our pivotal moment remains shrouded in mystery and cover-up. Like the wind, we can see its effects—moving the seemingly unmovable into action (the disciples). But no one on record saw Jesus' actual transformation from horizontal to vertical.

The moment is ripe with questions:

Did Jesus rise too soon? If we take his predictions literally, he should have stayed dead until Monday.

Looking ahead to his time in the tomb, Jesus had told the Jewish scholars harassing him for proof that God sent him, "You want a sign because you are evil and won't believe! But the only sign you will get is the sign of the prophet Jonah. He was in the stomach of a big fish for three days and nights, just as the Son of Man will be deep in the earth for three days and nights" (Matthew 12:39–40 CEV).

Jesus died at three in the afternoon on Friday, a few hours before sunset marked the start of the annual celebration of Passover. So why didn't he stay in the tomb for three full days and nights: Friday, Saturday, and Sunday—72 hours?

He stayed in the tomb only a tad more than half that time—about 40 hours. That's assuming he was buried soon after he died on Friday, April 3, AD 33, and that he rose before the 5:30 a.m. sunrise on April 5.

Bible experts offer a few theories about the discrepancy:

Fulfilling prophecy. The most popular theory is that Jesus was connecting his death and resurrection to an ancient prophecy: "After two days he will revive us; on the third day he will raise us up, that we may live before him" (Hosea 6:2 NRSV).

Three partial days qualify. Another popular theory spins around an ancient Jewish understanding: Any part of a day qualified as a full day. Writings confirm, for example, that if a Jewish traveler expected to be away on business for two days, he could leave on Monday and return as early as the next morning.

"A few days." Jesus may have been picking up on a common Jewish expression. "Three days" could mean "a few days," just as our expression "a day or two" could mean "a day or two or three or four."

Deliverance day. Jesus may have been referring to a common Bible theme that connected his resurrection to the number three, which symbolized deliverance. Several Bible stories feature God's deliverance on the third day. Jonah's story is the most famous. A big fish spit him ashore after three days.

Whatever Jesus had in mind, day three was important for another reason. Some rabbis taught that the soul could linger with the body for up to three days, hoping to reenter—until death began to disfigure the corpse. It was customary in some Jewish circles for survivors to visit the tomb on day three to make sure their loved one was still dead.

By staying dead until day three, Jesus was considered dead as dead could be.

Was Jesus resuscitated? After a soldier's spear had punctured Jesus' pericardial sac, releasing the serum and blood around the heart? That's how some physicians today explain what poured out of his wound: "Immediately blood and water flowed out" (John 19:34).

The first-century Jewish historian Josephus wrote that three people he knew were pardoned at the last moment, after being raised on crosses. Even with immediate medical treatment, and no spear to the chest, two of them died.

How did Jesus rise from the dead? No one on record witnessed the event. And there are pitifully few clues.

Manly men fainted. "Suddenly there was a great earthquake! For an angel of the Lord came down from heaven, rolled aside the stone, and sat on it. His face shone like lightning, and his clothing was as white as snow. The guards shook with fear when they saw him, and they fell into a dead faint" (Matthew 28:2–4).

Grave clothes neatly folded. When Peter rushed to the tomb, he saw "the linen wrappings lying there, while the cloth that had covered Jesus' head was folded up and lying apart from the other wrappings" (John 20:6–7). This description leaves Bible experts guessing whether someone removed the strips of cloth from his body, or whether Jesus simply passed through them and left them lying in place, folding the separate face covering.

The controversial Shroud of Turin feeds off the second theory. Some Christians have claimed that the shroud captured the brilliant burst of trans-figuration, imprinting the image of Jesus' body into the cloth.

Science begs to differ. In 1988, three labs in different countries tested a postage-stamp-sized piece of fabric from the Turin shroud. They carbon-dated the cloth to sometime between 1260 and 1390. The Catholic Church accepted these find-ings, confirming that the shroud wasn't genuine. Yet church leaders encouraged Christians to respect the shroud as a reminder of how Jesus suffered for humanity.

COVER-UP

Jesus' disciples took no action that would suggest they believed he would rise from the dead. But the Jewish leaders did.

On Saturday, "leading priests and Pharisees went to see Pilate. They told him, 'Sir, we remember what that deceiver once said while he was still alive: "After three days I will rise from the dead." So we request that you seal the tomb until the third day. This will preveant his disciples from coming and stealing his body and then telling everyone he was raised from the dead! If that happens, we'll be worse off than we were at first' " (Matthew 27:62–64).

Pilate, the Roman governor of the region, granted this request and placed a group of Roman soldiers at the disposal of these Jewish leaders.

Sometime after Jesus' predawn resurrection, the manly men soldiers, armed and dangerous, awoke from fainting.

Wisely, the soldiers decided not to report directly to Pilate or to their com-mander. Had they done so, what could they possibly have said to defend them-selves? "Sir, we saw something really, really scary and we fainted. And when we came to, the dead man was gone." Or how about, "We were really wiped out, so we caught some z's"? Either way, the soldiers could have anticipated their next mission: Go find the dead man—in Hades.

Gaius Petronius (AD 27–66), writing in *Satyricon*, tells of one Roman sol-dier slipping away from his post—guarding crucified corpses from being stolen for burial. He left to "comfort" a widow grieving for her husband in a nearby tomb. The soldier "comforted" her for three days and nights inside the tomb. But when he returned to his post, he found a body missing. He decided to kill himself rather than face the humiliating punishment, which could include be-ing beaten to death, beheaded, or exiled. The comforted widow came up with a better idea: Nail her dead husband to the cross.

Given the likely punishment, the soldiers guarding Jesus went to the Jew-ish leaders who might actually believe their story—and who might have good reason to keep the story from spreading among the Roman ranks.

It was a smart decision. The Jewish leaders bribed the soldiers to spread this story: "You must say, 'Jesus' disciples came during the night while we were sleeping, and they stole his body.' If the governor hears about it, we'll stand up

SCHOLARS ON THE RECORD WITH ABC'S 20/20

The ABC News program *20/20* grilled a team of Christian and Jewish Bible experts, asking what they thought about the resurrection of Jesus. Here are a few of their replies:

The first question is, do you believe in the Resurrection? My answer is, if you don't. . .you're not a Christian. But that's the easy question. The second question is well, what do you mean by the Resurrection? That's where the difference of opinions come in.

REV. RICHARD P. MCBRIEN
PROFESSOR OF ROMAN CATHOLIC THEOLOGY, UNIVERSITY OF NOTRE DAME

I don't believe it was a physical Resurrection exactly in the way we understand the body today—we have Jesus walking through walls—those kinds of experiences suggest not the physical body that we would see today. But something that if we have to use our categories would look much more like a visionary experience.

KAREN L. KING
PROFESSOR OF ECCLESIASTICAL HISTORY, HARVARD DIVINITY SCHOOL

I think definitely something happened. I don't know how they [followers of Jesus] convinced themselves. But the historical fact is, you've got people who are convinced he was resurrected.

DANIEL SCHWARTZ
PROFESSOR OF HISTORY, HEBREW UNIVERSITY IN JERUSALEM

I don't think there would have been a New Testament or a Jesus movement had there not been some astonishing experience of power. . . . I don't know exactly what that is. But it is clear to me that there was something that opened their eyes to see a dimension of reality that I believe is beyond the boundaries of normal.

BISHOP JOHN SHELBY SPONG
RETIRED EPISCOPAL BISHOP OF NEWARK, NEW JERSEY

If the body had been discovered, there would be no Christian church. . . and everybody would have laughed about a crucified criminal being the son of God.

PAUL L. MAIER
PROFESSOR OF ANCIENT HISTORY, WESTERN MICHIGAN UNIVERSITY

If God exists and created the universe, this is child's play for him.

LEE STROBEL
ATHEIST-TURNED-CHRISTIAN AUTHOR AND FORMER TEACHING PASTOR,
WILLOW CREEK COMMUNITY CHURCH

Jesus took off the grave clothes. . .and walked out of the tomb. He would be palpable. He would be physical. He would be tangible.

WILLIAM LANE CRAIG
RESEARCH PROFESSOR, TALBOT SCHOOL OF THEOLOGY

for you so you won't get in trouble" (Matthew 28:13–14).

Pilate and other Romans may have believed that line. But Bible experts say there are two good reasons no one else should.

Obsessive-compulsive neat thieves. Disciples or anyone else trying to steal a corpse from under the noses of a Roman guard probably wouldn't waste time undressing the body and then neatly folding the burial clothes.

Cowardly disciples turn fearless. Even some Jewish scholars today who deny that Jesus was God's Son admit that the disciples saw something dramatically transforming—perhaps a vision of Jesus alive and well. For on Passover, the disciples cowered in a locked house, fearing they might suffer the same fate as their master. Yet less than two months later, they were boldly continuing Jesus' work by spreading his teachings in Jerusalem—right in front of the Jewish leaders who had orchestrated his execution.

SUNDAY SURPRISE

All four Gospels—Matthew, Mark, Luke, and John—tell the astonishing tale of what happened on that first Easter Sunday morning. If only the sources they used would have gotten their stories straight, then maybe the Bible critics wouldn't flog Christians with the discrepancies.

Yet it's the discrepancies that smack of reality, some say. Multiple witnesses of any event usually tell different tales. They each see things from a different perspective and they report different details.

Matthew reports only two women going to Jesus' tomb that morning: Mary Magdalene and another Mary. Mark says there were three: Mary Magdalene, Salome, and Mary the mother of James. Luke says there were several women, including Mary Magdalene, Joanna, and Mary the mother of James. John reports only one woman: Mary Magdalene. Most Bible experts say there was probably a group of women. However many there were, there's a powerful element of truth buried in the fact that women were the first witnesses of the Resurrection.

Any well-intentioned Christian writer inventing a resurrection story about Jesus—and expecting people to believe it—wouldn't have rested his case on the reliable witness of women. Jews and Romans alike discounted the testimony of women, treating ladies like courts today treat minors—with caution.

When it came time to weigh testimony, first-century historian Josephus offered this advice: "Don't trust just one witness. You should have at least two, preferably three or more whose lives show they are trustworthy. Don't accept evidence from women. Rash and frivolous by nature, they shouldn't be taken seriously."

Another first-century historian, Philo (about 15 BC–AD 45), called women "irrational" and "untrustworthy."

RESURRECTED JESUS IN A ROMAN HISTORY BOOK

Jesus' resurrection shows up in a Roman history book written during his century. The writer was Josephus, a Jew who was also a Roman citizen.

There was a wise man who was called Jesus, and his conduct was good. . . . Pilate condemned him to be crucified. . . . His disciples didn't abandon their loyalty to him. They reported that he appeared to them three days after his crucifixion, and that he was alive.

JOSEPHUS (ABOUT AD 37–101), *ANTIQUITIES OF THE JEWS*

KNEE-JERK REACTION OF THE DISCIPLES

The disciples in hiding mimicked the era's macho attitude toward women.

Mary Magdalene and the other women rushed back from the tomb to tell the disciples that Jesus had risen from the dead. But the disciples treated this report "like nonsense" (Luke 24:11).

To their credit, two of the 11 went to check out the story: "Simon Peter and the other disciple, the one whom Jesus loved" (John 20:2). Most Bible experts speculate that the "other disciple" was John, brother of James. He's the only disciple not mentioned by name in this Gospel—an apparent, humble omission, because most Bible experts agree that John wrote this Gospel later named after him.

That evening, Jesus visited 10 of the disciples, suddenly appearing inside the locked house where they were still hiding from Jewish authorities.

"Peace be with you," he said, showing them the wounds in his hands and his side. John's Gospel says the disciples were filled with joy. Luke says that before the joy there was terror. "The whole group was startled and frightened, thinking they were seeing a ghost!" (Luke 24:37). Jesus ate some fish to prove he was more than a disembodied spirit.

Thomas missed that meeting and had to wait eight days to see the resurrected Jesus with his own eyes. Until then, he remained skeptical. "I won't believe it unless I see the nail wounds in his hands, put my fingers into them, and place my hand into the wound in his side" (John 20:25).

Thomas' show-me attitude dissolved the moment he saw Jesus and declared, "My Lord and my God!"

Self-preserving cowards and skeptics all, the disciples suddenly transformed into new creatures—brimming with faith and boldness. Some 50 days after the Passover crucifixion, these disciples would preach to Jewish pilgrims who had come to Jerusalem for the annual Pentecost festival. When the same Jewish leaders who had orchestrated the execution of Jesus ordered them to stop or risk Jesus' fate, the disciples preached on—starting what became the Christian movement.

The Bible reports the fate of only one disciple: James. "King Herod Agrippa began to persecute some believers in the church. He had the apostle James (John's brother) killed with a sword" (Acts 12:1–2). Church writers in the AD

100s said all the others were persecuted and most were martyred. Only John escaped execution for preaching about Jesus.

GABRIEL: "IN THREE DAYS LIVE, YOU PRINCE OF PRINCES"
—a new discovery from Jesus' lifetime

A 2,000-year-old inscription recently released to the public may tell the story of Jesus' resurrection—before it took place.

The stone slab, with a message written in ink, was discovered a decade ago in Jordan, but has only recently been translated. The style of the letters is the same as other documents from the end of the first century BC and into the early years of the first century AD—when Jesus lived.

Called "Gabriel's Revelation," because the writer often quotes the angel Gabriel, the message seems to come from a group of Jews who expected the Messiah to come from King David's descendants—and then to die and rise again. So say some scholars who have translated the inscription.

Many words are worn off or hard to read. But parts of the message that remain seem to hint of Jesus as the Messiah. The writer describes the Messiah as Ephraim, ancestor of one of the 12 tribes of Israel—and a son of Joseph.

In the inscription, Gabriel tells David to ask Joseph's son fore a sign. In context, some scholars say, the sign sounds like a reference to salvation. Key lines that follow:

- "This is what the Lord of Hosts, the God of Israel says: my gardens are ready to harvest."
- "By three days you will know, for this is what the Lord of Hosts, the God of Israel says: the evil has been broken."
- "I Gabriel command you, in three days live, you prince of the princes."

Some scholars say the discovery of this inscription threatens Christianity because it suggests that the idea of a Messiah rising from the dead after three days gradually evolved out of Jewish teachings.

Others say the translators are reading too much between the lines, and that there's no clear reference to the Messiah, salvation, or a resurrection.

Still others say if the translators got it right and the message tracks with Jesus' story, it's just one more prophecy Jesus fulfilled.

JESUS' ASSIGNMENT FOR HIS FOLLOWERS

"Go and make disciples of all the nations, baptizing them in the name of the Father and the Son and the Holy Spirit. Teach these new disciples to obey all the commands I have given you."
MATTHEW 28:19–20

What now?

That had to be a top question on the minds of the disciples after the resurrected Jesus stepped back into their lives on Easter Sunday—suddenly showing up inside the locked room where they were hiding in Jerusalem.

Jesus told them to get out of town and meet him on a mountain in Galilee. By Rocky Mountain standards, these weren't even foothills. Mountain men might call them speed bumps. The Galilean terrain consists of gently rolling hills for the most part, easily walked. Jesus probably had in mind one favorite hilltop, perhaps a spot he often taught his disciples in the past.

As the disciples walked the several-day journey north to Galilee, they must have thought the answer to their question waited for them there—and it did. But it wasn't the answer they expected.

Jesus spent 40 days with the disciples and other followers. The apostle Paul, writing a letter about 20 years later, said, "He was seen by more than 500 of his followers at one time, most of whom are still alive" (1 Corinthians 15:6). During those five weeks Jesus spent among his followers, he continued doing what he had done before: teaching them.

Given what had just happened, he probably focused a lot on prophecies he had just fulfilled through his suffering, death, and resurrection. His tutoring may be why the four Gospel writers were able to connect so many of the Old Testament prophecies with Jesus. (See "Prophecies Jesus Fulfilled in Dying," page 271.)

The disciples must have been intrigued by these new takes on old scripture. But one thing troubled them. They wanted to hear the answer to "What next?" Yet after 40 days of teaching, Jesus still hadn't confirmed their expectation about where all of this was headed. So moments before he ascended into the sky, they asked him to confirm what they expected to happen next: "Lord, has the time come for you to free Israel and restore our kingdom?" (Acts 1:6).

After everything they had seen and heard, they still couldn't let go of their preconceived notions about what the Messiah would do when he came. They still thought he would free Israel politically in the here and now rather than free all humanity spiritually, here, now, and forever.

Jesus responded with something known as the Great Commission— marching orders for conquering the world spiritually.

WHO DIED AND MADE PETER POPE?

Roman Catholics teach that the pope is God's voice box on earth. They say Jesus himself set up the system when he left Peter in charge: "I will call you Peter, which means 'a rock.' On this rock I will build my church. . . . I will give you the keys to the kingdom of heaven, and God in heaven will allow whatever you allow on earth. But he will not allow anything that you don't allow" (Matthew 16:18–19 CEV).

Many early church leaders in the generations that followed interpreted this as a mission statement for Peter and the elite churchmen who would follow in his footsteps. Church leaders also came to recognize the bishop of Rome—the city in which, tradition says, Peter was crucified upside down—as Peter's successor. That's why the pope lives at the Vatican in Rome.

After the Resurrection and shortly before leaving the planet, Jesus asked Peter three times, "Do you love me?" (John 21:15). Jesus may have intended that triple request followed by Peter's triple reply of "yes" to reflect a contract. In the ancient Middle East, solemn obligations were often repeated three times in front of witnesses.

Jesus followed each question with a commission: "Take care of my sheep" (John 21:16).

"Why does Jesus pass over the others?" asked John Chrysostom, a prominent Syrian preacher in the AD 300s. "Peter was chosen as. . .the mouth of the disciples—the head of the choir. . . . Jesus entrusts him with leadership over the others."

Most Protestants agree that Jesus put Peter in charge of what became the Christian movement. It was Peter's sermon during Jerusalem's Pentecost festival that jumpstarted the church, inspiring some 3,000 people to join.

But most Protestants stop short of portraying Peter or any human being as God's spokesman. As for what Jesus meant by implying that God would enforce any rules that Peter set up, Protestant scholars say that's a stretch. And they add it's an even bigger stretch to apply it to the church's long line of popes.

Instead, most Protestant Bible experts say, Jesus was simply giving Peter the authority to lead the church and to discipline its members as needed.

SPREAD THE WORD

Beyond ambitious, the job Jesus left to 11 men seemed over the edge and off the wall. Impractical. Impossible. Insane.

No money, no land, no army. Yet this motley crew, one traitor shy of a dozen, was to conquer "all the nations," a phrase that most Bible experts say refers not to countries with borders, but to all kinds of people everywhere: in country, out of country, Jew, non-Jew, men, women, kids, in-laws, even bosses.

Weapon of choice: the mouth. The disciples were to speak words of a new ideology that was based on a single, seemingly absurd premise: Jesus didn't stay dead, and we don't have to stay dead, either.

The closest Jesus came to giving his disciples a how-to-conquer-the-world manual was to offer them a three-point strategy: Go, baptize, teach.

Go. "You will be my witnesses, telling people about me everywhere—in Jerusalem, throughout Judea, in Samaria, and to the ends of the earth" (Acts 1:8). They would start in Jerusalem, spreading out to Judea in what is now southern Israel, and then to Samaria in what is now central Israel. In time, they would scatter abroad. Church leaders writing in the centuries that followed said most of Jesus' original disciples died as martyrs in other countries.

Baptize. "Baptize them in the name of the Father, the Son, and the Holy Spirit" (Matthew 28:19 CEV). The earliest Christian communities on record left documents showing that baptism was part of the initiation process for new Christians—a ritual welcoming newcomers into the faith. The Jews, too, started using a similar process to induct converts into the Jewish faith. The convert would wash in a ritual bath called a *mikveh* (MICK-vah). For Christians, however, baptism seemed more symbolic than essential for salvation—though some Christians argue otherwise. (See "Is Baptism a Must?" page 78.)

Teach. "Teach these new disciples to obey all the commands I have given you" (Matthew 28:20). In a way, the disciples were to clone themselves. They were to make more disciples. These 11 men, most of whom scattered and hid during Jesus' trial and execution, were to pick up where Jesus left off. They were to start in Jerusalem, within earshot of the same Jewish leaders who had orchestrated Jesus' crucifixion just a few weeks earlier.

Words alone probably wouldn't have gotten the job done. But Jesus promised them a little something extra.

He said he was well within his rights to do so: "I have been given all authority in heaven and on earth" (Matthew 28:18). Most Bible experts say Jesus was citing a prophecy: "I saw someone like a son of man. . . . He was given authority, honor, and sovereignty over all the nations of the world, so that people of every race and nation and language would obey him" (Daniel 7:13–14).

The little something extra: "In just a few days you will be baptized with the Holy Spirit" (Acts 1:5).

Jesus had led the men back to Jerusalem, ground zero for launching their spiritual, nonviolent crusade. "Do not leave Jerusalem until the Father sends you the gift he promised," Jesus told them. "You will receive power when the Holy Spirit comes upon you" (Acts 1:4, 8).

Then, standing on the ridge of hills called the Mount of Olives, somewhere near Bethany, Jesus "was taken up into a cloud while they were watching, and they could no longer see him" (Acts 1:9). His exit sounds a bit like that of the prophet whose predicted return to earth was to mark the beginning of the Messiah's ministry: Elijah, "carried by a whirlwind into heaven" (2 Kings 2:11).

The sequel to Jesus' story—the book of Acts—reports that the Holy Spirit gave miracle-working power to Jesus' followers. They preached in languages they hadn't studied and they healed the sick.

It's tough to ignore the words of people with power like that. On day one when the Spirit arrived, some 3,000 Jews, assembled in Jerusalem for the harvest festival of Pentecost, joined the messiah movement. For many Jews, this movement must have seemed like a new branch of the Jewish religion, one that said the promised Messiah had come.

Jewish purists branded the movement a heresy, arguing that there's only one God—and he didn't have a son.

Persecution chased off many Messiah-believing Jews. But they took their faith with them to distant lands. Within two decades, the apostle Paul was spreading Christianity as far away as Europe. By the end of the century, when most eyewitnesses of Jesus had died, seeds of the Christian faith had scattered throughout the Roman Empire—which most people at the time considered the extent of the civilized world.

Some Bible experts say the Great Commission ended there—a mission impossible, miraculously accomplished by Generation First. Most scholars, however, insist that spreading Jesus' teachings and making disciples are the mission of every follower in every generation.

Many scholars add that Jesus' final promise to his 11 surviving disciples was a promise to all followers throughout the ages: "I will be with you always, even until the end of the world" (Matthew 28:20 CEV).

THE LAST WORD
John—probably the last of the four Gospels, and likely written in the AD 90s—wraps up the story of Jesus with words of high praise: "Jesus also did many other things. If they were all written down, I suppose the whole world could not contain the books that would be written" (John 21:25).

Not the most creative way to end Jesus' dramatic story. But it does track with other writings of the time—including that of one rabbi who praised himself:

If every ocean became an inkwell, every tree a pen, and the sky from horizon to horizon a scroll, there wouldn't be enough of anything to preserve my wisdom, which I amassed from my study with the masters.

RABBI YOHANAN BEN ZAKKAI,
LEADER OF JEWISH COUNCIL FROM AD 70–90,
SOPHERIM (SCHOLARS) 16:8

BEYOND THE STORY
JESUS AND THE
SECOND COMING

"The Arrival of the Son of Man! It will fill the skies—
no one will miss it. . . . At that same moment,
he'll dispatch his angels with a trumpet-blast summons,
pulling in God's chosen from the four winds, from pole to pole."
MATTHEW 24:30–31 THE MESSAGE

When is Jesus coming back, and what's it going to look like?
That's what we want to know.

Bad news from the most respected Bible experts. Even with all the New Testament predictions about the Second Coming, experts aren't even close to agreeing on when Jesus is coming or what's going to happen when he gets here.

They're following a good precedent: his First Coming.

With all the Old Testament predictions about the Messiah—which turned out to be Jesus' First Coming—the most respected Jewish scholars of the day not only missed him as the Messiah, they killed him as a fraud.

The New Testament portrays those scholars as enslaved to preconceived notions based on what they thought were solid interpretations of prophecies about the Messiah. But expecting a warrior king, they got a pacifist rabbi. Expecting salvation from oppressors, they were offered salvation from sin. Expecting a restored nation of Israel, they were invited into the Kingdom of God.

CHRIST: NOT JESUS' FAVORITE TITLE

Christ is a title, not a last name. Jesus wasn't raised in the house of Joseph and Mary Christ.

The word is the Greek form of *messiah*, which means "anointed one," referring to a savior sent by God.

Jesus didn't usually call himself the Messiah, probably because he knew the Jews had misconceptions about what the Messiah would do. He preferred another title: Son of Man. It sounds so, well, human.

And that's exactly how God used it when he gave that nickname to the prophet Ezekiel: "Stand up, son of man. I want to speak with you" (Ezekiel 2:1). It was as if God was reminding Ezekiel, "You're a mortal, but I'm immortal. And don't you forget it."

But there was deity in the title, too: "I saw a human form, a son of man, arriving in a whirl of clouds. . . . He was given power to rule—all the glory of royalty. Everyone—race, color, and creed—had to serve him. His rule would be forever, never ending" (Daniel 7:13–14 THE MESSAGE).

That two-for-one meaning is what made the tag perfect for Jesus, who's portrayed in the Bible as both God and man.

Jesus must have realized how well the title fit.

With miserably few exceptions, most Jewish scholars refused to change their minds about Jesus. It didn't matter that his theological insights argued them silent. Or that he could heal the sick and raise the dead. Or even that he rose from the dead himself.

Some Christians today, say many scholars, seem just as stuck in a rut when it comes to notions of the Second Coming. These Christians will read a prophecy about the Second Coming like an engineer reads a blueprint.

For Christians like that, most Bible experts have one word of advice: Don't.

WHEN IS HE COMING?

Don't count on insights from the apostle Paul, many Bible experts say, for he got it wrong: "The time that remains is very short" (1 Corinthians 7:29).

Some of those scholars add that this belief of Paul's, early in his ministry, might have been why he offered this advice: "It's better to stay unmarried, just as I am" (1 Corinthians 7:8).

Other students of the Bible say, "Not so fast. It's not that simple."

Jesus, for example, made some apparently contradictory statements that could seem like they cover both sides of a coin toss on the timing of the Second Coming.

At one point, Jesus says, "No one knows the day or hour when these things will happen, not even the angels in heaven or the Son himself. Only the Father knows" (Matthew 24:36).

Yet just moments earlier he had said, "I tell you the truth, this generation will not pass from the scene until all these things take place" (Matthew 24:34).

Some pretty famous scholars thought Jesus got that wrong. Albert Schweitzer, for one—a famed theologian and winner of the Nobel Peace Prize for 1952. Schweitzer, who eventually jumped career tracks to practice medicine in Africa, argued that even though Jesus admitted he didn't know the hour of the Second Coming, he seemed to think he knew the generation.

That was about 50 generations ago, figuring 40 years to a generation.

Scholars who give Paul and Jesus the benefit of the doubt by assuming they weren't wrong tackle the problem in various ways.

Regarding what Jesus said, some scholars wonder if the Second Coming took place at the Resurrection, or perhaps when the Holy Spirit descended on the disciples a few weeks later, at the harvest festival of Pentecost.

But one of the most widespread views at the moment argues that when Jesus made his end-time statements, he seemed to be hopping back and forth between several events on the future timeline:

- the Roman decimation of Jerusalem fewer than 40 years later;
- the Second Coming; and
- the beginning of a new age.

Scholars call this speech of Jesus the Olivet Discourse because he delivered it on the Mount of Olives. And if Jesus was talking about the fall of Jerusalem when he said the current generation would witness it, he got that prediction right.

Regarding what both Jesus and Paul said, predicting a quick return, it seems that a growing number of scholars are teaching that prophecy isn't a matter of getting the future right or wrong.

"Salvation history is not a predetermined scheme," says Dr. Dale C. Allison Jr., a New Testament professor at Pittsburgh Theological Seminary. Writing in the *Dictionary of Jesus and the Gospels*, Allison says, "It is rather a dynamic relationship between God and his people. The Lord of the Gospels can shorten the interim. . .or lengthen it."

Prophecy isn't mainly about telling the future, Allison adds. It's mainly about showing one possible course of future events. It can be a warning "which may or may not be heeded." Or it can be a promise, "whose conditions may or may not be met." The response dictates what happens.

A great example is the story of Jonah, the Jewish prophet who traveled to the Assyrian city of Nineveh in what is now northern Iraq. His prophetic warning: "Forty days from now Nineveh will be destroyed!" (Jonah 3:4). But the Assyrians repented. So God spared the city.

If Allison and his kindred spirits are right—that prophecies are often metaphors conveying open-ended messages rather than chiseled timelines—then the first wave of Christians may not have missed the boat. God simply changed the schedule.

— WHAT'S TAKING JESUS SO LONG? —
"What happened to the promise that Jesus is coming again?" (2 Peter 3:4).

That was not a polite question. That was ridicule. And it was coming, warned the apostle Peter (or perhaps one of his students writing in his name—scholars debate which). If Peter wrote the warning, he probably did so shortly before his execution in the AD 60s. If one of his students wrote it, the letter may not have been written for another 20 or 30 years.

"God isn't late with his promise as some measure lateness," the letter writer explains. "He is restraining himself on account of you, holding back the End because he doesn't want anyone lost. He's giving everyone space and time to change" (2 Peter 3:9 THE MESSAGE). Some Bible experts seem mystified by this explanation.

Yet others use it as evidence for a first step in the direction of understanding that prophecies aren't chiseled in Jerusalem limestone. Timelines may be relatively unimportant to a God for whom "a day is like a thousand years. . .and a thousand years is like a day" (2 Peter 3:8).

WHERE DO THE DEAD GO?

It's fairly clear in reading the Gospels that when the apostles heard Jesus say he was coming back to get them, they expected to be there when he arrived.

"I am going there to prepare a place for each of you," Jesus told them. "After I have done this, I will come back and take you with me. Then we will be together" (John 14:2–3 CEV).

Most apostles apparently assumed they'd be alive when this happened. They weren't.

As Christians started dying and Jesus remained a no-show, survivors began asking questions like this one: "What happens to Christians who die before Jesus gets here?"

Paul tackled that question in what many say is probably the oldest document in the New Testament—his first surviving letter. He says that when Jesus returns, "Christians who have died will rise from their graves" (1 Thessalonians 4:15–16).

A great follow-up question would be, "Where are they in the meantime?"

Some Bible experts, such as Dr. Bruce L. Shelley, professor of historical theology at Denver Seminary, say there may not be a "meantime."

"All who die trusting in the Lord Jesus Christ die in his love and will probably be unconscious of any passage of time before Christ's return," Shelley writes in Christian Theology in Plain English. Much like we're unaware of sleeping the night away.

Whatever happens between death and the Second Coming, Paul writes in what many say was one of his last letters before his execution, "I long to go and be with Christ" (Philippians 1:23). By this time—perhaps 30 years after Jesus' ascension—Paul had come to realize that he would die before Jesus came back.

SECOND COMING SPECIALISTS BATTING ZERO

Throughout history, many end-time specialists have worked up the masses by predicting when Jesus would return. Some got rich doing it. But no one got the date right. A mere sampling:

PREDICTED DATE OF SECOND COMING	MAN BEHIND THE DATE	SOURCE OF AUTHORITY	BAD NEWS/ GOOD NEWS
1836	John Bengel (1687–1752), German theologian	Bible books of Daniel and Revelation	*Bad news:* Didn't happen. *Good news:* He didn't live to see his failure.
1843	William Miller (1782–1849), home-schooled New York farmer turned Baptist preacher	Daniel 8:14. Miller said Daniel's 2,300 days symbolized 2,300 years after Jews rebuilt Jerusalem's wall in what he said was 457 BC. 2,300 − 457 = 1843.	*Bad news:* Didn't happen. *Good news:* He had a backup plan.
1844	William Miller	See above. Then add one year for the year zero between BC and AD, which Miller said he had missed earlier.	*Bad news:* Ditto. And most of his 100,000 fans bailed. *Good news:* Die-hard followers helped start churches, including the Seventh-Day Adventist Church.
By 1988	Hal Lindsey, campus chaplain turned best-selling author of *The Late Great Planet Earth*	Lindsey said the 1948 rebirth of Israel is the landmark Jesus referred to when saying "this generation will not pass away" before he returns.	*Bad news:* The generation passed away. *Good news (for him):* Lindsey got rich. Prophecy teaching became a lucrative business for many.
1988	Edgar Whisenant, NASA rocket engineer turned author of *88 Reasons Why Jesus Will Come in '88*	Among his eighty-eight reasons: Though Jesus said no one knows the "day or hour" of the Second Coming, that doesn't mean we can't know the month and week.	*Bad news:* He couldn't back-pedal as well as Lindsey, and he lost his credibility. *Good news:* His "Rapture Report 1989" tanked.
October 28, 1992	Jang Rim Lee, South Korean minister and author of *Getting Close to the End*	Alleged interviews with South Korean children and adults said to have visions of Jesus' coming.	*Bad news:* He pocketed some of the donations he collected, investing in bonds that matured seven months after the date he set for the Second Coming. *Good news:* He got busted for defrauding his church of $4 million and was sentenced to two years in prison.
October 21, 2011	Harold Camping, California radio preacher	Bible prophecies, which he later said he misunderstood.	*Bad news:* The world didn't end as he had predicted— and he was bummed and apologetic about it. *Good news:* The world didn't end.

WHAT WILL HAPPEN WHEN HE COMES?

If God played baseball, he'd be a pitcher. And he'd be famous for his curveballs. We think we see it coming, but we miss it like we're waiting for yesterday's bus.

First-century Jewish scholars thought they had the Messiah's coming lined up perfectly. Christian scholars today caution that some Christians are doing the same thing with Jesus' Second Coming: reading too much into open-ended prophecies and building timelines and scenarios based on Bible metaphors. The scholars would say that's about as smart as building a skyscraper on a foundation of s'mores.

Take the Second Coming description offered by Paul, for example, written early in his ministry when he seemed to expect that Jesus would come back in his lifetime. Paul outlined the Second Coming itinerary like he was writing history:

- "The Lord himself will come down from heaven with a commanding shout, with the voice of the archangel, and with the trumpet call of God."
- "First, the Christians who have died will rise from their graves."
- "Then, together with them, we who are still alive and remain on the earth will be caught up in the clouds to meet the Lord in the air. Then we will be with the Lord forever."
- "The day of the Lord's return will come unexpectedly, like a thief in the night" (1 Thessalonians 4:16–17; 5:2).

To these graphic word pictures, Luke adds what some consider another element: location. As Jesus ascended to heaven from the Mount of Olives, his dumbfounded disciples stood staring into the sky. Suddenly, two white-robed men—angels, perhaps—appeared among them offering a promise. "Jesus has been taken from you into heaven, but someday he will return from heaven in the same way you saw him go!" (Acts 1:11).

The book of Revelation adds enough baffling visions about the Second Coming to make a stampede of end-time specialists richer than a tick on a bloodhound. That's assuming they convince enough people they have the code to unlock the secrets—and that Gabriel is wrapping up rehearsals with his celestial brass band. Many scholars certainly teach that those visions point to events—some cataclysmic—that must unfold before Jesus returns. But many others say most of those events were fulfilled during Roman times, and that the point of Revelation was to assure Christians during a time of Roman persecution that God was in control. The writer did this, scholars say, with coded images so the Romans wouldn't catch on and hammer the writer and his readers to a forest of crosses.

There are lots of ways to interpret all of these writings—Paul's letters, Luke's church history, John the Revelator's visions, along with other end-time material in the Old and the New Testaments.

Some interpreters take a literal approach. For example, when they read Ezekiel's vision that "the glory of the Lord" came into Jerusalem "through the east gateway" that faces the Mount of Olives, they put two and two together. Luke's angels implied that Jesus would descend back to the Mount of Olives, so it's logical to conclude that Jesus will enter Jerusalem through the nearest gate. Some Jews in ancient times speculated the Messiah would enter from this gate, too.

Sultan Suleiman the Magnificent, an Arab conqueror of Jerusalem, wasn't taking any chances. He sealed the east gateway in 1541, as if Jesus would stand there knocking till his knuckles wore off and then turn around and go home.

Other interpreters relax with the mystery. Dr. Rob Staples, a retired theology professor at Nazarene Theological Seminary, used to sum up his end-time lectures like this: "There are only two things we know about the Second Coming. Jesus is coming. And we don't know when."

Many would argue it's not quite that simple. But they would agree that Christians should focus on the who of the Second Coming, rather than on the what, when, where, and how.

WHAT SHOULD CHRISTIANS DO IN THE MEANTIME?

Paul answered that question about as bluntly as anyone.

Someone told him about a problem in the church he started at Thessalonica, in what is now northern Greece. For some reason, which many scholars guess was obsession over the Second Coming, a group of Christians had taken early retirement. Instead of working, they sat around waiting for Jesus. Working-class Christians took care of them.

Paul writes, "Don't you remember the rule we had when we lived with you? 'If you don't work, you don't eat.' And now we're getting reports that a bunch of lazy good-for-nothings are taking advantage of you. This must not be tolerated. We command them to get to work immediately—no excuses, no arguments—and earn their own keep" (2 Thessalonians 3:10-12 THE MESSAGE).

The Great Commission that Jesus left his followers wasn't "Just hang loose."

INDEX

Bold numbers: featured
Regular numbers: mentioned

A

Aaron, 13, 17, 23, 194
Abba, 249, 250
Abimelech, 34
Abortion, 56
Abraham, 12, 15, 23, 24, 25, 29, 84, 133, 159, 165, 175, 182, 202
Adam, 24, 84, 164, 265
Adonis, 40
Adoption, 24. **25**
Adultery, 26, 28, 33, 72, 117, 122, 123, 124, 152, 218, 220, 222
Afterlife (*see* Eternal Life)
Agriculture (*see* farming)
Alabaster, 223
Alexander Janneus, **17, 18**
Alexander the Great, **15, 18**, 19, 49, **71**
Aloe, 51, 208
Alpha, 204
Altar, 68, 165, 188, 217, 224, 226, 237, 242
Ambrose, 143
Andrew, 93, 94, **95**, 96, 99, 129, 184, 188, 189
Angels (*see also* Gabriel), 70, 175, 203, 205, 214, 231, 238, 255
  appearing to Joseph, 26, 33–34
  appearing to Mary, 32, 73, 89
  at Jesus' ascension, 238
  at Jesus' birth, 42, 46, 47
  at Jesus' resurrection, 10, 274, 275
  at Second Coming, 152, 173, 201, 285, 290
  at temptation of Jesus, 82–83
  during prayer in Gethsemane, 250
Anger,
  Jesus' views on, 120, **122**
  of Jesus, **209–10**
Animal sacrifice (*see* Sacrifice)
Annas, 252, 254, 255, 260
Anointed one, **13–14**, 132, 224, 233, 285
Anointing, 21, 51, 137, 209, 221, 225

Antigonus, **18**, 19–20, 49
Antiochus IV Epiphanes, **15**, **18, 185, 236**
Antipater, 18, 19, 55
Antonia Fortress, 60, 260, 266
Antony, Mark, 7, **18**, 20, 260
Apocalypse, 235
Apocalyptic literature, 235
Apocrypha, 103, 108, 115, 134, **202**
Apostle, (*see also* individual apostles by name), 91, **94**, 99, 288
Apostles' Creed, 39, 114
Apprenticeships, 62, 63, 92
Arabs, 12, 19, 129, 148, 223
Aramaic language, 95, 98, 114, 129, 250
Aretas, 72
Ark of the Covenant, 127, 137, 270
Aristobulus, 17, 18, 19, 55
Aristotle, 149
Armageddon, Valley of (*see* Jezreel Valley)
Assyria, 287
  defeats Jewish nation, 12, 14, 148, 165
Astrology
  Wise men as experts, 44, 45
Astronomy, 70
Athens, 115
Atonement (*see* Day of Atonement)
Augustine, 25
Augustus, Emperor (Octavian), 7, 18, 20, 25, 30, 37, 38, **71,** 73
  treated as a god, 37
Auranitis, 21

B

Baal, 132
Babylon
  city, 23, 24, 44, 45, 47
  destroys Jerusalem, 14, 137, 138, 139, 148, 166, 232, 249
  empire, 15
  jewish captivity in, 49, 54, 95, 114, 232
Balm, 208
Balthasar, 45
Baptism, 204, 283
  by John the Baptist, **72**, 85, 86, 207
  by other ancient cultures,

74–75
  chart of prophecies fulfilled by Jesus' b., **77**
  of Christian believers, 74, **78**, 141
  of Jesus, **72**, **76–79**, 80, 207, 250
  where it began, **74–75**
Bar mitzvah, 62
Barabbas, 262, 263, 264, 269
Barley, 22, 57, 66, 127, 157, **189**, 191
  poor man's bread, **189**
Bartholomew, 96
Batanea, 21, 207
Bathsheba, **26**, **27**, **28**, **29**, 137, 152
Battles (*see* Wars)
Beatitudes (*see also* Mount of Beatitudes), **118–20**
  chapel of the Beatitudes, 118
Bedbugs, 53
Bengel, John, 289
Bethany, 206, 215, 221, 226, 227, 228, 229, 283
Bethany beyond the Jordan, 80, 207
Bethesda, Pool of, 105, 111
Bethlehem, 35, 37, 38, 40, 50, **54**, 56
  birthplace of Messiah/Jesus, 38, 40, 42, 44, 89
  hometown of King David, 38
  hometown of Ruth's husband, Boaz, 29
  prophecy of Messiah's birthplace, 50, 89
  slaughter of young boys, 1, 8, 45, 50, 53, 54, 55
  star of B., 46
  tourists, 74
Bethphage, 226, 228
Bethsaida, 95, 96, 105, 186, 187, 188, 189
Betrothal (*see* Marriage)
Birth (*see also* Virgin Birth)
  control through infanticide, **56**
  of Jesus, 8, **35–37**, 38, 39, **40**
  techniques, rituals, **41, 42**
Blessings, 100, **118–19**, 121, 229, 240
Blind, 58, 103, 104, 105, 106, **107–8**, 110, 111, 114, 119, 154, 176, 206

Blood
 like drops of sweat, 247, 250
 of animal sacrifice, 226, 240, 265
 of Jesus, 226, 240, 242, 244, 245, 272, 275
 source of life, 265
Boats, ships, 92, 93, 183, 184, 185, 186, 188, 189
 "Jesus boat," 184
Boaz, 26, **27–28**, 29, 30
Body (at resurrection), 200, 275, 276
Born again, 80, 94, **204**
Bone box (ossuary), 208
Bread, 22, 81, 82, 127, 146, 150, 153, 160, 161, 191, 240, 242, 244, 245, 246
 Jesus as b. of life, 191
 Jesus miraculously feeds crowds, 95, 103, **187–90**
 live not by b. alone, 79
 manna, 82, 190, 191
 prayer for, **133–34**
 sacred, 146
 symbol of Jesus' body, 240, 244, 245
 yeastless (unleavened), 66, **67**, 146, 242, 243
Burial, 274, 276
 containers, 208
 Jesus, 51, 266, 271, 272
 jewish procedures, **208**, 209, 272
 Lazarus, 207, 209
 Moses, 193

C

Caesar, 18, 19, 25, 198, 253, 259, 260, 263, 264, 265
Caesarea, 20, 53, 181, 253, 266
 harbor town, 20, 181, 253
Caiaphas, 7, 211, 215, 218, 219, 252, 254, 255, 256, 257, 260, 261, 265
Caligula, 7, 230, 236, 246
Calvary, 266
Camel, 10, 53, 172
Cana, 96, **99**
 miracle of water into wine, 72, **99–103**
Canaan, 15, 28
Cannibalism, 232, **245**
Capernaum, 85, 86, 87, 95, 96, 97, 104, 105, 113, 116, **129**, 178, 180, 181, 183, 184, 186,

187, 188, 206
 Jesus' ministry base, 87, **129**, 179, 183
Caravan (*see also* Travel), 9, 40, 45, 49, 52, 57, 65, 68, 70, 223
Carpenter, 100, 115, 258
 Jesus as, 31, **62–63**, 113, 115, 116, 128
 Joseph as, 35, 50, **62–63**, 64
Celsus, 39, 115
Census, 37, 38
Centurion, 129, 179, 180
Children, 22, 25, 28, 30, 31, 41, 43, 55, 56, 58, **59–64**, 83, 104, 119, 122, 133, 151, 154, 159, 163, 169, 172, 178, 187, 205, 209, 222, 232, 235, 289
 chores, 22
 disease and injury of, **59**, 107–8
 education, **61–62**
 games, **60**
Christ (*see also* Messiah), 14, 36, 76, 78, 84, 129, 136, 200, 201, 205, 218, 234, 240, 242, 245, 246, 267, 272, **285**, 288
Christianity (Christians)
 critics of, 39, 115
 legalized, 36, 40, 143, 188, 195, 248, 266
 persecutions, executions, 7, 18, 85, 96, 97, 207, 279–80, 284, 287, 288, 290
 spreading the story of Jesus, **282–84**
Christmas holiday, **35–36**, 45
Chrysostom, John, 282
Church of All Nations, 248
Church of Gallicantu (Rooster Crowing), 257
Church of the Apostles, 242
Church of the Holy Sepulchre, 266
Church of the Nativity, **40**
Chuza, 221
Circumcision, 15, 42, 147, 180
Cisterns, 59, 92, 248
Clement of Alexandria, 35
Cleopatra, 7, 18
Colosseum, 8
Comet, **46**, **47–48**, 49, 237, 238
Commiphora bush, 51
Communion (Lord's Supper, Eucharist), 143, 240, 241, **245–46**
Constantine, Emperor, 36, 40,

143, 188
Conversion, 19, 75, 141, 259, 283
Covenant (Old/New), 42, 54, 76, 94, 121, 136, 140, 141, 147, 166, 194, 240
Creation, 66, 78, 81, 142, 151, 176, 234
Crime and punishment
 death penalty among Jews, 113, **117**
 death penalty among romans, 125, **264**
 jewish justice, 124
 penalties for criminals, 113, **124–25**, 222
 roman justice, **124–25**
Cripple (*see* Lame)
Cross, 43, 89, 95, 96, 102, 115, 124, 134, 173, 226, 246, 257, 265, 266, 267, 268, 269, 271, 272, 276,
Crucifixion, 7, 18
 description of, **267**
 of Jesus, 18, 21, 51, 67, 84, 89, 101, 109, 141, 154, 192, 210, 216, 218, 227, 233, 239, 240, 241, 259, 261, 262, 263, **265–72**, 277, 279, 283
 of other disciples, 95, 96, 97, 98
 of Peter, 95, 282
 of Pharisee leaders, 17
Cup of suffering, 134, 247, 250, **251**
Cyrene, 268

D

Daniel, 34, 46, 137, 174, 176, 202, 233, 236, 238, 289,
Daughter
 arranged marriages, 22, 30
 chores, 22
 education denied, **61**
 no inheritance, 22
David, 12, 14, 16, 17, 21, 29, 38, 42, 81, 137, 146, 166, 202, 215, 228, 229, 230, 280
 ancestor of Jesus, **23–25**, 49, 56, 89, 280
 sin with Bathsheba, 26, 27, 28, 29, 152
Day of Atonement (*Yom Kippur*), 66, 126, 136, 138, 140, 174, 237

Dead Sea, 9, 11, 16, 17, 52, 55, 74, 80, 126, 144, 201, 241
lowest spot on earth, 9
Dead Sea Scrolls, 16, 17, 50, 74, 126, 144, 201, 214, 241, 253
Deaf, 105, 111, 176
Death
Jesus conquers, 103, 210, 265
jewish beliefs about, **202–3**
Delilah, 254
Demons, 80, 81, 82, 164, 176, 221, 241
possession, exorcism, 105, **106–7**, 110, 168, 178, 253
Denarius, 32, 125, 180, 189, 196, 199, 223, 224
Desert (*see also* Judea), 9, 11, 16, 74, 78, 80, 140, 141, 158, 163, 191, 208, 224
Devil (*see* Satan)
Didache, 135, 140, 141, 245
Dio, Cassius, 48, 263
Dionysius Exiguus, 36
Disciple, (*see also* by name), 44, 70, 76, 78, 86, **91–98**, 99, 103, 110, 111, 119, 121, 128, 130, 131, 132, 136, 140, 142, 143, 146, 147, 150, 152, 154, 157, 159, 161, 173, 174, 176, 178, 183, 184, 186, 188, 189, 190, 193, 195, 198, 206, 218, 219, 227, 228, 229, 230, 231, 233, 236, 238, 240, 241, 242, 245, 246, 247, 248, 249, 251, 253, 255, 265, 271, 273, 274, 276, 278, 279, 281, 282, 283, 284, 286, 290
72 sent on mission, 94
Disease, 55, 59, 60, 104, 107, 108, 109, 110, 117, 179
chart of d. cured by Jesus, **105**
chart of remedies, **112**
cured by Jesus, **105**, 110, 117
relationship to sin, **110–12**, 119
skin disorders, 75, **106**
Divorce, 29, 32, 33, 72, 122
among Jews, **122–23**
letter of divorce, 22, 33, **123**
Doctors (*see* Medicine)
Dome of the Rock, 234
Donkey, 53, 89, 103, 109, 112, 172, **228–29**
hebrew word for, 258

of Jesus, 164
Domitian, 261
Dove, 42, 68, 74, 172, 212
Holy Spirit like a d., 39, **77–78**, 250
Dreams, 33, **34**, 50, 52, 56, 75, 76, 82, 83, **263**
Drought, 29, 116, 126, 157, 170, 171, 184, 191

E

Earthquakes, 10, 188, 235, 236, 270, 275
Easter, 67, 141, 226, 227, 278, 281
East Gate, 291
Eclipse, 269
Education, **61–62**
Egeria, 129, 188, 248
Egypt, 9, 12, 15, 18, 29, 30, 40, 46, 50, 65, 66, 67, 74, 82, 87, 97, 136, 177, 179, 219, 240, 241, 242, 243, 244, 245, 259
Jesus' family flees to, **52–56**
Eliezer, 25, 57, 147, 165
Elijah, 95, 116, 131, 132, 192, 193, 195, 203, 269, 283
Elisha, 116, 191
Elizabeth, 33, 73
Elysian fields, 175
Emmaus, 200, 274
En-Gannim, 166
England, 7, 19, 258
End times, 194, 202
chart of Second Coming specialists, **289**
comparison with crucifixion, **239**
second Coming theories, **285–91**
signs of, **231–39**
Enki, 75
Enoch, 174, 203
Ephesus, 96
Ephrathah, 38, 89
Ephraim, 258, 280
Epilepsy, 106
Eschatology, 235
Esther, Queen, 137, 138
Essenes, 16, 73, 126, 144, **203**, 207
chart about, **214**
Eternal life, 119, 161, 163, 174, 175, 191, 195, **200–205**, 234, 265

Eternal security (once saved, always saved), **161**
Ethiopia, 51, 97, 236
Eucharist (*see* Communion)
Eusebius, 25, 237
Eve, 81
Exodus out of Egypt, 12, 29, 46, 82
comparison with Jesus, **54**

F

Faith, 15, 39, 75, 78, 83, 95, 108, 118, 134, 161, 176, 178, 180, 181, 182, 202, 204, 279, 283, 284
heals, **110–11**
lack of, 186, 210
of a mustard seed, **127**
of Job, 134
produces good deed, 177
saves, 204, 206
Family life, **22**
honor parents, 122
Famine (*see* Drought)
Farming, 11, 57, 100
common crops, 57, 160
Festival of First Fruits, 66
in Galilee, 57, 158
parables about, 151, **157–61**
tenant, 150, 154, 158
wheat into bread, **160**
Fasting, **136–41**, 144, 272
calendar of Jewish fasting days, **138–39**
for public show, 126, **138–39**
jewish, 80, 126, **136–38**
of Jesus, 79, **80–81**, 108, 126
Father
role of, **22**
Felix, 125
Festivals (Jewish holy days), 53, 56, 65, 73, 217, 219, 241, 242, 253, 256, 262, 268, 279, 282, 284, 286
chart of, **66**
Fever, 15, 55, 105, 112, 180
Figs, 127, 153
Fish, 47, 91, 92, 95, 108, 172, 187, 189, 190, 200, 258, 274, 175, 179
saint Peter's, 189
Fishing, 47, 93, 95, 129, 142, 153, 183, 184, 185, 187, 188, 206
disciples' occupation, 91, 93
with nets, **92**

Flax, 22, 66, 127, 157

Flowers, 11, 127,

Food, 15, 22, 29, 53, 61, 67, 68,
74, 100, 101, 103, 120, 126,
127, 137, 138, 139, 142, 144,
145, 146, 153, 162, 170, 175,
178, 180, 189, 190, 191, 232
chart of kosher animals,
172
meal, 67, 80, 113, 123, 126,
139, 146, 152, 168, 189,
191, 197, 220, 232
passover meal, 219, 241, 242,
243
prayer for, 133, 135,

Foot washing, 22, **220–25**,
223, 246

Forgiveness, 72, 75, 76, 110,
123, 124, 131, 134, 135,
136, 139, 201, 217, 224, 225,
244, 265
of others, 134, 135

Frankincense, 45, 51, 269

Frog, 109, 172, 219

Fruit, 16, 56, 59, 66, 69, 100,
127, 155, 159, 160, 161,
243, 265

G

Gabriel, 290
announcing birth of Jesus,
32, 73
announcing birth of John
the Baptist, 73
predicting resurrection after
three days, 280

Galilee, 10, 33, 72, 93, 97, 103,
118, 129, 149, 157, 158, 160,
166, 178, 184, 188, 190, 281
accent, 258
fertile land, 10, 151
flowers,
homeland of Jesus' family,
10, 72, 260
Jesus' ministry center, **85–87**
pacified by Herod the Great,
19, 20
ruled by Herod Antipas,
7, 18, 21, 50, 56, 63, 72,
85, 221, 262

Gamaliel, 92, 180, 185

Garden of Eden, 81, 164

Garden Tomb, 266

Gaspar, 45

Gaul (France), 7, 17, 56, 179

Gaulanitis, 21, 188

Gaza Strip, 12, 162

Gemara, 62

Genealogies, 13
importance, **23–24**
of Jesus, 23, **24–25**, 29
inconsistencies, **24–25**

Gentile, 24, 28, 75, 76, 144, 162,
174, 180, 182, 216, 217
good Samaritan, **162–67**
in Galilee, 86, 87
Jesus helps, 117, 178
jews: a light to g., 91, 182
ritually unclean, 181
worshipping God,

Gerasenes, 183–84

Gethsemane, Garden of, 227
Jesus prays in, 95, 193,
247–51

Gnostic, 250

Goats, 43, 68, 90, 171, 172,
243, 272
parable of sheep and, 153,
173–77

God, 10, 12, 13, 14, 15, 16, 17,
21, 23, 25, 34, 35, 37, 38, 39,
41, 43, 49, 50, 52, 55, 57,
61, 64, 67, 69, 70, 72, 73, 76,
77, 78, 79, 80, 81, 82, 83, 84,
85, 87, 88, 89, 92, 94, 95, 96,
102, 107, 111, 113, 114, 117,
118, 119, 120, 122, 123, 126,
127, 128, 130, 131, 132, 133,
134, 135, 136, 137, 138, 139,
140, 141, 142, 143, 147, 149,
150, 151, 152, 153, 154, 155,
157, 159, 160, 161, 162, 163,
165, 166, 171, 172, 174, 176,
177, 178, 179, 180, 181, 182,
185, 187, 189, 190, 191, 192,
193, 194, 195, 198, 201, 202,
203, 204, 205, 206, 210, 212,
213, 214, 215, 216, 217, 218,
220, 222, 224, 225, 226, 228,
229, 230, 232, 234, 237, 239,
240, 241, 242, 243, 244, 245,
246, 249, 250, 251, 255, 256,
257, 260, 263, 265, 269, 270,
271, 274, 275, 277, 278, 279,
280, 282, 284, 285, 287, 290
communicates in dreams
(see Dreams)
father of Jesus (see Son of
God)
freed Jews from Egyptian
slavery, 54, 66, 67
hears prayer (see Prayer)

holiness of, 42, 132, 133
love for humanity, 204, 240
promises to the Jews (see
also Covenant), 13, 15,
42, 121
punishes Jewish nation and
other sinners, 29, 79, 110,
119
respecting his name, 117
seeks to save people from sin
(see also Salvation), 114,
177, 204, 230
source of life, 39
worship of, 65, 66, 68, 75,
114, 131, 133, 136, 142,
162, 165, 180, 181, 182,
201, 216, 217, 219, 242

Gold, 45, 51, 101, 137, 233, 234,
262, 270

Golden Rule, 120, **128**

Golgotha, 265, 266

Goliath, 12

Good Friday, 141

Gospel of Thomas, Infancy,
58, 69

Gospels, 32, 79, 85, 93, 94, 97,
113, 139, 146, 149, 151, 154,
183, 187, 201, 231, 235, 241,
246, 249, 252, 274, 278, 284,
287, 288
questionable sources, 278

Grapes, 22, 102, 127, 177

Great commission, 236, 282,
284, 291

Great Rift Valley, 10

Greece (Greeks), 9, 12, 14, 15,
17, 18, 27, 33, 36, 40, 78,
107, 116, 128, 133, 134, 140,
152, 155, 170, 175, 203, 207,
210, 291

Greek language, 31, 39, 40, 62,
84, 94, 95, 150, 170, 179,
192, 204, 207, 235, 238, 241,
245, 267, 285

H

Habakkuk, 249

Hades, 40, 276

Hadrian, Emperor, 12, 40

Halley's comet, 46, 47, 48

Hansen's Disease (see Leprosy)

Hanukah, 206

Harvest, 22, 51, 66, 68, 93, 100,
102, 152, 154, 155, 159, 160,
161, 177, 189, 196, 212, 248,
280, 284, 286

barley (*see* Barley)
figs (*see* Figs)
flax (*see* Flax)
grapes (*see* Grapes)
olives (*see* Olives)
wheat (*see* Wheat)
Hasmoneans (Maccabeans), 17, **18**, 19, 20, 49
Hate for enemies, **125–26**
Healing, 94, **104–12**, 116, 123, 147, 178, 179, 181, 215, 286
Heaven, 10, 14, 16, 49, 52, 70, 75, 76, 77, 85, 87, 88, 90, 95, 96, 109, 119, 120, 121, 123, 130, 132, 133, 134, 135, 150, 154, 170, 174, 176, 177, 180, 182, 187, 190, 191, 192, 193, 201, 203, 220, 229, 231, 234, 238, 243, 250, 256, 269, 272, 275, 282, 283, 286, 290
Hegesippus, 261
Helena, 40
Hell, 176
Heresy, 8, 245, 250, 284
Herod Agrippa, 96, 279
Herod Antipas, 7, 18, 21, 56, 63, 72, 85, 207, 221, 260, 262
Herod Archelaus, 21, 56
Herodias, 72
Herodotus, 12
Herod the Great, 7, 8, 18, **19–20**, 21, 35, 37, 44, **49–50**, 52, 53, 54, 55, 56, 57, 63, 72, 73, 148, 214, 232, 253, 260, 266
building projects, 166
death, **55**
slaughter of Bethlehem boys, 1, 8, 45, 50, 53, 54, 55
temple rebuilding, 69, **233**
wise men, **49–50**
Herod Philip, 18, 21
Herodians, 214
Herod's palace, 260
Hezekiah, 29, 148
High priests, 13, 18, 19, 20, 71, 105, 137, 144, 165, 212, 214, 215, 217, 237, 252, 254, 255, 258, 260, 270, 272
appointed by Romans, 13
ballad of the bad high priests, **254**
caiaphas, 7, 211, 215, 218, 219, 252, 254, 255, 256, 257, 260, 261, 265
descendants of Aaron, 13
Hyrcanus II (*see* Hyrcanus II)

Hillel, Rabbi, 123, 128
Hippolytus, 35
Holiness,
of God, 131, 132, 133
of people, 16, 138, 222
of Sabbath, 15
of sites (such as temples), 34, 40, 83, 217, 236
Holocaust, 12, 13, 137
Holy of Holies (Most Holy Place), 270, 272
Holy Spirit, 44, 78, 141, 204, 236, 281, 283, 286
at baptism of Jesus, 77, 250
at temptation of Jesus, 79, 80
coming as a dove, 77, 250
filling believers with power, 200
mary's pregnancy, 26, 32, 34, 39, 89
Horace, 53
Hospitality, 53, 101, 175, 223
Houses, 14, 22, 31, 50, 58, 59, 60, 62, 64, 70, 100, 101, 102, 116, 129, 144, 145, 146, 155, 180, 196, 198, 200, 208, 216, 217, 218, 220, 222, 223, 242, 252, 254, 256, 263, 278, 279, 285
Humanity
end of, 16, 81, 231
fall into sin, 164
of Jesus, 174, 251, 259
Humility, 246
of Jesus, 42
Hypocrisy, 141
Hyrcanus II, 17, 18, 19, 20

I
I Am (God's name), 14, 133, 255–56
Idols, 90, 117, 176
Idumea, 19, 56
Ignatius, 245
Immanuel, 39, 89
Infanticide (*see also* Herod the Great), **56**
Inheritance, 25, 73, 77, 119, 158
double share for oldest son, 41
nothing for daughters, 22
of Prodigal Son, **168–72**
Inns, 40, 53, 63, 164, 166, 222
Irenaeus, 39
Isaac, 12, 25, 77, 84, 165, 182
Israel (name of Jacob), 12
Israel (Jewish nation), 7, 9, 10,

11, 12, 14, 15, 17, 18, 19, 20, 23, 25, 26, 27, 28, 29, 33, 35, 38, 43, 44, 46, 47, 49, 50, 52, 53, 54, 56, 58, 65, 66, 74, 75, 80, 81, 85, 87, 88, 89, 90, 91, 94, 98, 102, 114, 117, 124, 127, 136, 137, 142, 148, 158, 160, 163, 165, 166, 167, 170, 174, 177, 178, 179, 180, 181, 182, 185, 187, 188, 190, 195, 196, 202, 209, 211, 215, 223, 224, 226, 229, 230, 233, 240, 243, 246, 253, 256, 257, 258, 259, 272, 280, 281, 283, 285, 289,
babylonians, 12, 14, 15, 24, 49, 54, 95, 114, 137, 138, 139, 148, 166, 232
defeated by Assyrians, 12, 14, 165
Jesus' homeland, **9–12**
modern state of, 10, 14, 20, 56, 69, 127,
northern Jewish nation, 10, 12, 14
occupied by Romans, 12, 13, 14, 16, 18, 19, 20, 65, 87, 190, 211
revolts against Rome, 15, 16, 17, 40, 48, 63, 98, 148, 166, 214, 215, 218, 233, 260, 268
source of name, 12
Isaiah, 39, 56, 87, 90, 104, 111, 114, 116, 151, 182, 202, 218, 230, 237,
Italy, 8, 17, 45, 53, 59

J
Jacob, 12, 25, 133, 182, 228
brother Esau, 19
father of twelve tribes of Israel, 12,
son Joseph, 24, 139
star from, 48
wives, 32
Jairus, 95, 210, 273
James (apostle), 93, 94, **95–96**, 129, 194, 249, 273, 274, 278
brother John, 93, 94, 95, 129, 184, 193, 194, 279
death, **96**
father Zebedee, 95
James (son of Alphaeus), **97**
James (brother of Jesus), 31, 58, 115, 177

Jehohanan, 268

Jehu, 229

Jericho, 69, 80, 105, 162, 163, 164, 207
  home of Rahab, 26, 27, 28
  home of taxman Zacchaeus, **196–97**
  road to, 69
  walls fall, 10
  winter home of Herod the Great, 55

Jerusalem, 7, 10, 11, 16, 17, 18, 19, 20, 21, 22, 23, 33, 40, 42, 44, 46, 48, 49, 50, 53, 55, 56, 57, 60, 65, 66, 67, 68, 69, 70, 73, 74, 82, 85, 86, 89, 90, 97, 106, 111, 126, 127, 137, 139, 140, 144, 148, 155, 162, 163, 164, 165, 166, 173, 176, 181, 182, 193, 195, 196, 203, 206, 207, 208, 211, 213, 214, 215, 217, 218, 219, 226, 227, 228, 229, 230, 231, 232, 233, 234, 235, 236, 237, 238, 239, 241, 242, 243, 247, 248, 253, 256, 258, 260, 262, 266, 268, 269, 270, 273, 277, 278, 279, 281, 282, 283, 284, 286, 287, 289, 291
  destroyed by Babylonians, 14, 137, 138, 139, 148, 166, 232, 249
  destroyed by Rome, 8, 48, 140, 203, 214, 215, **233–34**, 238, 242, 243, 270
  east gate, 291
  hilltop location, **9–10**
  passover crowds, 219, 248
  population, 219
  rebuilt after Jewish exile, 12, 15, 166, 289
  roman garrison, 233

Jesse, 29

Jesus Christ
  arrested, **252–58**
  as a child, **57–71**
  ascension, 95, 111, 238, 281, 290
  at age 12 with scholars, **65–71**
  baptism, **72–78**
  beating and mockery, **265–66**
  birth, 8, **35–43**, 46
  brothers and sisters, 31, 115
  burial, **272**

calms a storm, **183–86**
chart of main teachings, **120**
chart of Messiah prophecies fulfilled, **89, 271**
clears temple, 212, **216–18**
crucifixion, **267, 268–72**
divinity, 48, 51, 111, **174**, 251
family tree, **22–29**
feeds the crowds, **187–91**
great commission, 236, 282, 284, 291
heals the sick, **104–112**
helps Roman soldier, **178–82**
heresies about, 245, 250, 284
humanity, physical appearance, **90, 174**
infant dedication, 42, **43**
jews plot to kill, **212–19**
last supper, **240–46**
messiah, 14, 23, 24, 25, 27, 43, 48, 49, 52, 82, 83, 86, 88, **88–90**, 94, 95, 96, 111, 113, 115, 187, 211, 215, 255, 259, 260
modern scholars on the resurrection, **277**
palm Sunday, **226–230**
parables, **149–56**
prophecies about, (*see* prophecies)
raises Lazarus from the dead, **206–211**
resurrection, **273–80**
second Coming, **285–91**
selects disciples, **91–98**
sermon on the Mount, **118–129**
son of God, 77, 78, 82, 95, 103, 107, 111, 119, 132, 154, 191, 194, 195, 203, 204, 205, 206, 214, 225, 226, 231, 263, 265, 270, 278
starts ministry, **85–90**
stops a woman's bleeding, 105, **109–10**
talks with Mary in Bethany, 209
temptation, **79–84**
timeline of Jesus' resurrection, **274**
transfiguration, **192–95**, 273
trial, **259–64**
turns water to wine, **99–103**

visits hometown Nazareth, **113–17**
walks on water, **186**
washes feet of disciples, **246**

Jews
  chart of Jewish groups, **214**
  during World War II, 12
  God's chosen people, 50, 147, 154, 165, 179
  revolt against Rome, 15, 16, 17, 40, 48, 63, 98, 148, 166, 214, 215, 218, 233, 260, 268

Jewish religion,
  chart of Jewish groups, **214**
  essenes, 16, 73, 126, 144, 203, 207, **214**
  herodians, 214
  objections to Jesus as messiah, 284
  orthodox, 145
  pharisees, 17, 69, 86, 126, 137, 139, 141, 142, 144, 146, 147, 148, 151, 201, **203**, 213, **214**, 215, 220, 224, 225, 230, 234, 276
  sadducees, 86, **203**, 213, **214**
  scribes, 69, 142, 149, 214
  sicarii, 98, 214, 262,
  zealots, 91, 96, 97, 98, **214**, 236

Jezreel Valley (Valley of Armageddon), 10, 11, 69
  fertile farmland, 11

Joanna, 221, 278

Job, 46, 81, 84, 134, 249

Joel, 237

John (apostle), 72, 81, 86, 91, 93, 94, 95, **96**, 99, 100, 103, 104, 129, 146, 153, 184, 188, 189, 193, 194, 204, 221, 241, 248, 252, 255, 257, 261, 267, 269, 273, 278, 279, 280, 290,
  brother James, 93, 94, 95, 129, 184, 193, 194, 279
  close friend of Jesus, 99, 193, 249
  death, **96**, 236
  exiled to island, 8
  father Zebedee, 96

John (book), 105, 146, 153, 221, 226, 227, 241, 246, 248, 278, 284

John the Baptist, 33, **72–74**, 75, 76, 80, 85, 86, 93, 94, 111
  baptized Jesus, **72–78**

death, 18, 262
disciples of, 139
essene connections, 73, 207, 214
fulfilled prophecy about Elijah's return, 193
mother Elizabeth, 33, 73
Jonah, 285, 274, 275, 287
Joppa, 53, 69
Jordan (country), 18, 20, 26, 28, 29, 52, 86, 162, 280
Jordan River, 9, 10, 11, 55, 69, 72, 73, **74**, 78, 87, 183, 188, 207, 237
baptism of Jesus, 72
baptism of people today, 74
valley, 9, 10, 80, 164, 226
Joseph (husband of Mary, father of Jesus), 24, 25, 26, 28, **30–34**, 35, 38, 40, 41, 42, 43, 50, 52, 56, 58, 62, 63, 64, 67, 68, 70, 73
Joseph (brother of Jesus), 31, 115
Joseph of Arimathea, 271, 272, 274
Josephus, Flavius, 37, 48, 55, 56, 57, 82, 183, 184, 203, 207, 218, 237, 241, 278
about crucifixions, 262, 272, 275
about exorcism, **107**
about fall of Jerusalem, 233
about Galilee, 151
about Herod the Great, 55, 63
about Herod's temple, 233
about high priest, 212, 217
about himself, **71**
about Jesus, 267, 279
about John the Baptist, **72–73**
about prayer, 130
Judah (son of Jacob), 27
Judah (tribe), 166, 228
Judah (southern Jewish nation), 10, 12, 14, 38, 89, 240
Judaism (see Jewish religion)
Judas (apostle, son of James, aka Thaddaeus), **98**, 236
Judas (brother of Jesus), 31, 115
Judas Iscariot, 93, **98**, **252–53**
betrays Jesus, 98, 219, 227, 239, 252, 253, 254
death, **98**
treasurer of disciples, 98

Jude (aka Judas, brother of Jesus), 261
Judea, 7, 18, 32, 38, 44, 49, 50, 56, 85, 86, 90, 236, 237, 259, 260, 262, 264, 283
hills of, 9, 32, 69, 164, 165
roman province, 12, 18, 20, 21
wilderness (Desert, badlands) of, 17, 73, 79, 144
Judging others, **120**, 124, **128**
Judgment Day, 154, 173, 174, 175, 231, 234, 235, 237
Julius Africanus, 25
Julius Caesar,
Jupiter
planet,
roman god,
Justice (see Crime and Punishment)

K
Kaddish, 132
Kidron Valley, 82, 173, 229, 247, 268
Kingdom of God (Kingdom of Heaven), 14, 78, 85, 87, 88, 94, 119, 121, 147, 150, 151, 155, 182, 198, **201**, 204, 226, 234, 282, 285
Kiss, 48
for Jesus by Judas, 254
for Jesus by woman anointing his feet, 220, 224
for prodigal son, 171
hospitality, greeting, 223
Kosher (see Food)

L
Lamb, sheep, 16, 35, 36, 43, 67, 90, 147, 152, 158, 161, 172, 199, 262, 282
for Passover meal, **242**, 243, 244
for sacrifice, 42, 68, 241
hebrew word for, 258
parable of lost s., 153, 154, 168
parable of s. and goats, 153, **173–77**
pet, 152
symbol of Jesus (see Lamb of God)
Lamb of God (Jesus), 74, 86, 242
Lame, 103, 104, 105, 111, 112,

176,
Lamps, 100, 153, 173, 192, 220, 254
Landowner, 150, 154, 155, 158
Last Supper, 94, 96, 121, 219, 227, **240–46**, 247, 253
comparison with Passover meal, **244**
Law (Jewish rules), 15, 22, 27, 28, 30, 31, 33, 41, 42, 53, 56, 57, 61, 67, 68, 69, 70, 72, 75, 80, 83, 86, 88, 92, 93, 94, 106, 114, 117, 120, 121, 122, 123, 124, 125, 126, 126, 140, 141, 142, 143, 144, 145, 146, 148, 151, 160, 162, 163, 164, 165, 169, 172, 177, 180, 193, 194, 199, 201, 203, , 205, 212, 213, 214, 215, 216, 220, 222, 224, 240, 253, 254, 256, 257, 258, 263, 264, 265, 266, 267, 271, 272,
obsolete, 121, 136
of Moses, 15, 61, 80, 117, 121, 122, 205
of Pharisees, 220, 224
oral, 62
teaching to children, 61
ten Commandments, 61, 83, 122, 127, 136, 137, 38, 237, 240, 264, 270,
Law (five books of Moses), 61, 117
Lazarus, 72, 103, 153, 205, **206–11**, 213, 215, 221, 224, 227, 229, 273
Leah, 25
Lebanon, 11, 86, 116, 127, 178, 216
Lee, Jang Rim, 289
Lent, 137, 141
Leprosy, 105, **106**, 116
Levi, 93, **97**
Libya, 268
Lindsey, Hal, 289
Lord's Prayer, 126, **130–35**
Lord's Supper (see also Communion), 240
Lot, 29
Love, 34, 71, 77, 120 121, 124, 125, 131, 147, 150, 162, 163, 167, 205, 210, 224, 232, 240, 252, 282, 288
enemy, 120, 124
God, 121, 147, 163, 167, 205
neighbor, 121, 125, 150, 162,

163, 205
of God for people, 205, 240
of God for Son, 77
Luke (man), 40, **162**
Lust (*see also* Sexual
    Misconduct), **122–23**,
    222

M

Maccabees (*see also*
    Hasmoneans), 15, 18
    revolt, 15
Magdala, 188
Magi (*see* Wise men)
Magic (*see also* Sorcery), 44,
    210, 262, 264
    incantations, 44, 107, 210,
    264
Manger, 35, 40
Manna, 82, 134, 187, 190, 191
Mariamne, 20, 55
Marco Polo, 45
Marriage (*see also* Wedding),
    22, 26, 28, 30, 31, 32, 33, 38,
    41, 62, 72, 100, 101, 122,
    123, 205, 240
    bride, 30, 31, 32, 33, 100, 101
    bridesmaids, 100, 153, 173
    contract, 32, 33, **101**
    dowry, 31, **32**, 33, 100, 101
    engagement, 26, 30, 32, 33,
    101
    groom, 31, 32, 100, 101, 103,
    140, 173
    proposal, 28, 30, 81
    rabbis as m. counselors,
    122–23
Mars (planet), 11, 164
Mars (god of war), 39
Martha, 206, 209, 210, 221, 227,
    229, 273
Mary (mother of Jesus), 24, 25,
    26, 27, 28, 30, 31, 32, 33, 34,
    35, 38, 39, 40, 41, 42, 49, 50,
    52, 65, 69, 70, 71, 73, 89, 96,
    99, 100, 101, 115, 285
    at Cana wedding, 99, 100,
    101
    birth of Jesus, 8, **35–43**, 46
    pregnant, 26, 30, 32, 35, 38,
    39, 52
    purification after birth,
    42–43
    virgin, 26, 31, 32, 38, 39, 89
    visited by Gabriel, 32, 73
Mary (mother of James), 278

Mary (sister of Martha,
    Lazarus), 206, 209, 221,
    227, 229
Mary Magdalene, 105, 188, 221,
    274, 278, 279
Mass, 241
Massacres, 148, 166
Matthew (apostle), 93, **97**
    death, **97**
Meals, 113, 123, 139, 146, 152,
    168, 189, 191, 197, 219, 220,
    222, 240, 241, 242, 243, 244,
    245, 246, 253
Medicine, 70, 103, 127, 146,
    196, 213, 286
    chart of remedies, **112**
    Mustard seed as, 127
Mediterranean Sea, 9, 47, 52,
    53, 56, 58, 68, 74, 87, 158,
    184, 236
Medium (consulting the dead),
    117, 202
Melchior, 45
Messiah (*see also* Jesus), 13, 14,
    16, 17, 23, 24, 25, 27, 29, 34,
    35, 37, 42, 43, 48, 49, 50, 52,
    54, 56, 67, 74, 75, 76, 78, 82,
    83, 85, 86, 87, **88–89**, 90, 94,
    95, 96, 102, 111, 113, 114,
    115, 116, 132, 144, 182, 187,
    190, 191, 193, 195, 211, 214,
    215, 219, 224, 228, 229, 230,
    233, 253, 255, 259, 260, 261,
    269, 271, 273, 280, 281, 283,
    284, 285, 290, 291
    Jewish expectations, **13–14**,
    16, 50, 66–67, 75, 82, 88,
    191, 193, **215**, 228, 230,
    280, 285
    Jewish objections to Jesus as
    Messiah, **90**, 214, 284
    meaning, 224
    prophecies about (*see*
    Prophecies)
Midwife, **41**
Mikveh (bath for ritual
    cleansing), 283
Millennium, 47, 231, 238,
Miller, William, 289
Miracles of Jesus
    calms storm, **183–86**
    exorcism, **106–7**, 221
    feeding crowd with barley
    bread, **187–91**
    feeding crowds, **187–91**
    healing long-distance by

    prayer, 103, 206
    healing, **104–112**
    Jesus refusing, 101, 113
    jews demanding m., **82**
    legends from childhood, **58**
    raising the dead, **206–211**
    transfiguration, **192–95**, 273
    walks on water, **186**
    water into wine, 72, **99–103**
Mishnah, 62, 106, 114, 143,
    155, 169, 180, 181, 197, 198,
    213, 256,
Mithras, 36, 48
Moab, 26, 28, 29
Mold, 62
Monastery of Flagellation, 266
Money (*see also* Taxes), 17, 31,
    32, 33, 98, 100, 101, **120**,
    122, 127, 143, 146, 153, 168,
    170, 171, 173, 189, 190, 191,
    197, 198, 199, 212, 216, 224,
    252, 253, 282
    daily wage (denarius), 32,
    125
    wealth, 25, 26, 90, 119, 125,
    132, 159, 168, 198
Mother
    role of, **22**
Moses, 15, 23, 43, 46, 54, 61, 65,
    67, 79, 80, 92, 94, 95, 117,
    121, 122, 133, 136, 138, 142,
    163, 165, 166, 187, **190**, 191,
    192, 193, **194**, 195, 202, 205,
    213, 219, 222, 240, 242, 243,
    245, 255
    at Transfiguration, 192, 193
    comparisons to Jesus, **54**, 79,
    190, 194
Most Holy Place (Holy of
    Holies), 270, 272
Mount Carmel, 11
Mount Gerizim, 165, 166
Mount Hermon, 10, 74
    snow source of Jordan River,
    10
Mount Nebo, 193
Mount of Olives, 9, 89, 173,
    207, 226, 228, 229, 231, 233,
    234, 243, 247, 248, 268, 283,
    287, 290, 291
    ridge of hills, 173, 207, 226
Mount Seir, 162, 195
Mount Tabor, 195
Mount of Temptation (Jebel
    Quarantal), 80, 83
Mount of Transfiguration, 192

Mount Sinai, 79, 80, 136, 138, 192, 194, 195
Mount Vesuvius, 8, 59
Mourning, 119, 126, 137, 139, 208, 209, 210, 218, 243, 269
Mummy, 210
Music, 100, 171
Mustard seed, plant, 110, **127**, 150, 153
Mute, 105
Myrrh, 45, **51**, 208, 269

N
Nain, 210
Naphtali tribe, 87
Naomi, 28, 29
Nard (spikenard), 208, 221, 223
Nathan, 152
Nathanael, 94, **96–97**, 99, 115
Natural History, 108, 109, 121, 158
Nazareth, 9, 10, 35, 38, 42, 50, 56, **57–59**, 63, 65, 69, 85, 86, 87, 96, 99, 111, 113, 114, 115, 116, 129, 158, 273
distance to Cana, 99
distance to Jerusalem, 69
farms in, 57
hometown of Jesus, Mary, Joseph, 9, 10, 42, **57–59**, 86, 87, 99, 111, 113, 158
Jesus rejected in, 86, **113–17**
Negev, 11
Nero, 8, 48
Nicodemus, 272
Nile River, 74
Nineveh, 287

O
Obed, 29
Octavian (*see* Augustus)
Offerings, donations (*see also* Sacrifice, Tithe), 42, 43, **68**, 122, 137, 143, 147, 197, 198, 222, 242, 289
Olive oil, 41, 102, 116, 223, 224, 254
Pressing, **248**
Olives, 22, 74, 127, 248
Olivet Discourse, 231, 286
Omega, 204
Origen, 35, 46, 95, 115
Orphans, 176, 177
Ossuaries (*see also* Burial), 208

P
Panthera, 39
Palestine, **12**, 237
source of name, **12**
Palestinians, 12, 163
Palm branches, 107, 226, **229–30**
Palm Sunday, **226–30**
Parables, 40, 68, 69, 72, 100, 113, **149–56**, 157–205, 224
chart of, **153**
farmer planting seeds, 153
good Samaritan, 40, 68, 72, 149, 153, **162–67**
Jesus' favorite teaching technique, **149–56**
lost (Prodigal) son, 149, 151, 153, 154, **168–72**
lost coin, 153, 154, **168**
lost sheep, 153, 154, 168
man in debt, 153, **224**
mustard seed, 127, 150, 151, **152**, 153, **157–61**
Nathan's parable to David, **152**
of Plato, **155–56**
of rabbis, **155**
sheep and goats, 153, **173–78**
ten virgins (bridesmaids), 100, 153, 173
Paralysis, 105
Parthian Empire, 19, 49
Passion Week, 226
Passover, 53, 65, **66–67**, 69, 85, 166, 213, 217, 218, **219**, 226, 229, 230, 237, 241, 242, 243, **244**, 245, 248, 253, 256, 257, 260, 262, 268, 274, 278, 279
in Egypt, 67, 219
Jerusalem crowds during, 65, 219, 248, 253, 262
Jesus in Jerusalem during, 69, 85, 213, 226, 229
jewish festival, 53, 56, 65, 66, 219, 241–42, 244, 253, 256
last Supper on, 219, **241–42**
meal, 219, 241, 242, 243
Patmos, 8
Paul, 7, 78, 82, 84, 92, 122, 125, 136, 140, 141, 143, 177, 200, 201, 205, 245, 246, 265, 281, 284, 286, 287, 288, 290, 291
death, 7
jailed, 125

teachings, 78, 141, 177, 201, 205
Peace, 12, 14, 16, 38, 68, 78, 81, 87, 88, 90, 119, 124, 179, 191, 206, 216, 219, 229, 272, 279, 286
Pentecost, 66, 279, 282, 284, 286
Perea, 21, 207, 237
Perfume, 26, 27, 51, 144, 220, 221, 223, 224, 225
Persia (Persians), 15, 40, 44, 45, 48, 71, 137, 242, 250
Peter, Simon (apostle), 7, 53, 78, 83, 91, 93, **94–95**, 96, 99, 105, 109, 111, 129, 186, 188, 193, 194, 195, 239, 249, 252, 255, 257, 258, 273, 274, 275, 279, 282, 287
as first pope, **282**
at Transfiguration, 95, 193, 194, 195, 273
close friend of Jesus,
cuts off man's ear, 83, **255**
death, 7, **95**
denies knowing Jesus, 95, **257**
during prayer at Gethsemane, 95, 249
fisherman, 91, 93, 95, 129
house in Capernaum, 95, 129
Jesus washes his feet, 246
leader of disciples, 94
northern accent, **258**
renamed by Jesus, **95**
runs to tomb, 275
Phaesalis, 72
Pharisees, 17, 69, 86, 126, 137, 139, 141, 142, 144, 147, 148, 151, 172, 201, 203, 213, **214**, 215, 220, 224, 225, 230, 234, 276
chart about, **214**
criticize Jesus, 146, 147
Plot to kill Jesus, 148, 213
rules of, 137, 144, 201, 213
Phasael, 18, 19, 49
Pilgrimage, 66
at Passover, 66
Philip, 94, **96**, 99, 188, 189
Philistines, 10, 12, 137, 162, 202
Philo, 189, 222, 259, 278
Pisces, 7, 47
Pig, 20, 57, 91, 107, 112, 162, 170, 172, 236

Pilate, 7, **18**, 21, 88, 90, 124, 166, 219, 239, **259–64**, 265, 266, 267, 271, 272, 274, 276, 278, 279
  crucifixion of Jesus, 18, 21, 267, 279
  fired, 7, 166
  ruler of Judea, 7, 18
  saint, **259**
  trial of Jesus, **259–64**
Planting, 153, 157, **160**
Plato, 149, 150, 155, 156, 203
Pliny, 48, 53, 108, 109, 110, 121, 158, 159
Plowing, 145, 158
Plutarch, 267
Poetry, 119, 202, 228, 229, 264
Poor, 40, 42, 68, 104, 108, 111, 114, 119, 124, 125, 139, 152, 154, 170, 176, 177, 189, 196, 198, 201, 212, 222
  blessed by God, 119
  charity for, 176, 177
  don't worry, 120
  Jesus' ministry to, 42, 104, 111, 114, 176, 212
  unjustly treated, **124**, 125
Pompeii, 8, 59, 60
Pompey, 18, 19
Pope, 36, **282**
Potter, 63, 253,
Prayer, 80, 114, 120, 126, **130–35**, 136, 137, 153, 163, 180, 185, 189, 193, 210, 216, 217, **247–51**, 253
  complaining to God, **249**
  fasting, 80
  for show, 126, 131
  Lord's Prayer, 126, **130–35**
  of Jesus, **132**, 134, 193, **247–51**
  over food, 189
  stops a storm, **185**
Prefect (governor), 259
Priests (*see also* High Priests), 16, 17, 23, 43, 44, 51, 68, 71, 73, 106, 146, 147, 151, 167, 168, 198, **212–19**, 239, 241, 252, 253, 254, 255, 271, 276
  Aaron's dynasty, 17, 23
  corruption, 167, 212, 254
Plot to kill Jesus, **212–19**
Procurator (governor), 259, 267
Prodigal son, 149, 151, 153, 154, **168–72**
Promised Land, 13, 46, 81, 166,

187, 190, 191
Prophecies, 11, **13–14**, 38, 39, 43, 45, 50, 52, 56, 74, 75, 77, 78, 87, 88, **89**, 90, 91, 114, 117, 121, 147, 151, 167, 193, 194, 201, 202, 211, 215, 218, 226, 228, 230, 231, 236, 256, 262, 269, **271**, 275, 280, 281, 283, **285–91**
  end times, 194, 201, 231
  Jesus/messiah suffering, 14, 88, **89**, **271**
  Jesus' baptism, **77**
  Jesus' resurrection, **89**, 280
  Jesus' Second Coming, **285–91**
  messiah, **13–14**, 87, 88, **89**, 215, 228, 271
  messiah's birth, arrival, **14**, 38, 39, 50, **89**
  messiah's mission, 43
Prophets, 10, 13, 15, 16, 34, 39, 56, 69, 73, 76, 78, 82, 87, 88, 91, 92, 102, 104, 111, 113, 114, **116**, 117, 119, 121, 131, 137, 151, 152, 161, 174, 176, 177, 180, 182, 190, 191, 193, 195, 202, 211, 215, 217, 218, 223, 228, 229, 230, 233, 236, 237, 238, 249, 263, 269, 273, 274, 283, 285, 287,
  false, 81, 113, 117
  Jesus, 113, 116
  John the Baptist, 73, 111
Persecuted, killed, 113, **116**
Prostitution (*see also* Sexual Misconduct), 26, 27, 220, 222
Psalms, 45, 59, 61, 77, 83, 89, 90, 110, 114, 125, 133, 151, 155, 230, 243, 247, 249, 254, 256, 269–70, 271
  about Jesus/messiah, 45, 77, 90, 269–70, 271
  quoted by Satan, 83
Punishment, 73, 78, 124, 174, 176, 177, 185, 201, 211, 222, 267, 276
  criminals (*see* Crime and Punishment, Crucifixion)
  escaping p., 201
  sinful people, 78, 174, 176, 177, 185, 222
Purification, **42–43**, 75, 165, 198, 226
  after ritual contamination,

75
  from sin, 226

Q
Quirinius, 37
Qumran, 16, 17, 73–74, 75, 144, 163, 241
  dead Sea Scrolls, 16, 17, 74, 163, 241
  home of Essene Jews, 16, 73, 144

R
Rabbis, 32, 39, 47, 55, 57, 61–62, 91, 92–93, 109, 110, 114, **122–23**, 127, 128, 142, 144, 147, 150, 155, 165, 168, 169, 170, 178, 179, 180, 181, 185, 196, 197, 198, 199, 208, 209, 213, 213, 214, 222, 242, 246, 275, 284, 285
  as marriage counselors, **122–23**
  burned to death, 55
  Jesus as one, 91, 110, 150, 178, 179, 180, 196, 285
  teachings of, 61–62, 92–93, 114, 147, 169, 197, 208, 209, 242, 275
Rachel, 25
Rahab, **26**, **27–28**, **29**
Rapture, 289
Rebekah, 25
Red Sea, 11
Refugees, 12, 136, 142, 176, 237
Remus, 38
Repentance (*see also* Day of Atonement), 66, 75, 76, 126, 136, 270
Raphael, 108
Restitution, 124, 199
Resurrection, 7, 10, 13, 14, 17, 40, 58, 89, 95, 97, 103, 111, 121, 143, 195, 200, 202, 203, 205, 214, 227, 255, 265, **273–80**, 281, 282, 286
  adonis, 40
  all humans, 200, 202
  daughter of Jairus, 95, 273
  Jesus, 7, 10, 89, 95, 97, 111, 121, 143, 195, 200, 255, 265, **273–80**, 281, 282, 286
  Lazarus, 103, **206–11**, 229, 273
  modern scholars on the

resurrection, 277
timeline charts of Jesus'
resurrection, **227**, **273**
Revenge, 120, 123, 124,
Rhea Silvia, **38–39**
Righteousness, 14, 16, 29, 36,
73, 77, 89, 90, 140, 172, 175,
192, 202, 203, 228, 249, 271
of Jesus, 77, 89, 90, 228, 271
Rituals (*see also* Purification),
15, 16, 39, 42, 52, 61, 72, 74,
75, 76, 78, 80, 91, 102, 114,
130, 135, 140, 147, 165, 170,
181, 197, 198, 201, 236, 240,
244, 245, 246, 283
foot washing, 22, **220–25**,
223, 246
Lord's Supper, **240**
Rome (city), 7, 8, 9, 13, 17, 18,
19, 20, 36, 48, 53, 78, 95,
175, 205, 259
founders, **38**, 175
Rome (Roman Empire), 13,
17, 19, 20, 21, 48, 53, 55, 56,
67, 71, 96, 98, 124, 148, 155,
166, 179, 180, 181, 195, 197,
199, 205, 211, 214, 215, 218,
229, 230, 232, 233, 235, 236,
237, 241, 248, 260, 261, 263,
266, 267, 268, 282
armies, 49, 140, 144, **179**,
180, 197, 215, 232, 237,
265
destroys Jerusalem, temple,
15, 16, 17, 40, 48, 63, 98,
148, 166, 214, 215, 218,
233, 260, 268
invades Jewish homeland,
12, 13, 14, 16, 18, 19, 20,
65, 87, 190, 211
persecutes Christians, 7, 18,
85, 96, 97, 207, 279–80,
284, 287, 288, 290
Roads, 53
Romulus, 38
Rooster, 257
Ruth, **26**, **27–29**, 30

S
Sabbath
a good day to attack Jews,
148
day of rest, worship, 58, 61,
142, 213, 237
Jesus breaking S. laws, 58,
62, 103, **142–48**, 213, 237

Jewish rituals, practices, 62
laws about, 15, 92, 117, 142,
143, **144–45**, 213, 256
when S. became Sunday, **143**
Sacrifice (*see also* Offerings),
43, 67, **68**, 77, 84, 121, 130,
132, 140, 146, 147, 165, 167,
176, 212, 216, 217, 226, 236,
240, 241, 242, 243, 244, 264,
265, 270
animals, 43, 67, 212, 216,
242, 265
at Jerusalem temple, 67, 140,
216, 217, 242
good behavior is more
important, 147, 167
humans, 176, 264
obsolete, 270
Sadducees, 86, **203**, 213
chart about, **214**
on afterlife, **203**
other teachings, 213
Salome, 31, 278
Salvation, 27, 28, 42, 56, 76, 78,
91, 131, 132, 160, 161, 164,
177, 182, 194, 199, 201, 204,
205, 226, 230, 243, 244, 251,
280, 283, 285, 287
Samaria, 56, 68, 140, 165, 166,
283
Samaritan, 40, 68, 72, 86, 96,
149, 150, 152, 153, **162–67**
feud with Jews, 68, 162, 163,
165, 166
parable of Good, 40, 68, 72,
149, 153, **162–67**
Samson, 30, 254
Sanhedrin
top Jewish council, 20, 124,
212, 252
tries Jesus, 212, 252
Sarah, 25
Satan, **79–84**, 135, 159, 164, 252
accuser, 81
tempts Jesus, **79–84**
possesses Judas, 252
Saturn, 7, 36, 47
Saturnalia, **36**
Saul, King, 137, 146, 202
Savior, 13, 14, 21, 26, 35, 37, 42,
49, 89, 164, 229, 245, 285
Schools (*see* Education)
Schweitzer, Albert, 286
Scribes, 69, 142, 149, 214
non-Jewish, 34
Sea of Galilee, 9, 10, 58, 74, 85,

87, 95, 107, 127, 129, 160,
183, 184, 186, 189, 207,
fishing, 189
freshwater lake, 10, 87
Second Coming, 164, 174, 228,
234, 235, 238, **285–91**
failed predictions, **289**
Sejanus, 259, 264
Seneca, 36, 128, 261, 267, 268
Sennacherib, 148
Sepphoris, 63
Sermon on the Mount, **118–29**,
130, 179, 181
Sermon on the Plain, **118**
Servant (*see also* Suffering
Servant), 14, **22**, 25, 55, 60,
77, 88, 89, 95, 100, 102, 105,
110, 114, 153, 154, 170, 171,
173, 178, 179, 181, 182, 206,
212, 223, 246, 254,
role of, **22**
Sexual misconduct (*see also*
Adultery, Prostitution), 26
Shammai, Rabbi, 123
Shechem, 162, 166, 167
Sheep (*see* Lamb)
Shekel, 31, 43, 196, 216, 217,
253
Shelah, 27
Shema, 114
Sheol, 202
Shepherd, 22, 35, 42, 55, 63,
126, 153, 168, 173, 174, 178
parable of Goods, 153
Shibboleth, 258
Ships (*see* Boats)
Shroud of Turin, 208, 276
Sicarii, 98, 214, 262
Simeon, 43, 61, 144
Simon (brother of Jesus), 31,
115
Simon Magus, 44
Simon of Cyrene, 123–24, 268
Simon the Pharisee, 220, 221,
223, 225
Simon the Zealot, **97–98**
Sin (*see also* Forgiveness), 13,
14, 27, 28, 34, 54, 57, 66, 68,
72, 73, 74, 75, 76, 77, 81, 83,
86, 87, 88, 89, 99, 110, 111,
117, 119, 133, 134, 135, 136,
138, 141, 152, 164, 171, 174,
175, 176, 201, 204, 205, 206,
211, 217, 220 221, 224, 225,
226, 234, 237, 239, 240, 244,
245, 265, 269, 270, 285

capital offense, **265**
    relation to sickness,
        110–12, 119
Sinai, 79, 80, 136, 138, 190, 192,
    194, 195
Slaves, 22, 177, 181, 222, 243,
    246
Snake, 58, 81, 112, 172
Socrates, 150
Sodom, 29
Solomon, 12, 20, 26, 29, 81,
    107, 127, 137, 202, 228, 232
Sons
    adopted, **25**
    firstborn, **41**, 43, 244
Son of God (*see* Jesus)
Son of Man
    Ezekiel as, 174, 285
    Jesus as, 89, 101, 152, 173,
        174, 199, 218, 238, 239,
        256, 273, 274, 285
Soranus, 41
Sorcery (*see also* Magic,
    Medium), 257
Soul, 19, 43, 73, 81, 101, 119,
    121, 131, 152, 160, 161, 163,
    168, 172, 175, 187, 201, 203,
    205, 208, 219, 220, 222, 233,
    249, 251, 275
Spikenard (*see* Nard)
Spirit (*see* Holy Spirit)
Star of Bethlehem, 46
Stoning, 113, 257
Storms (on Sea of Galilee),
    183–85
Suetonius, 48, 49, 230, 246
Suffering servant, 14, 88, **89**
Suleiman the Magnificent, 291
Sumerians, 75
Supernova, 46, 47
Susa, 45, 137
Swaddling clothes, 41
Swearing oath, 122, **123**
Sychar, 162, 166
Synagogues, 22, 40, 57, 61, 63,
    86, 104, 105, 113, 114, 124,
    126, 129, 130, 131, 146, 147,
    180, 181, 210, 213, 239, 273
    Capernaum, 105, 181
    for religious education, 22,
        57, **61**, 63, 147,
    for trials, 124
    Nazareth, 104, 113

T
Tabernacle, 17, 66, 272

Tabgha, 188–89
Tacitus, 47, 56, 179, 233, 259,
    267
Talmud, 30, 81, 93, 109, 110,
    134, 170, 198, 209, 254,
    257, 258
Tamar, **26**, **27–29**
Tartarus, 175
Taxes, 13, 23, 38, 63, 91, 93, 97,
    129, 153, 154, 168, 171, 196,
    197, 198, 199, 216, 253, 260
    for Temple, 253
    Jesus' tax advice, **198**, 260
    rabbi tax advice, **197–98**
Tax brackets, **196**
Tax collectors, 13, 93, 97, 129,
    153, 154, 168, 171, 196, 197,
    198, 199
Toilet tax, **197**
Toll roads, 97, 196
    Zacchaeus taxman, 91,
        196–99
Tel Aviv, 10, 69, 163
Temple (Jewish, *see also*
    Sacrifice), 7, 8, 10, 15, 20 23,
    34, 42, 43, 48, 51, 55, 60, 65,
    67, 68, 69, 70, 73, 75, 76, 82,
    83, 95, 106, 127, 137, 138,
    139, 140, 146, 164, 165, 166,
    173, 181, 195, 196, 197, 203,
    206, 211, 212, 213, 214, 215,
    216, 217, 218, 219, 224, 227,
    231, 232, 233, 234, 236, 237,
    238, 239, 240, 242, 243, 252,
    253, 254, 255, 256, 260, 263,
    265, 266, 270, 273
    curtain torn at Crucifixion,
        10, 239, 270
    defiled by Samaritans, 166
    destroyed by Babylon, 137,
        232
    destroyed by Romans, 8, 15,
        16, 17, 40, 48, 63, 98, 148,
        166, 214, 215, 218, 233,
        260, 268
    gentile worship area, **216**
    Herod's, 7, 69, **232–33**
    Jesus chasing off merchants,
        212, 213, **216–18**
    Jesus teaching crowds, 173,
        218
    Jesus' temptation at, **82–83**
    police, 219, 253, 254
    Solomon's, 137, 232
    young Jesus with scholars,
        65–71

Temptation, 79, 80, 82, 83, 84,
    113, 134, 140, 141
    as spiritual test, 79
    God doesn't tempt, 134
    of Jesus, **79–84**, , 113, 140,
        141
Ten Commandments (*see* Law)
Thaddaeus (apostle), **98**, 236
Thomas (apostle), **97**, 173, 206,
    236, 279
    doubting, **97**
Thorns, crown of, 60, 127, 266
Threshing, 145, 146
Tiberius (emperor), 7, 25, 73,
    85, 259, 264, 267
Tiridates, 48
Tithe (*see also* Offerings), 196,
    212
Titus, 197, 233, 237, 248
Toilets, 197
Tombs, 10, 45, 57, 59, 206,
    208, 210, 227, 266, 267, 271,
    272, 273, 274, 275, 276, 277,
    278, 279
    of Jesus, 227, 271, 272, 273,
        274, 275, 276, 277, 278, 279
    of Lazarus, 206, 210
Trachonitis, 21
Transfiguration of Jesus,
    192–95, 273
Travel, **53**, 68, 164, 191, 207,
    223, 255
Tree of life, 115, 269
Trees
    acacia, 127
    boswellia, 51
    carob, 170
    cedars of Lebanon, 127
    eucalyptus, 10, 127
    fig, 57, 153
    life (*see* Tree of life)
    oak, 127
    olive, 248
    palm, 188
    pine, 109
    sycamore, 196
Tamarisk, 127
Tribes of Israel, 25, 28, 94, 137,
    165, 280
Tribulation, 235, 238
Trinity, 39

U
Uriah, 27, 28
Uzziah, 10

V

Vegetables, 57
Vespasian, 197, 233
Vesta, 38
Via Dolorosa, 266
Vineyards, 57, 102, 103, 151, 153, 154, 155, 177
Virgin birth of Jesus, 34, **38–39**, 89
Visions, 10, 34, 289, 290
Vitellus, 7

W

Wadi (dry stream bed), 164, 237
Wailing Wall (see Western Wall)
Wars (see also Babylon, Assyria)
　attacking Jews on Sabbath, **148**
　end times, 235
　Jews revolt against Rome, 15, 16, 17, 40, 48, 63, 98, 148, 166, 214, 215, 218, 233, 260, 268
　Jews revolt against Syria's antiochus, 15, 18, 236
　of Alexander the Great, 15
　roman civil war, 7, 17, 18
　romans kill Samaritans, 166
　rome destroys Jerusalem temple, 15, 16, 17, 40, 48, 63, 98, 148, 166, 214, 215, 218, 233, 260, 268
Water, 9, 10, 11, 16, 20, 22, 29, 40, 41, 53, 57, 58, 59, 64, 72, 74, 75, 76, 78, 87, 92, 93, 99, 100, 101, 102, 103, 107, 108, 109, 112, 127, 137, 144, 145, 153, 155, 165, 172, 180, 183, 186, 188, 204, 223, 224, 242, 243, 248, 252, 264, 270, 271, 275
　aqueducts, 20, 199
　"born of w.," 78
　cistern, 59, 92, 248
　irrigation, 11, 160
　israel's main source, 10–11
　Jordan River, 9, 10, 11, 55, 69, 72, 73, **74**, 78, 87, 183, 188, 207, 237
Wells, 22, 58, 59, 144, 147
Wealth (see Money)
Wedding (see also Marriage), 30, 32, 99, 100, 103, 117, 136, 140, 153, 154
　reception, **100**
　shotgun, 117
Wedding planner, **103**
Wells, 22, 58, 59, 144, 147
Western Wall (Wailing Wall), 233
Wheat, 22, 57, 66, 127, 151, 152, 153, 157, 158, 159, **160**, 189
　chart from planting to table, **160**
Whisenant, Edgar, 289
Widow, 26, 27, 28, 29, 32, 116, 117, 153, 176, 177, 210, 273, 276
　of Nain, 210
　social security program, 28
Wife, 17, 20, 22, 25, 30, 31, 32, 33, 34, 41, 44, 50, 55, 56, 72, 93, 101, 122, 123, 152, 169, 221, 263
Wine, 51, 57, 72, 99, 100, 101, 102, 103, 112, 121, 137, 139, 140, 153, 166, 170, 241, 242, 243, 244, 245, 258, 268, 269, 270, 271
　at Passover meal, 243
　hebrew word for, 258
　medical uses, 51, 122, 166
　new wine in old wineskins, 140, 153
　symbol of Jesus' blood, 121, 242, 245
Water into wine, 72, **99–103**
Winemaking, **102**
Winnowing, 145, 146
Wise men (magi), 40, **44–51**, 52, 53
　fleeing Herod, 52
　gifts of, 45, **51**
　names of, 45
Witchcraft (see also Magic, Sorcery, Medium), 117
Word (term for Jesus), 204
Work, 22, 23, 32, 35, 43, 50, 53, 61, 62, 63, 64, 76, 85, 92, 100, 102, 126, 142, 143, 144, 145, 146, 147, 153, 170, 171, 178, 183, 185, 192, 197, 201, 203, 213, 215, 222, 225, 243, 253, 278, 291
　categories of, **145**
When not to w. (see Sabbath)
Worry, 49, **120**, 126, 128, 143, 234

Worship (see also Sabbath), 15, 17, 36, 42, 44, 48, 50, 52, 62, 66, 67, 70, 82, 83, 90, 104, 106, 114, 130, 131, 132, 133, 135, 136, 142, 143, 146, 165, 166, 180, 181, 182, 201, 216, 217, 219, 242, 272
　at Temple, 36, 62, 67, 70, 165, 216, 219
　christian, 130, 135
　God alone, 83, 133
　idols, pagan gods, 36, 106
　synagogue order of w., **114**

Y

Yom Kippur (see Day of Atonement)

Z

Zealots, 91, 96, 97, 98, **214**, 236, Zebedee, 93, 95, 96
Zebulun tribe, 87
Zechariah, 73, 228, 229
Zerubbabel, 24
Zeus, 15, 36
Zion (Jerusalem), 89, 228, 247